Dedicated to

Rev. John P. Schlegel

Table of Contents

Jews in the Gym

Studies in Jewish Civilization
Volume 23

Proceedings of the
Twenty-Third Annual Symposium
of the Klutznick Chair in Jewish Civilization
and the Harris Center for Judaic Studies

October 24-25, 2010

Other volumes in the
Studies in Jewish Civilization Series
Distributed by the Purdue University Press

2010 – Rites of Passage:
How Today's Jews Celebrate, Commemorate, and Commiserate

2011 – Jews and Humor

Jews in the Gym:
Judaism, Sports, and Athletics

Studies in Jewish Civilization
Volume 23

Editor:
Leonard J. Greenspoon

The Klutznick Chair in Jewish Civilization

Purdue University Press
West Lafayette, Indiana

Acknowledgments

The Twenty-Third Annual Klutznick-Harris Symposium took place on October 24 and October 25, 2010, in Omaha, Nebraska. The title of the Symposium, from which this volume also takes its title, is "Jews in the Gym: Judaism, Sports, and Athletics."

All of the presentations made at the Symposium appear, in revised form, in this volume. In addition, Ori Z. Soltes composed a second article for this collection.

For many people in the academic as well as the general community, sports are a topic of perennial interest. In addition to tapping into this overall interest, we selected sports and athletes as our theme for two additional reasons: first, the year 2010 witnessed the very exciting Winter Olympics in Vancouver and was only two years away from the next Summer Olympics in London. In short, we were experiencing Olympic fever (to be fair, it's difficult to find a year or perhaps even a season lacking in this "malady"). Second, and closer to home, in the fall of 2010, the Omaha Jewish community hosted the JCC Maccabi Games, during which hundreds of Jewish teens met, competed, and had a great time. At least some of this enthusiasm, we reasoned, would survive the games themselves and give a boost to our admittedly more cerebral, but not entirely sedate, activities.

We were not disappointed. Enthusiastic, knowledgeable, and appreciative audiences greeted all of our presenters. Far be it from me to attempt to appropriate sports language, but I think it's safe to observe that each of our participants hit a homer, with nary a strike out or a walk in sight.

Although it is indeed the case that some athletic events favor or reward individual achievement over group effort, when it comes to planning and implementing a Symposium, success is definitely a team effort. Our successful team once again included my two colleagues, Dr. Ronald Simkins, director of the Kripke Center for the Study of Religion and Society at Creighton University, and Dr. Jean Cahan, director of the Harris Center for Judaic Studies at the University of Nebraska-Lincoln. We also had some outstanding assistance from Fran Minear, who worked with both Ron and me, and Mary Sue Grossman, of the Jewish Federation of Omaha's Center for Jewish Education. Although we did not know it at the time, this was to be Fran's last Symposium. Were she a player, we would retire her number. As a valued associate, we wish her and her family all the best in retirement.

This volume is the third in our collaboration with the Purdue University Press, all of whose staff, under Director Charles Watkinson, has made us feel welcome in every possible way.

In addition to the Harris Center, the Kripke Center, and the Jewish Federation of Omaha, this Symposium is nourished and supported by the generosity of the following:

The Ike and Roz Friedman Foundation

The Riekes Family

The Creighton College of Arts and Sciences

The Gary Javitch Family Foundation

The Center for Jewish Education

The Henry Monsky Lodge of B'nai B'rith

The Dr. Bruce S. Bloom Memorial Endowment and Others.

This volume is dedicated, with sincere thanks, to Father John P. Schlegel, S.J. As Creighton's twenty-third president, from 2000-2011, Father Schlegel was a steadfast supporter of the annual Klutznick-Harris Symposium.

Leonard J. Greenspoon
Omaha, Nebraska
May 2012
ljgrn@creighton.edu

Editor's Introduction

Okay, so I'm not a sports fan. But even I have a sports-related memory involving a Jewish athlete. This is what I remember: it was the summer of 1965, and I was still a teenager. Somehow or other, I was in New York City, with a choice: go to the World's Fair or go see Sandy Koufax pitch. Without hesitation, I chose the latter: Koufax vs. Tug McGraw, Dodgers vs. Mets. I went to Shea Stadium for what was surely my first Major League game. I watched it all. There wasn't too much scoring. Koufax lost. I may have been disappointed, but I never regretted the choice. After all, World's Fairs come and go, but there was only one Sandy Koufax!

Just this past year, I was telling a friend of mine this story. He objected: Tug McGraw was a relief pitcher, not a starter. We looked it up: McGraw was indeed a starter early in his career. I felt vindicated. Could we push it further? Yes, we found the exact date of the game, Thursday, August 26, 1965. Koufax vs. McGraw; final score 5-2, in favor of the Mets, who had, we discovered, won only forty-two games up until that point. Koufax pitched seven innings, giving up three runs (two of which were earned). Only one more detail was needed to cinch the deal: yes, indeed, the 1964 World's Fair had been an option for me, running as it did until October 17, 1965.

I still have no recollection of how I got to New York, where I was staying, and when I returned to my home in Richmond, Virginia. This was the summer between my sophomore and junior years as an undergraduate. Maybe that was the same summer I went to Italy. Who knows? Right now, who cares? I saw Sandy Koufax pitch, all of seven innings—a dream come true!

With these thoughts, as well as many others, in mind, I have decided in this introduction to highlight some of the memories that readers will come away with as they look through each chapter:

From my perspective, it is always memorable when an author succeeds in challenging long-held perspectives. Loren Spielman's efforts in this regard are evident from this statement of his: "Arguing for a more nuanced interpretation . . . I hope to demonstrate that . . . Jewish attitudes toward spectacle entertainments . . . were complex and variegated . . . through Antiquity. . . . I offer contrasting evidence for Jewish contact and interest in Greek and Roman theater and athletics during the Second Temple period."

Is it then possible that Jewish attitudes on related issues presented themselves in a more varied way than is generally recognized? Indeed so, argues Ori Z. Soltes in his first chapter for this collection: "In both cases, although this is not the norm in the Jewish tradition, the physicality of those saviors [the Golem and Esther] is emphasized, even as physicality alone does not drive the salvational course of either narrative. And that physicality may be seen not only as an adjunct to skill in sports, but in part, as a metaphor for Jewish visual artistic activity."

. But isn't it the case, we may ask, that Jews as athletes are invariably a source of derision in films? Not so, Nathan Abrams effectively argues: "While cinema . . . frequently depicts Jews playing sports, this is often for fun and not in any seriously competitive and/or professional sense. . . . There have been exceptions, however, and key and serious Jewish characters have been defined by their athleticism. For example, sport has been used in many films as a means for Jews to assimilate, charting the clash between ethnic specificity and the mainstream culture and the struggle to pass from the former to the latter."

Jews like a good fight, and wagering on a fight, as much as anybody else. Isn't that true? Emphatically no, stresses Steven J. Riekes, basing his contention largely on the work of the Anglo-Jewish writer Maurice Samuel: "Samuel argues that the Greek idea of competitive sports, or life is a game, is utterly foreign to Judaism. The Hebrew Bible has no trace of sports fixation. . . . The summation of life as a game, with the concomitant implication of life as a hideous tragedy, was completely unknown in the Jewish world."

It would, nonetheless, be possible for a Jewish athlete to maintain the highest levels of faith and competition. Doubtful, very doubtful indeed, in the opinion of Danny Rosenberg, on the basis of his sophisticated analysis of the writings of the influential Rabbi Joseph B. Soloveitchik: "The very structure and organization of virtually all elite and professional sports make it almost impossible for a Jewish athlete of faith to be a competitor. . . . In some ways there is almost an imponderable divide between sport and faith. . . . However much the Jewish athlete of faith excels in sports, she or he will have to limit her or his involvement to some degree by recoiling and retreating."

We might suppose that Jewish successes—of which there were many—on the playing fields would have led to their increased acceptance in board-rooms, classrooms, and drawing rooms. Alas, throughout nineteenth- and early-twentieth-century Europe, this was almost never the case. This is broadly demonstrated by the findings of Steven A. Riess: "At the turn of the twentieth century, Jewish achievement in sport, even the most elite, did not promote respect for them from the broader society or facilitate structural assimilation. . . . Winning a gold medal did not lead to acceptance. . . . There was no Jewish Jackie Robinson . . . whose great athletic performances made people look up and take notice."

Similarly negative conclusions arise from the study by Mihály Kálmán of the extraordinarily talented Jewish fencers who propelled Hungary to the highest ranks: "Despite its emphasis on demonstrating the achievement of the Magyar race, Hungarian officialdom did not exclude Jews from the Olympic team, although it was equally unprepared to grant even the least measure of recognition to the champions as Jews."

From such analyses, it would seem safe to conclude that few, if any Jewish athletes achieved any sense of professional, to say nothing of religious/ethnic satisfaction. But this is hardly the case. In their joint presentation, William Kornblum, Erin Sodmiak, and Phil Oberlander demonstrate that even those who grappled with ghosts felt they had the capacity to be victorious. Thus, Phil, himself an Olympic-level wrestler, recalls several vignettes from his childhood in England, where the family was led by his father, Fred, who was a champion wrestler throughout the 1930s and 1940s: "During the war [Phil writes] my father [Fred] set us up in England where he was a young businessman and a celebrity among the expatriate Austrian Jews. In his heart he remained a rough and ready street fighter. And he tried to impart that to us as kids. If someone calls you a dirty Jew, you go up to them and tell them to take it back."

Although there were admittedly some exceptions, did not most European Jews and their leadership essentially buy into the stereotypes of Jews as brainy but far from brawny? Not at all. A number of authors touch upon this point, including Nina Spiegel: "In 1898 at the Second Zionist Congress in Basel, [Max] Nordau called for the creation of a 'Muscular Jewry.' In order for Jews to disprove the image of being weak and feminized and to refashion themselves, he claimed that they needed to become physically strong, a quality that was associated with, and promoted, a masculine image."

Given the wealth of material available, we might imagine that the Jewish experience loomed large in the annals of early sports history and/or that sports were granted a central place by the first practitioners of Jewish studies. Alas, neither was the case. Jeffrey S. Gurock, the keynote presenter at the Symposium and himself a participant in the process he describes, constructs a necessarily corrective narrative that highlights these factors, among others: "The serious study of the Jewish sports experience in the United States had great difficulties getting out of its starting blocks. Historiographical traditions of apologetics and self-congratulation weighed down scholarly considerations of the Jews in the American gym."

Once serious study of Jewish participation in athletics was initiated, was it not the case that issues of gender evaporated? Sadly, the answer to this and related queries is in the negative. It is to redress imbalances of this sort that Linda J. Borish has dedicated much of her scholarly work: "Basketball for Jewish women, generally neglected by historians of American sport and women, and Jewish sport history scholars, represents a topic of considerable importance in understanding historical experiences of 'Jews in the Gym.' In the early twentieth century Jewish women played basketball at settlement houses [and] ladies auxiliaries of Young Men's Hebrew Associations, where women faced gender constraints on the male spaces of sporting facilities."

Because Jews have faced unique obstacles, as well as opportunities, within American life, their experiences within the realm of athletics do not parallel those of other ethnic or religious groups. But this is not accurate, as amply demonstrated by Ori Z. Soltes in his second contribution for this volume: "The importance of sports for Jews, particularly immigrants and the children of immigrants, as a mechanism for weaving one's self into the American tapestry would be felt by a succession of other groups . . . and similar patterns of participation would follow standout athletes within these groups from the boxing ring to the baseball field and beyond."

By now, we might imagine, there are few surprises for the modern researcher in Jewish sports history. Hasn't it all been covered, uncovered, or discovered? Most decidedly not. Aspects of the "surprises" that still await us are illustrated, among other places, by the last two articles in this collection. For the first, Rebecca T. Alpert writes: "When I began to research Jewish participation in black baseball I assumed I would be writing primarily about Syd Pollock, Abe Saperstein, and Ed Gottlieb, the white Jewish owners and promoters of Negro League teams, and the Jewish communist sportswriters who fought for baseball's integration. [A colleague of mine] was certain that the Jewish presence in the Negro League went beyond the white owners and sportswriters to include black players as well. I challenged him to find some for me, and he found not only individual players, but an entire team."

And finally, as David J. Leonard observes, Jewish sports history continues to be made as fast as (or faster than) we can record it: "One of the most hyped and media saturated stories of the 2009-2010 NBA season was the arrival of Omri Casspi, a rookie with the Sacramento Kings. Treated like a 'rock star' . . . Casspi as the first Israeli to play in the NBA has received ample support from the Jewish American community."

Thus, we recognize that the study of Jews and/in sports is dynamic. This dynamic quality accounts for the fact that the authors of these articles, all except one of which appeared as part of the Klutznick-Harris Symposium in October 2010, were encouraged to present new data and new insights prior to submitting their papers in final form for publication in this volume.

I hope that readers of this volume also partake in this dynamic quality, albeit in a more individualized way, when they incorporate into their appreciation of these articles insights of their own gained through other material with which they come into contact. As a reader of these articles, I cannot help but note that further data, in the form of stats and analysis, have become available for sports figures who are still active in their careers. And more examples come to the fore of ways in which Jewish religious, or more broadly communal, concerns are taken into account in the marketing and scheduling of sports events from middle schools to major leagues. Since most of us participate in, as well as observe, athletics in some form or other, our interaction with the authors of this volume can enhance our experience of center field or center court as well as the grandstands or the box seats.

Leonard J. Greenspoon

Contributors

Nathan Abrams

Bangor University
Gwynedd
Bangor, UK LL57 2DG
nabrams@bangor.ac.uk

Rebecca T. Alpert

Temple University
1114 W. Polett Walk
Philadelphia, PA 19122-6090
ralpert@temple.edu

Linda J. Borish

Western Michigan University
1903 West Michigan Avenue
Kalamazoo, MI 49008-5334
linda.borish@wmich.edu

Jeffrey S. Gurock

Yeshiva University
500 West 185th Street
New York, NY 10033
gurock@yu.edu

Mihály Kálmán

Harvard University
Cambridge, MA 02138
mkalman@fas.harvard.edu

William Kornblum

Graduate Center
City University of New York
365 5th Avenue
New York, NY 10016
wkornblum@gc.cuny.edu

David J. Leonard

Washington State University
Pullman, WA 99164
djl@wsu.edu

Steven J. Riekes

Marks Clare Richards
11605 Miracle Hills Drive
Omaha, NE 68154

Steven A. Riess
Northeastern Illinois University
5500 North St. Louis Avenue
Chicago, IL 60625
s-riess@neiu.edu

Danny Rosenberg
Brock University
500 Glenridge Avenue
St. Catharines, ON, Canada L2S 3A1
danny.rosenberg@brocku.ca

Ori Z. Soltes
Georgetown University
37th and O Streets, N.W.
Washington, DC 20057
orisoltes@aol.com

Nina Spiegel
Hadassah-Brandeis Institute
Brandeis University
415 South Street
Waltham, MA 02453
spiegeln@gmail.com

Loren R. Spielman
Portland State University
Portland, OR 97207
spielman@pdx.edu

Playing Roman in Jerusalem:
Jewish Attitudes toward Sport and Spectacle during the Second Temple Period

Loren R. Spielman

INTRODUCTION

Under the rule of the first few Roman emperors, games and spectacles, whether performances of comedy, tragedy, mime, or musical competitions in the theater, horse and chariot races held in the Roman circus, the Greek-style athletic competitions of the stadium or gladiatorial bouts or beast fights staged in the arena, played an increasingly important role in civic life.[1] These sports and spectacles performed far more complex social functions than mere entertainment.[2] They served as the most conspicuous displays of Romanitas, the very essence of being Roman.[3] Theaters and amphitheaters were often the first public buildings constructed in a new or resettled Roman city, and the extent of their diffusion often went far beyond any expectations based on population or need, stretching even beyond the urban network in some cases.[4] The festivals and games that were held in theaters and amphitheaters promoted predominantly civic values and loyalties among the spectators. Since seating in these entertainment structures was divided according to status, and tickets were often provided by patrons and voluntary organizations rather than by means of purchase, attending games and other spectacles also provided an unparalleled opportunity to express sub-group identities, whether as a client of a particular patron, a member of a guild, or a constituent of an ethnic or religious minority.[5]

Roman sport and spectacle also transcend categorization as purely political or religious phenomena. For example, a great deal of attention has been placed on the theater and amphitheater as a site of Roman disciplinary control.[6] Since theaters, amphitheaters, and stadiums could be used as settings for trials and punishments, Roman games served as an important locus for the demonstration of Roman power. But theaters and stadia were also often connected to temples or local festivals. Altars and statuary were common architectural features in monumental Roman circuses; many sporting events likely began with some sort of dedicatory sacrifice to a patron deity. There were strong links between these games, particularly the presentation of athletic competitions and gladiatorial bouts, and the cult of the Roman emperor.[7] Spectators at these events thus displayed not only the outward forms of Roman culture, but a whole set of accompanying meanings and assumptions as well.

It is perhaps because of these powerful linkages between Roman power, politics, religion, and identity that most scholarship emphasizes Jewish resistance and avoidance of sport and spectacle during the ancient period. The evidence for this view comes predominantly from literary sources, most notably the works of the Jewish historian Josephus, which contain sharp criticism of these sorts of popular entertainments.[8] Josephus, perhaps our best source for the history of the Jews before the destruction of the Second Temple in 70 CE, relates a number of incidents that appear to attest to Jewish antagonism toward Roman entertainments and the rulers who attempted to promote them.

In his Jewish Antiquities (AJ 15.264-291), the historian Josephus describes a set of games founded in Jerusalem by the Jewish king Herod, who had been appointed as the Roman client king of the Jews in 40 BCE. For Josephus, these games provide fodder to further vilify Herod as an impious tyrant. The Jewish historian stresses a certain degree of popular opposition to the games, and he levies harsh criticism against the theater and amphitheater that Herod constructed in Jerusalem. Traditional scholarship has tended to uncritically accept this passage as evidence for native Jewish aversion to sports and athletics, considering Josephus' accounts of Jewish resistance to Herod's games as trustworthy evidence for an "orthodox" or typical Jewish attitude toward Roman spectacle.[9] This common view assumes that Herod planned his games despite a complete lack of Jewish interest and in the face of almost certain and inevitable resistance. According to this view, Herod, blinded by his desire for self-aggrandizement and under pressure to ingratiate himself with his superiors in Rome, imposed his theater and amphitheater on an unwilling and uncooperative Jerusalem, offending Jews and leading to the ultimate failure of his Jerusalem games.

Arguing for a more nuanced interpretation of Josephus' account, I hope to demonstrate that, despite Josephus' claims, Jewish attitudes toward spectacle entertainments during the Herodian Period were complex and variegated, as they were throughout Jewish Antiquity. Re-evaluating Josephus' statements, I offer contrasting evidence for Jewish contact and interest in Greek and Roman theater and athletics during the Second Temple period. Given the serious political and religious importance of sport and spectacle in Roman society, I also re-consider Herod's motives for founding games in Jerusalem. I argue that Herod's Jerusalem games were not planned solely out of self-interest, but as a well-crafted political strategy, designed to publicize Jerusalem as the capital of Herod's realm and the center of the Jewish world.

HEROD'S JERUSALEM GAMES

> For this reason Herod went still farther in departing from the native customs, and through foreign practices he gradually corrupted the ancient way of life, which had hitherto been inviolable. As a result of this we suffered considerable harm at a later time as well, because those things were neglected which had formerly induced piety in the masses. For in the first place he established athletic contests every fifth year in honor of Caesar, and he built a theatre in Jerusalem, and after that a very large amphitheatre in the plain, both being spectacularly lavish but foreign to Jewish custom, for the use of such buildings and the exhibition of such spectacles have not been traditional (with the Jews). Herod, however, celebrated the quinquennial festival in the most splendid way, sending notices of it to the neighboring peoples and inviting participants from the whole nation. Athletes and other classes of contestants were invited from every land, being attracted by the hope of winning the prizes offered and by the glory of victory. And the leading men in various fields were assembled, for Herod offered very great prizes not only to the winners in gymnastic games but also to those who engaged in music and those who are called thylmelikoi. And an effort was made to have all the most famous persons come to the contest. He also offered considerable gifts to drivers of four-horse and two-horse chariots and to those mounted on race-horses. And whatever costly or magnificent efforts had been made by others, all these did Herod imitate in his ambition to see his spectacle become famous.[10]

In the early 20s BCE, almost a full decade before Herod the Great began his two most impressive construction projects—the reconstruction of the Jerusalem Temple and the founding of Caesarea—the Jewish king built a theater in Jerusalem and a building that Josephus describes as "a very big amphitheater" in the plain outside of the city.[11] These two civic buildings, like many others in the ancient Mediterranean, were initially constructed to house a series of games dedicated to the new Roman emperor, Octavianus Caesar.

The Jerusalem theater and amphitheater were not mere copies or imports of foreign cultural institutions. A few features specific to these buildings mark them as somewhat peculiar. Though monumental entertainment structures would soon dominate the urban landscape throughout the Roman empire, Herod's theater and amphitheater ranked among the very first of their kind not only in Herod's kingdom, but also in the entire Roman Near East. Moreover, Herod's decision to build them in Jerusalem should seem somewhat puzzling. Herod heaped civic benefactions—including temples, gymnasia, and theaters—on Greek cities, both in his kingdom and throughout the Mediterranean. But Herod constructed his first theater and staged his first set of games in Jerusalem, the same thoroughly Jewish city that later housed his magnificent Temple.[12]

The content of the games was also somewhat unique. They were modeled after the Olympic games at Elis and the other so-called "Crown Games" (Pythian, Nemean, and Isthmian), and so were meant to occur every five years in perpetuity. Additionally, they featured the types of events that were typical of a Greek festival. Theatrical and musical competitions were held in the theater, while discus throwing, javelin, and a variety of foot-races, boxing, and possibly the pankration, an event that featured a combination of punching, kicking, and wrestling moves, were staged in the structure that Josephus calls an amphitheater.[13] Most likely, this was in reality part hippodrome, part stadium, where both athletic events and races could be held.[14] The equestrian events were held according to the Greek style, with races for two-horse [biga] and four-horse [quadriga] chariots as well as for bareback riders, an event that rarely occurred in Roman circuses.

But Herod's games were also modeled after Octavian's Actian Games at Nicopolis, held to commemorate his naval victory against his rival Marcus Antonius. They therefore included more classically Roman entertainments alongside the characteristically Greek events. These included, according to Josephus, venationes, or live beast shows, and public executions.[15] Some suggest that Herod's games also included armed combat between gladiators, since these generally occurred as the main event in the afternoon, following a morning of beast fights and the noontime executions. Josephus, however, makes no mention of them.[16]

Josephus, a Jewish historian working under the patronage of the Flavian emperors near the end of the first century CE and our only source for a description of Herod's Jerusalem games, sharply criticizes Herod for introducing these sorts of spectacle entertainments into the city. The theater, decorated with inscriptions honoring Octavianus Caesar and adorned with trophies made of gold and silver, and the "very large amphitheater" according to Josephus were both "alien to Jewish custom." The use of such buildings and the presentation of spectacles within them, Josephus claims, were not traditional for the Jews. Though combat between beasts thrilled the "foreigners" who were impressed by the action and by the expense, Josephus adds that these venationes and executions ad bestias particularly disturbed the "natives" because "on the one hand, it seemed a glaring impiety to throw men to wild beasts for the pleasure of other men, and on the other hand, it seemed a further impiety to change their established ways for foreign practices." Beast shows and public executions, among the most characteristically and symbollically Roman of entertainments, according to Josephus, constituted "an open abrogation of the customs held in honor by [the Jews]."[17]

Lastly, Josephus remarks that the Jews were particularly irked by the thought that Herod had introduced images into Jerusalem, for "it was not ancestral for them to worship such things" and they could not bear "images of men" being brought into the city. Josephus begins to describe how Herod successfully managed to placate his detractors by demonstrating that these trophies were not "images of men" at all; they were merely panoplies of armor over wooden frames. Though the Jerusalemites and the Jewish king appear to have resolved their differences over nervous laughter, Josephus continues his narrative by suggesting that lingering resentment led a small group of zealots to make an attempt on Herod's life while he sat in the theater.

One of the real problems with using this passage from Josephus' Jewish Antiquities to accurately reconstruct the ancient Jewish reception of Herod's games stems from the markedly unbalanced nature of his account. On the one hand, Josephus claims that the games were an egregious affront to Jewish mores. For example, in his introduction to this passage Josephus claims that Herod, after eliminating his last few rivals, "gradually corrupted the ancient way of life, which had hitherto been inviolable. The Jews suffered considerable harm at a later time, because those things were neglected which had formerly induced piety in the masses." In other words, Josephus blames Herod for the catastrophe of the Jewish War some one hundred years later. The introduction of "foreign practices" and their subsequent popularity among the Jews caused neglect of the "ancestral customs." The punishment for this neglect, according to Josephus, was the complete destruction of Jerusalem and its sacred Temple, and the total disappearance of the traditional forms of Jewish life.[18]

On the other hand, Josephus' description appears to celebrate these games as a great achievement and boast of their magnificence. Herod's games were lavish, novel, and exciting. The games were well publicized and attracted participants from abroad. The prizes that Herod offered were lucrative enough to entice competitors "from every land." Objects made of gold and silver, expensive garments, and wild beasts were displayed before an awestruck crowd. And the theater itself was magnificently decorated—a tremendous spectacle in its own right.

The easiest explanation for this imbalance in the description of Herod's games is that the historian reworked a previous source that had an overwhelm-

ingly positive assessment of Herod's games. Josephus, like most ancient historians, used previous source materials to compose his narrative.[19] In this case,
his source was likely Herod's court historian, Nicholas of Damascus, who provides most of Josephus' material about Herod. [20] Nicholas, it seems, described
the games as a terrific success; Josephus added his own editorial comments
nearly a century later, emphasizing the problematic nature of Herod's Jerusalem games. These rhetorical and sometimes hyperbolic flourishes, common
strategies used by Josephus in Jewish Antiquities to present a darker and more
critical view of Herod, offer an image of Herod's games that is significantly
skewed by Josephus' own negative assessment of Herod's reign and may reflect
the author's deeply ambivalent attitude toward spectacles and other forms of
popular entertainment.

On the basis of Josephus' account, most modern scholars consider
Herod's Jerusalem games to have been a complete failure. In truth, there is
some external evidence to support this claim. The Jerusalem games were meant
to reoccur every four years, but they are mentioned in no other sources. Civic
inscriptions in cities elsewhere in the Roman Empire proudly list hometown
victors who traveled to compete in other contests in Syria and Palestine; none
of these mention the quadrennial games at Jerusalem. Josephus does not refer
to the theater, even in passing, in any other passage in either his Jewish War
or (Jewish Antiquities), though he describes Jerusalem in some detail as he
narrates the Roman siege and ultimate destruction of the city. Moreover, neither the theater nor the amphitheater built by Herod have been conclusively
identified in any of the archaeological surveys conducted in the area of ancient
Jerusalem and its environs.[21] In light of this, most assume that, either because
of disinterest or mass protest, the Jerusalem theater fell into disuse or was
dismantled.[22] More than a decade later, Herod founded a second set of games
dedicated to Augustus, which were inaugurated upon completion of his new
city, Caesarea.[23] It is generally assumed that Herod founded this second set of
games as a replacement for his failed games in Jerusalem. Having discovered
that the Jews were simply too resistant to theatrical and athletic competitions,
Herod relocated his games to a locale with a pagan population that would
ensure their perpetuation. While there is ample evidence that the Caesarean
games and the structures Herod built to house them lasted several centuries
after Herod's death, the theater and the so-called amphitheater of Jerusalem
left no trace.

To explain the failure of Herod's games, the only recorded instance of
such a failure in all of Roman history, most modern scholars uncritically accept
Josephus' view that Herod's games were "foreign" to the Jews and thus trans-

gressive. Jews, in light of their devotion to Torah law and their own peculiar set of values, were simply different from the other subjects of the Roman Empire and completely rejected the culture of Greek and Roman sport and spectacle.[24] According to this view, Herod planned his Jerusalem games only as a result of external pressure.[25] The historian Jean Juster, for example, assumes that Herod was obligated to offer games because he needed some way to ingratiate himself with his patron Augustus. Since the Jews would obviously be opposed to the imposition of the imperial cult in traditionally Jewish areas, Herod was forced to compromise, presenting the sorts of games that often occurred in the context of the imperial cult without any of the elements, such as sacrifice, that would have been glaringly offensive to the Jews.[26] However, given that during the early years of Augustus' rule the presentation of spectacles, not to mention participation in the imperial cult itself, was entirely voluntary, any explanation that stresses external pressure as Herod's primary motivation for founding games in Jerusalem ultimately fails to convince.[27]

Another explanation for Herod's games focuses on his particular devotion to Greek and Roman athletics and other entertainments. He was, after all, an intimate friend of some of the most important figures of his day and spent a great deal of time at Rome, where he no doubt was first introduced to the types of spectacle entertainment that he would later promote in Judaea. His devotion to the culture of spectacle entertainment went far beyond most of his contemporaries. He donated funds to erect theaters and other public buildings throughout the Greek East and played a significant role in rehabilitating the Olympic Games, a feat for which he received the honor of being appointed "a perpetual president" of the games.[28] At his winter palace in Jericho, Herod constructed a multi-purpose entertainment complex including a theater, a small hippodrome, and swimming pool that were apparently for his own personal use.[29] Recent excavations at Herodium have revealed another private theater built by Herod, complete with a private theater box decorated with lavish frescoes.[30] According to this explanation, Herod may have been so zealously devoted to Greco-Roman culture and so blinded by personal ambition that he either failed to forsee a negative Jewish reaction to these games or simply did not care about this reaction at all.

Herod's passion for Greek and Roman spectacle entertainments bordered on obsession; however, his excessive personal intertest in these diversions rarely compelled him to completely ignore Jewish taboos. Herod's attitude toward Jewish law was, to be brief, complex.[31] He built pagan temples at Caesaerea and Sebaste and helped to fund others in major cities throughout the Greek East.[32] But Herod appears to have been generally respectful of Jewish norms

in the Jewish areas of his kingdom, particularly in Jerusalem where he transformed the Jewish temple into a building that rivaled the temple of Artemis
in Ephesus and of Jupiter Capitolinus in Rome. He refrained from putting
human images on his coins, though under Augustus it became increasingly
more common for a portrait of the emperor to appear on provincial coinage
and for client kings to put their own likenesses on the coins that they mint-
ed.[33] Herod took pains to obey the second commandment even in his personal
villas and palaces, and possibly on his own sarcophagus.[34] There is little reason
to believe that Herod would have broken with his policy of respecting Jewish
law in Jerusalem, no matter how personally interested he was in Greek and
Roman entertainments.

Moreover, the success of his games was predicated on at least some Jewish
participation, and it is unlikely that Herod would have devoted considerable
personal resources to an enterprise that would so predicably fail. If in fact
Herod's construction of a theater and amphitheater in Jerusalem violated Jewish law, it stands out as uncharacteristic and costly miscalculation in the career
of an otherwise shrewd monarch.

Nor is it certain that Herod's games were a failure. Recent research provides some challenges that necessitate a reassessment of the fate of the Jerusalem games. Archaeologists Ronny Reich and Ya'akov Bilig have excavated a
group of stone slabs that they interpret as the remains of theater seats from
either Herod's theater in Jerusalem or the theater mentioned in the Chroni-
con Pascale as part of Hadrian's Aelia Capitolina.[35] Achim Lichtenberger and
Joseph Patrich disagree that these seats belonged to the Herodian theater in
Jerusalem. In their view, Herod's theater and amphitheater were not built as
permanent stone buildings, but were temporary wooden structures erected
for the games and then subsequently dismantled.[36] Wooden theaters and
amphitheaters were actually the norm at Rome. The gladiatorial games were
held in a wooden amphitheater constructed out of bleachers that were erected
in the Roman Forum. Though Pompey built the first permanent theater
there in 55 BCE, temporary theaters and amphitheaters continued to be used
until the construction of the Flavian Amphitheater, commonly known as the
Coliseum, in 79 CE.[37] Reich's and Bilig's identification of theater seats and
Lichtenberger's and Patrich's theory about wooden theaters, though neither is
universally accepted, remove the disappearance of the Herodian entertainment
buildings in Jerusalem from the rather short list of evidence for the failure of
the Jerusalem games.

JEWISH ATTITUDES TOWARD SPORT AND SPECTACLE IN THE SECOND TEMPLE PERIOD: A REASSESSMENT

In light of some the arguments advanced above, I would like to return to Josephus' claims about the innapropriate nature of Herod's games while perhaps recognizing the Jerusalem games as something other than a terrific blunder. Since these claims appear to have been added by Josephus to a previous source that considered the games a great success, and because Josephus lived more than a century after the events he describes, it is worthwhile to evaluate his claims about Jewish attitudes toward spectacle entertainment one by one. Close attention to a wider body of evidence reveals that there were at least some Jews who might have been interested in participating in or attending athletic and dramatic performances in Herodian Jerusalem.

GREEK ATHLETICS AND THEATER: FOREIGN TO JEWISH CUSTOM?

While Josephus claims that the theater and amphitheater were "foreign implants" in Judaea, what the Jewish historian fails to tell readers is that the theater and amphitheater were equally foreign to the non-Jewish residents in Herod's realm. The buildings that Herod constructed in Jerusalem were among the first of their kind in the Near East. No theaters, amphitheaters, hippodromes, stadia, or odea that date from before the Herodian period have been discovered in either the predominantly Jewish or non-Jewish areas of Hellenistic Palestine. Few public structures are preserved at any of the major settlements that date to the Hellenistic period, and where public buildings do exist they are particularly difficult to identify. No gymnasia or assembly houses have been uncovered. In fact, none of the buildings that were characteristic of the Classical Greek city, which the principal political institutions of the Hellenistic polis were meant to mimic, appear in the archaeological record.[38] This lack of civic architecture leaves the impression that the residents of the so-called Greek cities of Hellenistic Palestine had little interest in or experience with spectacle entertainments.[39] At the very least, they lacked the funds to support these festivals themselves.

The sole evidence for the existence of gymnasia or athletic festivals in Hellenistic Palestine comes from Jewish sources that appear to be hostile to these sorts of institutions. First and Second Maccabees rail against the construction of a gymnasium in Jerusalem, though they also let slip the ugly secret that the Jerusalem priests frequently attended the wrestling matches and discus throwing that took place in the palaestra.[40] Second Maccabees dwells on the wickedness of the high priest Jason who sent a delegation to the isolympic games in Tyre. The priests in the delegation were apparently uncomfortable with the 300 silver drachmae that Jason had allegedly earmarked as a gift to the festival and diverted this money to outfit triremes for the Tyrian navy instead. Second Maccabees seems concerned about the appearance of supporting an idolatrous cult but has no real opinion about the priests' attendance at the games. Though the authors of First and Second Maccabees were hostile to gymnastic, athletic, and theatrical festivals, their writings betray the fact that others clearly were less so.

The fact that Second Maccabees was intimately familiar with several technical terms from Greek athletics also suggests that Jewish interaction with this culture survived the uprising.[41] The Hasmonean high priest Hyrcanus I descended from a dynasty that circulated the story about the high priest Jason's construction of a gymnasium as propaganda to legitimate their own rival claim to Jewish leadership. Despite this fact, when Hyrcanus was offered a gold crown by the city of Athens in 105/6 BCE, the honor was to be announced "in the theater at the Dionysian festival, and at the Panathanaean and Eleusinian festivals as well as at the gymnastic games."[42] Whether the Hasmonean high priest would have actually attended any of these festivals is difficult to say. The possibility remains intriguing. It should also be noted that Josephus, who lambasts Herod's founding of a similar festival at Jerusalem, considers Hyrcanus' invitation to be a high point in Jewish-Greek relations, rather than something to be censured. The fate of the gymnasium itself is unknown. Neither First Maccabees or Second Maccabees mentions the destruction of the gymnasium at any point during the Hasmonean revolt. It is highly possible that the gymnasium in Jerusalem continued to exist for several centuries until the destruction of the city by the Romans in 70 CE.[43]

Despite Josephus' claim that gymnastic and theatrical entertainments were "not traditional" among the Jews, Jewish attitudes toward the theater and other entertainments were far from monolithic. No verse from the Pentateuch specifically outlawed these sorts of entertainments.[44] In fact, in the Jewish Diaspora, at least, Jews appear to have been particularly open and accepting, if not enthusiastic about dramatic performances. The Letter of Aristeas, written presumably by an Alexandrian Jew sometime during the second century BCE, actually recommends the theater as an edifying pastime.[45] Ezekiel the Tragedian, most likely another Alexandrian Jew from the same century, composed a tragedy based on the Exodus story, called the Exagoge. Philo, the Alexandrian Jewish philospher, frequently attended the theater, including a production of a Euripidean tragedy.[46]

Philo also admits to attending the games on several occasions; he appears to have been particularly interested in the footrace, the subject of many of his metaphors. Philo's works are permeated with imagery drawn from contests in the stadium, organizations of local games, and the training routines of athletes.[47] For example, he compares a virtuous man to a pancratist in the public games, who endures "all kind of blows with hands and feet . . . being thoroughly hardened with great firmness of flesh, and being tough and unyielding, and filled with the true spirit of an athlete."[48] Philo's pious man is like a runner, who must keep his course straight without stumbling or losing his breath.[49] Philo's references to sport cannot simply be explained away as representing the conventional language of the day. On at least one occasion, Philo provides a unique insight into an ancient sport, offering the only evidence for a boxing referee stepping between the contestants to stop the fight. In general, Philo demonstrates more than a casual familiarity with the gymnasium. On occasion he seems to have firsthand knowledge regarding athletic training and competition.

The evidence from Philo and other Jewish authors from the Second Temple Period argues against Josephus' generalizations about Jewish attitudes toward sport and spectacle. His claims that the theater and amphitheater were "foreign implants" and that they were "not traditional" or perhaps even "not permitted" among the Jews should be treated with a healthy dose of skepticism. At best, we can say Josephus felt that mentioning Herod's theater in Jerusalem served as a ripe opportunity to criticize the Jewish king for violating Jewish norms. Other Jews, however, may not have agreed with him.

In addition to the theatrical, musical, and gymnasitic events, which were common features of festivals elsewhere in the Greek East, Herod's games at Jerusalem featured a number of events that were of decidedly Roman origin:

> When the practice began of involving them [the beasts] in combat with one another or setting condemned men to fight against them, foreigners were astonished at the expense and at the same time entertained by the dangerous spectacle, but to the natives it meant an abrogation of the customs held in honor by them. First, it is a glaring impiety to throw men to wild beasts for the pleasure of other men as spectators. And it is a further impiety to exchange customs for foreign practices.[50]

Josephus exhibits particular disgust at the fact that Herod pit beasts against each other in the arena and threw condemned prisoners to be ripped apart for the entertainment of the crowd. But Jewish attitudes toward these specifically Roman entertainments were probably more complex than Josephus admits. Jews in some circles, especially those connected with the Hasmonean and Herodian houses, were apparently undisturbed by these combat sports. Among other honors, Julius Caesar granted to Hyrcanus II, high priest and ethnarch of the Jews, his sons, and any men who were sent as their ambassadors the right to sit among the senators at bouts between single gladiators and beast shows.[51] Hyrcanus' ancestors had been among those who opposed the gymnasium in Jerusalem, but in Caesar's decree Hyrcanus seems to have received this privilege as a great honor. Such decrees were often granted in response to specific requests, and it is hard to see why Caesar would have offered such a privilege if he felt that it would not have been appreciated. At the very least, Caesar's grant to Hyrcanus and his associates demonstrates that Herod's games did not constitute the first contact between the Jews and the games.[52] Even before the reign of Herod, the Hasmonean monarchs and their emissaries considered attending spectacles an invaluable and essential means for remaining connected to their patrons at Rome.

As Josephus points out quite clearly, the real problem with Herod's games were not the events that were held or the types of entertainments that were displayed, but the prospect that the trophies that adorned the theater violated the second commandment by depicting images of living beings:

> Most of all the trophies were distressing; for thinking these things to
> be images dressed up in weapons, since it was not ancestral for them to
> revere such things, they were completely unable to endure them. . . .
> but Herod seeing that they were riled up and would not easily be
> convinced, if some persuasion were not supplied, summoned the most
> prominent of them to the theater. He led them there and showing
> them the trophies asked them what in the world they thought these
> things were. When they cried out, "images of men," ordering the
> removal of their outer adornment, Herod pointed out to them the
> bare wood. When these were stripped there was laughter.[53]

This story about Herod's rebuttal of the Jewish protests against the trophies in the theater clearly rests on the assumption that these trophies made of wood and armor did not actually violate the biblical prohibition against graven images. Herod had likely been quite careful to avoid the sorts of statuary that normally adorned the front of the stage, erecting panoplies around the theater instead.

That the Jews would have been particularly disturbed by the trophies because they mistakenly assumed that they were statues accords well with the rather copious evidence that from the early years of Herod's reign until the destruction of the Temple, the prohibition against images was one of the most widely respected and deeply felt biblical norms. The almost complete lack of representational art in Jerusalem during the first century BCE until the destruction of the Temple in 70 CE demonstrates that Jerusalemites, not merely radicals, but a large segment of the population, rigorously observed the prohibition against the making of any likeness, whether of humans or of animals, represented two-dimensionally or three-dimensionally in relief or as fully carved sculpture.[54] Herodian Jerusalem experienced a major construction boom and a massive influx of foreign wares. The taste for imported pottery or local imitations grew. The homes of Jerusalem elites were decorated with geometric mosaics and frescoes with architectural motifs. Despite all this, iconic art was scrupulously avoided.[55]

Even Herod took care to avoid violating the second commandment, at least in areas that were populated predominantly by Jews. As his Hasmonean predecessors had done, Herod refrained from placing images of human figures on his coins despite the obvious disadvantages that this would have caused.[56] At Caesarea, the temple dedicated to Roma and Augustus, and the colossal cultic statues it contained, formed the visual focal point of the city.[57] Caesarea must have been saturated with images. The sanctuaries at Sebaste and Panais no doubt featured similar statuary and decorations. The public buildings that Herod constructed in Jerusalem, however, lacked any decoration that might have violated Jewish norms against figurative representation.[58] His villas at Jericho, which featured among other Roman refinements a private athletic entertainment complex, contained no statues or figurative mosaics.[59] A sarcophagus recently discovered by Ehud Netzer at Herodium, which may very well have been Herod's final resting place, appears to have been decorated only with rosettes. In the Western Palace at Masada, a mosaic featuring geometric designs and images of olive branches, figs, and vine leaves gives the impression that Herod did not stray too far from Jewish decorative schemes even in his private residences. When a group of Jewish radicals seized the fortress during the first Jewish revolt against Rome, they encountered no offensive images and apparently refrained from the sort of iconoclasm that their contemporaries exhibited in the destruction of Antipas' palace in Tiberias.[60]

The general absence of iconic imagery in Jewish areas, the numerous anecdotes relating the severity of Jewish protests against the erection or entrance of images into Jerusalem, and the fact that Herod himself avoided figurative representation in the decorative schemes that adorned his numerous building projects, even in the most intimate and personal settings, suggest that the trophies, and not any of the other features of Herod's games, provoked real resentment in some Jewish circles. Herod appears to have been sensitive to Jewish opinions about figurative representation in a number of different contexts, including the private seclusion of his personal residences.[61] Why, then, would Herod have risked offending his Jewish subjects by erecting trophies in the most public context imaginable, in the cavea of a theater that he constructed in the heart of Jerusalem?

Actually, Herod appears to have based his decorations not on a whim, but on precedent. The funeral monument that Simon the Hasmonean constructed in memory of his father and brothers in Mode'in in the 140s BCE, likely still standing in Herod's day, had been constructed as a set of seven pyramids surrounded by pillars supporting carved ships and full suits of armor. The trophies in Herod's theater had the advantage of straddling both worlds. They were already part of Hasmonean iconography but they also celebrated the victory of the Roman emperor in a way that would have been readily understood at Rome.

Once we strip Josephus' anti-Herodian rhetoric away from his description of the Jerusalem games, the inevitability of their failure seems less profound. There was at least some Jewish interest in the sorts of entertainments that Herod provided, even if it appears as though most of this interest was located in Jewish Diaspora communities like Alexandria. Herod cultivated a deep interest in these areas and tried to court their support as he transformed Jerusalem into the capital of world Jewry.[62] Marcus Antonius and the senate at Rome, and later Augustus, had crowned him not only king of Judaea, but king of the Jews. This was a title that he took rather seriously. Herod appointed high priests from the sizeable diaspora communities in Alexandria and Babylonia. This not only de-emphasized the power of the Judaean elites who had traditionally monopolized the high priesthood, but also helped to create new ties with these communities and, ultimately, new sources of income. Herod also defended the rights of the Ionian Jews who were being forced to appear in court on the Sabbath, participate in military service, and perform other civic liturgies although, as they claimed, "the Romans had always allowed them to live in accordance with their own laws."[63] It did not hurt, of course, that in defending the rights of these Ionian Jews, Herod also ensured that their donations to Jerusalem would arrive unimpeded.

Herod appears to have gone out of his way to accommodate Jewish mores when he planned his games at Jerusalem, not simply to minimize resistance to his games, but to ensure that there would be Jewish participation in an event that was, like most festivals in the Greco-Roman world, designed to promote its host city as an international destination and a center of culture and sophistication. Trophies, instead of statuary, were the main decorative feature in Herod's theater. Though these trophies were generally a part of a sophisticated iconographic program that included figurative representations of conquered peoples or provinces, Herod replaced these potentially offensive features with inscriptions that commemorated Augustus' victories without violating the second commandment. The overall message remained the same:

the known world was united by Augustus' victories into a solitary empire, promising peace over land and sea amongst all of the peoples who were subject to Roman rule. Augustus had used his games at Actium to convey a similar message. By reviving an ancient Greek festival at the site of his greatest victory, he offered the inhabitants of the Greek East, who had previously backed his rival Antony, an oportunity to join in his new political enterprise. Combining Greek and Roman entertainments under the banner of a united Rome, Augustus used the games at Actium as a symbol of wholeness and universal peace.[64]

It is also possible that Herod avoided presenting bouts between gladiators because he suspected that Jews would have found these sorts of entertainments particularly disturbing. One of the main features of Agrippa I's games at Berytus included armed battle between condemned men. Herod's games at Caesarea may also have included gladiatorial combat. Though Josephus mentions beast fights and executions as events that took place in Herod's Jerusalem games, gladiatorial combat is conspicuously absent from this list. The three events were generally presented as a set program at munera from the Republican period through the late Principate. The omission of armed battle between single gladiators at Herod's games may have been a concession to the delicate sensibilites of Herod's Jewish subjects, though it is difficult to say this with any certainty.

Herod knew full well that games served not only to strengthen ties with Rome, but that they also instilled a sense of civic, sometimes national or ethnic, pride in their spectators. At Rome, Augustus, Herod's patron and friend, transformed spectacle entertainments into a powerful tool for statecraft.[65] In what were essentially state spectacles, Augustus and the imperial family, "functioned not simply as revered leaders, but as dynamic emblems that attracted and inspired deep patriotic and religious sentiment."[66]

At roughly the same time that Herod was planning his games in Jerusalem, Augustus passed the Lex Iulia Theatralis, which "carefully controlled the allocation of seats and even the appearance of the audience." The newly constructed Theater of Marcellus was designed to flaunt these divisions of class and status, with special passageways for honored attendants and color-coded flags to mark off each section of seats according to the status of the spectators. This arrangement of the seating in the theater had two effects. On the one hand, it controlled the webs of patronage that distributed seats as gifts to clients and friends, reinforcing the strict divisions of the Roman social order. On the other hand, it turned the audience itself into a spectacle. With people from every status visibly represented in the cavea, the disparate crowd in the theater "conveyed the sense that the whole of society was taking part."[67] Herod seems to have been as keenly aware as Augustus that the crowd, though it might consist of vastly different elements from the social order, could be fashioned into a coherent whole, when they sat and cheered in the theater.

CONCLUSION

By throwing quadrennial games in Jerusalem, Herod was without doubt looking outward, toward the imperial court at Rome, a court with whom his relations at this point were somewhat tenuous. But Herod was also apparently looking inward as well. He had inherited a country that was marked by civil strife, not only between Jews and non-Jews, but between the different factions of Jews, the supporters of Hyrcanus II and Aristobulus II, who had been embroiled in a rather lengthy civil war, the remnants of his own Idumaeans, the Ituraeans, and other ethnicities, who had been subjected to Hasmonean rule through a policy of military expansion and in some cases subjected to forcible circumcision.[68] In the same manner that Augustus attempted to use games and festivals as a means to integrate an empire that had been plagued by decades of civil war, Herod may have thrown his own set of games in an attempt to integrate his own fractured country and to focus the attention of Jews worldwide toward his capital, Jerusalem.

NOTES

[1] Richard C. Beacham, *Spectacle Entertainments of Early Imperial Rome* (New Haven: Yale University Press, 1999); Donald G. Kyle, *Spectacles of Death in Ancient Rome* (London: Routledge, 1998); idem, *Sport and Spectacle in the Ancient World* (Malden: Blackwell, 2007); Thomas E. J. Wiedemann, *Emperors and Gladiators* (London: Routledge, 1992); Alison Futrell, *Blood in the Arena: The Spectacle of Roman Power*, 2nd ed. (Austin: University of Texas Press, 2001); Katherine E. Welch, *The Roman Amphitheatre: From its Origins to the Colosseum* (Cambridge: Cambridge University Press, 2007).

[2] See the extremely helpful overview of sociological or anthropological approaches to Roman spectacle in Garrett Fagan, *The Lure of the Arena: Social Psychology and the Crowd at the Roman Games* (Cambridge: Cambridge University Press, 2011), 13-22; Kyle, *Spectacles of Death*, 7-10; Welch, *The Roman Amphitheatre*, 1-8; Keith Hopkins, *Death and Renewal* (Cambridge [Cambridgeshire]: Cambridge University Press, 1983), 1-30; Roland Auguet, *Cruelty and Civilization: The Roman Games* (London: Routledge, 1972); K. M. Coleman, "Fatal Charades: Roman Executions Staged as Mythological Enactments," *Journal of Roman Studies* 80 (1990): 44–73; Marcus Wistrand, *Entertainment and Violence in Ancient Rome: The Attitudes of Roman Writers of the First Century A.D.* (Göteborg: Acta Universitatis Gothoburgensis, 1992); Wiedemann, *Emperors and Gladiators*; Paul Plass, *The Game of Death in Ancient Rome: Arena Sport and Political Suicide* (Madison: University of Wisconsin Press, 1998), 3-77; E. Gunderson, "The Ideology

of the Arena," *Classical Antiquity* 15, no. 1 (1996): 113–51; Futrell, *Blood in the Arena*; Catharine Edwards, *Death in Ancient Rome* (New Haven: Yale University Press, 2007), 46-77; David Potter, "Performance, Power and Justice in the High Empire," in *Roman Theater and Society: E. Togo Salmon papers I* (ed. William J. Slater; Ann Arbor: University of Michigan Press, 1996), 129-61.

[3] Wistrand, *Entertainment and Violence in Ancient Rome*, esp. 55-80.

[4] Greg Woolf, *Becoming Roman: The Origins of Provincial Civilization in Gaul* (Cambridge: Cambridge University Press, 1998), 121-22; Futrell, *Blood in the Arena*, 53-76.

[5] Fagan, *The Lure of the Arena*, esp. 80-154.

[6] Potter, "Performance, Power and Justice in the High Empire"; "Coleman, "Fatal Charades."

[7] See S. R. F. Price, *Rituals and Power: The Roman Imperial Cult in Asia Minor* (Cambridge: Cambridge University Press, 1984); M. J. D. Carter, "The Presentation of Gladiatorial Spectacles in the Greek East: Roman Culture and Greek Identity" (PhD diss., McMaster University, 1999), 144-238, 286-92; Futrell, *Blood in the Arena*, 79-92.

[8] Harold Arthur Harris, *Greek Athletics and the Jews* (Cardiff: University of Wales Press on behalf of Saint David's University College, Lampeter, 1976); Manfred Lämmer, "Griechische Wettkämpfe in Jerusalem und ihre politischen Hintergründe," *Jahrbuch der Deutschen Sporthochschule Köln* (1973): 182-227; idem, "Griechische Wettkämpfe in Galiläa unter der Herrschaft des Herodes Antipas," *Kölner Beiträge zur Sportwissenschaft* (1981): 37–67; idem, "The Attitude of King Agrippa I toward Greek Contests and Roman Games," in *Physical Education and Sports in Jewish History and Culture* (Netanya: Wingate Institute, 1973), 7-17; idem, "The Introduction of Greek Sports into Jerusalem through Herod the Great and its Political Significance," in *Physical Education and Sports in Jewish History and Culture* (Wingate Institute, 1973), 18-38.

[9] Gedalia Alon, "Me'Halakhot Rishonim," in *Mehkarim Be-Toldot Yiśra'el Bi-Yeme Bayit Sheni Uvi-Tekufat Ha-Mishnah Veha-Talmud* (Tel Aviv: Hotsa'at Ha-Kibuts Ha-Me'uchad, 1970); E. Mary Smallwood, *The Jews Under Roman Rule: From Pompey to Diocletian* (Leiden: Brill, 1976); Jean Juster, *Les Juifs dans l'Empire Romain; Leur Condition Juridique, Économique et Sociale* (Paris: P. Geuthner, 1914); Louis H. Feldman, "The Orthodoxy of the Jews in Hellenistic Egypt," *Jewish Social Studies* 22, no. 4 (1960): 215–37; Martin Goodman, *State and Society in Roman Galilee, A.D. 132-212*, 2nd ed. (London: Vallentine Mitchell, 2000); idem, *Rome and Jerusalem: The Clash of Ancient Civilizations* (London: Allen Lane, 2007); Lee I. Levine, *Jerusalem: Portrait of the City in the Second Temple Period (538 B.C.E.-70 C.E.)*, 1st ed. (Philadelphia: Jewish Publication Society, 2002); Arthur Segal, *Theatres in Roman Palestine and Provincia Arabia* (Mnemosyne, bibliotheca classica Batava 140; Leiden: Brill, 1995).

[10] AJ 15:264-71. All translations of Josephus are based on the Loeb Classical Literature series with my own occasional emendations and corrections.

[11] AJ 15:264-91. The date of the first Jerusalem games is not firm. Heinrich Graetz, *Geschichte der Juden von den Ältesten Zeiten bis auf die Gegenwart*, vol. 3 (Leipzig: Leiner, 1908), 218, assumes that the games were given in 28 BCE in conjunction with Augustus' Actian games. See also Abraham Schalit, *Hordos Ha-Melekh: Ha-Ish U-Po'alo*, 3rd ed. (Yerushalayim: Mosad Byaliḳ, 1964), 193; Emil Schürer et al., *The History of the Jewish People in the Age of Jesus Christ (175 B.C.-A.D. 135)*, revised (Edinburgh: Clark, 1987),

I.290, assumes that the games took place sometime between the death of Costobarus in 28/27 BCE and the rebuilding of Samaria as Sebaste in 25 BCE. Smallwood, *The Jews Under Roman Rule*, 84 n. 78, who follows a corrected date for the first Actiad (27 instead of 28), says that "the order of the Josephus' narrative suggests the early 20's for the festival." 28/27 serves as a *terminus post quem* for the construction of the theater and the amphitheater, but not as a fixed date.

[12] See the list of Herod's benefactions in Peter Richardson, *Herod: King of the Jews and Friend of the Romans* (Columbia: University of South Carolina Press, 1996), 186-88, 197-203, 272.

[13] Josephus mentions that Herod offered prizes to those "who were engaged in the musical arts and the so-called *thymelikoi*." The latter were apparently a guild of actors and musicians. They are mentioned alongside mimes and kithara players by Plutarch (*Sulla* 36). See Ralph Marcus and Allen Wikgren, *Josephus in Ten Volumes Jewish: Antiquities Books XV-XVII* (Cambridge: Harvard University Press, 1963), 129d; Michael Ivanovitch Rostovtzeff, *The Social and Economic History of the Hellenistic World*, vol. 3 (Oxford: The Clarendon Press, 1941), 1048-50; Walter Puchner, "Acting in the Byzantine Theater," in *Greek and Roman Actors: Aspects of an Ancient Profession* (ed. P. E. Easterling and E. Hall; Cambridge: Cambridge University Press, 2002), 313; Jane Lightfoot, "Nothing to do with the Technitai of Dionysus?," in *Greek and Roman Actors: Aspects of an Ancient Profession* (ed. P. E. Easterling and E. Hall; Cambridge: Cambridge University Press, 2002), 210. It seems that they are mentioned here as choral actors in distinction with those who excel at the art of music, i.e., the principal singers and actors. For the events held in the so-called amphitheater see Joseph Patrich, "Herod's Hippodrome-stadium at Caesarea and the Games Conducted therein," in *What Athens Has to Do with Jerusalem: Essays on Classical, Jewish, and early Christian Art and Archaeology in Honor of Gideon Foerster* (ed. Gideon Foerster and Leonard Victor Rutgers; Leuven: Peeters, 2002), 29–68.

[14] In the late Republican and early Imperial period, the term amphitheater could designate any number of entertainment structures that were built, in contrast to a theater, with "seats for spectators all around." Josephus appears to have used the term amphitheater to describe several of the Herodian hippodromes. It is very likely, then, that the hippodrome that the rebels occupied in 4 BCE was the same structure that Josephus calls an amphitheater at AJ 15:267. See Harris, *Greek Athletics and the Jews*, 37-39; Lämmer, "Griechische Wettkämpfe in Jerusalem," n. 90; Ehud Netzer, *The Architecture of Herod, the Great Builder* (Tübingen: Mohr Siebeck, 2006), 280; J. H. Humphrey, "Amphitheatrical Hippo-Stadia," in *Caesarea Maritima: A Retrospective after Two Millennia* (ed. Avner Raban and Kenneth G. Holum; Leiden: Brill, 1996), 126; Joseph Patrich, "Herodian Entertainment Structures," in *Herod and Augustus: Papers Presented at the IJS Conference, 21st-23rd June 2005*(ed. David M. Jacobson and Nikos Kokkinos; Leiden: Brill, 2009), 189; Levine, *Jerusalem*, 205 n. 73, assumes that Herod constructed three entertainment structures in Jerusalem.

[15] The Actian Games were held by Augustus in September 28/27 BCE near the site of his victory over his rival Marcus Antonius. On the games and their significance see Robert Alan Gurval, *Actium and Augustus: The Politics and Emotions of Civil War* (Ann Arbor: University of Michigan Press, 1995), 19-65; K. Zachos, "The 'Tropaeum' of Augustus at Nikopolis," *Journal of Roman Archaeology* 16, (2003): 64. Achim Lichtenberger, "Jesus

and the Theater in Jerusalem," in *Jesus and Archaeology* (ed. James H. Charlesworth; Grand Rapids: Eerdmans, 2006), 248, notes, "The traces of two models for the event can be shown: one with a Roman influence and the other following Hellenistic form. Not only do the inscriptions in honor of Octavian point to Rome, but also the agitation of animals, which is of Roman character and, as such could be seen as a diminished form of gladiator games, which Herod felt confident enough to hold only in pagan Caesarea. But also the Hellenistic character of the event is clearly evident. It had as its goal the display of wealth and opulence (*polyteleia* or *tryphē*) and sought models in the Hellenistic representation of royalty."

[16] See e.g., Lee I. Levine, *Judaism and Hellenism in Antiquity: Conflict or Confluence?* (Seattle: University of Washington Press, 1998), 55. Lämmer, "Griechische Wettkämpfe in Jerusalem," 201, suggests that Herod may have intentionally eliminated gladiators from the standard repertoire in order to avoid offending Jewish sensibilities.

[17] AJ 15.274-75.

[18] Lichtenberger, "Jesus and the Theater in Jerusalem," 285; Tamar Landau, *Out-Heroding Herod: Josephus, Rhetoric, and the Herod Narratives* (Leiden: Brill, 2006), 167, ranks this among other "authorial comments" that attest to Herod's impiety, "a prominent theme in the narrative."

[19] See Shaye J. D. Cohen, *Josephus in Galilee and Rome: His Vita and Development as a Historian* (Leiden: Brill, 1979), esp. 48-66.

[20] Ben Zion Wacholder, *Nicolaus of Damascus* (Berkeley: University of California Press, 1962), 5-7; idem, "Josephus and Nicolaus of Damascus," in *Josephus, the Bible, and History* (ed. Louis H. Feldman and Gōhei Hata; Detroit: Wayne State University Press, 1989), 147-72.

[21] C. Schick, "Notes from Jerusalem," *Palestine Exploration Fund Quarterly Statement* 19 (1887): 161-66, identified what he believed to be the remains of the Herodian amphi-theater in Abu Tor, though the features he describes are more fitting for a theater. Harris, *Greek Athletics and the Jews*, 38. Schürer et al., *History of the Jewish People*, 304-5 n. 56, accept this identification. Gustaf Dalman, *Jerusalem und sein Gelände* (Gütersloh: C. Bertelsmann, 1930), 149-50, and A. Kohler, "Abu Tor- the 'Theater,'" *Hadashot Arche-ologiyot* 50 (1974): 14, were among the first to reject Schick's identification of the site. More recently, Ronny Reich and Ya'akov Bilig, "A Group of Theatre Seats Discovered near the South-Western Corner of the Temple Mount," *Israel Exploration Journal* 50, no. 2 (2000): 175-85, have suggested that the Herodian theater might have been located near the Temple mount but are hesitant to date their discoveries. Most likely these the-ater seats belonged to the Hadrianic theater mentioned in the *Chron. Paschale* 1:474 (ed. Dindorf, Bonn, 1832). See also Ronny Reich, "Jerusalem: The Robinson's Arch Area," in *New Encyclopedia of Archaeological Excavations in the Holy Land* (ed. Ephraim Stern, vol. 5; Jerusalem: Israel Exploration Society, 2008), 1809-11, 1836; cf. Lichtenberger, "Jesus and the Theater in Jerusalem," 190-91; Joseph Patrich, "Herod's Theatre in Jerusalem: A New Proposal," *Israel Exploration Journal* 52, no. 2 (2002): 231-39.

[22] Segal, *Theatres in Roman Palestine*, 4; M. Lämmer, "Griechische Wettkämpfe," 287, believes that the games were moved to Sebaste because Herod felt that a non-Jewish population would be more appreciative of his benefactions—though this is little more than conjecture.

[23] AJ 16.138; On the history of the Caesarean games see Patrich, "Herod's Hippodrome-stadium."

[24] See e.g., Feldman, "The Orthodoxy of the Jews in Hellenistic Egypt," 226; Schürer et al., *History of the Jewish People*, II:54-55; S. L. Ari, "The Origins of Theater in Hellenic and Judaic Cultures," in *Hellenic and Jewish Arts* (ed. Asher Ovadiah; Tel Aviv: Ramot Pub. House, Tel Aviv University, 1995), 385-93.

[25] According to Schalit, *Hordos Ha-Melekh*, 144-60, Herod, as a client king of Rome, was pressured or even obliged to demonstrate his allegiance to Augustus, the emperor who had relatively recently confirmed the appointment given to Herod by Marcus Antonius. Schalit continually stresses that Herod, as *rex sociusque et amicus*, essentially a political appointee to a royal post, was completely subject to the will of Rome. The Jewish client king acted with only limited autonomy and was under great pressure to impress his imperial patron. His games, according to Schalit, were largely an attempt to flatter Augustus and demonstrate his loyalty to the new emperor's regime.

[26] Juster, *Les Juifs dans l'Empire Romain*, 338-54.

[27] Simon Price argues powerfully that emperor worship in Asia Minor and elsewhere in the East was never strictly obligatory. Theaters frequently housed rites related to the imperial cult. The celebration of games in honor of the emperor continued to be an important feature of emperor worship through the Severan period and beyond. Imperial priests frequently functioned as sponsors of agonistic festivals or *munera* involving gladiators and *venationes*. Sacrifice before images of the emperor and his family may have preceded some of the most important games. But this sort of civic worship of the emperor was never required. In every case, impetus for the establishment of the imperial cult in urban settings came not from the emperor or his ministers, but as a voluntary responsibility taken on by the urban aristocracy, either a wealthy freedman or a member of the civic council. Even in cases where the emperor seems to have served as the benefactor of local games or cult, his involvement may have been minimal. Often the emperor did little more than agree to the request of a city to hold a festival in his honor. See Price, *Rituals and Power*, 101-32.

[28] See the list of Herod's benefactions in Richardson, *Herod*, 186-88, 197-203, 272.

[29] Ehud Netzer et al., *Hasmonean and Herodian Palaces at Jericho: Final Reports of the 1973-1987 Excavations* (Jerusalem: Israel Exploration Society, 2001), 195-225.

[30] Ehud Netzer, "Additional Discoveries from Herod's Tomb at Herodium [Hebrew]," *Ariel* 186 (2009): 46-57; idem, "Excavation of Herod's Tomb at Herodium [Hebrew]," *Judea and Samaria Studies* 17 (2008): 56-67; idem, "Herod's Tomb and a Royal Theater on the Slopes of Herodium [Hebrew]," *Qadmoniot* 42, no. 138 (2009): 104-17.

[31] Gideon Fuks, "Josephus on Herod's Attitude toward Jewish Religion: The Darker Side," *Journal of Jewish Studies* 53, no. 2 (2002): 238–45; Richardson, *Herod*, 240-62; idem, *Building Jewish in the Roman East* (Waco: Baylor University Press, 2004), 225-40.

[32] BJ 1.403-25; AJ 15.326-41. See also Richardson, *Herod*, 174-96; Barbara Burrell, "Herod's Caesarea on Sebastos: Urban Structures and Influences," in *Herod and Augustus: Papers Presented at the IJS Conference, 21st-23rd June 2005* (ed. David M. Jacobson and Nikos Kokkinos; Leiden: Brill, 2009), 217-33; Donald Ariel, "The Coins of Herod the Great in the Context of the Augustan Empire," in *Herod and Augustus: Papers Presented*

at the IJS Conference, 21st-23rd June 2005 (ed. David M Jacobson and Nikos Kokkinos; Leiden: Brill, 2009), 113-26; Patrich, "Herodian Entertainment Structures."

[33] For a brief catalogue of Herodian coins see Richardson, *Herod*, 203-16. See also Ariel, "The Coins of Herod the Great in the Context of the Augustan Empire"; Samuel Rocca, *Herod's Judaea: A Mediterranean State in the Classical World* (Tübingen: Mohr Siebeck, 2008), 57-60.

[34] On Herod's Sarcophagus see Ehud Netzer, "Uncovering Herod's Grave [Hebrew]," *Ariel* 182 (2008): 6-31; idem, "Excavation of Herod's Tomb at Herodium [Hebrew]," *Judea and Samaria Studies* 17 (2008): 56-67; idem, "Additional Discoveries from Herod's Tomb at Herodium [Hebrew]," *Ariel* 186 (2009): 46-57; idem, "Herod's Tomb and a Royal Theater on the Slopes of Herodion [Hebrew]," *Qadmoniot* 42, no. 138 (2009): 104-17. See also Netzer, *The Architecture of Herod, the Great Builder*, 240-70; Richardson, *Building Jewish in the Roman East*, 225-39; Duane W. Roller, *The Building Program of Herod the Great* (Berkeley: University of California Press, 1998), 270-78.

[35] Ronny Reich and Ya'akov Bilig, "A Group of Theater Seats from Jerusalem [Hebrew]," *Qadmoniot* 122 (2001): 88-92; idem, "A Group of Theatre Seats Discovered near the South-Western Corner of the Temple Mount"; Ronny Reich, "Excavations near the Temple Mount and Robinson's Arch, 1994-6; Appendix: A Group of Theater Seats from Jerusalem," in *Ancient Jerusalem Revealed* (ed. Hillel Geva; Jerusalem: Israel Exploration Society, 2000), 340-52. Reich and Bilig interpret the inscriptions ΔI and ΔIO as numbers for marking off rows and sections within the theater. They connect these inscriptions to a set of two ornamental bone disks that Avigad had originally interpreted as theater tickets. See Nahman Avigad, *Discovering Jerusalem* (Nashville: T. Nelson, 1983), 193-94; idem, *The Herodian Quarter in Jerusalem: Wohl Archaeological Museum* (Keter, 1989), 65; cf. Elizabeth Alfoldi-Rosenbaum, "The Finger Calculus in Antiquity and in the Middle Ages: Studies on Roman Game Counters I," *Frühmittelalterliche Studien* 5 (1971): 1-9. who believes these so called "theater tickets" were actually game pieces and have no relationship to the theater. See also Lichtenberger, "Jesus and the Theater in Jerusalem," 294 n.50.

[36] Lichtenberger, "Jesus and the Theater in Jerusalem," 190-91; Patrich, "Herod's Theatre in Jerusalem," 231-39.

[37] The use of wooden buildings for spectacle entertainment has a long and distinguished history. The Dionysia at Athens were performed in the agora while spectators watched seated on wooden bleachers. When the bleachers collapsed in 498 BCE, seats were made by digging into the hillside and later constructed out of stone. See Margarete Bieber, *The History of the Greek and Roman Theater* (Princeton: Princeton University Press, 1939), 54. By the later fourth century, Greek theaters were constructed in stone, but the *skene* and other features of the theater building continued to be constructed out of wood. During most of the Republican period, Roman senators were hesitant to allow the construction of permanent theater buildings. Permanent theaters or amphitheaters provided unruly plebs a place to assemble as a mob and demonstrate their displeasure. Theatrical displays served as powerful political propaganda; permanent buildings would demonstrate honors that no one man should enjoy. According to Livy (*Epitome* XLVIII), the censors Valerius Messala and Cassius Longinus were forced to abandon plans to construct a stone theater.

Pompey managed to overcome this taboo against stone theaters and constructed the first theater in Rome in 55 BCE, though wooden theaters continued to be utilized until 17 BCE. See Richard C. Beacham, *Spectacle Entertainments of Early Imperial Rome* (New Haven: Yale University Press, 1999), 51-74; idem, *The Roman Theatre and Its Audience* (Cambridge: Harvard University Press, 1991), 56-84. *Munera* took place in makeshift wooden structures in the *Forum Romanum* from the second century BCE on. During his quadruple triumph in 46 BCE, Julius Caesar presented gladiator matches in a wooden amphitheater. See Welch, *The Roman Amphitheatre*, 38-42. Augustus built wooden seats in the Campus Martius for athletic games (Suetonius *Vit. Aug.* 43.1). The first permanent amphitheater in Rome, that of Statilius Taurus, was not constructed until 29 BCE. When this burned down in 64 CE, Nero constructed a wooden amphitheater as a replacement. This was soon followed by the construction of the massive Flavian Amphitheater (the Colosseum) in 79/80 CE. The chariot races in the Circus Maximus lacked permanent facilities until the first quarter of the second century BCE. Augustus' reconstructions transformed the Circus Maximus into a monumental building with seating that extended around three sides of the track. Still, wooden bleachers accounted for nearly two thirds of the available seating. See John H. Humphrey, *Roman Circuses: Arenas for Chariot Racing* (London: B.T. Batsford, 1986), 64-76. See also Lichtenberger, "Jesus and the Theater in Jerusalem," 294; Patrich, "Herod's Theatre in Jerusalem," 233-35.

[38] Oren Tal, *The Archaeology of Hellenistic Palestine: From Tradition to Innovation [Hebrew]* (Jerusalem: Mosad Byalik, 2006), 41-46,325-27; Segal, *Theatres*, 4.

[39] Schürer et al., *History of the Jewish People*, I.24, acknowledges that there is no evidence that the celebration of games took place in the cities of pre-Roman Palestine, but suggests that they occurred nonetheless "given the general character of the age"; cf. Victor Tcherikover, *Hellenistic Civilization and the Jews*, 1st ed. (Philadelphia: Jewish Publication Society of America, 1959), 105-16. Nearby Hellenistic Syria lacked proper monumental theaters, though inscriptions do mention *agonothetes* and *theoroi* and a number of literary references suggest that gymnasia were common. Polybius mentions a hippodrome at Daphne near Antioch where isolympic games were held (30.26.1) and at Seleucia-Pereia (5.59.1). See Fergus Millar, "The Problem of Hellenistic Syria," in *Hellenism in the East: The Interaction of Greek and Non-Greek Civilizations from Syria to Central Asia after Alexander* (ed. A. Kuhrt and S. Sherwin-White; London: Duckworth, 1987), 117. Nothing suggests that these hippodromes consisted of anything more than flat plains for racing horses. In any event, the horse racing events in both of these areas were probably exceptional, since they were connected to the imperial court. See Humphrey, *Roman Circuses*, 456, 529. Theater-temples existed in Hellenistic and early Roman Syria but these seem to have been a local phenomenon. See Malcolm Colledge, "Greek and non-Greek Interaction in the Art and Architecture of the Hellenistic East," in *Hellenism in the East: The Interaction of Greek and Non-Greek Civilizations from Syria to Central Asia after Alexander* (ed. A. Kuhrt and S. Sherwin-White; London: Duckworth, 1987), 151.

[40] 1 Macc 1:14; 2 Macc 4:12.

[41] Harris, *Greek Athletics and the Jews*, 29f.

[42] AJ 14.151-55.

[43] Rocca, *Herod's Judaea*, 129-31.

[44] Though Lämmer, "Griechische Wettkämpfe in Jerusalem," suggests that Leviticus 18:3 might have served as a prooftext, he clearly has the rabbinic interpretation of this verse in mind (Sifra *Achare Mot* 13.9 [ed. Finkelstein, 372]).

[45] *Let. Aris.*, 284.

[46] *Ebr.*, 177; *Prob.*, 144.

[47] See Harris, *Greek Athletics and the Jews*, 72-91; Pierluigi Lanfranchi, *L'exagoge d'Ezéchiel Le Tragique* (Leiden: Brill, 2006), 42; Feldman, "The Orthodoxy of the Jews in Hellenistic Egypt," 227; idem, *Jew and Gentile in the Ancient World: Attitudes and Interactions from Alexander to Justinian* (Princeton: Princeton University Press, 1996), 62-63; John M. G. Barclay, *Jews in the Mediterranean Diaspora: From Alexander to Trajan (323 BCE-117 CE)* (Edinburgh: T&T Clark, 1996), 160-61.

[48] *Prob.*, 26.

[49] *Ebr.*, 177.

[50] AJ 15.274-75.

[51] AJ 14.210. A similar right was granted to the ambassadors of Aphrodesias and Plarasa in Rome. See Joyce Maire Reynolds, *Aphrodisias and Rome: Documents from the Excavation of the Theatre at Aphrodisias* (Journal of Roman Studies Monographs 1; London: Society for the Promotion of Roman Studies, 1982), 60, 63, 88 esp. insc. #8 lines 76-77. Patrich, "Herod's Hippodrome-stadium at Caesarea," 56 n. 43, assumes that this demonstrates that "there were Jews who were curious enough to want to watch precisely these shows many years earlier [than Herod introduced them]"; cf. Lämmer, "Griechische Wettkämpfe in Jerusalem," 195.

[52] Patrich, "Herod's Hippodrome-stadium," 56.

[53] AJ 15.276-79

[54] A few exceptions can be noted, which perhaps prove the rule. See e.g., Levine, *Jerusalem*, 390 n. 75.

[55] Levine, *Jerusalem*, 142-43; Schürer et al., *History of the Jewish People*, 2.81-82.

[56] Coins served more than just pecuniary functions in antiquity. Ancient money frequently portrayed portraits of the rulers responsible for their issue, representations of their divine patrons, pictures of monuments dedicated to their military exploits, or other key symbols of their sovereignty. Because of their wide circulation, royal coinage provided an unrivaled opportunity to communicate the propagandistic interests of the monarch and served as the most powerful physical representation of the king in his realm.

[57] BJ 1.408-15; AJ 15:331-41; AJ 16:136-37.

[58] The sole exceptions to this are the eagle that he erected over the gate in the Jerusalem Temple (BJ 1.649-55; AJ 17.151) and the trophies that are currently under discussion.

[59] See e.g., Netzer et al., *Hasmonean and Herodian Palaces at Jericho.*

[60] See *Vita* 65.

[61] To this list of contexts, we can now add his sarcophagus, which appears to have been completely absent of figurative representation. See Netzer, "Excavation of Herod's Tomb at Herodium [Hebrew]"; idem, "Uncovering Herod's Grave [Hebrew]"; idem, "Herod's Tomb and a Royal Theater on the Slopes of Herodium [Hebrew]."

[62] Seth Schwartz, *Imperialism and Jewish Society, 200 B.C.E. to 640 C.E.* (Princeton: Princeton University Press, 2001), 45-46; Michael Grant, *Herod the Great* (New York:

American Heritage Press, 1971), 178-82; Smallwood, *The Jews Under Roman Rule*, 82; Schalit, *Hordos Ha-Melekh*, 424-28. For a different perspective on Herod's relationship to the Jewish Diaspora, cf. Erich Gruen, "Herod, Rome and the Diaspora," in *Herod and Augustus: Papers Presented at the IJS Conference, 21st-23rd June 2005* (ed. Nikos Kokkinos and David M. Jacobson; Leiden: Brill, 2009), 13-29.

[63] AJ 16.28.

[64] Gurval, *Actium and Augustus*, 19-65. For Herod's appropriation of Augustan ideology, see Rocca, *Herod's Judaea*, 36-60.

[65] Beacham, *Spectacle Entertainments*, 92-155.

[66] Ibid., 113.

[67] Ibid., 124.

[68] Schwartz, *Imperialism and Jewish Society*, 32-48.

Sports and the Graphic Novel from Diaspora to Diaspora: James Strum's *The Golem's Mighty Swing* and JT Waldman's *Megillat Esther* in the Tree of Contexts

Ori Z. Soltes

At first glance, James Strum's 2001 *The Golem's Mighty Swing* and JT Waldman's 2006 *Megillat Esther* would seem to have little in common aside from the fact that they are both graphic novels. Strum creates a story *ex nihilo*, a fiction based on a range of interlocking historical realities. Waldman takes on a story that already exists as an ambiguous part of the biblical canon. The two works are visually different in style from each other, but both grow out of common issues.

Both works partake of the graphic re-invention of the novel as a radical re-statement of Jewish artistic identity. The People of the Text can also be a People of the Image, as Jewish artists in Paris and New York have been making clear since the late nineteenth and early twentieth centuries. But that double identity can co-exist in one frame. While Jews have produced illuminated manuscripts for centuries,[1] both Strum and Waldman do more than this by making the image the equal of the text.

More than that, both further the larger questions of Jewish identity as a minority community within often hostile or at best tolerant majorities. Both authors deal with a Jewish "community" at risk that is saved by a methodology conceptually connected to messianic thinking. That thinking also asks questions with regard to divine-human interaction, especially *for* the purposes of salvation. Both Strum's and Waldman's saviors—in opposite ways—might be called "crypto-Jews." And in both cases, although this is not the norm in the Jewish tradition, the physicality of those saviors is emphasized, even as physicality alone does not drive the salvational course of either narrative. And that physicality may be seen not only as an adjunct to skill in sports, but in part, as a metaphor for Jewish visual artistic activity.

For like art, sports and physicality were both long disassociated from the Jewish experience. Where art is concerned, the graphic novel proves to be only among the latest explosive output in a long series of Jewish visual accomplishments—from the wall paintings in the Dura Europas synagogue (ca. 240-5 CE) on the bank of the Euphrates River; to lush illuminated and illustrated *haggadot* such as the Golden Haggadah (ca. 1320) and the Sarajevo Haggadah (ca. 1400) from Aragon, Spain; to Pissarro's late nineteenth century Impressionist landscapes; to Mark Rothko's mid-twentieth century chromatic abstractions. Thus, if graphic novels such as these are of particular interest because they combine visual and textual elements so intimately, they are also a reminder of the range and variety of Jewish art because of the profound differences between their respective approaches to visualizing their respective subjects, and not only because of the radical differences between the two narratives and narrative-sources that they offer.

Like visual art, sports and physicality also have a longer Jewish history than might be commonly supposed. There are, of course, as with every aspect of Judaism, the obvious biblical bases for both—from Jacob's epic night-long wrestling match, to Samson's unprecedented strongman act (a career that included a weaponless defeat of a hungry lion—no Roman amphitheater warrior would ever match that feat—and the singular defeat of a thousand Philistine opponents with not much more of a weapon; and that culminated with his bringing the house down—literally). But there is also the emphasis on attributes other than pure size and/or strength. When David destroys *his* gargantuan Philistine opponent, he does so with speed and skill and—in his own words—by coming "in the name of the Lord of hosts."

The Judaean descendants of the Israelites would turn both to speed and skill, clever stratagems, and also divine assistance to fend off their opponents. Thus, the righteous and attractive widow, Judith, would save Jerusalem by using her beauteous wiles to gain access to the Assyrian general, Holofernes, and lop off his head. Esther would save the Persian Judaeans with similar skills—but in the end it was also the Judaeans themselves, armed by royal decree and allowed to defend themselves, who were skilled enough to defeat their armed enemies by matching sword for sword and tooth for tooth. And, of course, Judah the so-called Maccabee and his brothers used both intelligence and martial skills to achieve success against an opponent more numerous and better outfitted for battle than they—and if 1 Maccabees emphasizes their skills, 2 Maccabees emphasizes God's miraculous contributions to their victory.[2]

These biblical and post-biblical, Israelite and Judaean precedents would both lead into and contrast with the first eighteen centuries of Jewish Diasporic life. For the most part, during those centuries, to be fair, Jewish survival was rarely based on athletic skill, but on using stratagems to outsmart more numerous and better-equipped opponents. On the one hand, the ultimate wrestling matches prove to be verbal disputations, in which (consider Nachmanides in Barcelona in 1263), even in victory, the Jewish winner could lose (Nachmanides was exiled after his stunning triumph over his Dominican opponent). On the other hand, sporting events like jousting and its martial concomitants were by definition limited to Christians,[3] so Jews could hardly excel if they could not participate in becoming or being knight-athletes and their competitions. In addition, since the vast majority of medieval athletic heroes remain anonymous (like the vast majority of medieval artists and craftsmen), then we cannot know for certain whether there were Jews who bucked the odds and participated and even succeeded in such a mode of life.

There were, in any case, the occasional real or imagined exceptions—beginning with Bar Kokhba, who was not only a brilliant strategist in his three-year-long struggle against the Romans, but apparently a physical giant of a man. But these exceptions tend to end up as cautionary tales for Jews against using physicality as a survival mechanism. There is—apropos of the larger history of the novel of which the graphic novel is also part—the quintessential picaresque novel (often also regarded as the first "modern" novel), Miguel de Cervantes' *Don Quixote*. In it, the eponymous hero, a knight (of sorts), is implied (in a conversation with his loyal peasant acolyte, Sancho Panza) to be of crypto-Jewish extraction.[4] But to whatever extent we might therefore embrace him as a Jewish hero, we must recognize that, from the perspective of real, everyday knights, he hardly fits the mold—he tilts at windmills and flocks of sheep, after all—and his knight-errant career is based on an excessively large library and being buried too long in too many texts.[5]

By the time Cervantes was penning his *Quixote*, "Jewish" literature had expanded and diversified. In the very Spain in which Cervantes would eventually write his masterwork, some Jews were earlier drawn to a side of Jewish literature, mystical literature, which reached its classical kabbalistic zenith with Moses de Leon's renowned 1305 *Zohar*. By the time of Cervantes, one finds later kabbalistic literature growing. One of the places where late kabbalah developed was in Prague, whose key figure was Rabbi Judah Loew (1525-1609), an older contemporary of Cervantes (1547-1616).

Judah Loew was known for writings that further expanded the esoteric side of kabbalah. More astonishing, perhaps, he carried practical kabbalah to a new level by using its most abstruse formulae to create a creature to serve and protect the Jewish community of Prague. This might be considered a second medieval exception to Jewish non-physicality. The creature was called simply "Golem"—a Hebrew term extracted from Psalm 139:16 that means "unformed." It was contrived by emulating the creation by God of the first human, Adam, from the red [*adom*] earth [*adamah*] itself, as described in Genesis 1. Rabbi Loew shaped his creature out of earth, reciting the necessary formulae and then placing the ineffable name of God on a piece of paper in the Golem's mouth to animate it.[6]

The Golem can be understood within the vague messianic terms found in Jewish literature and thought over the centuries:[7] its strength makes it messianic to Prague's Jews, albeit localized and purely physical. But unlike Adam, it is soulless, and in the end, Rabbi Loew has to de-commission it (by removing the divine name from its mouth/forehead) because only he knew how to control it, and uncontrolled, such a creature could wreak unintended havoc.[8] Thus, this second exception to the largely non-physical emphasis in medieval Jewish history and culture also ends up as cautionary: physicality can get out of hand, even if it is informed by the ineffable name of God, and is not the proper prescription, after all, for Jewish survival.

* * *

It is the story of Judah Loew's Golem from which James Strum's *The Golem's Mighty Swing* derives its title and part of its content. Strum interweaves aspects of the shapeless story of that soulless creature (yet animated by the divine name) with a number of historical, literary, and mythological matters into his fictional account of a Jewish baseball team barnstorming across the belly of the United States in the 1920s. Among these matters is the shifting attitude toward physicality and toward violence as a response to a violent world that began to take shape with Jewish emancipation in the late eighteenth century. The facilitating moment of change for Jews was the emergence of the English Jewish boxer—Daniel "Battling" Mendoza (1764-1836)—as a star. Mendoza won the British heavyweight boxing crown in 1792—the only middleweight ever to do so[9]—and is regarded as the father of modern, technique-powered boxing that emphasizes strategic thinking, defensive moves, side-stepping, and other footwork.

Physicality, as a Mendoza-inspired Jewish desideratum, broadened by the end of the following century toward the evolution of "muscular Judaism." The idea—also connected to emergent back-to-the-earth Zionism—was to further overturn both the stereotype and the tradition of non-physicality that had defined Jews for most of the previous eighteen centuries. Cognate with this idea, there emerged an array of Jewish sports individuals and teams in the early twentieth century extremely successful in athletic competitions that ranged from fencing to soccer.[10]

By the time of Mendoza, a small but growing Jewish community was beginning to find its way within the nascent United States. Here Jews would have the opportunity to be reshaped as from the beginning they were involved in influencing the new United States. By the time of "muscular Judaism" and broader Jewish sports successes, millions of European Jews were braving the difficult journey from inland village to port city and across the ocean to America. Like all immigrants of every religious, ethnic, and national background, Jews asked: how shall we become Americans?

One means of responding to that question was—in a manner that echoed the ethos of "muscular Judaism"—by joining the effusive American enthusiasm for sports. By the aftermath of World War I, the ultimate goal was becoming participation and success in baseball, the "American pastime," whether playing in street games, little league games, or aspiring to big league games. The ultimate hero for American Jews, as the manic 1920s eventually pushed into the Great Depression of the 1930s, was Hank Greenberg, who starred in Major League Baseball from 1933 to 1947 (with time out to serve in the armed forces during World War II).

Greenberg arrived in messianic fashion—like the Golem, but with neither rabbinic intermediation nor dire counter-consequences—when he was most needed to uplift the spirits of a community less sure of its position by the 1930s than it had been a generation or two earlier. America had by then shown itself possessed of ethnocentric and other prejudices familiar from centuries of European history. From Leo Frank's lynching in 1913 in Georgia to the Sacco and Vanzetti executions of 1927 (the year of Babe Ruth's sixty home runs and of Nazi-sympathizing Charles Lindbergh's solo flight across the Atlantic), the American people and legal system had demonstrated a distinct ability for injustice.

And as fascism grew in Europe, particularly that brand shaped by Adolph Hitler in Germany, the United States found itself host to an expanding array of Nazi sympathizers (Charles Lindbergh was hardly alone). The vast belly of America between the coasts, where Strum sets his tale, was marked by significant Judaeophobia, nowhere more intensely than in and around Detroit—the very city for whose Tigers Hank Greenberg played—where on the one hand, Henry Ford was stirring Judaeophobic poison in his *Dearborn Independent,* and printing thousands of copies of *The Protocols of the Elders of Zion,*[11] and distributing them to his workers; and on the other hand, the notorious Catholic priest Father Coughlin was spewing antisemitic venom every week from his radio pulpit. So Hammerin' Hank held up more than a baseball bat on his broad shoulders when he played.

By then, two other parallel developments relevant to this discussion were also taking shape for American Jewry. One was its movement toward prominence in the visual arts. In New York, an array of Jewish painters and sculptors, from Max Weber to Ben Shahn and Raphael Soyer, emerged between the time just before World War I and the era of the Great Depression.[12] But a number of Christian American critics saw the work of New York artists—implicitly, Jewish artists—as questionably "American."[13] So the notion of an America of wide-open acceptance of religious and ethnic variation was challenged even on the level of the visual arts.

The other relevant development was the marriage between sports writing—particularly baseball writing—and the novel and short story that found its first serious exponent in Ring Lardner in the 1920s. The figure who most conspicuously carries Lardner's mode of writing forward in American letters is Jewish novelist Bernard Malamud. His 1952 *The Natural* was the first full-scale novel not only focused on baseball, but also offering an internal matrix of interlocking issues that include what is endemic to Judaism and Jewish thought: questions without answers, particularly the question of why inexplicable things happen as they do.[14]

A generation after Malamud's *The Natural*, Philip Roth would play on the entire idea of what it means not only to write a novel, but to write one definitive enough, in a distinctly American idiom, to be considered *the* great American novel.[15] Tongue-in-cheek (or perhaps not), Roth titled his 1973 work *The Great American Novel*. Roth stands on Malamud's shoulders with regard to baseball writing as quintessential American writing: the subject of *The Great American Novel* is actually a fictional baseball league—the Patriotic League—and the Communist conspiracy to efface the recollection of its existence from history. So his novel chooses the grandest American sport, depicted during the World War II period when many of its best players were serving in the armed forces and thus AWOL from baseball, and interweaves it with the grandest twentieth-century American fear—the "red peril"—with which Jews in particular were suspected of being associated.[16]

* * *

These varied issues—the novel in its picaresque origins, marranism, messianism and the story of the Golem, the question of Jewish physicality, the matter of fitting into America in spite of American prejudices, the rise of Jewish American artists and authors in America—all resonate through Strum's *The Golem's Mighty Swing* that, as a novel, might be said to stand on Malamud's and Roth's shoulders. He takes on the all-American sport and interweaves the matter of the American struggle to define itself as open to diverse cultures, religions, and also races—or as mired in prejudice and closed-mindedness—and places these issues in the setting of the 1920s. He thus places them in the decade in which America was rethinking its international role after World War I, was reconsidering its "nation of immigrants" role with the articulation of a refined quota system under the Johnson-Reed Act of 1924,[17] and was exulting in Charles Lindberg's conquest of the skies during the same year that the Babe singlehandedly pushed baseball into the ultimate sports spotlight by slamming those sixty home runs.

Strum places them in a decade when, to repeat, Jews were also arriving as a force on the American visual art scene and on the American sports scene, while in one part of Europe—Germany, socioeconomic and cultural *goldene medina* for many Jews over the previous few generations—a new art was being shaped. German Expressionist cinema developed in the 1920s, in which one of the most popular films, directed by Paul Wegener, played on the old Bohemian Jewish story of Rabbi Judah Loew and his creation: *Der Golem und Wie er in der Welt Kam* [The Golem and How He Came into the World].[18] Meanwhile, the previously-mentioned rise of fascism was becoming embodied in a real-life Golem, Hitler—a shapeless destroyer presenting himself to Germany as a secular messiah.

Strum weaves all of these issues and more into his tale in simple, straight-forward prose, narrated in the first-person and in an understated and effective drawing style that emphasizes rectilinearity (like the baseball diamond and its bases) [Fig. 1]. His barnstorming Jewish baseball team makes itself stereotypically Jewish by giving everyone a beard, even (with boot-polish) the sixteen-year-old younger brother of the manager-narrator. The team endures a range of complications that are mostly traceable to the antisemitism that they encounter in various ways, offering echoes of the experience of African American players during the same era playing games in the Negro League created because the American pastime would not allow blacks into its mainstream until 1947. Thus, he encompasses not only the question of the place of Jews as feared outsiders in the Middle America of that era, but also the question of the relationship between Jewish Americans in their struggle and African Americans in theirs, and the question of whether that relationship offers team camaraderie or competition.

Jews and blacks—one black, anyway—are on the same team that moves together through the hateful atmosphere of America. Strum's story reflects on the historical partnership of common interests that would carry through the 1960s, where it unraveled, in part because it was never an equal partnership, in part because the nature of the prejudices against both was never exactly the

Figure 1.

same. In Strum's tale, there are subtle suggestions of that imbalance. The opening page offers a poster announcing the arrival of the team to Forest Grove; along the bottom of the image are the words "Reserved Seating For Whites," a category that presumably could include Jews; on the other hand, when Henry Bell, the African American teammate competes, there is an entire section of the stands filled with African Americans who cheer him and who will lionize him after the game, while the only interface with the locals possible for the Jewish players is getting stoned by children or beaten up by adults [Fig. 2].

As the Stars of David struggle to survive financially, the manager-narrator, Noah Strauss, reluctantly agrees to allow a promoter, Paige, to dress one of them up—their biggest, most powerful player—in the costume of the Golem from the Wegener movie. Paige claims to have brought the very costume worn in that role "all the way from Germany"—and the viewer will recognize that familiar film still in Strum's drawings. The idea is to stir up greater interest by playing even more profoundly on the fears of their small-town audiences than the mere fact that the team's members are Jewish. Strum accompanies Paige's quotations from newspaper headlines—"Crowds held in awe by the mythical Jewish Legend . . . The Golem has captivated New York"—with one frame showing a mesmerized audience in a darkened theater and a second filled with the fierce creature raked by severe lighting and casting a giant shadow [Fig. 3].

Acceding to this proposal will turn serious entertainment defined by athletic skill into a form of circus-like entertainment, but Coach Strauss—the Zion Lion, former Boston Red Sox star—gives in out of desperation. The biggest, most powerful player happens to be the one non-Jew on the team: Henry Bell, former Negro League star, who has an array of tales to tell about baseball and America and his own experience as a member of a feared and despised minority. Henry has been a crypto-Jew of sorts—he has been offered to the public as "Hershl Bloom (member of the lost tribe)." He will now carry the complexity of his "hiddenness" further: a feared Negro playing a feared Jewish batter playing the feared mythic Golem. A dark version of the Golem's story was alive in movie theaters from Germany to the United States at the very time when Hitler was planning and leading a failed *putsch* and then writing in *Mein Kampf* about how fearful as betrayers of Germany the Jews are, all of whom "descended" from the betrayer, Judas.

The parallels between the story we are reading/seeing and those told by Henry reflect the parallels between Jews and African Americans as objects of fear. The team is an entire team of Golems to a frightened Middle America—or rather, a team of devils, with horns and cloven hooves. More ironically, its star player is and is not one of them, but another form of Golem and so can

Figure 2.

Figure 3.

serve, in costume, as the Golem [Fig. 4]. That is, for the team he can play the role of the local messianic figure who will offer salvation on the baseball field and in the bank; while for the fans he can be a particular manifestation of "golem," like his teammates are, a creature that does not possess a genuine, fully realized human soul and wreaks havoc among civilized, fully human folk. Both Jews and Africans (and Asians and Native Americans) fell into the not-fully-human category for white, Christian Europeans in the nineteenth century and early twentieth century.[19]

It certainly does not require a profound study of Freud to recognize the baseball bat as a phallic symbol, so this Golem plays both to stereotype with regard to his weapon of choice and to the most particular and perverse form of fear directed by white Middle American males to males of Henry's race before, during, and after the 1920s with respect to the sexual safety and sanctity of their women. Irony within irony: he who is stereotypically sexually over-endowed and uncontrollable with respect to that endowment plays disguised as a Jew on a Jewish team (he's kind of an anti-marrano); the stereotypical Christian view of Jewish males is that the circumcision experienced by them on the eighth day after birth has diminished their sexual endowment and enjoyment.

But the further irony is that, in the end, the Golem's mighty swing fails at the crucial moment, falls short of the hype, when the team is up against a squad with serious players, and his final hit is a trickle to the mound. (Note the continued punning Freudian implications of the terms "trickle" and "mound" in the last clause.) Conversely, his mighty pitch, which beans an opposing player, provokes a pogrom-like riot that might have destroyed the Jewish players had he not (irony now further wraps around irony) stood by the entrance to the dugout intimidatingly, with his mighty bat and its threatening swing, as his teammates quietly and calmly intoned the *Shma*. This is the most fundamental of Jewish prayers, affirming belief in God's uniqueness and God's covenantal (and soteriological) relationship with Israel—and the "last words" of choice for generations of Jewish martyrs.

But the Golem's bat might not have saved these Jews in the long run; they still might have been destroyed by the angry crowd, had God not ultimately intervened with the sudden thunderstorm that rains out the game and drives the crowd home. The only image that fills an entire page of Strum's novel is that of the water pouring down, accompanied by the text, "for thousands of years Jews have tried to die with the *Shma* on their lips" [Fig. 5].

So God, not the Golem, is the savior, who intervenes with flooding water—as God had first "intervened" to destroy all the evil inhabitants of the

Figure 4.

Figure 5.

world, while saving the righteous few, led by Noah (whose name is borne by Strum's narrator/manager), in Genesis 6-9; as God had later intervened with flooding water to rescue the Israelites led by Moses along the dry bottom of the Sea of Reeds, while drowning the Egyptians, in Exodus 14; as God still later saved the Israelites, led by Deborah and Barak, with a sudden downpour that transformed the hillside along which the Canaanite Sisera had held such a strategic advantage before the rains came, in Judges 4-5.

In the epilogue beyond the end of Strum's tale of survival, when the Stars of David have long broken up, Noah finds himself at a game promoted by Paige that disgusts him because it has completely reduced the serious effort of baseball to a caricature. Rather than leave the ballpark, he stays, "curious to see how it all plays out." And we might wonder, is "it" the tug-of-war that has developed in the last frame over a goat? Is "it" the particular game that Noah is watching? The extended joke to which the game has been reduced? Jewish history? American history? American Jewish history? Simply: history? And what role does God play in any of that now, in the era beyond Noah, Moses, Deborah, and Barak?

What role do we humans play, who have so often believed that our own creations could be our salvation and seen them turn into destructive golems—like the technology turned horrific in World War I and in the Holocaust/Hiroshima destructions, between which historic events Strum's story is sandwiched?

* * *

All of these questions connect Strum's graphic novel to that by JT Waldman. For there is a story in the Jewish tradition in which no Golem but a human being, a conceptual descendant of Deborah, rescues a Judaean community in danger of destruction at the hands of an angry crowd filling 127 states within a large empire. This is the story of Esther, who risks her life to save the Judaeans in the fanciful Persia of Ahasuerus. Waldman retells this story in his graphic novel, *Megillat Esther*. He picks up where Strum leaves off, for his heroine expands the role of Strum's "hero." Where Strum's Golem saves barely a minyan of Jews whom he had endangered with his one wild pitch, Esther saves a far-flung community of Judaeans endangered by her uncle Mordecai's refusal to kowtow to the villainous Haman.

Like Strum, but with different emphases, Waldman weaves his tale with other, parallel figures and events in the Jewish narrative. Esther is like Moses, redeeming her people by going before the ruler—in his case, as an Egyptian

prince who is not really Egyptian but an outsider Israelite, to the Pharaoh; in
her case, as a Persian queen who is not really Persian but an outsider Judaean,
to the Shah. Both squeeze success out of disaster, one in the passage through
the Sea of Reeds and the destruction by drowning of the Pharaoh (or his
son), and the other through the counter-royal-declaration she achieves, which
allows the Judaeans to defend themselves and to encompass the destruction
of Haman and his sons. Both Esther and Moses are, like Strum's Henry Bell,
crypto-Jews of sorts—but from the opposite perspective. Where Henry masquerades as a Jew and then as a Jewish Golem, Esther masquerades as a non-
Judaean Persian and Moses as a non-Israelite Egyptian.

All three stories are set outside *Eretz Yisrael* [the Land of Israel]. Those
of Moses and Esther are the only ones in the Hebrew Bible to be thusly set,
and the two narratives divide the lion's share of the Jewish tradition of manuscript illumination and illustration between them. One offers the *Haggadah*, a
book of telling that puts the biblical story in an extra-biblical textual context;
the other offers *Megillat Esther* that puts the biblical story in a separate scroll
outside the biblical text in which it is yet part of the canon.[20]

The same rabbinic tradition that struggled to find a place for the uplifting story of Judaean redemption within the canon—because of its failure even
to mention God or the land of Israel—also understood the story of Esther to
be part of the larger story of exile and return, disaster and redemption that
connects biblical to Jewish history. Waldman enhances this rabbinic tradition
in his work.

Strum's vision is so very sober and straight-laced (this is an observation,
not a criticism), as if to underscore that the "game" is not to be mistaken for
merely a game. It is about the lives and identities of these people and the
people that they represent in the struggle for acceptance, and the serious-
ness quotient of the drawing echoes the serious mien of the narrator and his
frustration at efforts to turn the game into a circus act. On the other hand,
Waldman's vision is inebriated, in a manner consonant with his subject. He
tells his story with a swirling dynamism that encompasses the calligraphized
text as part of an abstract pattern of images that are both lyrical and expres-
sionistic [Fig. 6]. His style evokes the swirling lights and action of the circus
and its atmosphere that are eschewed by Strum and his characters.

Where a single poster-image offers a prelude to Strum's first-person
narrative, in Waldman, a succession of prologue images leads into the text.
These are like the introductory images in the illuminated *Golden Haggadah*
and *Sarajevo Haggadah*.[21] Waldman leads us into the story of Esther by way
of the story of Timna, the wannabe Israelite, rejected by the Israelites, without

Figure 6.

justification according to the rabbis (as Waldman reminds us). She became the concubine of Esau's son, Eliphaz, the mother of Amalek—who stands out as a source of Israelite pain in the time of Moses and the wandering through the wilderness. She is also the ancestor of Haman, who is the villain of the story.[22] The prologue is devoid of text until its very end, when the Talmudic tractate *Sanhedrin* is quoted to verbalize what we have just seen.

So Waldman follows the tradition of rabbinic enhancement, but on his own terms. Once entered, the entire text of the *megillah* is there in Hebrew, and most of it translated into English, though not all of it. There are places where Waldman deliberately wanders from literally translating to allow the words of his characters to articulate the sense of the Hebrew narration. Moreover, the involvement of the reader is intensified by Waldman's swaying interweave of passages from the story with passages commenting on the story that reinforce the notion that it is part of a larger narrative. So we step out of the text by seeing others reading and reacting to it, as in the interlude that comes after 10:1. There—after the words asserting that Esther's decree established the rituals of Purim and that it was written in the book—the biblical Ezekiel, spouting messianic prophecies, joins a contemporary congregation reading the book of Esther and celebrating Purim.

The viewer is drawn into the images by those that stare out at us (as Esther does, when she is declared beautiful in 2:15, and we see her from the perspective of the king who will shortly choose her) [Fig. 7], and those with their backs to us (so that we stand with them, looking over their shoulders—as when Esther stands in the entryway to the royal throne room in 5:1). Sometimes we see, literally, into the heart of a protagonist, as most strikingly when Haman thinks about the king's question regarding "what should be done to the man whom the king desires to honor," in 6:6 [Fig. 8].

From Timna in the prologue we move to the first part of the narrative that culminates with the king's decision to choose a successor to Queen Vashti with a beauty contest-by-force including every unattached young woman throughout the 127 states that he governs. Vashti has been removed from the court for reasons directly related to Strum's *Golem*: Persian males' fear of losing their position of sexual domination in the one case and the same fear by white, Christian American males in the other. Isn't it ironic that a fragile woman will successfully rescue the Judaeans of Persia where the mighty male "Golem" would fail to rescue the Stars of David without divine intervention?

Where physicality in Strum pertains to strength, speed, and athleticism, in Waldman it pertains to aesthetics, sex appeal, and visual beauty. In actuality, Esther's athleticism is ultimately not even due to her beauty as much as to her intellect: her sport is that of outsmarting her enemy by lulling him into believing himself still the Judaean-hunter and not the hunted—her repeated invitations to dinner are her version of the rope-a-dope trick used so effectively by Muhammad Ali when boxing against a younger, stronger George Foreman.[23] She may sweat—both in the locker room of self-preparation and when she gains her audience with the king—and Haman surely sweats when he begs her not to deliver the coup de grâce, but the battlefield is more subtle than an athletic field and the final blow will be administered with naught but words.

In fact, Esther, as fairest of them all, looks more like Bette Midler (and remarkably like Vashti) than like the latest *Playboy* centerfold, so Waldman plays with whatever conceptions and preconceptions shape the concept of "beauty" in history and art history, in Persia then or America now—especially when he reminds us in his endnotes of the Talmudic tradition that she was seventy-five years old when she first stood before Ahasuerus. And he therefore emphasizes that her ultimate weapon is really her intellect.

The issue of interpreting and defining beauty, which offers a centerpoint both for the biblical story and for Waldman's churned-up swirls of imagery, is the analogue of interpreting God and defining the most beauteous path

Figure 7.

Figure 8.

to God. Put otherwise, it focuses on the oldest Jewish sport: interpretational gymnastics.

So Waldman's interludes all revolve around the relationship between God and ourselves, and how that relationship flounders and rights itself. The first turns on who best understands that relationship, from the House of Saul (physically king-like, "head and shoulders above the people") and the House of David (small and "ruddy" but fast and smart). This is a contest of spiritual beauty, "*Mashiah* [Messiah] for a Day," that encompasses matters of the family tree begun with Abraham and Sarah and the descendants of their descendants, Judaism and Christianity, each of which believes it has the true franchise on covenantal correctness and beauty.

Another interlude follows to the story of Joseph, who, like Esther, is an outsider in a strange land in which he achieves power through his beauty, both physical and spiritual, and through his interpretive intellect. Joseph brings the children of Israel to the Egypt from which Moses will, Esther-like, redeem their descendants. The interlude further connects to Judah (whose descendants are the Jews), whose story in Genesis 38 runs parallel to that of Joseph in Genesis 39, which parallel is played on in the interlude—Haman's wife is at home reading a comic book "version" of these parallel tales—that comes just after Haman's humiliation in 6:12 [Fig. 9].

Interludes are thus essential and not mere interludes for Waldman. They are like baseball for Strum: a game that is not merely a game. They encompass a passage from Deuteronomy 31:18—visually shaped by Waldman as a tear drop—which passage is a link between two contexts. The first is to an undefined future. The line ". . . and I will surely hide My face in that day because of all the evil which they have done in that they turned to other gods" is quoted (from God through Moses to the Israelites, in Moses' valedictory speech to them before he dies) as part of the prophecy regarding how, in the future, the Israelites and their descendants "will forsake Me and break My Covenant which I have made with them."

The second "context" is the figure of Esther within that future, who, in hiding her Judaean identity until the moment when she must reveal that identity in order to save her people and herself, could be said to have come perilously close to forsaking God. In Esther's story, the name of God is never mentioned, and the very name "Esther" is built from the same Hebrew root as "I will hide" [*astheer*].

That is, who she truly is remains hidden (even when, as Waldman plays with the Talmudic play on Esther 2:18, the king asks her outright what her heritage is) until the salvational moment—when both her crypto-Judaeanism

Figure 9.

and her hidden heroism are revealed—just as God remains hidden throughout the narrative. But God's hand might be said to be active, albeit in hiding, through the actions of Mordecai and Esther.

These actions turn upside down at the outset of chapter six. Waldman physically flips the novel at the middle point of the narrative's conceptual flip. We are between the moment when Esther, rising to Mordecai's challenge, has gone before Ahasuerus and, having "found favor in his eyes," invites him—and Haman—to dinner; and the moment when, unable to sleep well after too much food and drink, Ahasuerus decides to have some passages from his annals read to him. He is thus reminded of Mordecai's act of having saved his life and decides to reward him—in a manner suggested by an unwitting Haman, who ends up thereby shaping his own humiliation.

Waldman flips the text and its images—the images and their text—so that the reader is turned topsy-turvy, as if inebriated, and must read English thereafter from right to left, page by page, and frame by frame. He thus plays on a rabbinic tradition that enjoins the celebrant to consume enough wine on this festive holiday to help continue the storyline in which everything is turned upside down; in which the oppressed and downtrodden emerge victorious over their oppressors; in which, in the hyper-textual world of *gematria* that Golem-maker Judah Loew espoused, one cannot distinguish the phrase "blessed is Mordecai" from "cursed is Haman."[24] Waldman turns the phrase "reversal of fortune," which is endemic to the novel throughout its history, and which is, after all, endemic to the story of Esther, Mordecai, and Haman, into a literal reversal of the book that the reader reads, so that we share "reversal" with the characters within the book.

We are the descendants to whom Mordecai "speaks peace" at the end of the biblical *Megillat Esther*—having achieved the sort of success that Joseph in Egypt had, in becoming "second only to King Ahasuerus." *We* are the descendants shown as ghost figures responding to the narrative at the end of Waldman's *Megillat Esther* [Fig.10], brought out of hiding, illuminated by Waldman in his dynamic graphics.

In the end of the epilogue in Strum's story, the narrator sits back down in the stands to see how it all turns out, and we ask what "it" is. The epilogue of Waldman's narrative overtly expands "it" by leading directly out into the vast seas of diasporic Jewish history. There the "turning out" includes the narrative of Esther and Mordecai and the question of how to be a Jew in the diasporic world; of how to assert oneself as a Jew and at the same time as part of the majority Christian or other society of which one wants to be a part—whether in Judah Loew's Prague, Germany in its Golden Age, or the United States in

Figure 10.

the 1920s and 1930s—as an athlete, as an artist, or just as an everyday person on Main Street. Or in the twenty-first century. How do we "pass" without passing beyond the border of the Jewish self? The real and the imagined—by Philip Roth or James Strum or many others—meet in Waldman's Persian Empire of twenty-five centuries ago as in the America of yesterday and today.

Both Strum and Waldman have added new branches to the double tree of the history of the novel and the history of the Jews as a people of paradox: surviving in a world where drunk and sober can be indistinguishable, interludes can carry the essence of a narrative, images can be text, games can offer the most serious of enterprises, and sports can be played by exercising the muscles of mind and tongue. They offer Jews as a people of books, images, athletic acumen, and balancing-act diasporic experiences and questions with and without answers. And of course wrestling both with divine inscrutability and with questions that have multiple answers—or no answers at all—is the consummate Jewish sport, in which athletes from Esther to Judah Loew to James Strum and JT Waldman have excelled.

NOTES

[1] The purpose of the imagery has always been (as with non-Jewish illuminated manuscripts) to bring to light important points being made by the words of the text (in Latin: "light" = *lux*, which word is at the heart of both "illumination" and "illustration"). So, too, any number of twentieth-century Jewish artists have embedded words literally or figuratively within their images. Thus Marc Chagall, for example, often offers what amount to Yiddish puns in his paintings. See Ori Z. Soltes, "Language, Art and Identity: Yiddish in Art from Chagall to Shalom of Safed," in *Yiddish Language and Culture: Then and Now* (ed. Leonard J. Greenspoon; Studies in Jewish Civilization 9; Omaha: Creighton University Press, 1998).

[2] The story of Judith, like that of the Maccabees, is not found within the accepted Jewish or Protestant canons, but within the Catholic and Orthodox Bibles. And of course, Esther, as we shall see below, was only reluctantly accepted into the canon—because, among other issues, the name of God is never mentioned in the text, making it, in a sense, the mirror opposite of 2 Maccabees with the latter's emphasis on divine involvement.

[3] See the specific Christian religious component of the making of knights and jousting in Ori Z. Soltes, *God and the Gold Posts: Sports, Religion, Politics and Art* (Laurel: Bartleby Press, forthcoming).

[4] Sancho Panza proudly asserts that he is an Old Christian; Don Quixote, surprisingly, does not respond that he, too, is one—in fact responding that even if he were not one, it would make no difference. The implication seems to be that as a *hidalgo*—a member of the lesser noble class—Don Quixote himself must undoubtedly have Jewish blood flowing through his veins, thereby rendering him less purely "Spanish" than the earthbound Sancho Panza. There has been considerable discussion, which falls outside the scope of

this essay, that Cervantes himself may have been of *converso* stock. For an elegant and eloquent summary, see Michael McGaha, "Is there a Hidden Jewish Meaning in Don Quixote?," *Cervantes: Bulletin of the Cervantes Society of America* 24 (2004):173-88.

[5] But how stereotypically Jewish of him, even if the texts are medieval Christian chivalric tales and hardly rabbinic literature or even secularized *piyyutim*.

[6] Or he inscribed it on his forehead, or he did this with the Hebrew word for "truth"— *emet*. There are different versions of the story that have trickled down through the last four centuries.

[7] This vagueness—who will be the messiah? What exactly will the messiah be and do? Will it be a particular individual at all, or a condition? How will that individual or condition be brought about? Through whose actions?—contrasts dramatically with the Christian notion: the messiah has been here once before and is known therefore to be Jesus of Nazareth, who is God incarnate. The only Christian question is: "When will he return?"

[8] The Golem's popular legacy reflects the dual, positive/negative potential inherent in its nature: a salvational symbol to Bohemian and Moravian Jews, it also served the non-Jewish community through the centuries as a kind of bogeyman, as a Christian mother might warn her children that, if they fail to perform some assigned task, "the Golem will get you!" See Byron L. Sherwin, *Mystical Theology and Social Dissent: The Life and Works of Judah Loew of Prague*, (Rutherford: Fairleigh Dickinson University Press, 1982).

[9] He was all of 5'7" tall and weighed 160 pounds.

[10] There is a growing literature on this subject. The 1985 catalogue of an exhibition, *Jews in the World of Sports*, organized by Beth Hatfutsoth: The Nahum Goldman Museum of the Jewish Diaspora, Tel Aviv, offers a concise introduction, but oddly excludes America from the discussion. One might also see Joseph Siegman, *Jewish Sports Legends* (Washington and London: Brassey's Publishers, Second Edition, 1997), and Robert Slater's oddly named (are they necessarily great Jews?) *Great Jews in Sports* (Middle Village: Jonathan David, 1983).

[11] A spurious "record"—created in Tsarist Russia in the 1890s but with possible antecedents in France as far back as the eighteenth century—of "meetings" of a worldwide group of Jewish leaders intent on taking control of the world.

[12] As in sports, so in the visual arts, things began to change dramatically by the late eighteenth century with Emancipation. The volume of recognizable Jewish visual artists working outside the context of illuminated *haggadot, megillot,* and the like expanded dramatically over the next 150 years—from portraiture and genre paintings to Pissarro's Impressionism and Moses Jacob Ezekiel's sculpture to artists like Shahn and Rothko. That expansion has been slowly explosive since the mid-twentieth century.

[13] See Ori Z. Soltes, *Fixing the World: Jewish American Painters in the Twentieth Century* (Hanover: Brandeis University Press, 2004), 33-4 and 14n.

[14] Who shot the hero, Roy Hobbs, early on in the story, thereby short-circuiting his career—and why? Did he strike out intentionally in the last scene and, if so, *was* it for the money or some other reason? We can read and reread the passages pertinent to these two key events again and again and not come up with a definitive answer. Within the Jewish tradition, if the beginning point of this is the tale of biblical Job, the latest, most intense chapter was written by the Holocaust's swallowing up of over a million Jewish children. Where was God? Where were humans? Both Strum and Waldman create in a

post-Holocaust world and one in which these questions have been raised by theologians since the early 1970s.

[15] This discussion has layers of course: perhaps the Great American Novel was written—two or three times—in the nineteenth century, by Herman Melville (*Moby Dick*) or Mark Twain (*Huckleberry Finn* and/or *Tom Sawyer*), so that the question really being addressed is: what is the Great American Novel of the twentieth century, when the United States became the major power on the planet? There have been any number of pretenders to that designation, but that would carry us beyond the point I wish to make here, concerning Roth's thoughtful tongue buried in his cheek.

[16] One might also mention in this discussion the 1996 novel, *The House of Moses All-Stars,* by Charley Rosen, a former basketball player and coach and the author of a number of works with a sports and particularly a basketball focus. Set in the Great Depression era of the 1930s, Rosen's narrative follows a Jewish basketball team as it barnstorms across America—in a refitted 1932 hearse. This America is, to its western edges, rife with anti-semitism, fears of the unknown personified by anyone who is different, and confusion about its (America's) identity simultaneously as a land of openness and a land of closed-mindedness. The most obvious exceptions to this for Rosen's team's experience are African Americans and Native Americans. With regard to associating Jews with Communism, see the ever-increasing volume of literature on the trial and execution of Julius and Ethel Rosenberg, and also the chapter on that topic in Ori Z. Soltes, *Jews on Trial: From Jesus to Jonathan Pollard* (Laurel: Bartleby Press, 2012).

[17] The Johnson-Reed Act all but slammed the door on Eastern European and Southern European immigration to the United States—precisely at a time when fascist forces were on the rise and immigration from those parts of Europe was most sought after.

[18] The film came out in 1920 and was the third of Wegener's films playing on the Golem theme, in all of which he played the lead role, besides directing. It was based on the 1915 work by Gustav Meyrink that took the earlier legend and fleshed it out into a novel.

[19] I am thinking not only about colonialism and slavery, but also of the words and works that served to de-Europeanize and thus de-humanize Jews, such as Wilhelm Marr's 1878-79 coinage of the term "Semite" to refer to Jews as a race, and the range of nineteenth century writings discussed and summarized in Maurice Olender, *The Languages of Paradise: Race, Religion, and Philology in the Nineteenth Century* (trans. Arthur Goldhammer; Cambridge: Harvard University Press, 1992).

[20] For a fuller discussion of the exclusion/inclusion of *Megillat Esther* from/in the Hebrew biblical canon and its illumination and related art, see Ori Z. Soltes, "Images and the Book of Esther: From Manuscript Illumination to Midrash," in *The Book of Esther in Modern Research* (ed. Sidnie White Crawford and Leonard J. Greenspoon; London and New York: T&T Clark International: Continuum Press, 2003), 137-75.

[21] Arguably the most significant medieval illuminated manuscripts in the Jewish tradition, they were both created in northeastern Spain and were carried—presumably due to the Expulsion of 1492 (or emigration earlier in the fifteenth century due to the complications for Jews throughout Christian Spain that set in after 1391)—to Italy (*Golden Haggadah*) or the Ottoman-controlled Balkans (Sarajevo *Haggadah*). The first ended purchased in Italy by the British Museum, the latter emerged (and remains) in Sarajevo, Bosnia-Herzegovina, in the nineteenth century. These *Haggadot* illuminate in rich color,

offering a lead-in from Creation to *b'deekat hametz* [the search for leavened foods] and the slaughtering of and preparation of sheep for Passover *(Golden)*; or to the moment when the family is depicted coming home from the synagogue to open the *Haggadah* and begin the telling (Sarajevo). Waldman's *Megillat Esther*, in comic-book-style black and white, uses Timna's story as the lead-in to the story of Esther.

[22] There is the chronologically intermediating irony, as the rabbinic tradition understands history, that, had King Saul hearkened to God's command and destroyed all of the Amalekite descendants of those who had plagued his ancestors in the wilderness, Haman would never have been born to plague his own descendants. Saul was soon replaced by David as God's anointed—*mashiah* in Hebrew, and *christos* in Greek, the English versions of which words are, of course, "messiah" and "Christ," respectively.

[23] For the boxing-benighted, this was during the "Rumble in the Jungle" that took place in Zaire on October 30, 1974. Muhammad Ali is usually regarded as the consummate practitioner/developer of Mendoza's "scientific" style of boxing.

[24] *Gematria* is that aspect of (particularly mystical) Jewish literature in which, by recognizing a numerical value for every Hebrew letter, esoteric relationships between words and phrases that are not apparent on the surface are ferreted out from underneath the words. Thus, the two Purim phrases, so opposite in meaning—how drunk would one need to be not to be able to distinguish them?—both add up to the same number in *gematria* (the number is 502): so even on this day actually one should not be that drunk because one is enjoined to be able not to distinguish two phrases that are actually identical to each other.

The Jew in the Gym: Judaism, Sports, and Athletics on Film

Nathan Abrams

Air Stewardess: Would you like something to read?
Passenger: Do you have anything light?
Air Stewardess: How about this leaflet, "Famous Jewish Sports Legends"?

INTRODUCTION

As the above joke from *Airplane* (dirs. Jim Abrahams and David Zucker, 1980) demonstrates, it has long been a tenet of Jewish humor that Jews do not do sports. In *The Hebrew Hammer* (dir. Jonathan Kesselman, 2003), for example, members of "the Coalition of Jewish Athletes" are, entirely predictably, nowhere to be seen. Although this stereotype is clearly inaccurate, the representations of Jewish sportsmen and women in cinema have been surprisingly few and far between. While cinema in the United States frequently depicts Jews playing sports, this is often for fun and not in any seriously competitive and/or professional sense, such as the "Jewish Children's Polo League" in *A Mighty Wind* (dir. Christopher Guest, 2003) that rode on Shetland ponies instead of horses.[1] There have been exceptions, however, and key and serious Jewish characters have been defined by their athleticism. For example, sport has been used in many films as a means for Jews to assimilate, charting the clash between ethnic specificity and the mainstream culture and the struggle to pass from the former to the latter.

Building upon the "corporeal turn" in Jewish textual studies, which has led to the growth of scholarship addressing the connections between Judaism, Jewishness, sexuality, and gender in ancient, early modern, modern, and contemporary Jewish cultures, I will explore male Jewish "bodies qua bodies"[2] in the contemporary sporting film—for what better way is there to explore the Jewish male body than in a genre that emphasizes its representation? In doing so, I will take the United Kingdom, and specifically a film about sport, *Chariots of Fire* (dir. Hugh Hudson, 1981), as my case study. I am interested in how the film's use of sport allows us to view the Jew and his body, something that, ironically in a film about physical exertion, is not particularly evident in the writing about it. In so doing, I will consider the English Jew through the prism of post-colonialism, in particular the work of Homi K. Bhabha.

WEAK, UNNATURAL BODIES

Before I turn to *Chariots of Fire*, however, I wish to establish some wider and cinematic context for the film. Self-images of the Jew's body have traditionally fallen into two opposing categories, both of which were "openly resistant to and critical of the prevailing ideology of 'manliness' dominant in Europe."[3] First, the "tough" Jew, which is the idealized hyper-masculine, macho, militarized, muscled, and bronzed, though not very intellectual, Jew of the Zionist project[4] with its variations of the "Muscle-Jew"[5] and, later, the *sabra* [Hebrew: lit. prickly pear; a native-born Israeli].[6] Second, the "queer" or "sissy" Diaspora Jew, who can be defined as the intellectual yet insufficiently, incompetently, and inadequately masculine Ashkenazi [central and eastern European] body found in the Diaspora. This Jew's body was "nonmale." He was an "unmanly man," feminized, effeminate, gentle, timid, studious, and delicate. He never used his hands for manual labor, exercised, or paid attention to maintaining his body. The Diaspora Jew of traditional Ashkenazi Jewish culture who devoted his life to the study of Torah embodies him.

For centuries the Diaspora Jew, especially his physiognomy and physiology, was tenaciously intertwined with notions of unmanly passivity, weakness, hysteria, and pathology, all bred by the lack of outdoor and healthy activity. The Jew's legs and feet in particular were characterized as nonathletic, unsuited to nature, sport, war making, brutality, and violence. At the same time, rabbinic culture and *Yiddishkeit* [Yiddish: lit. Jewish culture] valued timidity, meekness, physical frailty, and gentleness, privileging the pale, scholarly Jew who studied indoors, excluded from the worlds of labor and warfare. This resulted in a number of self-images of the Jew: the *nebbish* [Yiddish: an unfortunate simpleton; an insignificant or ineffectual person; a nobody; a nonentity], the *yeshiva-bochur* [Yiddish: a religious scholar], the *schlemiel* [Yiddish: a sort of cosmic fool combined with cosmic victim], the *mensch* [Yiddish: a decent, upstanding, ethical, and responsible person with admirable characteristics], and the *haredi*.[7] All of these images were defined by their softness, gentleness, weakness, and nonphysical activity.

This queer/sissy Jew was characterized as "hysteric," the result of prominent nineteenth century antisemitic prejudices. Psychoanalysts such as Sigmund Freud and Jean-Martin Charcot worked toward understanding the Jew's hysteria. The male Jew as an unmanly hysteric seeped into the Jew's own self-consciousness and identity. Daniel Boyarin noted how "by focusing on hysteria, especially in light of his own self-diagnosed hysteria, Freud was fashioning a self-representation that collaborated with one of the most tenacious of anti-semitic topoi—that Jews are a third sex: men who menstruate."[8]

Franz Kafka, for his part, was morbidly preoccupied with his own insubstantial physicality, especially in relation to his physically imposing father.[9] Otto Weininger concluded in his *Sex and Character* (1903) that "Judaism was saturated with femininity" and that the Jew was "found to approach so slightly and so rarely the ideal of manhood." Like women, the Jew shared an "exaggerated susceptibility to disease."[10] Adding repressed homosexuality to his fragile self-consciousness, Weininger's self-hatred was so acute that he committed suicide shortly after the publication of his work. Boyarin noted the conflation between homosexual and Jew, that the same constructs were attached to both, namely, "hypersexuality, melancholia, and passivity . . . the Jew was queer and hysterical—and therefore not a man."[11] Sander Gilman summarized that "the Jew is the hysteric; the Jew is the feminized Other; the Jew is seen as different, as diseased."[12] The Jew was both hysterical and homosexual; at once a man who menstruates, with menstruation a signifier of illness, incompletion, and incapability, and not a man at all.

In line with these representations, Jewish cinematic stereotypes, dating back almost as far as the birth of the medium itself, portrayed the Jew as a weak, frail, small, nonathletic, urban (ghetto) businessman, perpetuating the link between Jewishness and particular trades, predominantly depicting the Jew as a tailor, peddler, pawnbroker, or Shylockesque moneylender, and rarely as anything else.[13] The Jew was marked by his intelligence, cunning, and quick-witted verbal, rather than physical, skills. He had more brains than brawn.[14] The Jew did not do manual labor; rather he used his cleverness to make others do it for him. The "queer" Jewish male intellectual, what we can call *Yiddishe kopf* or "Jewish brains," dominated bodily values in cinema. Since superior intelligence was considered to be a stereotypical Jewish trait, it was deployed as a fairly standard cinematic device to create the representation of "smart Jews."[15]

For decades cinema reflected these dominant stereotypes, consequently downgrading Jewish involvement in sport no matter how extensive it was in reality. In line with this paradigm, "the one sport in Britain in which Jews had any real history of participation," boxing, has not been represented in British film[16] The late eighteenth century was often described as a golden age of Jewish boxing; by the turn of the twentieth century, it had undergone a resurgence in London as renewed immigration from Eastern Europe filled the East End with "a new eager breed of working-class pugilists."[17] During the 1920s and 1930s, Jews again achieved national and widely acknowledged prominence, including the world champions Kid Lewis and Kid Berg.[18] Other champion Jewish boxers included Daniel Mendoza, "Dutch" Sam Elias, Barney Aaron,

Aschel Joseph, Sid Burns, and Matthew Wells. It is hard to prove why cinema has chosen to omit this history, but perhaps it can be speculated that the reason lies in its clear contradiction of two long-held, engrained, and intertwined stereotypes: the weak and unathletic Jew. The passive Jew is supposed to be powerless; he does not victimize or humiliate.[19]

MIMICRY

Jews have not been thought of as colonized subjects largely because they have not been deemed as subjects of colonial domination. Furthermore, the elision of intra-Jewish difference in popular culture means that Diaspora Jewry is unprobematically considered to be "white" (i.e., Ashkenazi), which has in turn led to the erasure of any Jewish colonial histories at least in the dominant British-Jewish narratives. There are, however, Jews of colonial descent, such as those from Persia, the Asian subcontinent, or the West Indies, who must be considered at least doubly Othered (once as Jewish; twice as colonial subject) and who are decidedly not white.

In this context, Homi K. Bhabha's analysis of the colonial subject is useful in considering the status of the British Jew: "almost the same, *but not quite.*"[20] At one level, it can be used to refer to the primary signifier of Jewish male difference—circumcision—but on another it (albeit unwittingly, I would suggest) invokes a racialized schema in which Jews were never "whitened" as they were in the United States during the 1950s.[21] Where "Jews were, more or less, accepted as white" in the United States, the "imperative to whiten the Jews," owing to a lack of large-scale immigration and economic need, did not occur in the United Kingdom.[22] Consequently, Jews could be considered as "[a]lmost the same *but not white.*"[23] with the result that, in cultural terms, they have adopted a form of mimicry.

According to Bhabha, "mimicry is like camouflage not a harmonization or repression of difference, but a form of resemblance."[24] Mimicry "is never a simple reproduction of those traits. Rather, the result is a 'blurred copy.'"[25] Mimicry has long been a Jewish strategy. For Max Horkheimer and Theodor Adorno, it is "engraved in the living substance of the dominated and passed down by a process of unconscious imitation in infancy from generation to generation, from the down-at-heel Jew to the rich banker."[26] Using Bhabha's notion of mimicry, I will explore how these ideas are played out in *Chariots of Fire*, in particular how the Jewish male body bears the brunt of "the difference between being English and being Anglicized,"[27] with specific reference as to how it seeks to disguise itself or perhaps to make it more interesting to the mainstream by miming "the forms of authority."[28]

SPORT AND MIMICRY

Sport provided Jewish youngsters with the means to prove their athletic prowess and shoot down traditional stereotypes of Jews as physically weak, effete, intellectual, frail, and bookish. In the United Kingdom specifically, between 1874 and 1914, sport and physical recreation played a key role in the "Anglicization" of the children of the thousands of Eastern European Jewish immigrants who permanently settled in London, as English Jews enthusiastically mimicked the codes of Muscular Christianity as an assimilatory strategy. Their objective was to produce "Englishmen of the Mosaic Persuasion." The first initiative to be set up was the Jewish Working Men's Club and Institute in 1874, which initially introduced athletics and drill, followed by cycling, football, and cricket, among Jews.[29] A newly created network of youth clubs and social and sporting organizations was established in the belief that the introduction and promotion of British sport among the "alien" children was an effective means of "Anglicization"; success in the physically demanding sports was the "perfect retort to accusations surrounding the immigrant physique and its 'negative' effect on the British 'stock.'"[30] At the same time, it was felt, the English values of sportsmanship, fair play, and teamwork could be instilled. Yet sport betrayed that almost-the-same-but-not-quite-ness, as tension between being a good Englishman and being a good Jew arose. Sections within the Jewish community soon began to fear that the focus on physical recreation was undermining traditional Jewish culture and contributing to a "drift" toward religious indifference and apostasy, for sportsmen often had to contravene the Sabbath and dietary laws to train and compete.

Middle-class sports, in particular, functioned as assimilatory devices. They were part of that subtle and diffuse cultural shift that Norbert Elias described as "the civilizing process" in which those changes in manners that underpinned what is today called "decent behaviour" evolved.[31] Furthermore, with their strict codes of conduct, forms of dress, rules, and behaviors, sports provided the perfect raw material for mimicry, surrogation, and racial cross-dressing. Clothing allowed the male Jewish body to hide the primary marker of Jewish identity—circumcision. In some sports, such as cricket, extra cover was provided through the need to wear a protective "box" around the genitals. Sports also literally afforded the opportunity to "whiten up," to pass as white both literally and figuratively, in that many middle- and upper-class sports demanded the wearing of pristine and spotlessly white attire (running, fencing, tennis, cricket; the English football and rugby teams play in white).[32] This use of sartorial whiteness splendidly reflects the essence of Frantz Fanon's *Black Skin, White Masks.*[33] Having now provided the critical framework, as well as the filmic and historical context for the English Jew, I shall now turn to the film.

CHARIOTS OF FIRE

Released in 1981, *Chariots of Fire* is based on actual events. It is a story of social exclusion and class privilege, focusing on the experiences of two athletes, both outsiders, in Britain in the 1920s. Harold Abrahams (Ben Cross) is an intense and driven Jewish law student at Caius College, Cambridge, in 1919. A gifted athlete, he desires material success and social acceptance, as well as gold at the Olympics of 1924, in order to smash the antisemitism that he encounters. Meanwhile, Eric Liddell (Ian Charleson), a devout Scot, seeks to proclaim the "Glory of God" through success on the athletics track. Abrahams is the son of a Lithuanian Jewish immigrant. His father, whom Abrahams describes as "alien" and "as foreign as a frankfurter," desired for his children to fit in, to assimilate. As Abrahams tells his friend Aubrey Montague (Nicholas Farrell), "He worships this country. From nothing he built what he believed was enough to make true Englishmen of his sons." Like his father, Abrahams also wishes to pass within the dominant culture; he "desires more than anything to become part of the system."[34] Through mimicry he attempts to take on the mantle of whiteness. In doing so, he appropriates the prevailing English cultural habits, assumptions, institutions, and values.

Abrahams is, outwardly, the perfect copy/imitation of the well-educated English gentleman of 1919 in speech, behavior, manners, and dress. Indeed, in scene after scene, there is little to distinguish him visually from any of the others in the film whom he resembles in appearance. Other than his name (which in itself is not a solid basis for assuming Jewishness) and being told that he is Jewish, the audience is never offered any other explicit visual evidence of Abrahams' ethnicity. The opening sequence is of a memorial service, which takes place in a chapel, and hence contains no outward signs of Abrahams' Jewishness or Judaism. Indeed, in the next scene, the title sequence of the British team running together on the beach set to Vangelis' celestial synthesized score, there is nothing "to suggest this character is a Jew." The "tall and lithe" English runners' "appearance in white shirts and shorts contributes to an image of a nation which is aligned with whiteness that is undisturbed. Wearing the same white attire, embroidered with a British flag over his heart, Abrahams is indistinguishable from the other runners."[35] He is the same; he is white.

Indeed, as portrayed by Cross, Abrahams does not fit the filmic stereotype of the Jew. In a changing room sequence, for example, we see Abrahams topless. He is lithe and muscled, the polar opposite of the stereotypical *schlemiel*.

He has "the poker-faced glare of a professional boxer and the gait of a basket-ball player. Tall and angular, he dispenses challenges in a way that advertises arrogance."[36] The viewer, therefore, is not given the possibility of reading him as a Jew by the typical signifiers—looks, physiognomy, behavior, profession, or location. Thus, while we are told Abrahams is Jewish (and history certainly bears this out), his filmic persona gives no certainty.[37] Abrahams is thus, out-wardly, the perfect mimic because nowhere does he externally behave as a Jew.

Yet the film reveals Abrahams' Jewishness in more subtle ways. Physi-cally, as portrayed by Cross, Abrahams is Orientalized with his dark hair and dark eyes, resembling Rebecca, *la belle Juive* [the beautiful Jewess] of Walter Scott's novel *Ivanhoe* (1819). His dark eyes and hair mark him out as a subject of difference among his largely blond, Gentile counterparts. The darkness of his complexion reminds us that he is not white. Abrahams is *le beau Juif* [the handsome Jew], the male equivalent of Rebecca. Although we never see him fully nude, which, if we did, may provide an unequivocal physical marker of his Jewishness (in that I presume he would be circumcised), other clear signi-fiers are present. What we do see, for example, is Abrahams' naked ambition and desire for success and assimilation, very much fitting into the notion of the pushy, impudent, grubby, professional, social parvenu Jew. In the title and credits sequences, Abrahams is intense, driven, and determined, all of his but-tons, including the very top one, are done up. In contrast, Lord Lindsay (Nigel Havers), the embodiment of the Corinthian gentleman amateur, is shown smiling and all of his shirt buttons are undone. Unlike Abrahams, Lindsay is competing for the sheer enjoyment of it ("To me the whole thing's fun"). Such a figure, who "tried at a bound to bridge the gap between his aspiration and his real social status," was a permanent fixture on the stage, "much laughed at by the gentiles and resented by Jews."[38]

This is reinforced by the clear contrast to the training "regime" of the nonchalant, leisurely Lindsay. As a privileged member of the elite, Lindsay does not need to struggle. The differences between the two men are fur-ther dramatized in the theatrical sequence in which Lindsay practices in the grounds of his country estate, Highbeck House, a stately home set in an Eng-lish pastoral idyll.[39] Wearing an expensive white dressing gown (a similar one is later worn by Abrahams at the Olympics) over his white athletics slip and shorts, Lindsay is smoking a cigarette while his servant brings him his spikes. On an immaculate lawn that sweeps down from the front door to an ornamen-tal pond bordered by blossoming trees, a full glass brimming with champagne is balanced on the edge of each hurdle (if he sheds a drop he wants to know), as Lindsay leaps over them at speed but without spilling a single drop. Abrahams' thirst for success is an example of his excess, of his desire to be like everyone else, only more so. At the same, time the juxtaposition of Abrahams' "thirst" with Lindsay's literal quenching of it is a mockery of the gentleman-amateur athletic values of the English elite of the 1920s in its reliance on a conspicuous level of wealth and leisure.

Single-minded in his goal, Abrahams literally has a one-track approach. His training sequences are puritanical, serious, strict, disciplined, and rigorous, as he grinds out the punishing miles under the dictatorial supervision of his coach. He is typically shown training and racing in straight lines—running around the edges of the quad, within the walls of the college, down a tree-lined approach, on a gravelly path.[40] Often, the setting is the countryside, and in one scene he is depicted running alongside foxhounds and their master dressed in hunting attire. Such sequences juxtapose Abrahams with the English pastoral, highlighting that, as a Jew, he does not belong. Abrahams is thus depicted as extraterritorial. Where Liddell is shown with the backdrop of Scottish landscapes or churches, Abrahams is never depicted as a part of anywhere else or any religious institution. The result is that he remains continually apart from England.[41] The film, as *Jewish Chronicle* reviewer Pamela Melinkoff put it, "delicately conveys that sense of perpetually being on the periphery of the ancient and beautiful English heritage that afflicts so many first-generation English Jews."[42]

In true cinematic tradition, Abrahams is defined by his mind. He has *Yiddishe kopf.* As a graduate of the great public school Repton and a student at Cambridge (which Abrahams characterizes as "the finest university in the land"), he is of superior intelligence. And he can sing. He is studying to be a lawyer (a stereotypically Jewish profession) and is fast-talking and quick-witted; the "gift of the gab," which he reluctantly admits, is "a rare ethnic advantage." His father is described as a "financier," tapping into the antisemitic stereotype of the Jewish banker in late-nineteenth-century literature and thereafter film, whom Henry H. Weinberg described as "shifty, cosmopolitan, cleverly manipulating . . . single-minded [in his] quest for money."[43] Abrahams' pursuit, and conquest, of the *shiksa* [Yiddish: a non-Jewish woman bearing derogatory connotations that objectify and sexualize her] Sybil (Alice Krige) similarly conforms to filmic stereotype. These queer qualities mark him out as a subject of difference, so while Abrahams may appear the same, he is not quite.

Abrahams is acutely aware of his alien Otherness, his ethnic difference, his same-but-not-quite/white-ness. Abrahams may be Anglicized but he is certainly not English, and many scenes establish this key difference as they relay the various antisemitic comments from college faculty, staff, and students. For, as he tells his friend Aubrey, he is a Jew in a Christian and Anglo-Saxon England. Located in between two cultures, Abrahams is structurally ambivalent. He bears "the doubled consciousness of the colonized subject,"[44] as well as the weight of this twin legacy, symbolized by the film's refrain of the hymn "Jerusalem," which juxtaposes Abrahams' dual origins.[45] Similarly, Abrahams' first and last names signify this liminal and ambivalent status, in that Harold [an Old English name meaning heroic leader] was the last Anglo-Saxon king of England (c. 1019–66) before the Norman invasion, while Abrahams refers to the biblical patriarch from whom all Jews trace their descent and whose name translates as "father of a great multitude." In this way, Abrahams is caught between what David Daiches called "two worlds."[46] As Laura Levitt has written of Al Jolson in *The Jazz Singer* (dir. Alan Crosland, 1927) but which is just as apt for *Chariots of Fire*, "He neither gets all of the benefits of 'whiteness' nor can he escape the responsibilities that still tie him to the ghetto."[47] Recognizing this fact, Abrahams tells his girlfriend Sybil he is "semi-deprived": "they lead me to water but they won't let me drink" because "This England of his is Christian and Anglo-Saxon. And so are her corridors of power. And those who stalk them guard them with jealousy and venom." When his coach Sam Mussabini (Ian Holm) initially refuses to coach Abrahams until he is sure that he has what it takes physically, saying "You can't put in what God's left out," it also reinforces Abrahams' status as a mere mimic, that he cannot compensate for being Jewish by being more English than the English.

CONCLUSION

In the final analysis, despite his athletic prowess, Harold Abrahams' body, in particular the inescapability of his somatically inscribed Jewishness, means that he can never fully pass as English or white. He will forever remain "almost the same." His position is one of structural ambivalence. Neither English nor foreign, he occupies the liminal space between the worlds of Englishness and Anglicization. In this way, Abrahams stands as a metonym for an ambivalent English Jewishness that is not entirely at home within the English body politic, or with itself even, because it cannot fully pass.

NOTES

[1] As evidence of this, a variety of Jews play recreational basketball in films such as *Eight Crazy Nights* (dir. Seth Keasley, 2002), *Along Came Polly* (dir. John Hamburg, 2004), *Prime* (dir. Ben Younger, 2005), and *Keeping the Faith* (dir. Edward Norton, 2000). Wal-

ter Sobchak (John Goodman) in *The Big Lebowski* (dir. Joel Coen, 1998) is dedicated to ten-pin bowling but this is done as a leisure activity.

[2] Joshua N. Lambert, "Unclean Lips: Obscenity and Jews in American Literature" (PhD dissertation; University of Michigan, 2009).

[3] Daniel Boyarin, *Unheroic Conduct: The Rise of Heterosexuality and the Invention of the Jewish Man* (Berkeley: University of California Press, 1997), 23.

[4] Paul Breines, *Tough Jews: Political Fantasies and the Moral Dilemma of American Jewry* (New York: Basic Books, 200), and Raz Yosef, *Beyond Flesh: Queer Masculinities and Nationalism in Israeli Cinema* (New Brunswick: Rutgers University Press, 2004).

[5] Max Nordau, speech delivered at the Second Zionist Congress (Basel, August 28-31, 1898), in *Stenographisches Protokoll der Verhandlungen des II. Zionisten-Congresses* (Vienna: Verlag des Vereines "Erez Israel"), 14-27; and Todd Presner, *Muscular Judaism: The Jewish Body and the Politics of Regeneration* (London: Routledge, 2007).

[6] Oz Almog, *The Sabra: The Creation of the New Jew* (Berkeley: University of California Press, 2000).

[7] *Haredi* (plural: *haredim*) literally means "one who trembles," deriving from Isaiah 66:5, in which the prophet admonishes his people to, "Hear the word of the Lord, you who tremble [*haredim*] at His word." It is often translated as "ultra-Orthodox," a definition that does not do justice to an extensive and nuanced term, which covers a range of Jews who fall into this category but not all of whom are "Orthodox" in the strictest definition of that term

[8] Daniel Boyarin, "Freud, Sigmund (1856-1939)," in *Gay Histories and Culture: An Encyclopedia* (ed. George E. Haggerty; New York: Garland, 2000), 354.

[9] Sander L. Gilman, *Franz Kafka: The Jewish Patient* (London: Routledge, 1995); and Ernst Pawel, *The Nightmare of Reason: A Life of Franz Kafka* (New York: Farrar, Straus and Giroux, 1997).

[10] Quoted in Jonathan C. Friedman, *Rainbow Jews: Jewish and Gay Identity in the Performing Arts* (Lanham: Lexington Books, 2007), 15.

[11] Boyarin, "Freud," 355.

[12] Sander L. Gilman, *The Jew's Body* (London: Routledge, 1991), 76.

[13] Nathan Abrams, *The New Jew in Film: Exploring Jewishness and Judaism in Contemporary Cinema* (London: IB Tauris, 2011).

[14] David Desser, "Jews in Space: The 'Ordeal of Masculinity' in Contemporary American Film and Television," in *Ladies and Gentlemen, Boys and Girls: Gender in Film at the End of the Twentieth Century* (ed. Murray Pomerance; Albany: State University of New York Press, 2001), 269.

[15] Sander L. Gilman, *Smart Jews: The Construction of the Image of Jewish Superior Intelligence at the Other End of the Bell Curve* (Lincoln: University of Nebraska Press, 1996), 179.

[16] David Dee, "'Nothing Specifically Jewish in Athletics?' Sport, Physical Recreation and the Jewish Youth Movement in London, 1895-1914," *The London Journal* 34.2 (2009): 90.

[17] Ibid.

[18] Tony Collins, "Jews, Antisemitism, and Sports in Britain, 1900-1939," in *Emancipation through Muscles: Jews and Sports in Europe* (ed. Michael Brenner and Gideon Reuveni; Lincoln: University of Nebraska Press, 2006), 149.

[19] It must be pointed out, however, that there have been films about Jewish boxers and Jewish boxers in film respectively, including *His People* (dir. Edward Sloman, 1925), *Body and Soul* (dir. Robert Rossen, 1947), *Métisse* (dir. Mathieu Kassovitz, 1993), and *Cinderella Man* (dir. Ron Howard, 2005), all of which are obvious exceptions to the Jewish weakling syndrome, reflecting Jewish domination of the sport in the eighteenth and early twentieth centuries.

[20] Homi K. Bhabha, *The Location of Culture* (London: Routledge, 1994), 123.

[21] Karen Brodkin, *How Jews Became White Folks and What That Says about Race in America* (New York: Rutgers University Press, 1998), 10.

[22] Jon Stratton, *Jewish Identity in Western Pop Culture: The Holocaust and Trauma Through Modernity* (New York: Palgrave Macmillan, 2008), 198.

[23] Bhabha, *Location of Culture,* 128.

[24] Ibid.

[25] Bill Ashcroft, et al., *Post-Colonial Studies: The Key Concepts* (London: Routledge, 2000), 139.

[26] Max Horkheimer and Theodor Adorno, *Dialectic of Enlightenment* (trans. John Cumming; London: Allen Lane, 1973), 182.

[27] Bhabha, *Location of Culture,* 128.

[28] Ibid., 130.

[29] Harold Pollins, *A History of the Jewish Working Men's Club and Institute, 1874-1912* (Oxford: Clarendon, 1981), 198; Collins, "Jews, Antisemitism, and Sports."

[30] Dee, "Nothing Specifically," 90.

[31] Norbert Elias, *The Civilizing Process: The History of Manners,* (vol. 1; trans. Edmund Jephcott; New York: Urizen Books, 1968).

[32] The reasons for this are not entirely clear. Suffice it say that the whiteness of such sporting kit would have cost a great deal to maintain, thus excluding those too poor to afford such attire.

[33] Frantz Fanon, *Black Skin, White Masks* (trans. Charles Lam Markmann; New York: Grove Press, 1967).

[34] Ed Carter, "*Chariots of Fire:* Traditional Values/False History," *Jump Cut* 28 (1983) [online version].

[35] Cheryl Alexander Malcolm, "Heritage, Nation, and the Other," in *Widening Horizons: Essays in Honour of Professor Mohit K. Ray* (ed. Rama Kundu; New Delhi: Sarup & Sons, 2005), 288-89.

[36] Ellis Cashmore, "*Chariots of Fire:* Bigotry, Manhood and Moral Certitude in an Age of Individualism," *Sport in Society* 11.2/3 (2008): 163.

[37] Jon Stratton, *Coming Out Jewish: Constructing Ambivalent Identities* (London: Routledge, 2000). There is a significant contrast between the filmic portrayal of Abrahams and the reality of his life. David Dee ("Jews and British Sport: Integration, Ethnicity and Anti-Semitism, c. 1800-c. 1960" [Unpublished PhD thesis; De Montfort University, 2011]) argues that was driven by integration and "Anglicization" and that, in reality, his Jewish "difference" did not really play a significant part in his life or athletic career.

[38] Jacob Katz, *Out of the Ghetto: The Social Background of Jewish Emancipation 1770-1870* (Cambridge: Harvard University Press, 1973), 86.

[39] Martyn J. Bowden, "Jerusalem, Dover Beach, and King's Cross: Imagined Places as Metaphors of the British Class Struggle in *Chariots of Fire* and *The Loneliness of the Long-Distance Runner,*" in *Place, Power, Situation, and Spectacle: A Geography of Film* (ed. Stuart C. Aitken and Leo E. Zonn; Lanham: Rowman and Littlefield, 1994), 78.

[40] Ibid.

[41] Malcolm, "Heritage, Nation, and the Other," 288.

[42] Pamela Melinkoff, "Conflict on Heritage," *The Jewish Chronicle* (3 April 1981): 29.

[43] Quoted in Jon Stratton, *Jews, Race and Popular Music* (Farnham: Ashgate, 2009), 166.

[44] Boyarin, *Unheroic Conduct*, 243.

[45] Sheila Johnston, "Charioteers and Ploughmen," in *British Cinema Now* (ed. Martin Auty and Nick Roddick; London: BFI, 1985), 102.

[46] David Daiches, *Two Worlds: An Edinburgh Jewish Childhood* (Edinburgh: Canongate, 1987).

[47] Laura Levitt, "Redressing Jewish Difference in Tania Modleski's 'Cinema and the Dark Continent,'" *Journal of Religion and Film* 1.2 (1997) [online].

Is Life a Game? Athletic Competition as a Metaphor for the Meaning of Life

Steven J. Riekes

If someone made the statement: "Athletic competition is very important because it has lessons for playing the game of life," I suspect that most people would, at least initially, concur.

Our American culture is completely immersed with sports. Our very language is imbued with terminology either derived from or associated with sports. These terms are used in almost every field of human activity. As an example of this immersion, consider the words written by columnist Nicholas Kristof: "We journalists tend to cover politics the way we cover sports; Republicans are gaining yardage on their immigration play. The Tea Party is stealing second base! A bench-clearing brawl over health care!"[1]

In the world of finance, Warren Buffett has commented: "Risk is a part of God's game, alike for men and nations."

Even in religion, these terms are used. Consider the title of a book by Dov Moshe Lipman, *Timeout: Sports Stories as a Game Plan for Spiritual Success.*[2]

One could effortlessly make a huge list of words, terms, and phrases from the world of sports that we apply to all sorts of activities.

The purpose of this presentation is to reflect on whether athletic competition is or should be thought of as a metaphor for living. In this process, I will present some very uncommon perspectives. Some of them may be uncomfortable, particularly to those for whom competitive sports are a passionate preoccupation and an essential part of their persona. I present these ideas for discussion and examination because I find them interesting, and not necessarily because I agree with them.

Because sports are so significant an activity in our culture, an examination of the relationship between sports and our society, including our belief systems, should be a worthwhile undertaking. This presentation has nothing to do with physical exercise or health. Instead, it has to do with perceptions, values, masculinity, popular culture, and religion, and their intersection with competitive sports.

My initial interest in the subject of this presentation started many years ago when I attended a lecture presented at the Jewish Federations of North America's General Assembly in Kansas City. The lecture was given by Mervin

Verbit, then professor of sociology at Brooklyn College, and now at Touro College in New York. Neither he nor I now remember what the title of the lecture was, but its basic essence was as follows:

A Christian minister observed that, on a regular basis, significantly more women attended church services than did men. In examining and experimenting with this phenomenon, the minister realized that Jesus could be viewed, particularly in the eyes of Western culture, as a rather feminine figure. After all, in both Luke and Matthew, Jesus advises: "If someone strikes you on the right cheek, turn to him the other also." On the other hand, to some, more manly advice would be to stand one's ground. Further, Jesus advises that the meek will inherit the earth. If so, what virtue is there in being strong?

Therefore, it would appear that Jesus is in direct contradiction with the popular notion of what an ideal man should be. In other words, in current parlance, Jesus is a wimp.

This contradiction, while not often openly discussed, creates a disturbance, particularly just below the surface, in the social psychology of Western civilization. The contradiction between the exemplar of the Savior and the cultural expectations for manhood seems unresolvable. How then can the enormous tension created by such a clash be possibly relieved? Professor Verbit proposed that this tension was subconsciously redirected by some molders of Western civilization. They placed fault upon the Jews. After all, it was from the Jews and their religion that Jesus came forth. Thus, it wasn't deicide for which the Jews were blamed (although that's what was said); rather, they were faulted for foisting Jesus upon them in the first place (even though this was not publicly said).

In regard to this idea, consider, for example, the German composer Richard Wagner. In his opera, *Tannhäuser*, while not dealing with the character of Jesus, as such, Wagner has Christian salvation as a major theme. It also has the pagan goddess Venus as a major character. From a logical perspective, this seems to be a very odd farrago. The Christian Wagner was preoccupied with pagan myths (i.e., his famous ring cycle). He was also known as a rabid antisemite: "The old Jewish god always ruins the whole thing," Wagner was quoted as saying.[3] Later, I will suggest what Wagner actually may have meant.

After this single lecture, Professor Verbit never developed this theme any further. However, he did recommend that I read a book entitled *The Gentleman and the Jew* by Maurice Samuel. While not directly furthering this particular theme of the basis of antisemitism, it deals with ideas that may have some relationship to Verbit's thesis.

Samuel was a novelist, translator, and lecturer. Born in 1895 in Romania, he came with his family to Great Britain in 1900. His book, *The Gentleman and the Jew*, was published in 1950. It is a hodgepodge of biography, philosophy, and Samuel's views on a number of different subjects, including Christianity, nationalism, Yiddish, and Zionism.

The major theme of this book is Samuel's argument that the concept of an ideal man, as embedded in Western civilization, is the gentlemanly combatant who fights in the athletic arena and in all other venues. According to Samuel, this concept's origins lie in the pagan Greco-Roman view of life. It is antithetical, he argues, to Christianity and, most definitely, to Judaism.

As a child of immigrants, Samuel wanted to assimilate into English society. There was a type of juvenile literature that he and his friends devoured. The literature was about young men, such as a fictional "Tom Merry," who attended "Greyfriars" and "St. Jim's." These fictional heroes displayed the English ideals of fair play, honesty, patriotism, pluck, and cheerfulness; and above all else, they participated in cricket. Cricket was more than a game—it was a symbol. If something was not cricket, it did not simply imply that it was morally wrong, but that it would also be disapproved by "the right people" who attended Greyfriars and St. Jim's, "all other people being outsiders."[4] The Jewish boys wanted to be insiders.

All this, however, was beyond the understanding of Samuel's parents and their generation:

> Our parents remained, till the end, incapable of understanding that a game was more than a game, and that "playing the game"—untranslatable concept!—was morality itself. They had a more somber attitude toward youth than did their Christian neighbors. At most they were willing to concede to youth a certain playfulness, a coltish need to scamper about and make unnecessary noises. But to invest this release with a tremendous moral function, on a level with the law of Moses, was wholly beyond their capacity. They lived out their lives in England, from early middle to old age, without so much as a glimpse of the English attitude toward sports; and until the end they were baffled by the extraordinary phenomenon of grown-up, often elderly people passionately addicted to football and cricket.[5]

(A personal anecdote: While my dad played football, his parents never saw a game. One day, in her later years, my Yiddish-speaking *bobeh* [grandmother] saw "All-Star Wrestling" on television. She thought it was hilarious that grown men would act so ridiculously, and she said to my aunt, "For the first time in my life I am seeing American football.")

Like many other boys, Samuel felt that he was "robbed" of several hours each day by being force to attend *cheder* or Hebrew school. Nevertheless, the lessons he learned at *cheder* stuck with him. When he matured intellectually and began to appreciate what he learned in Hebrew school, he was amazed at the incompatibility between his Jewish world and the English world of his boyhood:

> The mutual incompatibility of those two worlds comes back to me with peculiar vividness as I reconstruct, with inescapable certainty, the moral instruction I received in *cheder*. This was both general, as issuing from the study of the Pentateuch, and specific, as condensed in *The Ethics of the Fathers*. When I place it side by side with the moral instruction that I derived from the *Union Jack* books, I am astonished not to find myself in the care of a psychiatrist.[6]

In this maturing process, Samuel came to the realization, through his examination of English literature, that there was a strong connection between sports and war. As an English boy, Samuel learned the following poem by Sir Henry Newbolt, who connected the playing field with the battlefield:

> To set the cause above renown,
> To love the game beyond the prize,
> To honor, while you strike him down,
> The foe that comes with fearless eyes.

Samuel contrasted this with what he learned as a Jew:

> When Jews used to go to war, thousands of years ago, they did not kill their foes in that fine spirit. And Jews, teaching and learning their own history, did not begin to understand the deficiency. How could one convey [to his parents] the spirit in which an Englishman did his killing? It was almost not killing. It was—well, it was rather like cricket.
>
> "A good clean fight, no hitting below the belt, may the best man win, and no hard feelings": on the battlefield as in the ring. One could put these words accurately into Yiddish, but they would be gibberish. Jews looked on all fighting, private and public, personal and historic, as such a disgusting business that they could not associate it with an affirmative code; and I felt this so strongly even in my boyhood that I despaired of ever giving my parents a glimpse into the sunny combativeness of the St. Jim's *Weltanschauung*. How could I begin to reconcile it with the somber thoughtfulness of the Pentateuch and *The Ethics of the Fathers*? Where, within that subtle and perceptive discipline, could you find room for the dashing buccaneer type, who could make his prisoners walk the plank, but who, beneath everything, was something of a gentleman because he knew the meaning of "a fair fight"?[7]

Samuel could not reconcile these clashing worlds. At one point, he assumed that Christianity somehow had the ability to make this reconciliation. One day he saw a Christian girl, whom he liked, playing cricket with a minister. Therefore, he was sure that the church would put the two worlds together. So he snuck into a church and listened to the sermon. There, he received a shock:

> The sermon, in which the name of Jesus appeared and reappeared with—to me—terrifying frequency, had nothing whatsoever to do, in spirit or in substance, with that gay, magnanimous, adventurous and gamesome world which I had come to hear glorified. It did not proclaim, in new and unimaginably attractive phrases, the cosmic rightness of Greyfriars . . . and the cricket team. In a most unbelievable way it rehearsed what I had been learning in *cheder*! It appeared that among the Christians, too, the meek and the humble were blessed. It appeared that when someone hit you, you did not answer laughingly with a straight left, and you did not invite your friends to stand around in a circle while you carried on with the Marquis of Queensberry rules. Not a bit of it! You turned the other cheek! . . . It appeared that the peacemakers, not the soldiers, not the manly, laughing killers, were the blessed. This was not Tom Merry's world at all. It was my *Rebbi's*.[8]

Samuel developed his theme further by examining English literature, such as that of Rudyard Kipling:

> Oh, East is East, and West is West, and never the twain, shall meet,
> Till Earth and Sky stand presently at God's great Judgment Seat.
> But there is Neither East nor West, Border nor Breed, nor Birth,
> When two strong men stand face to face, though they come from the ends of the earth![9]

And:

> If you can fill the unforgiving minute
> With sixty seconds' worth of distance run,
> Yours is the Earth and everything that's in it,
> And—which is more—you'll be a Man, my son.[10]

He examined Shakespeare and other English authors. But it is not only literature by which Samuel tries to prove his point. He cites Oliver Wendell Holmes, the American jurist and justice of the Supreme Court. Holmes said: "I believe that the struggle for life is the order of the world, at which it is vain to repine." More to the point of Samuel's thesis, he quotes Holmes as stating: "I rejoice at every dangerous sport which I see pursued. The students at Heidelberg with their sword-slashed faces inspire me with sincere respect."[11] Indeed, although not quoted by Samuel, Holmes went on to state: "I gaze with delight upon our polo players. If once in a while in our rough riding a neck is broken, I regard it, not as a waste, but as a price well paid for the breeding of a race fit for headship and command."[12]

Also, Samuel could have added remarks by a contemporary of Holmes, President Theodore Roosevelt, who said: "Aggressive fighting for the right is the noblest sport the world affords."

General Douglas MacArthur put the following words on the doors to the gym at West Point: "Upon the fields of friendly strife / Are sown the seeds / That upon other fields, on other days / Will bear the fruits of victory."

Further, lest one think that Samuel must surely be exaggerating when he declares such an ideal man as a gentlemanly killer with a smile, consider the words of Winston Churchill: "War is a game that is played with a smile. If you can't smile, grin. If you can't grin, keep out of the way until you can."

Samuel further develops this line of thinking by examining the ideal man according to the culture of the Italian Renaissance, focusing on Castiglione's *The Courtier*. The renaissance courtier was a cultured, refined, well-mannered, and multi-talented man. Yet above all else, he was always a swordsman.

Samuel then traces the origins of the courtier back to the ideal man according the ancient Greeks, founders of the Olympic Games. To them, the ideal man had grace, manners, a decorative attachment to intellectual values, adoration of the physical, and the worship of the combative and the competitive. Samuel concludes that: "The gentleman is the noblest ideal of man in a society which immorally accepts competition and rivalry as the basis and meaning of life."[13] Then he states: "That one man can kill another man in combat on a high level of mutual regard is perhaps the most fantastic and perverse notion that has ever sprung from the human brain."[14]

Samuel's thesis is, at least in part, based upon his reaction to and revulsion with a view common in the British Empire in the nineteenth century to the middle of the twentieth century. That cultural philosophy is examined by Patrick F. McDevitt in a book, *May the Best Man Win: Sport, Masculinity, and Nationalism in Great Britain and the Empire, 1880-1935.*[15] According to McDevitt, organized sport was perceived as a great bond of the Empire:

> "May the best man win" was a common sentiment in imperial Britain and the Empire, but this was not simply a paean to fair play and clean sport. It was also an expression of a worldview which held that participation in and success at athletic endeavors were primary measures of the worth of a man *as a man*.[16]

McDevitt points out that there was an instant connection between the playing field of the English schools and the battlefield. It was a "belief that games created the hardy, quick-thinking men who would run the empire, dominated elite education throughout the realm in the second half of the nineteenth century through World War II."[17]

McDevitt also notes that, while games were popular among all social classes, there were important differences. The British ideals of sportsmanship that Samuel discusses were very much the product of an elite and middle-class view of how sports should be played (i.e., as a "gentleman"). Even the game of cricket, which Samuel characterizes as having the values of gentlemen, when played by working classes, "was not a matter of how one played the game, but rather whether one won or lost."[18] In the English village contests, matches would frequently wind up with fistfights on and off the field. Many times visiting teams had to make a dash from the vicinity when pursued by a hostile crowd.

Now, at the beginning of the twenty-first century, few leaders in the Western world glorify war as did Teddy Roosevelt or conflate it with sports as did Justice Holmes. In addition, the notion of the "gentleman," as portrayed by Samuel, is probably passé in this age of the celebrity and the dumbing down of culture. The concept of masculinity can also be a changing one, as McDevitt observes:

> [V]aried communities continually enlisted sport to demonstrate and display the "appropriate" characteristics of a man at any given time. While in the nineteenth century, the term "manliness" was often used to describe characteristics of the ideal of a moral and civilized man, increasingly in the twentieth century there was a noticeable shift from a dominant discourse of "upright manliness," to one of "virile masculinity." Masculinity can be seen as the more expansive terms of the two since it generally speaking takes into account the traits, good and bad, which are to be seen in real men.[19]

In my opinion, the foregoing changes do not mean, however, that Samuel's insights no longer apply. Some of them may be even more relevant today. While the values of the gentlemanly sport of cricket may have faded, they may have been replaced by something much more sinister. Consider the quote widely attributed to football coach Vincent Lombardi: "Winning isn't everything. It's the only thing." That statement is also based upon the philosophy that life is a game and that competition is what life is about.

Indeed, that idea, so current in American culture today, may be traced back to the ancient Greeks. In this view, winning was the only thing that counted in those ancient events. Along these lines, Rabbi Richard J. Israel commented:

> The root of the term "athletics" means prize, and winning was an athlete's sole goal. Greek athletic games were not "sports." They implied no concept of sportsmanship. There was no value attached to doing one's best, no notion of coming in a close second. There was only one

issue, winning. All else was disgrace. No silver or bronze medals were given to the also-rans. The man who came in second was just one of many losers.

Since the games were confrontations and not sports contests, there was nothing considered wrong with maiming or killing an opponent. Death was not such a bad outcome for a loser. It didn't earn him a hero's burial, but in dying, he could salvage a few scraps of honor even though he had lost.[20]

The gentlemanly killer with a smile may have been only a British upper-class affectation, but, in any case, it appears that, at bottom, it is only winning that counts, smile or not. So powerful and pervasive has the Lombardi maxim become that our entire culture is infected by it:

"Winning is the only thing" acquired meanings on both the symbolic and literal levels that transcended the realm of sport. S.W. Pope noted that individuals and groups construct, revise and reshape the interpretations of sports events that are subsequently digested by a wider audience. Sporting traditions are then presented to the public in a variety of ways, as part of a collective experience, to popularize and legitimize particular philosophies and political ideologies. The lexicon of sport pervades American institutions from the barbershop and bar room to the corporate board room and political arena. Lombardi's slogan on winning was applied widely to business, politics and life in general. This was consistent with Lombardi's own philosophy. In his speech, "What it takes to be No. 1", he stated: "Running a football team is no different than running any other kind of organization—an army, a political party or a business. The principles are the same. The object is to win—to beat the other guy".

This observation was made by Steven J. Overman in a very interesting essay, "'Winning Isn't Everything. It's the Only Thing': The Origin, Attributions and Influence of a Famous Football Quote."[21]

Overman comments that in 1968, Lombardi was featured in a motivational film for the business community that became the largest selling industrial film in history. He concludes that "America's corporate executives have been quite willing to believe that football experience equates with business experience."[22] It also infected politics:

In 1971, President Richard Nixon launched a national fund raising drive to build a memorial to the late Vince Lombardi, who had ended his coaching career in Washington. The 1972 Republican Campaign's Committee to Re-elect the President hung a sign in their office with the motto "Winning politically is not everything. It's the only thing." The committee's subsequent actions personified the belief that the end of winning justified virtually any means. The resulting Watergate scandal did not weaken the American belief in the importance of winning. A month before succeeding Richard Nixon as President, Gerald Ford commented, "We have been asked to swallow a lot of home-cooked psychology in recent years that winning isn't all that important anymore. . . . I don't buy that for a minute. It is not enough just to compete. Winning is very important. Maybe more important than ever."[23]

Samuel argues that the Greek idea of competitive sports, or life is a game, is utterly foreign to Judaism. The Hebrew Bible has no trace of sports fixation. The only positive reference to athleticism that arguably occurs in the Bible is contained in Psalm 19, which compares the glory of the Lord to one "who is like a groom coming forth from the chamber, like a hero, eager to run his course." But that sole positive reference is negated elsewhere. For example, Psalm 147 claims that the Lord "does not prize the strength of horses, nor value the fleetness of men."[24]

While Judaism is not a pacifistic religion, there is no glorification of those who must fight. Indeed, those who are commanded to fight and kill in a just war must also bring a sacrifice to atone for the necessity of doing so.[25] Only God, never man, is described as a heroic warrior. The greatest Hebrew warrior, King David, was not allowed to build a temple because he shed so much blood. While hunting was the sport of kings in the ancient world, no such activity is mentioned in regard to the kings of Judah or Israel. The Talmud has no mention of the regulation of public games. Samuel states:

> The rejection of sports was not an ingenious even if unconscious stratagem in the struggle for survival. It was the result of a moral fixation . . . there is no evidence anywhere in the Bible of a Jewish bent toward the sporting expression of life. Nowhere do the prophets and teachers have to prohibit the practice of sports. The sins of the Jews were many, and whether native or imported they were denounced in great detail. Neither of their own accord nor under foreign influence did the Jews in Biblical days ever fall into the error of glorifying and enhancing the competitiveness of life with the symbolism of games, or of refining and idealizing military combat with punctilio.[26]
>
> The enmity of man for man had no uniforms, arenas, heralds, and trumpets to dazzle or deafen the moral perception. There was no intoxicating or hypnotic ritual to put the intelligence to sleep. Above all, there was no recognized philosophy of contest, and no traditions of canonized contestants.
>
> The summation of life as a game, with the concomitant implication of life as a hideous tragedy, was completely unknown in the Jewish world. . . . Fighting was not a lark, armies were not masquerades; and sporting contests, the charades of war, with their wild practice

excitations, were an abomination to the Hasideans who fought Antiochus the Fourth, and a foolishness to the Jews among whom I grew up. If competitive brutality existed among them in the ordinary daily struggle—and it did—there was no philosophy to make it seem the proper order of the universe.[27]

If the maxim "winning is everything" is what life is about, where has that taken us? Has not sports itself been corrupted by such a philosophy? Is this why so many athletes use steroids? Is this why athletes are no longer role models, if they ever were, but instead simply vacuous celebrities? Is this why loutish behavior occurs so often, around the world, by both athletes and fans, on and off the field? As one wag put it, he went to a fistfight and a hockey game broke out.

According to Ted Turner: "Life is a game. Money is how we keep score." That may be fine for financial moguls and the wizards of Wall Street, but what happens to thousands of working people who are laid off when the factory is shut down because buying from China is more profitable? What shall we say to those people? Do we call them "losers"?

If winning is everything, then it is not surprising that we are beset with Enrons and Bernie Madoffs.

If winning is everything in politics, then has that not only brought us Watergate, but also "Swift Boating," attack ads, unconscionable sums of money for political publicity, and a dysfunctional and polarized Congress? If winning is everything, then anger, fear, and hate can be so easily manipulated to stir the populous.

If winning is everything, then surely it should not be surprising that education is rife with cheating and plagiarism. Indeed, what is the meaning of grades? Do they measure what anyone has in fact learned or simply which students are more competitive than their peers?

The American concept of jurisprudence, which we inherited from Britain, is known as the adversarial legal system. It is premised that out of the clash of legal gladiators, truth will emerge. However, if winning is everything, does the victory belong to those who can afford the best champion?

"May the best man win." What does that phrase really mean?

Samuel states:

The modern Olympiad is a faithful continuation of the ancient, not only in name, but in function and effect. The roar that goes up from Wembley or the Yankee Stadium or the Rose Bowl is the one that went up from the Colosseum, the Circus Maximus, or the racing-track of the New Rome on the Bosporus. Its spiritual content, expressed in universal mob language, is what it has always been: the intoxicating affirmation of the exclusive rightness of the combative ethic; the sub-limation of frustrated individual ambition into group assertiveness, focusing in the hero; the surrender or evasion of moral perception in favor of the automatism of a Yes-or-No loyalty; the substitution of a simple functional test for a difficult, thoughtful approach to the meaning of personality. The intelligence is put to rest while the most easily manipulable emotions take charge.[28]

Is there not a valid message in such a sentiment?

There are those who see life as strife and struggle, man against man, and group against group. So why not think of it as a game and enjoy the combat and embrace the fight? This idea was recognized by a German Jewish poet, Heinrich Heine, in a chilling prediction of what would happen in Germany ninety-eight years before the Nazis actually took power:

> Some day there will awake that fighting folly found among the ancient Germans, the folly that fights neither to kill nor to conquer, but simply to fight. Christianity has—and that is its fairest merit—somewhat mitigated that brutal German lust for battle. But it could not destroy it; and once the taming talisman, the Cross, is broken, the savagery of the old battlers will flare up again, the insane Berserk rage of which Nordic bards have so much to say and sing. That talisman is brittle. The day will come when it will pitiably collapse. Then the old stone gods will rise from forgotten rubble and rub the dust of a thousand years from their eyes; and Thor will leap up and with his giant hammer start smashing Gothic cathedrals. . . .
>
> Then when you hear the rumble and clatter—beware. . . . Our German thunder . . . rolling up pretty slowly, but come it will—and when you hear a crash as nothing ever crashed in world history, you'll know that the German thunder has finally hit the mark. . . . A play will be performed in Germany that will make the French Revolution seem like a harmless idyll in comparison. Now, of course, all is rather quiet. And if one or the other over there acts a little frisky, don't think these will soon appear as the real actors. They are the little dogs that run about the empty arena barking and snapping at each other, before the hour strikes and the host of gladiators arrive who shall fight for life or death.
>
> And the hour will come. As on the tiers of an amphitheater, the nations will range round Germany to watch the great games.[29]

What is most disturbing and hated by some who advocate this view of life is not the "foe that comes with fearless eyes" or the enemy from the East or the West, as the case may be. After all, one cannot play a game without an opponent. Instead, what is utterly despised is the rejection of the game itself.

Adolph Hitler said: "Those who want to live, let them fight, and those who do not want to fight in this world of eternal struggle do not deserve to live."

What was intolerable to the Nazi mind, and others of similar view, was the rejection of the game by Judaism, and the moral constraints that it, and its daughter religion, Christianity, wished to impose upon the fighting spirit. As Hitler also said: "Conscience is a Jewish invention. It is a blemish like circumcision." It is this Jewish God that ruins everything, as Wagner thought.

If the view that life is a competitive game is a core belief, then those who reject the same should be utterly loathed and despised far beyond the emotional hatred that may be aroused in having a "good" fight. Further, if masculinity is also defined by this core belief in combat, then a very toxic brew begins to boil. If some believe that the very essence of their manhood is under attack, then extreme passion may be engendered. One doesn't have to be a Freudian to suggest that the strident and single-minded passion of some members of the National Rifle Association may be thus explained.

Samuel expressed the Nazi hatred of the Jews as follows:

The Jewish episode in human evolution had to be repudiated, and the most spectacular way of beginning it was with the extermination of the Jews.

This was not genocide as such, and it was not systematic bestiality, whatever play it gave to both of these. It was a call to arms against the restraints of the moral law; it was an offer to lead western man out of the labyrinth of the moral problematic, and back into the lost paradise of the primitive, pre-Christian world. Therein lay its appeal; therein still lies its appeal to millions of men and women who do not understand, have never quite understood, its explicit purpose, but have felt and feel its attractiveness none the less.[30]

There is a song attributed to Hitler youth: "We are the joyous Hitler youth. We do not need any Christian virtue. Our leader is our savior. The Pope and Rabbi shall be gone. We want to be pagan once again."

Perhaps this explains why antisemitism has been the most virulent and persistent of all the prejudices that man has indulged. Antisemitism is not the exclusive product of a Christian Europe that, claiming the Jews killed Jesus, actually resented them for the rejection of core cultural values concerning man as a man. Antisemitism can be found in many non-Christian places such as in a pagan fascism, in an atheistic Communism, in the Arab world, in the ancient world of Greece and Rome, and in ancient and modern Persia.

Maurice Samuel believed that the culture of competitive sports inevitably leads to nationalism and to war. Therefore, he argues that competitive sports are incompatible with Judaism.

I would agree with Samuel that Judaism rejects any notion that life is a game. It is Torah and its commandments that are our life and the length of our days. However, given this understanding, that does not mean that participation in games is therefore precluded by Judaism. On this point, I disagree with Samuel. Judaism and competitive sport are not mutually exclusive activities. Judaism is not an ascetic religion. It is a way of life that promotes the enjoyment of living. Enjoyment, in turn, may surely include recreation. Note, for example, that the game of chess, a board game of war, albeit mental and not physical, has been played for centuries by very observant Jews. Also, in the news of late is boxer Dmitriy Salita, who is aspiring to be an Orthodox rabbi. Obviously, he and his many supporters see no contradiction.

We have so often heard it proclaimed that participation in competitive sports is character building, that it is a fountain of morality. At the very least, it would appear that such a proclamation should be turned the other way around. Sports is not a source of morality, but rather, it is morality that must be brought to our participation in sports. Life is not a game. Manliness means being a *mensch*, not a competitor. So, perhaps, living rightly and morally can be brought to the games that we want to enjoy playing.

NOTES

[1] *New York Times* (October 2010).

[2] New York: Devora, 2008.

[3] Reported in the diary of his wife, Cosima Wagner, 112, *Time Magazine* (27 November 1978).

[4] *The Gentleman and the Jew* (New York: Behrman House, 1977), 22.

[5] Ibid., 24.

[6] Ibid., 27.

[7] Ibid., 31.

[8] Ibid., 34-35.

[9] Ibid., 36.

[10] Ibid., 37.

[11] Ibid., 42.

[12] Memorial Day Address, May 30, 1884.

[13] Samuel, *Gentleman,* 56.

[14] Ibid., 57.

[15] Gordonsville: Palgrave Macmillan, 2004.

[16] Ibid., 2.

[17] Ibid., 11.

[18] Ibid., 6.

[19] Ibid., 8.

[20] Richard J. Israel, *The Kosher Pig And Other Curiosities of Modern Jewish Life* (Los Angles: Alef Design Group, 1994), 131

[21] *Football Studies* 2:0 (October 1999):88.

[22] Ibid., 88.

[23] Ibid., 89.

[24] Psalm 147:10.

[25] Exodus 30:11-16, Numbers 31:50.

[26] Samuel, *Gentleman*, 108.

[27] Ibid., 205-06.

[28] Ibid., 100.

[29] *The Wisdom of Israel* (New York: Browne, Random House, 1945),611-12, quoting a passage from Heine's *Religion and Philosophy in Germany*, published in 1834.

[30] Samuel, *Gentleman*, 278.

The Jewish Athlete of Faith: On the Limits of Sport

Danny Rosenberg

INTRODUCTION

The subject of this essay speaks to my deep involvement in sport personally and professionally, and to a way of life that guides and influences me every day. The meaning, character, and nature of being a contemporary person of faith, and the perspective I will be discussing, derive from a modern Orthodox Jewish viewpoint that I trust will resonate to some degree with the reader. In developing this theme, a main question I want to pose and probe is, what sort of individual is the person of faith? A second pertinent question I want to consider is, to what extent can a Jewish athlete of faith engage in elite sport and remain a person of faith? Finally, what limits, if any, does high-performance sport set and impose upon a Jewish athlete of faith?

As will become evident shortly, I describe the person of faith as one who experiences a deep sense of loneliness. The source for this phenomenological account, originally given as an oral address, is found in a short, elegant book titled, *The Lonely Man of Faith*, by Rabbi Joseph B. Soloveitchik, perhaps the most important Talmudist and Jewish thinker of the twentieth century who bridged strict Orthodox Jewish understanding, knowledge, and practice with the conditions of modernity.[1]

I will proceed by providing a biographical sketch of Rabbi Soloveitchik and then turn to explore his thoughts on the person of faith and loneliness, and the parameters that guide the life of a person of faith. This will be followed by a description of the athlete of faith in the context of contemporary sport. I will provide examples in sport where the Jewish athlete of faith in particular approaches experiences of loneliness, perhaps loneliness itself, and the circumscribed world of sport with its strictures. This effort will not provide solutions to the many problems found in sport for the person of faith; however, it may stimulate a deeper comprehension of one segment of the sport community and the struggles some athletes encounter. As Rabbi Soloveitchik asserts, "I have no problem-solving thoughts. I do not intend to suggest a new method of remedying the human situation I am about to describe. . . . for there is a redemptive quality for an agitated mind in the spoken word, and a tormented soul finds peace in confessing."[2]

A BIOGRAPHICAL SKETCH OF RABBI SOLOVEITCHIK

Rabbi Joseph B. Soloveitchik was born in Pruzhan, Poland, in 1903, to a pre-eminent Lithuanian rabbinic family whose stature in traditional Jewish religious knowledge and erudition was and is highly acclaimed. The Soloveitchik name commands immense respect in the Orthodox Jewish world, so much so that the Rabbi Soloveitchik here is often referred to as just the *Rav* [Rabbi par excellence]. He was schooled at home mainly by his father and mastered the Talmud and *halacha* [Jewish law] in the tradition of his grandfather, who founded a unique method of study, the Brisker school, which emphasized razor-sharp analysis, exact categorizations, fierce independence, and a reliance on the works of the Rambam, Maimonides. The Rav was a widely recognized child prodigy and ordained in his late teens. He also received a high-school-level education from tutors. At the age of twenty-two, Rabbi Soloveitchik enrolled at the University of Berlin, where he studied philosophy and was attracted to the neo-Kantian school of thought. In 1931, he submitted a dissertation on the epistemology and metaphysics of Hermann Cohen.[3]

In 1932, Rabbi Soloveitchik immigrated to the United States and settled in Boston, where he became the leader of the Orthodox Jewish community. He established the Maimonides School in Boston in 1937, the first modern Orthodox Jewish day school in New England, and gave advanced Talmud classes to postgraduate students. In 1941, he succeeded his father as head of the rabbinical college of Yeshiva University in New York City, where he was a professor of Talmud. He also taught Jewish philosophy at Yeshiva University's Bernard Revel Graduate School. In a career that spanned over four decades, Rabbi Soloveitchik ordained over two thousand rabbis and was mentor to thousands of others, thus spreading modern Jewish Orthodoxy throughout the United States and around the world.[4]

During his lifetime the Rav published very few works. Most of his writings today derive from unpublished manuscripts, and notes and recordings of his classes and public lectures that were given in Yiddish, Hebrew, or English that could draw thousands of students and laypeople. Rabbi Soloveitchik was an eloquent orator and original thinker who could speak for hours and keep his audience spellbound. His Talmudic and halachic discourses were meticulously crafted, intellectually inspiring, and rooted in a relentless, honest search for truth. His knowledge of mainstream philosophy was exceptional and woven brilliantly into his treatises dealing with Jewish philosophy. He was also committed to serving the Jewish community not only in Boston, but throughout America, and was a guiding force in many national and international organizations. When the Rav died in 1993 at the age of ninety, the modern

Orthodox Jewish world mourned the loss of one of its greatest spiritual leaders and teachers, who continues to inspire thousands of people of faith to this day.

AN EXPLICATION OF *THE LONELY MAN OF FAITH*

One of the few works that Rabbi Soloveitchik did publish and in English was *The Lonely Man of Faith,* which appeared as an essay in the Orthodox Jewish journal *Tradition* in the summer of 1965. While almost impossible to summarize, it is to this work that I will now turn to describe and explain, as best I can, the predicament and character of the person of faith.

Before I begin, two caveats are in order. The title and content of *The Lonely Man of Faith* clearly utilizes masculine language and references. I will try to avoid this language as much as possible, although it will be extremely difficult to bypass when referring to Rabbi Soloveitchik's narrative. In no sense could the Rav be accused of being motivated by sexism even though his words might lead one to draw this conclusion. Second, *The Lonely Man of Faith* is framed exclusively in the tradition of Western religions.

In the opening words of this remarkable essay we learn that Rabbi Soloveitchik will elucidate "a personal dilemma" rather than tackle questions related to faith and reason, Bible criticism, and theoretical conundrums.[5] He encapsulates his own experiential predicament in three words: "I am lonely."[6] He makes clear that he is not alone in the sense that he is lacking intimate relationships with family, friends, and colleagues. Even in their company the experience of loneliness is felt as rejection, despair, frustration, and pain, which is also invigorating. As for the source of loneliness, it is "in the experience of faith itself. I am lonely," explains Rabbi Soloveitchik, "because, in my humble, inadequate way, I am a man of faith for whom to be means to believe."[7] The person of faith experiences loneliness on an ontological level as a solitary individual and on a historical level influenced by overpowering social and cultural forces. Interestingly enough, one would think ontological loneliness is the Rav's main concern, but instead his focus is on the struggles of the contemporary person of faith who experiences a unique sense of loneliness in the modern age.

Here is Rabbi Soloveitchik's description of the encounter between the person of faith and contemporary life: "He [the person of faith] looks upon himself as a stranger in modern society, which is technically minded, self-centered, and self-loving, almost in a sickly narcissistic fashion, scoring honor upon honor, piling up victory upon victory, reaching for distant galaxies, and seeing in the here-and-now sensible world the only manifestation of being."[8] The modern world appears antithetical to the person of faith whose ideals and beliefs cannot be tested in a laboratory, held with mathematical certainty, and are void of technical merit. Historical loneliness today is a unique experience for the person of faith and compounds the alienation and solitude felt onto-logically. Rabbi Soloveitchik reminds us that this dilemma, this paradox as he calls it, is insoluble, yet defining, describing, and exploring the predicament are in themselves worthwhile pursuits.

As for the frame of reference for this inquiry, to the person of faith "self-knowledge has one connotation only—to understand one's place and role within the scheme of events and things willed and approved by God."[9] One of those pivotal "events and things" was the creation of human beings as depicted in the Hebrew Bible.

In the first two chapters of Genesis there are two seemingly inconsistent accounts of the creation of Adam. Rabbi Soloveitchik points out the discrep-ancies as follows. In the first chapter, Adam I is created in the image of God, while in the second account in chapter two, Adam II is formed from the ground and God breathes life into him. Adam I is commanded to fill the earth and subdue it; Adam II is to cultivate and preserve the Garden of Eden. Eve is created together with Adam I, while Adam II is fashioned alone and later Eve is created as a helpmate and companion. In the first account, the name *Elokim* [God] appears, while in the second account, the name *Hashem* [Lord] also appears.[10] Unlike Bible critics who claim these two accounts refer to a dual tradition, Rabbi Soloveitchik explains they refer to two distinct personal-ity types, two typological or ideal categories that describe the dual character of human beings.

The nature of Adam I is to control and master the environment. The likeness to God is expressed through the creative urge by assuming a pragmatic and utilitarian approach to the world.[11] Adam I is interested in the question, "How does the cosmos function?" as a practical, technical matter.[12] Adam I strives to achieve dignity and majesty through subduing nature. Rabbi Soloveit-chik asserts, "to be human means to live with dignity. . . . Human existence is a dignified one because it is a glorious, majestic, powerful existence."[13] This is the way Adam I discovers his identity and what it means to be human. Mastery over the environment compels human beings to assume responsibility for their technical accomplishments. It is also the way they acquire recognition. In this regard, "Adam the first is aggressive, bold, and victory-minded. His motto is success, triumph over the cosmic forces. He engages in creative work, trying to imitate his Maker (*imitatio Dei*)."[14] As well as being a scientific theoretician, Adam I is also an aesthete. The first Adam's quest includes aesthetic creativity, orderliness in society, an emphasis on the pleasant and functional, and not necessarily on truth and goodness. Reaching for the stars intellectually and aesthetically is part of the nature of Adam I as God intended.

Adam II is also concerned about the cosmos, but he is interested in the metaphysical question, "Why does the cosmos exist at all and what message does it carry?"[15] Adam II explores the given world and "encounters the universe in all its colorfulness, splendor, and grandeur, and studies it with the naiveté, awe, and admiration of the child who seeks the unusual and wonderful in every ordinary thing and event."[16] In this fascinating world, Adam II establishes an intimate relationship with and a "genuine living experience of God."[17] The motivation of both Adams is identical, to be human as willed by God, but each selects a diverse approach in finding one's identity. Adam I chooses a dignified, majestic route where ruling the environment is supreme, whereas Adam II elects another mode of existence, namely, a redemptive one.

Rabbi Soloveitchik describes the qualitative differences between dignified and redemptive existence. The person who seeks dignity is involved in "a technique of living" and tries to impress others, makes her presence felt, and commands respect and attention.[18] Dignity is measured by one's achievements, noble gifts, talents, and successes that are shared publicly "through the medium of the creative majestic gesture."[19] In short, "dignity is linked with fame."[20] Adam I is simultaneously created with Eve in a given community where social etiquette, practical accomplishments, communication, creative endeavors, and aesthetic pursuits are publicly recognized activities. Adam I is never alone, even on the day of creation, and together with Eve they both form a single community.

This collective is a natural community guided by biological and instinctual characteristics that promote the interests of Adam I. Faced with a hostile environment, Adam I realizes that acting jointly, in cooperation with others, assists him in leading a dignified life.[21] In this sense Adam I cannot relate to loneliness but the superficial, practical experience of aloneness. The relationship with Eve is similar to a coworker not an existential life partner. As Rabbi Soloveitchik explains, "Male and female were summoned by their Creator to act in unison in order to act successfully. Yet they were not charged with the task of existing in unison, in order to cleanse, redeem, and hallow their existence."[22] In sum, "the natural community fashioned by Adam I is a work community, committed to successful production, distribution, and consumption of goods, material, and culture."[23]

In turning to Adam II, who seeks a cathartic redemptive life, being redeemed is "an ontological awareness" that penetrates the depths of one's

personality. The individual recognizes her existence is unique, singular, legitimate, and grounded in that which is stable and constant. Unlike dignity that
results from one's control over the environment, cathartic redemptiveness is
the outcome of a person controlling himself.[24] This requires a person to be
disciplined, humble, to serve, recoil, retreat, and accept defeat before God.
Recall, Adam II is formed from the dust of the earth and placed in the garden
to cultivate and keep it. With every success and redemptive step forward to
find a secure existence, Adam II experiences his exclusivity and ontological
isolation from every other person. He is existentially insecure and struggles
with the tragic awareness of his loneliness. Even the creation of and relationship with Eve, who is singular and unique, emerges in sacrifice, defeat, and
surrender for Adam.[25]

Unlike Adam I, Adam II communicates and communes through sacrifice
and distress to create a new community, a covenantal faith community. Such
a community is not grounded in utilitarian, functional, or performance terms,
but instead with awareness that its individual members are unique, exclusive,
lonely, and insecure. Adam II seeks an existential community where one is
committed to embracing others tormented by loneliness. The covenantal faith
community contains three participants: the "I," "thou," and God. Unlike
the natural work community of Adam I, the existential community is never
separated from the presence of God and is a full partner with God. As Rabbi
Soloveitchik explains, "God is never outside the covenantal community. He
joins man and shares in his covenantal existence. Finitude and infinity, temporality and eternity, creature and creator become involved in the same community. They bind themselves together and participate in a unitive existence."[26]

There are two ways the covenantal faith community is constituted. God
"speaks" to people by creating a covenantal-prophetic community, and people
approach God by forming a covenantal-prayer community. The prophet is
God's agent and interacts within the covenantal community, while people
who comprise the prayer community encounter God through prayer and others via love, sympathy, and communal behavior.[27] The prophetic and prayer
communities, therefore, involve a confrontation between God and human
beings; they consist of the three-fold structure of the I, thou, and God, and the
encounter of God in both communities confirms that if human beings are to
be redeemed, it is through "a normative ethico-moral message."[28] Unqualified
commitment to the covenantal faith community results in "the final objective
of the human quest for redemption"; that is, relief from, but not an overcoming of, loneliness and isolation.[29]

As mentioned previously, the two accounts of the creation of Adam refer to two ideal or typological individual personalities. Both personality types are divinely mandated and exist not only on different communal levels, but within each human being. Rabbi Soloveitchik states, "In every one of us abide two *personae*—the creative, majestic Adam the first, and the submissive, humble Adam the second."[30] It is our nature to quest for both dignity and redemption. However, in doing so, we oscillate between these two dimensions of our character and modes of existence, knowing that we can never realize completely the aspirations of Adam I and Adam II. The result of this constant dialectic for Adam I is unproblematic as long as a functional, utilitarian community is sustained. Adam II, or the person of faith, on the other hand, is tormented by this oscillation, the outcome of which is a deep and profound experience of loneliness and the realization that complete redemption is impossible.

Recall, for the contemporary person of faith, historical loneliness, together with ontological loneliness, compounds the level of frustration and alienation in one's life. In contrast, the contemporary Adam I tries to deny his dual character, rejects Adam II, and dismisses the covenantal faith community as something anachronistic and obsolete. In Rabbi Soloveitchik's assessment of contemporary Western society, the person of majesty is part of the religious establishment and belongs to a religious community but not to a covenantal faith community. This individual seeks dignity and success by valuing the usefulness of religion, where the religious act is a means for acquiring happiness. Just as majestic, creative Adam is achievement-oriented in the material world; he appropriates elements of the covenantal-redemptive community to be successful in the spiritual world. The contemporary Adam I engages in aesthetic gestures and upholds ethico-moral norms based on human ideals and principles. But such aesthetic creations are not sublime and redeemed, and the norms are not sanctioned "by a higher moral will . . . capable of lending to the norm fixity, permanence and worth."[31]

It is the duty of the person of faith to show dignity-seeking Adam aspects of the transcendental experience that cannot be converted to mere cultural categories. For example, prayer is considered uplifting, cohesive, and purifying for Adam I, but for Adam II, conversing with God is an awesome confrontation with another member of the covenantal community where God demands complete surrender and self-sacrifice. The message of faith is incompatible with the doctrine of utilitarian society. In Rabbi Soloveitchik's own words, "This unique message speaks of defeat instead of success, of accepting a higher will instead of commanding, of giving instead of conquering, of retreating instead of advancing, of acting 'irrationally' instead of being always reasonable."[32] Today's practical and efficient society has deteriorated to such a level that the majestic person "has developed a demonic quality: laying claim to unlimited power. . . . His pride is almost boundless, his imagination arrogant, and he aspires to complete and absolute control of everything."[33] Contemporary Adam I has built a religious cultural edifice that is comfortable, aesthetically pleasing, and socially functional where success, reciprocity with God, and a mercantile covenant of give-and-take exchanges are sought. The prime goal of the act of faith, unlike the religious act, "is redemption from the inadequacies of finitude and, mainly, from the flux of temporality," yet majestic Adam cannot accept this message."[34]

Contemporary people of faith, therefore, suffer a special kind of loneliness. They experience not only ontological loneliness, but also social isolation whenever they try to communicate the language of faith to the person of culture. Their estrangement is acutely felt because most people in modern society are unable or unwilling to speak the language of those in the faith community and have mostly forgotten or abandoned the faith element of their dual character. Rabbi Soloveitchik concludes his essay by declaring that inasmuch as contemporary people of faith experience both senses of loneliness, they have a unique task to continuously convey the message of faith to majestic, dignity-seeking people.[35]

THE JEWISH ATHLETE OF FAITH AND THE EXPERIENCE OF LONELINESS

The following will attempt to answer the second question I posed in the introduction. Contemporary modern sport is clearly part of the natural work-community of Adam I. Sport today is structured and appropriated to fulfill those elements of the pragmatic, creative, and mastery-seeking athlete. The goals of victory, success, beauty, achievement, the quest for records, and overcoming the environment and the challenges of competitors are relentlessly pursued by virtually all means possible. These include crass commercialism, political interference, bureaucratic manipulation, media exploitation, superficial cultural categories, and unstoppable rational, scientific, and technological innovations. Modern athletes find it enormously difficult to resist the "culture of narcissism" so prevalent in sport. They are mostly "intoxicated with [their] own adventures and victories and . . . bidding for unrestricted dominion."[36] This state of affairs of contemporary sport has been researched historically, sociologically, and philosophically on many fronts and is familiar to most. Therefore, I will not refer to any specific works that focus on the ills and moral shortcomings of sport and their remedies. Recall, problem-solving is not part of my agenda.

Instead, I want to focus on contemporary athletes of faith, mainly Jewish ones, who may be tormented by the oscillation between the dual character of Adam I and Adam II and as a result may experience loneliness in their engagement in sport. These same athletes also confront the structurally prohibitive nature of contemporary sport. Finding examples of such athletes can be difficult, but I will try.

The first I want to mention is Eric Liddell, the "Flying Scot," a non-Jew who was the winner of the men's 400-metre race at the 1924 Paris Olympics and who was portrayed in the popular film *Chariots of Fire*. As many know from the movie, Liddell was a devout Christian who refused to run in the 100-metre race, his best event, on Sunday, the Christian Sabbath. However, there is an inaccuracy in the film where Liddell learns that one of the heats of the race was to be held on Sunday just as he was boarding the boat with the British Olympic team to make their way to Paris. The truth of the matter is that the schedule and Liddell's decision were known a few months in advance. Liddell was also selected as a member of the 4 x 100 and 4 x 400 relay teams at the Olympics, but he refused his spots because the heats were held on Sunday.[37]

The important point of the story, the true one that is, is that a person of faith like Liddell did not have to weigh or calculate the advantages or disadvantages of making his decision to compete on Sunday. Once the circumstances were known, it was a foregone conclusion what he would do, or more accurately not do. Recall, the person of faith must recoil, retreat, and accept defeat before God. Contrast Liddell with Christian athlete Jonathan Edwards, a British triple jumper, who did not compete in the trials for the 1988 Seoul Olympics because they were held on a Sunday. Many compared him to Liddell, and his decision met with mixed responses. He later changed his mind about observing the Sabbath and started competing on the day of rest, which elicited further mixed reactions.[38] I would say that Adam I got the better of Edwards, who succumbed to the trappings of the religious community and abandoned the covenantal-redemptive faith community.

Turning to past and present Jewish athletes who encountered issues of sport and faith are notable professional baseball players like Hank Greenberg, Sandy Koufax, and more recently Shawn Green, who faced the decision whether or not to play on Rosh Hashanah or Yom Kippur, Jewish High Holy Days. In these instances, the stakes were much higher, the obligations more serious, and the pressures far greater. It is also the case that each of these athletes played in a different era, when religious sentiments in society generally, and in the Jewish community specifically, were quite disparate, the level of antisemitism was dissimilar, and the meaning of Jewish identity had changed drastically. A recent analysis of Shawn Green not playing on Yom Kippur in 2001 and a compromise decision he made in 2004 to not play a night game on the evening of Yom Kippur but then play an afternoon game the next day on Yom Kippur is quite revealing.[39]

In 2001, the media, commentators, fans, and the Jewish community all praised Green for skipping the game on Yom Kippur. However, in 2004, the compromise decision resulted in certain sectors of the Jewish community being critical of Green. As expected, comparisons to Greenberg, who played in the 1930s and 1940s, and Koufax, who played in the 1950s and 1960s, were part of the public discourse of such judgments. In 1934, Greenberg played on Rosh Hashanah but did not play ten days later on Yom Kippur, and he received positive responses in and out of the Jewish community. In 1965, Koufax sat out the first game of the World Series that fell on Yom Kippur, and he received widespread support for his decision, especially in the Jewish community. Green, on the other hand, was criticized for not paying tribute to who he was, not making a sacrifice, and not being a good role model for Jews and non-Jews.[40]

Two points intrigue me about these cases. First, all three athletes do not express ultimate loneliness felt by the person of faith. Instead, their decisions were influenced by cultural categories like assimilation, acceptance, Jewish identity, antisemitism, religious sentiments, loyalty to tradition, communal and public responses, and the place of baseball in the American imagination. The very notion of a compromise position and being selective in religious observance reflects the prognostications of Adam I. Religion is made to fit one's personal conscience in making individual judgments. Second, all Jews understand and know, as these athletes certainly knew, that any expression of faith or call to prayer requires a formal separation from the playing field. In the practice of Judaism, the sanctity of time and place, the holy as opposed to the profane, are explicitly demarcated from the everyday. Since sport is part of mundane life, it can never be appropriated as a place of worship, of conversing with God, and certainly not in terms of petition and thanksgiving. This, of course, makes the pre- or post-game prayer unheard of in traditional Jewish athletic circles.

Another story, lifted mostly from Jeffrey Gurock's fine book on Judaism and American sport, took place about a decade ago and concerns Baltimore-area basketball player Tamir Goodman. Goodman was one of the best sixteen-year-old point guards in the country, and in early 1999 he made a verbal commitment to play for the University of Maryland. He also happened to be an Orthodox Jew. Maryland was prepared to petition the NCCA to play as few games on Saturday (the Jewish Sabbath) as possible. Additionally, it would turn to other ACC teams to change dates and times to accommodate Goodman, and it would make sure the young star had a kosher training table and tutors to continue his religious studies. Goodman was widely covered in the local and national press, a rap song was dedicated to him called "The Kid with the Lid," and he was touted as the "Jewish Jordan."[41]

The euphoria over Goodman in the Jewish community reached fever pitch. Many held him up as the ideal role model of one who could live a strictly observant, Orthodox Jewish way of life and also pursue the highest echelons in sport. On the other hand, Goodman's religious high school took the bold decision not to accommodate his basketball needs, so he transferred to a Seventh Day Adventist School to hone his skills and fulfill his ambitions. This led to serious public clashes between Jewish school officials and Goodman supporters who felt the school was hypocritical in its stance. Meanwhile, Goodman had a stellar year with the Christian school and fully maintained his Orthodox way of life. In a move shrouded in mystery, in September 1999, Goodman turned down the Maryland offer, claiming the university had reneged on accommodating him. A month later he signed with Baltimore's Towson State University where all his needs as an Orthodox Jewish player were met until a new coach was hired who was not impressed with his talent and his special treatment. In 2002, Goodman left to play professional basketball in Israel, where he turned out to be a mediocre player, yet still held firm to his faith in a secular, sport-minded society.[42]

The Tamir Goodman saga perhaps demonstrates how difficult it is for the person of faith to participate and integrate into elite sport, especially team sport. The concessions and tolerance needed on both sides of the equation are nearly impossible to meet. On the one hand, how far should sports teams and organizations alter their rules and regulations to accommodate the religious beliefs and practices of individual athletes? On the other hand, is the pursuit of high-performance sport and certainly professional sport antithetical to a person of faith? In Goodman's case, he never compromised or relinquished the dedication to his faith or his practice obligations. Officials at his Jewish high school drew a line, however, when his basketball ambitions and the alterations needed to support his sport endeavors interfered with the Orthodox Jewish message it was mandated to uphold. I cannot be certain Goodman experienced loneliness as an athlete of faith in the Soloveitchik sense, but he was certainly thrust into circumstances where that experience was a genuine possibility.

The final and most extraordinary example I want to address is that of professional boxer, and former world super welterweight champion, Yuri Foreman, who is an Orthodox Jew and studying to be a rabbi. Foreman is an only child who was born to Jewish parents in Gomel, Belarus, in 1980. He was brought up in a nonreligious home, and the family was relatively poor. His first experience in sport was in swimming, where he was bullied by older boys. This turned out to be a blessing in disguise. As a result of the bullying, at the age of seven he switched to boxing and took to fighting. He started to compete at eight years old, and after a disheartening loss in his first fight, he returned to the ring to win a string of victories.[43]

In 1991, the Foreman family moved to Haifa, Israel, for economic reasons with little money and no knowledge of the language. For the next few years, Yuri attended school and worked part-time with his father who cleaned offices. In the summer he worked eleven hours a day in construction with Arab workers. There were no boxing gyms in Haifa at the time, so Foreman trained in boxing clubs in Arab villages, which was initially awkward until he earned the respect of the Arab fighters. When Mike Kozlovski, a proper boxing trainer from Russia, arrived in the city, he set up a makeshift outdoor training camp behind a local high school. Foreman began to train under pretty severe circumstances with practically no equipment, and after three months he fought his first amateur bout at 132 pounds. For the next five months he continued to compete and win in local boxing gyms against Jews and Arabs, and he qualified for the Israeli National Championship tournament that earned him a spot on the Israeli National Boxing Team. Foreman eventually won three Israeli national titles, in 1997 at 132 pounds, and in 1998 and 1999 at 148 pounds. Sadly, his mother passed away in 1998. After his third national title he decided to pursue a boxing career in the United States and moved to Brooklyn, New York, under the tutelage of Kozlovski, who was also his manager.[44]

Foreman did not have it easy when he first arrived in America. He worked as a laborer in the garment district in Manhattan and trained afterward at Gleason's Gym in Brooklyn. His discipline and determination paid off when he won the New York Golden Gloves in 2001 at 156 pounds. While an amateur, he compiled a record of seventy-six wins and five losses and was a sparring partner to several rising stars at Gleason's. He turned professional in 2002, and by 2003 he was 12-0 with six knockouts. He also encountered financial and personal difficulties with Kozlovski and with other managers and handlers.[45] A group of Jewish investors heard about Foreman's troubles and bought out his contract with no expectation they would receive an immediate return on their investment.[46]

At around this time at Gleason's, Foreman met his future wife, Leyla Leidecker, a non-Jewish, Hungarian-born model, filmmaker, and former amateur boxer. They married in 2003, and both became interested in Judaism and started taking classes with Rabbi DovBer Pinson at IYYUN, a Lubavitch Jewish institute in Brooklyn.[47] In 2006 Leyla converted; she and Yuri had a second wedding, a Jewish one; and in August 2010 they had their first child, a boy. Yuri turned out to be an exceptional student, and in early 2007 Rabbi Pinson suggested he enroll in a program to become a rabbi, a five- to six-year process. As a result, the boxer's training regimen became quite strict and disciplined. To this day Foreman studies Jewish law and mysticism in the morning, he works out in the gym in the afternoons, attends prayer services daily, strictly adheres to kashrut and the Sabbath and all Jewish holidays, and leads a complete Orthodox Jewish life. In the New York area, he became and still is a popular sports figure, especially in the Orthodox Jewish community. Moreover, throughout his Jewish re-awakening, he continued to dominate in the ring, started to wear a Star of David on his trunks, and referred to himself as an Israeli boxer.

By mid-2009, Foreman compiled a professional record of 27-0 with eight knockouts, and he was the World Boxing Association's (WBA) number one contender in his weight division. He also received some criticism for the cautious and low-risk way he fought by avoiding getting hit and the fact he hadn't had a knockout in about three years. Some called him Yuri "Boreman." Despite these criticisms, Foreman was given a title shot against heavily favored Puerto Rican Daniel Santos for the super welterweight championship on Saturday night, November 14, 2009, on the Miguel Cotto-Manny Pacquiao undercard at the MGM Grand Garden Arena in Las Vegas. Foreman's twelve-round unanimous decision victory, which could be seen as a pay-per-view HBO telecast, silenced his critics and gave Israel its first major world title holder in boxing. Many in Israel and in the Jewish community worldwide took pride as Foreman, the first Orthodox Jew to win a world championship in seventy-five years, carried an Israeli flag in front of the cameras after the victory.[48]

Foreman was once again in the limelight when he defended his title against three-time champion Miguel Cotto in the first boxing match at the new Yankee Stadium on Saturday, June 5, 2010. The fight was scheduled after sundown and was set to go at 11:30 pm. In front of over 20,000 mostly Puerto

Rican fans, Cotto won all but one round and defeated Foreman with a technical knockout (TKO) in the ninth round under the most bizarre circumstances. In the seventh round, Foreman slipped twice and was limping noticeably, plus he sustained a cut and was bleeding over the eye, yet he managed to get to his corner after the bell. It was questionable whether or not he should have continued, but he came out for the eighth round only to be dominated by Cotto until his knee locked up. Suddenly, a towel was thrown into the ring from Foreman's corner and people started entering the ring. The referee decided the fight was not over because he did not see who had thrown the towel, and after clearing the ring the fight resumed. Somehow a courageous Foreman lasted until the end of the round. After a few punches by Cotto in the ninth round, Foreman dropped to his knee and the referee stopped the fight. Some claim it was one of the most chaotic endings in boxing history. A week or so later, Foreman had knee surgery, and there was speculation he would be back in the ring by the end of 2010.[49] He did return to the ring in March 2011, losing to Polish light middleweight boxer Pawel Wolak.

As a world champion and now former world champion as well as a rabbi-in-training, Foreman garnered greater media attention than he had previously received and also renewed questions about whether or not boxing is an ethically defensible sport and whether or not a Jewish athlete of faith can and should be a professional boxer. As one columnist wrote in the *Jerusalem Post*, "How can we delight in a sport where the specific aim is to beat someone up so badly that they can't carry on?"[50] In Jewish circles, several rabbis in the press responded to questions that boxing is contrary to Jewish principles, such as the prohibition to harm oneself and others, and to avoid situations of potential danger. Although Foreman tries to schedule his fights on weekdays other than Friday night, Saturday night fights require that Sabbath laws and many prohibited activities be observed during the day. For example, even though Foreman usually stays at a hotel within walking distance of the arena on Shabbat, he must not violate any biblical and rabbinic laws related to things like wrapping his hands, ripping tape, tying knots, applying creams, and the like. Such activities are also related to the law that prohibits one to prepare anything on Shabbat for something after Shabbat.[51]

The question of whether or not boxing is ethically indefensible is complex and beyond the scope of this essay; however, it is fair to say there is no clear and definitive answer to the question. As for the status of boxing in terms of Jewish law and principles, let me state that a competent and knowledgeable rabbi must be consulted on these issues, and I presume Foreman has done so. Still, I discussed the questions posed above with a friend who is an Orthodox rabbi, and what follows is a summary of our discussion.[52] Physically harming another person can, under specific circumstances, be permitted provided a mutual, explicit agreement is in place whereby one foregoes one's honor not to be harmed. As for the ultimate harm, the knockout, Foreman has not done so in over four years, and his trainer suspects that piety may be responsible for this as well as his defensive, conservative style.[53] Putting oneself in a dangerous situation can sometimes be permitted if, for example, the situation is part of one's livelihood and thereby one can assume higher levels of risk. Now clearly a person of faith or anyone need not box professionally, but in Foreman's case he was a professional boxer before he became religious and perhaps boxing is his "only" viable means to earn a living at this point in his life. This same reasoning applies to exposing oneself to physical harm. That is, if one's livelihood involves potential harm to oneself, one may be open to greater risks.

The preceding basically claims that an Orthodox Jew can take up professional boxing from a halachic perspective. On the other hand, should a Jewish athlete of faith be a professional boxer? The answer to this question depends on one's *hashgafa* [philosophical outlook]. Perhaps in Foreman's case, if he gave up boxing when he became religious, it could have negatively altered his personality, led to less satisfaction in another job, resulted in a missed a chance to excel in boxing, and adversely influenced his spiritual development. In fact, Foreman and Rabbi Pinson do not encourage Jewish youngsters to take up boxing with the goal of becoming a professional.

As for the Sabbath-related questions and prohibited activities, there are many technical and subtle ways to alter what one does and remain within the strict letter of the Shabbat laws, but this would likely require one to compromise the spirit of Shabbat itself. As I said, I presume Foreman has addressed these dimensions with his rabbi and such detailed inquiry is interesting but may miss a larger point. A Jewish athlete of faith like Foreman, who is known as the "Lion of Zion," has achieved the very pinnacle of boxing while remaining true to his religious convictions. In the many accounts I've read, he describes his athletic life and spiritual quest as unified and harmonious, and both provide him with inner strength and greater focus.[54] One may still ask, is Foreman's successful career a rare exception as far as being a Jewish athlete of faith? I think so.

CONCLUSION

The very structure and organization of virtually all elite and professional sports make it almost impossible for a Jewish athlete of faith to be a competitor. Notwithstanding Tamir Goodman's brief foray, I cannot think of a team sport that does, could, or should accommodate an Orthodox Jewish athlete from division I colleges, to the Olympic level, or within the professional ranks. As for individual sports like tennis and golf, the tournament structure alone would make it unworkable for an Orthodox Jew to compete. Therefore, in one sense, it is remarkable that in a sport like boxing, with its dubious ethical character, a Jewish athlete of faith can rise to the very pinnacle of the sport. On the other hand, professional boxing has always played the ethnic card, and in Foreman's case, being an Israeli Orthodox Jew studying to be a rabbi and originally from Belarus, the script can't get much better than that. And yet, I am almost certain Foreman has experienced some level of loneliness as described by Rav Soloveitchik, given his bipolar oscillation between the world of sport and the world of faith. Both these domains offer defining moments of truth and navigating his life in each has likely led to encounters of loneliness.

I have tried to describe the person of faith generally and the contemporary Jewish athlete of faith in particular. In some ways there is almost an imponderable divide between sport and faith, between the world of Adam I and the community of Adam II. However much the Jewish athlete of faith excels in sport, she or he will have to limit her or his involvement to some degree by recoiling and retreating. Perhaps this is why Jeffrey Gurock observes there are fewer Orthodox Jewish students at Yeshiva University showing an interest in campus and intercollegiate sports and more are spending extracurricular time in Torah study.[55] The Jewish athlete of faith is a rare person who experiences a special kind of loneliness and perhaps reminds us that to preserve the best modern sport has to offer may require that we curb our hubris and place reasonable limits on the relentless drive to achieve the seemingly boundless ends of sport.

NOTES

[1] Joseph B, Soloveitchik, *The Lonely Man of Faith* (foreword by D. Shatz; New York: Doubleday, 2006), vii.

[2] Ibid., 2.

[3] Pinchas H. Peli, *On Repentence: The Thought and Oral Discourses of Rabbi Joseph Dov Soloveitchik* (Lanham: Rowan & Littlefield), 1.

[4] Alan T. Levenson, *An Introduction to Modern Jewish Thinkers* (2nd ed.; Lanham: Rowan & Littlefield, 2006), 197-99.

[5] Soloveitchik, *Lonely Man*, 1.

[6] Ibid., 3.

[7] Ibid., 4.

[8] Ibid., 6.

[9] Ibid., 8.

[10] Soloveitchik, *Lonely Man*, 11; Moshe Sosevsky, "The Lonely Man of Faith Confronts the *Ish Ha-Halakhah*," in *Exploring the Thought of Rabbi Joseph B. Soloveitchik* (ed. M. D. Angel; Hoboken: Ktav, 1997), 92.

[11] Ronnie Ziegler, "Introduction to the Philosophy of Rav Soloveitchik", n.p. [cited 8 July 2009]. Online: http://www.vbm-torah.org/archive/rav/rav15.htm

[12] Soloveitchik, *Lonely Man*, 13.

[13] Ibid., 14-15.

[14] Ibid., 17.

[15] Ibid., x.

[16] Ibid., 21.

[17] Ibid., 22.

[18] Ibid., 24.

[19] Ibid., 25.

[20] Ibid.

[21] Sosevsky, "Lonely Man Confronts," 93.

[22] Soloveitchik, *Lonely Man*, 32.

[23] Ibid., 31.

[24] Ziegler, "Introduction."

[25] Soloveitchik, *Lonely Man*, 38.

[26] Ibid., 42.

[27] Sosevsky, "Lonely Man Confronts," 94.

[28] Soloveitchik, *Lonely Man*, 59.

[29] Ibid., 66.

[30] Ibid., 80.

[31] Ibid., 91.

[32] Ibid., 96.

[33] Ibid., 97.

[34] Ibid., 99.

[35] Sosevesky, "Lonely Man Confronts," 95.

[36] Soloveitchik, *Lonely Man*, 97.

[37] Eric Liddell, Wikipedia entry, n.p. [cited 25 August 2009]. http://en.wikipedia.org/wiki/Eric_Liddell

[38] Nick J. Watson, "Muscular Christianity in the Modern Age: 'Winning for Christ' or Playing for Glory?" in *Sport and Spirituality: An Introduction* (ed. J. Parry, S. Robinson, N. J. Watson, M. Nesti; London: Routledge, 2007), 87, 89.

[39] David J. Leonard, "To Play or Pray?: Shawn Green and His Choice Over Atonement," *Shofar: An Interdisciplinary Journal of Jewish Studies* 25:4 (2007): 152-53.

[40] Ibid., 155-62.

[41] Jeffrey S. Gurock, *Judaism's Encounter with American Sports* (Bloomington & Indianapolis: Indiana University Press, 2005), 160-61.

[42] Ibid., 164-70.

[43] Yuri Foreman Bio, n.p. [cited 11 August 2010]. http://www.toprank.com/ViewArticle.dbml?SPSID=592850&SPID=73995&DB_LANG.html

[44] Ibid.

45 Geoffrey Gray, "Jewish Boxers are Looking to Make a Comeback," *New York Times* (27 December, 2003), D4.

46 Geoffrey Gray, "On Saturday, Rabbi-to-be Throws Jabs," n. p. *New York Times* (11 November 2009) [cited 18 August 2010]. http://nytimes.com/2009/11/11sports/11boxer.html

47 Zachary Braziller, "The Tale of the Tape and the Talmud," n. p. *New York Times* (3 April, 2008). [Cited 18 August 2010]. http://nytimes.com/2008/04/03/sports/othersports/03boxing.html

48 Gray, "On Saturday."

49 Corey T. Willinger, "WBA Junior Middleweight Championship," n. p. (5 June 2010) [cited 21 July 2010]. http://insidefights.com/2010/06/05/yuri-foreman-vs-miguel-cotto-live-round-by-round-coverage.html

Dan Rafael, "Foreman Expected Back in 6 Months," n. p. (11 June 2010) [cited 18 August 2010]. http://sports.espn.go.com/espn/print?id=5277694&type=story

50 Jeremy Last, "Boxing: Israel's Foreman Outspars Santos to Win Historic World Title," n. p. *The Jerusalem Post* (18 August 2010) [cited 18 August 2010]. http://www.jpost.com/LandedPages/PrintArticle.aspx?id=60505

51 Braziller, "Tale of the Tape."

52 Danny Rosenberg, interview with Rabbi Aaron Selevan, October 2010, Hamilton, ON.

53 Wallace Matthews, "Foreman Preps for Yankee Stadium Bout" n. p. (25 May 2010) [cited 18 August 2010]. http://sports.espn.go.com/espn/print?id=5219919&type=story

54 Dave Skretta, "Yuri Foreman: Boxing Champ and Rabbinical Scholar," n. p. (15 May 2010) [cited 7 July 2010]. http://ca.sports.yahoo.com/box/news?slug=ap-talmud to the title

55 Jeffrey S. Gurock, "The American Orthodox Athlete: From Contradiction in Terms to Institutional Standard-Bearer," in *Jews, Sports, and the Rites of Citizenship* (ed. J. Kugelmass; Urbana and Chicago: University of Illinois Press, 2007), 211.

Antisemitism and Sport in Central Europe and the United States c. 1870-1932

Steven A. Riess

Historians on both sides of the Atlantic have become increasingly interested in Jewish participation in sport in the early twentieth century, exploring their motivation, uncovering evidence of Jewish participation, and documenting antisemitism. One of the most famous episodes of antisemitism occurred in Russia in 1890, when four-time Canadian figure skating champion Louis Rubenstein went to St. Petersburg to compete in a world championship. However, the sponsors refused to permit him to participate because he was Jewish; Rubenstein was imprisoned. Only the intervention of Governor General Lord Stanley of Canada and the British Foreign Office got him back into the competition, which he won.[1]

This paper focuses on Jewish athletics in Germany, Hungary, Austria, and the United States from the late nineteenth century to 1932. These were all relatively urban and modern nations with large middle classes, where Jews were distinct minorities and encountered antisemitism. Central European sporting systems differed from the United States. They were based on privately organized sports clubs that originally focused on physical culture and martial arts until the rise of soccer, the first professional working-class sport. Americans, on the other hand, followed the English model of competitive amateur sports for the middle and upper classes, the commercialization of spectator sports, and the professionalization of working-class athletics.

Jewish achievements in central Europe were quite extensive and surpassed Jewish athletics in the United States. The first athletes were mainly fencers, highly assimilated upper-middle-class individuals who participated in an elite sport, or middle-class gymnasts. They attained a high level of achievement, reflected by numerous Olympic medals, but failed to gain the acceptance they craved. Then after the turn of the century, a significant working-class sports movement emerged, often in Zionist organizations that directly contested prevailing prejudices, and became a strong source of community identification. In the more democratic United States, Jews were also discriminated against by the upper class who barred them from most high-prestige sports organizations, especially by the 1880s when the influx of eastern European Jews began. Consequently, athletically minded German Jews formed their own ethnic (non-

Zionistic) sports clubs where they could display their prowess among people of similar background and class. Second-generation, working-class Eastern European Jews were introduced to sports that fit in well with their environment in streets, public parks, settlement houses, and boxing gymnasiums. The best Jewish American athletes, especially boxers, could become professionals, an option that only emerged in Central Europe in the 1920s with the professionalization of soccer.

Central European Jewish participation in physical culture was expected to provide a venue toward securing greater acceptance and recognition of their citizenship, especially in Central Europe, where unlike the United States, citizenship was tied to the "volk," and gymnastics and sport was a prime nationalistic venue. Many upper-class Jews by the mid-nineteenth century were viewing membership in the preeminent gymnastic movements and sports clubs, and competing in major competitions as part of their "emancipation" from unmanly physical inadequacies. They saw sport participation as a means to destroy long-held negative stereotypes about the Jewish body that included deformed feet, a hooked nose, a vile smell, and described them as weak, unmanly, and effeminate.[2] Jewish participation in the *Turnerschaft*—aristocratic sports such as fencing, middle-class contests like swimming, and masculine, working-class sports such as boxing and soccer—was expected to empower Jews by making them functional and equal members of society. Sport would provide a vehicle for assimilation, or at least evidence of acculturation, and immersion into the host countries' national priorities and goals. When that did not happen, an alternative response was to use sports to shape their own world, promoting Jewish identity and Zionism.[3]

While Jews were a negligible part of the European and American elite, they rapidly constituted a significant portion of the middle class and consciously cultivated sport as a means for social and psychological integration and acceptance into the nation. Ironically, however, as Jews became successful in sports, they inadvertently promoted antisemitism by becoming greater threats to prevailing ideas of national identity.

SPORT AND THE JEWS OF CENTRAL EUROPE

GERMANY

Jews identified wholeheartedly with German culture and the nation. There were about 550,000 Jews in Germany in 1910, just 1 percent of the national population of 64.9 million. Eighty percent of German Jews were citizens, heavily urban, and middle class. They were intensely patriotic, and in World

War I, 18 percent of them fought in the war, more than any other subcommunity. Nearly 80 percent served in the front lines, and 12,000 died for the Fatherland.[4]

German Jews employed sport as a vehicle to achieve and demonstrate assimilation. Health was equated with patriotism in Imperial Germany. As historian Patricia Vertinsky pointed out, "German Jews began to embrace the sport and physicality deemed necessary for 'Germanness.'" Jews sought to achieve the high standards of excellence that reflected positively on "the bearing, fortitude and sports abilities of young people. They also desired to appear robust and 'German' in contrast to the pale, unhealthy image which anti-Semites foisted upon them." Paul Yogi Mayer has argued that gaining recognition was a motivating factor for Jewish athletes: "It appears that the main drive of German Jews was the deep yearning to prove their *Gleichwertigkeit,* their equality in worth as individuals or as a group." However, the goal of assimilation was doomed to failure by increasingly intense nationalism and antisemitism.[5]

DUELING AND ANTISEMITISM

One Jewish response to antisemitism was student engagement in the elite sport of fencing and its rituals of duels, in spite of any religious or secular criticisms. Such engagement by Gentiles meant recognition of their claims to equality, honor, admiration, and respectability. Historian Ute Frevert claims that German Jewish college students fought as many duels as their Protestant peers. Jewish integrationists hoped that by fencing they would become more acceptable to Gentile students, whereas Jewish nationalists (who opposed total assimilation and Zionism) took up fencing for self-protection. The *Burschenshaften* [nationalistic student fraternities] emphasized duels with sabers in which rivals tried to wound opponents on the face, producing horrific scars. The duel was a testing ground for honor and manliness, rather than a venue to kill opponents. However, the Gentile did not want to duel Jewish students and thereby recognize their status as gentlemen. As historian George Berkley pointed out, "It angered the German nationalists still more by depriving them of the one activity in which they had heretofore demonstrated an absolute superiority to the Jews." Some *Burschenshaften* members in the late nineteenth century had fought duels with Jews, and lost them. As a result, the fighting fraternities adopted the Waidhofen Resolution in 1896: "Every son of a Jewish mother, in whose veins circulate Jewish blood, is by dint of birth without honor. . . . He cannot distinguish between dirtiness and cleanliness. . . . Since any Jew cannot be insulted, he can therefore not ask for satisfaction." Consequently, they would not have to fight, and possibly lose to a Jew, thereby losing face. Berkley noted that the resolution "also allowed the Jews to see that their efforts to prove themselves in any area would not create greater regard and rapport with the German students, but would only encourage greater animosity."[6]

Viennese Jewish students responded with their counter declaration: "The Jewish students dismiss the charge of being without honor with contempt. Honor does not depend on belonging to the German people or the Aryan race. The Jewish students are firmly resolved to defend their status as fully equal citizens with all the means at their command." Members of Kadimah, the first Zionist fraternity, studied saber for eight hours a day for six months in preparation for entering the assembly hall of the University of Vienna in full dress. This led to violent brawls, followed by a series of duels condoned by a leading Viennese rabbi.[7]

Between 1882 and 1914, 4.9 percent of Germans convicted of the crime of dueling were Jewish, five times their share of the national population. This certainly reflected the likelihood of Gentiles being more likely to be acquitted, but also that there were significant numbers of Jewish duelists, despite the Waidhofen Resolution. Nonetheless, Germany had fewer (antisemitic) duels compared to Austria and France because German Jews had little access to the principal dueling societies in the army and the university clubs, were all but barred from becoming Prussian officers until World War I, and there were no outbreaks of violent antisemitism in Germany universities until 1920. Any duel with a Jew meant some recognition of his honorable status, or, as historian Kevin McAleer indicates, that he had a claim to certain esteem.[8]

Banished from the major German dueling societies, Jewish students formed their own organizations. McAleer argues that by 1914, "in an undoubted attempt to obliterate the 'coffee house Jew' stereotype, they had carved out a ferocious reputation as duelists." The father of future novelist Arthur Schnitzler made sure his son became a trained swordsman, and young Arthur considered dueling an integral part of his Jewish identity. Zionist Theodor Herzl, who resigned from his Viennese fraternity because of antisemitic restrictions, was such a strong believer in dueling, that he argued, "A half dozen duels would very much raise the social position of the Jews," and dreamt of challenging leading Austrian antisemites to duels.[9]

JEWS AND THE TURNERS

German Jews had long participated in physical culture, dating back to the first Jewish members of the Turnverein in 1816, and by mid-century they were overrepresented among German gymnasts. In 1880, when Jews comprised only 1 percent of the German population, they were 5 percent of the Turners. Sixteen years later, at the first modern Olympics in Athens, Alfred Flatow won the individual parallel bars and teamed with Felix Flatow (unrelated) and their cohorts to win the team parallel and the team horizontal bars. Felix took second in the individual horizontal bars. Nonetheless, Jews would in the future be excluded from the German gymnastic movement, barred from country clubs, and discriminated against at in ski resorts and hotels.[10]

The first major threat to Jewish acceptance by the predominantly lower-middle-class Turners did not occur in Germany, but in Austria, mainly from the *Ersten Wiener Turnverein*, whose membership was nearly half Jewish. In 1887, the club added an "Aryan paragraph" to its constitution, making it free of Jews [*juden frei*]. Other Austrian societies soon copied this ploy. The *Deutsche Turnerschaft* (*DT*) expelled the Vienna club, which in 1889, together with about 15 percent of the other Turner clubs formed the antisemitic *Deutscher Turnerbund*. Most gymnastic societies in the liberal *DT* refused to add any Aryan restriction, adhering to a definition that Jews were "'of German stock,' but of the Mosaic faith."[11]

Jewish assimilationists agreed they were "Germans of the Mosaic faith" and should join German organizations. However, sport participation also drew many German Jews toward Zionism. In 1898, middle-class Zionists formed the Berlin Bar-Kochba club, described as a "national Jewish" society, at a time when most German Jews opposed exclusively Jewish societies (that could hasten antisemitism) in general, and Zionism in particular. At the Second Zionist Congress in Basel that year, Dr. Max Nordau advocated "Muscular Judaism" [*Muskeljudentum*], which, along with Zionism, would revive the Jewish people. Nordau was an assimilated Hungarian Jewish journalist, who self-identified as a German. He lived most of his life in Paris and turned to Zionism in reaction to the Dreyfuss affair. In 1900, anti-assimilationist Zionist advocates of Muscular Judaism, who believed they were good German citizens, created the *Judische Turnzeitung* to raise the Jewish national spirit and consciousness.[12]

Three years later, the *Judische Turnerschaft* [League of Jewish Gymnasts] was organized to rehabilitate the Jewish body. The *Turnerschaft* emphasized Jewish nationalism without embracing Zionism to accommodate German Jews concerned that a sport society organized along devotional lines would promote antisemitism. As one Jewish letter writer explained, "the German Jew is first of all a German and a good patriot, and does not consider the possibility to be a Jew first and then a German."[13]

The *Turnerschaft* informed the press that it sought to regenerate the Jewish people, but not at the expense of German feelings. Its constitution stated:

The *Juedische Turnerschaft* aims at the development of gymnastics as a means of the physical improvement of the Jewish people in the spirit of the national Jewish idea. Under national Judaism we understand the consciousness of belonging together of all Jews on the basis of their common origin and history, as well as the wish to preserve the Jewish people on this basis.[14]

In 1907, the *Turnershaft* clarified this further: "We are not a Jewish religious organization, but a Jewish national one, just as the *Deutsches Turnerschaft* is a German national organization. . . .The term 'Jewish' however, is not a religious concept like 'Catholic' or 'Protestant,' but a definition of stock, like 'German' or 'Slav.'"[15]

The Jewish Turners compared themselves to German Americans who loved their homeland, but also their traditional culture. However, the *Turnerschaft*'s founding principles caused problems for the *DT*, its Jewish members, and most German Jews. Historian Helmut Becker argues that in the early 1900s, most opposition to Jewish gymnastics clubs came from Jews, worried that it would harm relations with Gentiles: "The assimilated Jew, who had fought hard to gain German citizenship, considered Judaism to be merely a religion and saw in the Jewish gymnastic clubs religious organizations only. He could permit no discussion concerning Jewish nationalism, because this would have undermined his own position. On the other hand, the national Jew could not consider German nationality at all." By about 1911, as political Zionism matured, the *Turnerschaft* would ardently oppose assimilation.[16]

German Jews were less distinguished than other Central European athletes, earning just three Olympic medals from 1900-1932. Nonetheless, they were active participants in competitive sport, which supplanted the old interest in fencing and gymnastics. Historian Jacob Borut argues that in Weimar Germany, where young people looked to athletes for their cultural heroes, success in sports was an important means to enable Jews to assimilate and gain recognition from the host society. Jews mainly participated in non-Jewish clubs and faced little overt antisemitism (though it did exist) except for riding and alpine clubs, the latter led by the *Deutsch-Österreichischer Alpinverein*'s adoption of an Aryan-only clause.[17]

In the 1920s, Zionist sports became much stronger, and Jews were prominent members of the rapidly growing left-wing workers' sports movement that opposed discrimination. The patriotic *Reichsbund Jüdischer Front-soldaten* [Jewish Front-Line Soldiers, RJF] was organized in 1919 to combat antisemitism and claims of Jewish cowardice in the war. The RJF established *Schild* [Shield] four years later, partly to secure protection against antisemitic violence. It emphasized martial and militaristic sports like boxing, jujitsu, shooting, and gliding.[18]

Jewish Turners also saw themselves standing up for Jewish people. In 1927, according to Edgar Marx, a member of Bar Kochba Hamburg:

> Every fight that our team wearing the Mogen Dovid wins against our opponent is a fight for the Jewish club, and every time it is then somehow a Jewish matter . . . . Every match which our team with the Star of David on their chest plays is a match of the Jewish association and in some way becomes a Jewish matter . . . . Every single member of the team . . . feels . . . it is not merely a victory for you, your team, your association, but that it is much more a matter of victory to increase Jewish prestige, to prove the Jewish ability to perform in the area of gymnastics and gymnastics as well. And that nothing can more quickly, nicely, and objectively constrain anti-Semitism.[19]

By the 1920s, Jewish sportswomen were just as driven as their male counterparts to excel. Historians Gertrud Pfister and Toni Niewerth assert that the eminence of Jewish women among ranking German tennis players was a way to prove they belonged. They felt they had to be better than their rivals to be accepted.[20]

AUSTRIA

The liberal Basic Law of 1867 guaranteed Austrian Jews equality. They were free to live where they wished, become civil servants, attend university, and own property in Vienna, where in 1900 they were about 10 percent of the population and one-third of its university students. Despite the official policy of tolerance, endorsed by the aging Emperor Franz Joseph, Austria, a multinational and polyglot empire, provided a more fertile ground for virulent antisemitism than a more homogenous Germany, typified by the regime of Mayor Karl Lueger (1897-1910). Viennese Jews included titled bankers and industrialists, middle-class businessmen and professionals, impoverished Orthodox Galicians, and ethnic Hungarians, Bohemians, and Moravians. After World War I, when the Empire was disassembled, Austria's population was 6.5 million, 3 percent of which was Jewish. The breakup stunned Austrians, whose once proud realm became a powerless small state that suffered from economic depression, corruption, class conflict, political instability, and virulent antisemitism.[21]

Jewish young men and women participated in sport at all levels, mainly in mixed clubs. However, certain clubs like the *Ersten Wiener Turnerbund*, the *Wiener Sportklub* and the *Deutsch-Österreichischer Alpinverein* excluded Jews. Elite Jewish athletes were prominent at the 1896 Olympics where Paul

Neumann earned a second in the 400 meter freestyle, and Otto Herschmann came in third in the 100 meter freestyle. In 1900, Otto Wahle captured two silver medals in swimming, and Siegfried Flesch, a bronze in fencing. Wahle also medaled in 1904, a rarity for a European when the Games were in St. Louis. Otto Scheff took two swimming medals at the Games in Athens. A Jew medaled in swimming in London in 1908. Then in Stockholm, Herschmann got a silver in fencing, and three Jewish women, Margarete Adler, Klara Milch, and Josephine Sticker, silver in swimming (4 x 100 meters), becoming the first female Jewish medalists.[22]

Yet despite their success, Jews encountered enormous prejudice in the world of sport, beginning in 1886 when banned from the Austrian branch of the Turners. Jews responded to antisemitism by founding, in 1897, the first Jewish sports organization, later known as Maccabi. The creation of exclusively Jewish sports clubs was supported by prominent Zionists like David Wolffsohn and Max Nordau. Historian Marsha L. Rozenblit argues that the Jewish sports clubs were probably the most important Zionist youth organizations in Vienna, which had an "opportunity to fulfill the Zionist dream of 'normalizing' the Jewish people through physical exercise." However, anti-Zionist and liberal Jews felt such organizations would promote antisemitism and hinder Jewish participation in other sports clubs. The best Jewish athletes mainly played for non-ethnic clubs.[23]

In 1909, Viennese Zionists who advocated Muscular Judaism formed Hakoah ["strength" or "power" in Hebrew], a predominantly working-class club, following a visit by the first exclusively Jewish eleven, Budapest's *Vivó és Atlétikai Club* [VAC, or Fencing and Athletic Club] to play a reserve team of the Vienna Cricket and Football Club (reorganized in 1911 as Wiener Amateure SV, and in 1925 renamed FK Austria when the team became professional). The Hakoah eleven was national champion in 1924 and 1926, making Jewish teams national champions for three straight years. Its fan base was mainly comprised of old, established Viennese Jews.[24]

Hakoah's goals were to provide opportunities for Jewish athletes banned from antisemitic clubs to train and improve their physical strength, promote Jewish defense and self-confidence, prove that Jews were not inferior in physical strength, and advance Jewish national awareness. Team members wore the Star of David on their uniforms. Hakoah soon became the most important Jewish social institution in Vienna, and eventually had 5,000 members. The club sponsored fencing, football, field hockey, track and field, wrestling, and swimming. The soccer team started off modestly in the lowly Fourth Division, working up to Second Division by 1913, gaining the admiration of Jewish youth and their parents. It provided a valuable model for other Jewish sports clubs in Europe like Prague's *Hagibor*.[25]

After World War I, working-class Jews organized soccer and other athletic clubs. One popular goal was to rout the Gentiles and put them in their place. Jewish labor unions and the Association of Jewish War Veterans in Austria, Germany, Poland, France, Czechoslovakia, and Hungary all organized sports groups to protect synagogues and Jewish-owned property against pogroms and antisemitic riots.[26]

In 1920, Hakoah was promoted to the First Division. Austrian soccer was a violent sport in the 1920s, especially in games involving Jewish players, who were regularly insulted. Hakoah also played rough and purposefully challenged the prejudices of the opposition. Beginning in the summer of 1923, their games often ended in fights with Gentile players. That year, Hakoah dropped out of a league match because of attacks during matches and the behavior of antisemitic spectators assaulting presumably Jewish fans.[27]

The violence actually started even earlier in the stands between spectators. Matches were vigorously contested because of antisemitism from competitors and hostile spectators, and Hakoah backers identified the club as the champion of Jewish honor and symbol "of the fighting Jewish spirit and national ability." The first notable disturbance came in 1920, when an entourage of 8,000 Jewish fans attended a late-season match that enabled Hakoah to get promoted. The angry, defeated Germania foes attacked the Jewish team after the game. But on their way to their locker room, "The pugnacious players from *schwechat* were then given their just deserts by the [Hakoah] supporters and Hakoah needed a large number of mounted watchmen to keep order."[28]

But there were also episodes when Hakoah fans were the instigators, as when they threw bottles at opponents at one game that resulted in police intervention. Such behavior led the club management to bring in extra security for home games.[29]

Then in 1924-25, when the league went professional, Hakoah won the championship. The team took several tours, having already been to London in 1923, and then Palestine. In 1915, the soccer club went to the United States, where a match in New York drew 46,000, the largest crowd in American soccer history until 1976. By the end of the 1920s, Hakoah had won national titles in track, boxing, wrestling, swimming, fencing, and tennis.[30]

Hakoah in 1925 also captured national crowns in water polo and hockey. The Maccabee Club applauded its accomplishment: "Jewish dignity and Jewish self-confidence are indeed in good hands now; the ludicrous caricature of the bandy-legged, timid, contemptible Jew is already an anachronism, since countless Jewish victories have borne witness to the superb condition of the powerful Jewish physique."[31]

Hakoah had a huge impact on the Viennese Jewish community. Historian George Berkley found that it was a unifying force, attracting both integrationists and Zionists to its games. Edmund Schecter wrote, "Each Hakoah victory became another proof that the period of Jewish inferiority in physical activities had finally come to an end."[32]

Hakoah also played a vital role in the physical defense of fellow Jews being harassed in the streets. In his memoirs, Walter Frankl, a former track and field athlete, reminisced, "In Hakoah we were one big family. When the organized anti-Semitic demonstrations started in Vienna, we from Hakoah formed 'Haganah groups' (defense units), which were ready at all times to protect the Leopoldstadt Jewish quarters with their might."[33]

Jewish Austrian athletes encountered considerable ill-will from supporters of the National Socialists. In 1931, for instance, the water polo championships of Upper Austria in Linz were cancelled because the antisemitic Wiener Athletik und Sportklub (EWASK) squad refused to compete against a Hakoah team. Hooligans attacked the Jewish team at the railroad station. One year later, the teams did compete in a meet, during which time EWASK fans chanted "death to the Jews." Also in 1932, the river swimming championships at Krems ended with a riot. Local thugs attacked a Jewish swimmer in the locker room, and when he escaped, his teammates were stoned.[34]

Gaining success in sport hardly led to acceptance in (antisemitic Austria). It mattered little that through 1932, Jews won nineteen of Austria's forty-six Olympic medals (41.3 percent), nearly fourteen times their share of the population. In 1936, a number of Jewish athletes, including national swimming champion Judith Deutsch, boycotted the Olympics to protest antisemitism in Germany.[35]

HUNGARY

The highly assimilated (about one-eighth of whom converted to Catholicism) and well-off Hungarian Jews were Emperor Franz Josef's favorite ethnic minority. The population of 21 million in 1910 (8 million in 1920), which was just 54.5 percent Hungarian, included 910,000 Jews. There were very urban and comprised over 20 percent of Budapest and other major cities. Over half of the industry in Hungary was owned or operated by a few closely related Jewish banking families. In Budapest, Jews comprised 88 percent of the members of the stock exchange, 91 percent of the currency brokers, 60 percent of the physicians, 51 percent of attorneys, and 34 percent of editors and journalists. Nearly one-third of all university students were Jewish. On the other hand, Jews comprised a major segment of the leaders of the short-lived Hungarian Soviet Republic of 1919, and the counterrevolutionary White Terror, led by Admiral Miklós Horthy, targeted Jews with individual reprisals and pogroms. The average Hungarian was very jealous of Jewish success, which provoked enormous antisemitism. Many antisemitic laws were passed (the Numerus Clausus set a quota of 5 percent for Jews in universities), and Zionist activities were banned for most of the 1920s.[36]

Hungarians were sports fanatics and believed that to be a Magyar meant participating in sport. According to historian Andrew Handler, "participation in sports was not only a respected and popular fulfillment of patriotic duty, it was also believed to be as fundamentally Christian as it was unmistakably Hungarian."[37] Hungarian Jews were themselves major participants in all sports except for aristocratic equestrianism and rowing. In 1895, Dr. Henrik Schuschny, a respected physician, asserted in the *Izraelita Magyar Irodalmi Társulat* [Hungarian Jewish Literary Association] that physical education could foster Jewish assimilation. Strong, self-confident, and self-respecting Jews would be no different from other Hungarian citizens except for their religious preference. As Handler further noted, "many Jewish athletes kept quiet about, concealed, and even denied their religious background" because their ethnicity was "a serious impediment to advancement, success and acceptance."[38]

Jews attained prominence in Hungarian sport by the mid-1890s, yet the Hungarian Athletic Club [*Magyar Atletikai Club, MAC*], the nation's most prestigious, accepted no Jews. Most elite-level Jewish athletes belonged to the Hungarian Gymnastics Club [*Magyar Testgyakorlok Kore, MTK*], an outstanding sports club founded in 1888 by wealthy liberal Jews, open to anyone who could afford membership. *MTK* was never exclusively Jewish, yet was always labeled as a "Jewish" club and had more Jewish members than all other clubs combined.[39]

The Jewish eminence in sport was reflected by their accomplishments in Olympic and national competitions. For instance, Jews monopolized the formerly aristocratic sport of figure skating from 1908 to 1922. Hungary's first member of the International Olympic Committee was Ferenc Kemény, a renowned pedagogue, and three of the nation's seven competitors at the 1896 Games in Athens were Jews. Swimmer Alfred Hajos-Guttmann, an all-around sportsman, who was a member of Hungary's first national soccer team, as well as an eminent gymnast, sprinter, discus thrower, and boxer, captured gold in the 100 meter and 1,200 meter. An architect by profession, he captured first prize in architecture at the 1924 Paris Olympics. Eight years later, he became president of the Hungarian Olympic Society. Overall, between 1896 and 1932, Jewish athletes captured 38 of 123 summer Olympic medals (30.1 percent), including 22 of the 65 gold medals (33.8 percent) given to Hungarians, a remarkable accomplishment. In addition, Emilia Rotter and László Szollás won bronze in pairs figure skating in 1932, the first winter medal ever for Hungary.[40]

Upper-class Jews were particularly successful in fencing, which reflected their obsession with adopting aristocratic norms and gaining respect from their economic and social peers. Fencing had strong affinities with the military, and in 1900, Jews comprised 18.3 percent of the Empire's reserve officer corps. By custom, reserve officers (typically university students) had to challenge any gentleman who insulted them, and the recipient was expected to accept the challenge to preserve his honor and his commission.[41]

Hungarian fencers at times employed their skills in duels, not only to defend personal honor, fight antisemitism, and document their equality with Christian gentlemen. In 1888, when Jews were 4.5 percent of the population, they comprised 13 percent of men convicted for dueling. Miksa Szabolcsi, editor and publisher of *Equality*, the nation's most influential Jewish weekly, originally opposed dueling, but later became a fervent advocate: "The epidemic of Jew-hatred has to be combated by duels. Today our Jewish youth will convince the Jew-haters of our right only with the sword." Paul Sandor, the only Jew in Parliament in the early 1930s, reputedly fought 103 duels, often to demand satisfaction for antisemitic slurs.[42]

Jewish success in fencing was remarkable given the antisemitism of the Hungarian fencing establishment. *VAC*, founded in 1906 by *Lajos Dömény-Deutsch*, a Zionist lawyer, who also founded Kadimah, an organization of Jewish boy scouts, was Hungary's only exclusively Jewish sports club. *VAC* was a product of Nordau's philosophy of Muscular Judaism and Zionism, rather than of Jewish Hungarian leadership, who emphasized assimilation and expected Jews to participate in nonethnic organizations.[43]

Alfred Brull, president of *MTK* from 1905 to 1940, led the 1908 Hungarian Olympic delegation. Jewish athletes fared well in the competition. Jewish swimmers won three medals in swimming relays, and world record holder Richard Weisz of *MTK* (20" neck, 50" chest), a seven-time national champion in wrestling and weight lifting, took the gold in heavyweight Greco-Roman wrestling. The Hungarian athletes were led by the fencers, especially Dr. Jenö Fuchs, who belonged to no fencing club. He took gold in the individual saber and was one of four Jewish fencers on the victorious saber team. At the 1912

Olympics in Stockholm, Jewish Hungarians won seven medals, led again by Fuchs, who repeated his earlier feats at the London Olympiad, winning the individual saber event and the team saber, with three other Jewish fencers.[44]

Hungary, like the other Central Powers, was banned from the 1920 Olympics. In 1924, János Garay won an individual bronze in saber and a team silver as well, keeping up the Hungarian Jewish tradition in the sport. Then four years later, in Amsterdam, the fencers recaptured the gold in saber, with three Jews on the squad. Attila Petschauer also came in second in the individual saber. In 1932, Hungary repeated as saber champions with Petschauer and Endre Kabos, who also came in third in the individual competition. Jews also were becoming renowned in water polo with three on the national team that took the gold. Four years later, at the Berlin Games, Hungary again shined, winning ten gold medals (third behind Germany and the United States). Jews captured five gold, led by Kabos with victories in the individual and team saber.[45]

Hungarian Jews were prominent in non-Olympic sports as well in the interwar era. They were exceptionally strong in table tennis, a more plebeian sport, first introduced in Budapest in 1905. Jewish Hungarians from 1926 through 1939 virtually monopolized the world championships for men and women. The greatest player in the world was Viktor Barna, born Győző Braun, but he changed his name because of antisemitism. Barna won twenty-two world championships (including a sweep of singles, doubles, and mixed doubles in 1935) between 1929 and 1939, when he moved to England. Overall, he won forty medals in world play, his last in 1954.[46]

Finally, Hungarian Jews were also especially well regarded in soccer, Europe's most popular team sport, which they learned to play at public parks in middle-class Jewish neighborhoods. They played for heavily Jewish teams like *VAC*, BTC, FTC, and *MTK*, the greatest stage to showcase their talent. About thirty Jews played for the national team between 1901 and 1918, and in 1911, the team was predominantly Jewish. In the period 1919-1926 (the first year of professional play), seven starters on the "Golden Team" were Jews. The Jewish eminence was further reflected by their comprising a majority of Hungary's 1924 Olympic team. Handler claims that "no sport revealed the Jews' assimilationist ambitions as much as soccer," a questionable assertion by comparison to fencing. Nonetheless, Handler also points out that "the public's acceptance of Jewish players and appreciation of their performances had no remedial effect on the traditional relations between Jews and Christians."[47]

SPORT AND JEWISH IDENTITY IN THE USA

Unlike in Europe, Jews in the United States had no problem gaining citizenship. As Eric Foner points out, the founding fathers envisioned the nation as a community based on shared political institutions and values, open to all residents: "To be an American, all one had to do was commit oneself to an ideology of liberty, equality and democracy." This differed from countries like Germany and France, which emphasized that citizenship was based on ethnic nationalism. They defined the nation as a community of descent based on a shared ethnic and linguistic heritage.[48]

There was a long history of antisemitism in the United States, but it was largely benign until the late nineteenth century, which reflected the small Jewish population in the country of over 150,000 in 1860 out of 31,443,321. It rose to about 240,000 by 1880, mainly urban German Jews, who established a full array of communal institutions such as synagogues, lodges, and athletic clubs. They became assimilated, but also fully partook of German culture, joining organizations like the *Schutzenfest* and the *Turnvereine,* open to all German men, regardless of class or religion. As one San Francisco Turner noted in 1867, "Wir fragen keinen, bist du Jude, Protestant oder Katholik; oder gehst du in die Kirche und welches?" [We do not ask, are you Jewish, Protestant or Catholic, or do you go to church, and which one?].[49] In comparison to the success of Austrian and Hungarian athletes at the Olympics, American Jews did not fare as well. Americans earned 1,317 Summer Olympic medals (1896-1932), of which just 27 were by Jews, mainly in boxing and track.

The first great Jewish athlete was immigrant Philo Jacoby of San Francisco, publisher of *The Hebrew,* whose victory at the 1868 Berlin Shooting Championships made him the first individual American international titleholder. However, the most accomplished was Lon Meyers, born in Richmond, holder of every national running record from fifty yards to the mile, who in one day won the US national championship in the 100-, 220-, 440-, and 880-yard runs. He won fifteen United States championships, three British championships, and held world records in the 100, 220, and 880. There were just a handful of Jewish professional ballplayers, starting with Lipman Pike, a Dutch Jew, who was first paid to play in 1866 and went on to be a star player and manager in the first pro league, the National Association of Professional Base Ball Players (1871-1875), and then the National League. He led the majors in home runs four times. However, a number of middle-class Jewish entrepreneurs, like Barney Dreyfuss of Louisville, did own professional baseball teams in the Minor and Major Leagues. This provided an opportunity to make money and demonstrate public spirit. Jews were quite important as sports entrepreneurs, starting with the Swiss immigrant John Brunswick, a carpenter who built billiard tables in the 1840s and founded a sporting goods dynasty.[50] Wealthy German Jews encountered overt elite antisemitism by the late 1870s; shortly thereafter, many social and athletic clubs like the New York Athletic Club (founded in 1868) and The Jockey Club (1894) barred them from membership through restrictions in their constitutions, by blackballing applicants, or common consent. Ski lodges and vacation resort advertisements regularly specified "Christian clientele only," "Jews are not welcome," and "No Dogs, No Jews, No Consumptives."[51]

The German Jews responded by looking inward and forming their own sports organizations. The Young Men's Hebrew Association, established in 1854 in imitation of the YMCA, began promoting physical fitness in the 1870s. More secular status organizations were subsequently established to promote track and field, like New York's City Athletic Club (1906), whose original roster included a Morganthau, a Gimbel, and a Warburg. Wealthy German Jews formed country clubs that featured sociability and expensive sports, especially golf, as a haven for "Our Crowd."[52]

The arrival of two million impoverished, Yiddish speaking, Orthodox Eastern European Jewish immigrants between 1882 and 1914 resulted in heightened antisemitism. They came from the static premodern world of the *shtetl* and had no familiarity with sport, which was largely unknown in their homelands. Russian Jewish immigrants were stereotyped as weak, unhealthy, physically unfit, unaccustomed to "manly" labor, and unable to meet the standards of American citizenship. Harvard University President Charles Eliot described Jews in 1907 as "distinctly inferior in stature and physical development . . . to any other race." Sociologist E. A. Ross belittled Jewish immigrants in 1914 as "the polar opposite of our pioneer breed. Not only are they undersized and weak-muscled, but they shun bodily activity and are extremely sensitive to pain."[53] Such critics had no awareness of past Jewish achievements in sports, going back to English boxing champion Daniel Mendoza in the 1790s or the contemporary achievements of Central European Jews in Olympic competition.

While adult immigrants had no interest in American sport, belittled as childish, immoral, and wasteful, their sons flocked to athletic activities that they identified as fun and as a positive feature of American society. The youths did not want to be "greenhorns," but real Americans, who played sports, attended sporting contests, and talked about sports with their friends. Talented Jewish athletes gained recognition and status among their peers in the neighborhood and expected, because sport was supposedly democratic

and meritocratic, that their achievements would earn them personal acceptance and recognition for Jews in general from the broader society. Jewish
sportsmen displayed manliness, like other Americans, through strength and
courage, not like their fathers who sought to be a *mensch* who took care of his
familial, community, and religious responsibilities.[54]

Second-generation Eastern European Jews were most successful in
inexpensive sports like boxing, basketball, and track and field, which already
provided role models, fit their inner-city lifestyles by requiring little space or
costs, and held out the promise of a better life. They were less accomplished
at sports like baseball and football, like other recent immigrants from eastern
and southern Europe, that required large playing fields and high school and
college varsity experience. Inner-city youth often got their first athletic experience at German Jewish-sponsored settlement houses, established to help the
newcomers adjust to urban America, discard their old-world ways, sustain
their Judaic identity, and become good citizens. New York's Educational
Alliance, founded in 1892, became a model for the seventy-five Jewish settlements and community centers in 1910, and an additional fifty that mainly
catered to Jewish clients.[55]

Youth workers at settlement houses taught, among other things, self-
defense, dribbling, and patriotism. Sports kept youths off the streets, promoted good health, and taught self-discipline, cooperation, and respect for
authority. Boxing classes were very popular since it was a practical skill for
life on the streets, and youths could model themselves after such heroes as
heavyweight Joe Choynski, who had fought, all the top fighters and defeated
future champion Jack Johnson. In 1901, bantamweight Harry Harris became
the first modern Jewish world champion, the first of twenty-three Jewish
American titleholders. Harris was soon followed by featherweight champion
Abe Attell (1905-1905, 1906-1912), and his brother Monte, bantamweight
champion (1909-1911). There were a few more Jewish champions in the
1910s, like Al McCoy and Benny Leonard, who fought under pseudonyms,
sometimes to avoid parental disapproval, but usually because the public did
not see Jews as tough guys. In the 1920s, the sport enjoyed a major boom
after New York State legalized prize fighting under the Walker Act. There were
eight Jewish champions, including all-time great lightweight Benny Leonard,
and they also dominated the ranks of leading contenders. Jewish dominance
was so great that many fighters in the 1920s had Jewish trainers and managers, and up-and-coming Gentile fighters sometimes took Jewish names to
publicize their toughness.[56]

Basketball, which, like boxing, required little space, was very popular with Jewish youth, who dominated the sport for decades. They were among the first pros in the early 1900s and by the 1920s were prominent in college All-American selections. Jewish young men were also very successful in track, learning the sport at settlement houses and public elementary schools. They were largely barred from the most prestigious clubs, and consequently Olympic medalists Myer Prinstein, Abel Kiviat, and Alvah Meyer all competed for the Irish-American Athletic Club.[57]

Inner-city sport promoted ethnic rivalries in the ring and on baseball courts. In addition, neighborhood municipal parks became contested terrain After World War I, Chicago's Douglas Park was a "no-man's land," situated between Jewish North Lawndale and the mainly Polish Lower West Side. There were frequent fights, sometimes abetted by Jewish roughnecks from local poolrooms, eager to "Wallop the Polack."[58]

By contrast, there were few Jewish Major Leaguers in the early 1900s, and they were mainly German Jews from small communities far from New York City. These Major Leaguers, like other second-generation new immigrants, encountered a lot of discrimination, and the first five Jews in Major League Baseball, surnamed Cohen, all played under pseudonyms. Their absence from big-league rosters provided evidence to (antisemites) that Jews were unmanly.[59]

Antisemitism on the playing field, as well as the broader society, remained a problem in the postwar era. Jewish women encountered discrimination in tennis, being barred from the Western Open in the early 1920s. On American campuses, there was significant antisemitism, most notably in quotas at Ivy League colleges. Harvard students supported restrictions because they thought Jews had poor hygiene, were too competitive, and not into sports. Ironically, at Yale, the antisemitic basketball coach was compelled by the administration to recruit Jews because the team needed a stronger roster.[60]

Another notable example occurred at the 1932 Winter Olympics at Lake Placid. Irving Jaffee, who won two gold medals in speed skating, was bodily and orally abused by his own teammates. Afterward, he was invited to a celebration at the antisemitic Lake Placid Club that organized the festival. However, he did not attend.[61]

JEWS AND THE BLACK SOX SCANDAL

Suspected Jewish involvement in the 1919 World Series fix reinforced negative stereotypes of Jews. According to *The Sporting News,* the Bible of Baseball,

"There are no lengths to which the crop of lean-faced and long-nosed gamblers of these degenerate days will go." The conventional wisdom was that Arnold "the Brain" Rothstein, the leading American gambler, had hatched and financed the plot. He reportedly won $350,000 betting on the Cincinnati Reds. His role was depicted through the character Meyer Wolfsheim in F. Scott Fitzgerald's *The Great Gatsby* (1925), the most famous novel of the 1920s.[62]

Antisemite Henry Ford's *Dearborn Independent* blasted the Jewish complicity in two articles published in September 1921 by W. J. Cameron, titled "Jewish Gamblers Corrupt American Baseball" and "The Jewish Degradation of American Baseball." Cameron asserted, "If fans wish to know the trouble with American baseball, they have it in three words--too much Jews."[63] Furthermore, he claimed "[T]he Jews are not sportsmen. . . . The Jew saw money where the sportsmen saw fun and skill. The Jews set out to capitalize rivalry and to commercialize contestant zeal. . . . If it [baseball] is to be saved, it must be taken out of their hands until they have shown themselves capable of promoting sports for sports sake."[64]

Antisemitism was very strong in the postwar era, and the Black Sox Scandal exemplified to many bigots how Jews were insidiously destroying the inner fabric of American society by ruining the national pastime, just as they were harming the nation through their influence in Hollywood, Wall Street, and left-wing politics. Such attitudes helped justify the passage of immigration quota acts in the 1920s aimed against Russian Jews and other recent immigrants.[65]

CONCLUSION

At the turn of the twentieth century, Jewish achievement in sport, even the most elite, did not promote respect for them from the broader society or facilitate structural assimilation any more than did success in business, banking, education, or the profession. Accomplishments in middle- and upper-class sports were seen as threatening to Germans, Austrians, and Hungarians, who all prided themselves on their manliness, which they felt kept them above the effete Jews. On the other hand, Jews enjoyed beating the dominant groups at their own games, which made victory that much more sweet. Yet winning a gold medal did not lead to acceptance. There was no Jewish Jackie Robinson in Central Europe, nor even a Jesse Owens or Joe Louis whose great athletic performances made people look up and take notice, which says more about prejudice of Central Europeans than about star Jewish athletes. A few assimilated Jews chose to convert and join "the club," but mostly they joined less prestigious, and more democratic, sports organizations that welcomed them as outstanding athletes.

For the most part, athletically minded German, Austrian, and Hungarian Jews formed their own sports clubs, which historian George Eisen describes as a parallel sports universe.[66] Central European Jewish sports clubs were ethnic, rather than devotional, and stressed Muscular Judaism and Zionism. The first Jewish clubs were middle class, but by the end of the first decade of the century, working-class Jewish sports clubs emerged, notably Hakoah Vienna, that similarly emphasized secularity and Zionism. The Jewish clubs still promoted swimming and gymnastics, but increasingly supported competitive team sports, particularly the newly popular plebeian sport of soccer. These inclusive organizations promoted ethnic pride, manliness, and women's rights, while contesting prejudice.

In the United States, where there were no völkisch requirements for citizenship, the meritocratic institution of sport seemed more successful in integrating Jews into the mainstream culture. Sport has never been a social panacea, could never be expected to alone undo social injustice, and did not pave the way for complete assimilation into the core society's elite institutions. Jewish athletes in the United States were less reliant on explicitly Jewish sports organizations than in Central Europe, where the club system was more dominant and Jews did not have such options as settlement houses or intercollegiate sports. Nonetheless, there was still a real need for such organizations because of antisemitism at all levels of society. However, unlike in Europe, American Jewish sports clubs were neither Zionist nor political. They provided opportunities to engage in sport with other athletes who shared a sense of peoplehood.

A big difference between sport in the United States and Central Europe was the cash nexus. European sport was largely amateur until the boom in soccer in the 1920s. However, in the United States, commercialized sport provided opportunities for Jewish athletes to secure college scholarships and for Jewish athletes and entrepreneurs to earn a living. This was a big inducement for inner-city youth looking for an alternate avenue of social mobility.

NOTES

[1] Sandy Young, Danny Rosenberg, and Don Morrow, "A Quiet Contribution: Louis Rubenstein," *Canadian Journal of History of Sport* 13 (1982): 1-17.

[2] On the Jewish body see Sander Gilman, *The Jew's Body* (New York: Routledge, 1991); Patricia Vertinsky, "The 'Racial' Body and the Anatomy of Difference: Anti-Semitism, Physical Culture, and the Jew's Foot," *Exercise and Sports Sciences Review* 4 (1995):38-59; Patricia Vertinsky, "Body Matters from Goethe to Weininger: Race, Gender and Perceptions of Physical Ability," in *Identity and Intolerance: Nationalism, Racism and Xenophobia*

in Germany and the United States (eds. Norbert Finzsch and Dietmar Schirmer; Cambridge: Cambridge University Press, 1998), 332-34, 339-41, 354-70.

[3] For compilations of Jewish success in sport, see Bernard Postal, Jesse Silver, and Roy Silver, eds., *Encyclopedia of Jews in Sports* (New York: Bloch, 1965) (hereafter cited as *EJS*); Andrew Handler, *From the Ghetto to the Games: Jewish Athletes in Hungary* (Boulder: East European Monographs, 1985); Joseph Siegman, *The International Jewish Sports Hall of Fame: Jewish Sports Legends*, (2nd ed.; Washington: Brassey, 1997). On Jewish sports historiography, see George Eisen, "Jewish History & the Ideology of Modern Sport: Approaches and Interpretations," *Journal of Sport History* 25 (Fall 1998):482-531, and George Eisen, "Jews and Sport: A Century of Retrospect" Special Issue: "One Hundred Years of 'Muscular Judaism': Sport in Jewish History and Culture," *Journal of Sport History* 26 (1999): 225-39. On citizenship, see Pierre Birnbaum and Ira Katznelson, *Paths of Emancipation: Jews, States, and Citizenship* (Princeton: Princeton University Press, 1995), 59-93; Jack Kugelmass, ed., *Jews, Sports, and the Rites of Citizenship* (Urbana: University of Illinois Press, 2007).

[4] Bryan Mark Rigg, *Hitler's Jewish Soldiers: The Untold Story of Nazi Racial Laws and Men of Jewish Descent in the German Military* (Lawrence: University of Kansas Press, 1992), 72.

[5] George Eisen, "The Maccabiah Games: A History of the Jewish Olympics," (Ph.D diss., University of Maryland, 1979), 19; Vertinsky, "The 'Racial' Body and the Anatomy of Difference," 49-50 (quote); Marion A. Kaplan, *The Making of the Jewish Middle Class: Women, Family, and Identity in Imperial Germany* (New York: Oxford University Press, 1991), 56; Paul Yogi Mayer, "Equality-Egality: Jews and Sport in Germany," *Leo Baeck Institute Year Book* XXV (1980): 222. See also Vertinsky, "Body Matters," 332-70.

[6] Ute Frevert, *Men of Honour: A Social and Cultural History of the Duel* (Cambridge: Policy Press, 1995), 113. George E. Berkley, *Vienna and its Jews: The Tragedy of Success 1880s-1980s* (Cambridge: Abt Books, 1988), 81 (quotes).

[7] Quoted in Julius H. Schoeps, "Modern Heirs of the Maccabees: The Beginnings of the Vienna Kadimah," *Leo Baeck Institute Year Book* 27 (1982): 167. See also Frevert, *Men of Honour*, 113. On the memories of a Jewish Austrian fraternity brother on the consequences of the "Waidhofener principle" in the early 1920s, see Arthur Koestler, *Arrow in the Blue, an Autobiography* (New York: Macmillan, 1954), 109. Koestler belonged to *Unitas*, one of several other Jewish fencing fraternities.

[8] Kevin McAleer, *Dueling: The Cult of honor in Fin-De-Siècle Germany* (Princeton: Princeton University Press, 1994), 155; Frevert, *Men of Honour*, 235; Daniel Wildmann, "Jewish Gymnasts and Their Corporeal Utopias in Imperial Germany," in *Emancipation through Muscles: Jews and Sports in Europe* (ed. Michael Brenner and Gideon Reuveni; Lincoln: University of Nebraska Press, 2006), 33.

[9] McAleer, *Dueling*, 155. Jewish prominence in and preoccupation with dueling is noteworthy. People of Jewish background like Heinrich Heine, Karl Marx, Ferdinand Lassalle, and Theodor Herzl saw dueling as an integral part of Jewish life.

[10] Hartmut Becker, *Antisemitismus in der Deutschen Turnerschaft* (Sankt Augustin: Verlag Hans Richarz, 1980); Hajo Bernett, "Alfred Flatow—Vom Olympiasieger zum Reichsfeind," *Sozial-und Zeitgeschichte des Sports* 1:2 (1987):94-102. For an analysis of the role of the Turners in promoting German nationalism, see Arnd Kruger, "Deutschland, Deutsch-

land Uber Alles? National Integration through Turnen and Sport in Germany 1870-1914," *Stadion* 27 (2001): 109-29.

[11] Hajo Bernett, "Opfer des 'Arierparagraphen': der Fall der Berliner Turnerschaft," *Stadion* 15 (1989): 29-44; Harmut Becker, "The Jews and Anti-Semitism in the German Gymnastics Movement, 1810-1933," in *Physical Education and Sport in the Jewish History and Culture*, Proceedings of the Second International Seminar, July 1977 (ed. Uriel Simri; Netanya: Wingate Institute, 1977), 70-71; Hartmut Becker, "The Jeudische Turnerschaft Between Nation and Religion," in *Physical Education and Sport in the Jewish History and Culture*, Proceedings of an International Seminar, July 1981 (ed. Uriel Simri; Netanya: Wingate Institute, 1981), 66; Kruger, "Deutschland," 115.

[12] George Eisen, "Zionism, Nationalism and the Emergence of the Judische Turnerschaft," *Leo Baeck Yearbook* 26 (1983): 247-62. On Muscular Judaism, see Todd Samuel Presner, *Muscular Judaism: The Jewish Body and the Politics of Regeneration* (London: Routledge, 2007). On Max Nordau, see P. M. Baldwin, "Liberalism, Nationalism and Degeneration: The Case of Max Nordau," *Central European History* 13 (1980): 99-120; and on his concept of "Muscular Judaism," see Sander Gilman, *The Jew's Body* (Routledge, 1991), 53-54. Max Arendt in the early 1900s was the chairman of the Konigsberg city parliament, which passed a motion barring members of Maccabi from using the city's facilities because it was a Zionist group. Amos Elon, *The Pity of it All: A History of Jews in Germany, 1743-1933* (New York, Henry Holt, 2002), 289.

[13] Becker, "Judische Turnerschaft," 67; Wildmann, "Jewish Gymnasts," 29; Hans-Jurgen Konig, "Zwischen Marginalisierung und Entfremdung: Zum Nationalismus der Judischen Turn-Und Sportbewegung in Wilhelmischen Kaiserreich," *Stadion* 18:1 (1992): 106-25.

[14] *Juedische Turnzeitung* 4 (1903): 167, cited in Becker, "Judische Turnerschaft," 66

[15] *Juedische Turnzeitung* 8 (1907): 17-23, 96, cited in ibid., 68.

[16] Ibid., 69. Four of the 11 association (with 1,500 members) in 1903 were German. There were 89 in 1914 (9,300 members), but only 21 were German. See Wildmann, "Jewish Gymnasts and Their Corporeal Utopias in Imperial Germany," 27.

[17] Jacob Borut, "Jews in German Sports during the Weimar Republic," in *Emancipation through Muscles: Jews and Sports in Europe* (ed. Michael Brenner and Gideon Reuveni; Lincoln: University of Nebraska Press, 2006), 79.

[18] Ulrich Dunker, *Der Reichsbund Jüdischer Frontsoldaten 1919-1938. Geschichte Eines Jüdischen Abwehrvereins* (Düsseldorf: Droste, 1977); Donald L. Niewyk, *The Jews in Weimar Germany* (New Brunswick: Transaction Press, 2001), 90-92; Gertrud Pfister, "Sports in Germany: 1898-1938," *Jewish Women: A Comprehensive Historical Encyclopedia*, 1 March 2009, Jewish Women's Archive, http://jwa.org/encyclopedia/article/sports-in-germany-1898-1938.

[19] Edgar Marx, "Ideological Self-Determination of Bar Kochbar: The New Year of the Jewish Gymnastics and Sports Association Bar Kochbar," in *The Weimar Republic Sourcebook* (ed. Anton Kaes, et al.; Berkeley: University of California Press, 1994), 263.

[20] Gertrud Pfister and Toni Niewerth, "Jewish Women in Gymnastics and Sport in Germany, 1898-1938," *Journal of Sport History* 26 (Summer 1999): 294, 301. On Jewish women and German sport, see Pfister and Niewerth, "Sports in Germany: 1898-1938."

In 1928, the first year that women's gymnastics was an Olympic sport, five members of the gold medal team from the Netherlands, and their coach, were Jewish. All but one died in concentration camps in World War II.

[21] On Jews in Vienna during the age of Franz Joseph, see, for example, Steven Beller, *Vienna and the Jews, 1867-1938* (Cambridge: Cambridge University Press, 1989); Robert S. Wistrich, *The Jews of Vienna in the Age of Franz Joseph* (New York: Oxford University Press, 1989).

[22] Berkley, *Vienna and Its Jews*, 130; Marsha L. Rozenblit, *The Jews of Vienna, 1867-1914: Assimilation and Identity* (Albany: State University of New York Press, 1983), 165; Erich Juhn, "The Jewish Sports Movement in Austria," in *The Jews of Austria: The Jews of Austria: Essays on Their Life, History, and Destruction* (ed. Josef Fraenkel; London: Vallentine, Mitchell, 1967), 161-64; Harriet Pass Freidenreich, *Jewish Politics in Vienna, 1918-1938* (Bloomington: Indiana University Press, 1991), 5; Michael John, "Anti-Semitism in Austrian Sports Between the Wars," in *Emancipation through Muscles* (eds. Brenner and Reuveni; Lincoln: University of Nebraska Press, 2006), 136-37. Some sources claim that Hedwiga Rosenbaumová (also known as Hedwig Rosenbaum), who won medals in singles and mixed doubles tennis in 1900 representing Bohemia, a Czech province of Austria-Hungary, was Jewish, and the first Jewish woman to win an Olympic medal. See, for example, "Olympic Medal Winners," *Jewish Women: A Comprehensive Historical Encyclopedia.*

[23] Rozenblit, *Jews of Vienna*, 165; Berkley, *Vienna and Its Jews*, 130; John, "Anti-Semitism in Austrian Sports," 161-64.

[24] John, "Anti-Semitism in Austrian Sports," 122-23.

[25] Rozenblit, *Jews of* Vienna, 165; Juhn, "Jewish Sports Movement in Austria," 161-64; Berkley, *Vienna and Its Jews*, 130; John Bunzl, "Hakoah Vienna: Reflections on a Legend," in *Emancipation through Muscles* (ed. Michael Brenner and Gideon Reuveni; Lincoln: University of Nebraska Press, 2006), 109. See also Walter Frankl, "Erinnerungen an Hakoah Wien, 1909-1938," *Bulletin des Leo Baeck Instituts* 64 (1983): 55-84.

Soccer historian William J. Murray reported that Hakoah's soccer team "roused the anger not only of the anti-Semites but of the liberal Jews who opposed Zionist activity because they feared it would encourage anti-Semitism." William J. Murray, *The World's Game* (Urbana: University of Illinois Press, 1996), 26, 54 (quote); *EJS*, 417-18. After the war, Czechoslovakia, created out of the old Austrian empire, had a Jewish soccer league. For a recent history of the club, see Susanne Betz, Monika Löscher, and Pia Schölnberger, *100 Jahre Hakoah 1909-2009* (Innsbruck: Studien Verlag, 2009).

[26] Berkley, *Vienna and Its Jews*, 81; Murray, *World's Game,* 54. There were seven Zionist clubs in Austria, as well as other teams with a large Jewish presence like Wiener Austria, which was more of an assimilated squad. See John, "Anti-Semitism in Austrian Sports," 119-41.

[27] Murray, *World's Game*, 54; John, "Anti-Semitism in Austrian Sports," 131.

[28] John, "Anti-Semitism in Austrian Sports," 131, 136; Berkley, *Vienna and its Jews,* 169 (quote).

[29] Murray, *World's Game,* 54; John, "Anti-Semitism in Austrian Sports," 131.

[30] Karen Propp, "Hakoah Vienna: 100 Years Old and Still Powering On: Jewish Sports Club Founded in Adversity Goes from Strength to Strength," *Jewish Daily Forward,* November 17, 2009, http://www.forward.com/articles/119116/. On the American reac-

tion to the 1926 Hakoah tour, see Jeffrey Gurock, "Pride and Priorities: American Jewry's Response to Hakoah Vienna's U.S. Tour of 1926," in *Jews and the Sporting Life: Studies in Contemporary Jewry*, Vol. 23 (ed. Ezra Mendelsohn; Oxford: Oxford University Press, 2009), 70-86.

[31] *Judischer Sport*, 11 June 1925, 1, quoted in John, "Antisemitism in Austrian Sports," 131.

[32] Murray, *World's Game*, 54; John, "Antisemitism in Austrian Sports," 131; Berkley, *Vienna and Its Jews*, 169-70 (quote). My father was a member of Hakoah in the interwar era, and it was one of the few pleasant memories he had of life in Vienna in that era.

[33] Quoted in John, "Antisemitism in Austrian Sports," 133. John cites additional memoirs for the late 1930s.

[34] Ibid., 124-25. On Vienna's Jews, see Berkley, *Vienna and Its Jews*, 225, 342; *EJS*, 402. Growing antisemitism in Austria in 1936 led to the collapse of the nation's film industry with the mass exodus of Jewish artists. After *Anschluss*, anyone who could escape the country tried to emigrate. See Bruce F. Pauley, *From Prejudice to Persecution: A History of Austrian Anti-Semitism* (Chapel Hill: University of North Carolina Press, 1992).

[35] The Jewish medal winners are drawn from George Eisen, "Jewish Olympic Medalists," http://www.jewishsports.net/medalists.htm. Identifying Jews is an imperfect science. He based his decisions on the religion of the mother or the individual's self-identification as Jewish (religious or ethnic). For an alternate list, see Yogi Mayer, *Jews and the Olympic Games: Sport-A Springboard for Minorities* (London: Vallentine Mitchell, 2004), 209-15. Eisen does not identify Ellen Preis, gold medalist in fencing in 1932, as Jewish; however, she was of Jewish descent and would have been arrested and deported in World War II had she not gone into hiding. "Jewish Athletes—Helene Mayer," US Holocaust Museum, "The Nazi Olympics Berlin 1936," http://www.ushmm.org/museum/exhibit/online/olympics/detail.php?content=jewish_athletes_mayer&lang=en.

[36] On the Hungarian situation, see T. D. Kramer, *From Emancipation to Catastrophe: The Rise and Holocaust of Hungarian Jewry* (Lanham: University Press of America, 2000); Yuri Slezkine, *The Jewish Century* (Princeton: Princeton University Press, 2004); Raphael Patai, *The Jews of Hungary: History, Culture, Psychology* (Detroit: Wayne State University Press, 1996), 379-85, 546; William O. McCagg, Jr., *Jewish Nobles and Geniuses in Modern Hungary* (New York: East European Monographs, Columbia University Press, 1972); John M. Efron, *Defenders of the Race* (New Haven: Yale University Press, 1994); Eisen, "Jewish History and the Ideology of Sport," 508. For a discussion of Hungarian Jews and conversion, see the correspondence, "Duels in the Sunshine," George Eisen, reply by István Deák, *New York Review of Books*, October 19, 2000, http://www.nybooks.com/articles/archives/2000/oct/19/duels-in-the-sunshine.

[37] Patai, *Jews of Hungary*, 437-38; Handler, *From the Ghetto to the Games*, 35-41, 49; Andrew Handler, ed., *The Holocaust in Hungary: An Anthology of Jewish Response* (Tuscaloosa: University of Alabama Press, 1982), 10 (quote).

[38] Handler, *From the Ghetto to the Games*, 35-41, viii (quotes), 15.

[39] Eisen, "Maccabiah Games," 19; Handler, *From the Ghetto to the Games*, 26-27, 34-35. *MTK* began as a soccer club. Its main rival was Ferencvaros, which had a more Catholic and working-class base. In 1912, *MTK* built a 20,000 seat stadium. See Murray, *World's Game*, 27.

[40] Handler, *From the Ghetto to the Games*, 17-19, 26-27, 49, 53-55, 78. Kemény perished in the Holocaust. George Eisen, "The 'Budapest Option': The Hungarian Alternative to the First Modern Olympic Games," *International Journal of Sport History* 8 (1991):124-32. On Kemény, see Katalin Szikora, "Ferenc Kemény and the Hungarian Olympic Ideal," *in Coubertin et l'Olympisme, questions pour l'avenir: Le Havre 1897-1997: Rapport du Congrès du 17 au 20 sept. 1997 à l'Université du Havre* (ed. Norbert Müller; Lausanne: Comité international Pierre de Coubertin, 1998), 132-37. Jewish Hungarian medalists were drawn from a list of Olympic medals winners in George Eisen, "Jewish Olympic Medalists," International Jewish Sports Hall of Fame, http://www.jewishsports.net/medal-ists.htm. An additional eight gold medals were earned by Hungarians of Jewish descent that Eisen implies had no recognizable Jewish self-identity. Yogi Mayer included on his listing of Jewish Hungarian athletes fencer Zoltan Schanker as a "disputed" Jew. See Mayer, *Jews and the Olympic Games*, 209-15. Schenker is listed in other compilations as Jewish.

For my computation of Hungarian medalists, I did not use the normal lists of medals awarded nationally because such lists credit a team winner as achieving one medal, while in reality all members of those teams received medals. Consequently, I counted instead the number of all athletes (individuals and team members) who won medals.

[41] Erwin A. Schmidl, "Jews in the Austrian-Hungarian Armed Forces, 1867-1918," in *Jews and Other Ethnic Groups in a Multi-Ethnic World* (ed. Ezra Mendelsohn; New York: Oxford University Press, 1987), 138; Eisen, "Jewish History and the Ideology of Sport," 509; "Duels in the Sunshine."

[42] Handler, *From the Ghetto to the* Games, 26-27; Patai, *Jews of Hungary*, 342, 379, 383 (quote).

[43] Eisen, "Maccabiah Games," 27-31; Handler, *From the Ghetto to the Games,* 42-44.

[44] Handler, *From the Ghetto to the Games*, 21-32, 34-35, 38; Patel, *Jews of Hungary,* 384. Fuchs was 22-2-1 in his Olympic competition. Brull, who died in the Holocaust, was president of the International Amateur Wrestling Federation between 1924 and 1928, and president of the Hungarian Soccer League. See "Alfred Brull," International Jewish Sports Hall of Fame, http://www.jewishsports.net/PillarAchievementBios/AlfredBrull. htm. Dr. Oskar Gerde, who was on the winning saber teams in both 1908 and 1912 as a gold medalist, died in Mauthausen-Gusen Concentration Camp in 1944.

[45] Handler, *From the Ghetto to the Games,* 79-85. Janos Garay, gold medalist, team saber, died in 1945 at Mauthausen–Gusen Concentration Camp. Handler points out that Kabos often felt out of place, discouraged by teammates who were antisemitic army officers and fencing officials. The Jewish success in fencing was particularly notable because there were not a lot of Jewish men or women in the sport. Ibid., 83, 87. *EJS*, 393, reported that Jewish Hungarian athletes won seventy-two medals in all, or one-third of all medals won by Jews in the Olympics. In addition, Hajos-Guttmann won a silver for architecture in 1924, and Dr. Ferenc Mezo won a gold for literature in 1924. Ibid., 391-95. The female medalists in fencing in the 1936 Berlin Olympics, Elona Elek of Hungary (gold), Helene Mayer of Germany (silver), and Ellen Preis of Austria (bronze), were half-Jewish and did not consider themselves "Jewish."

[46] Gulu Ezekiel, "Down Memory Lane: The Magnificent Magyar," *Sportstar* 28:45 (October 18-24, 2005). http://www.hinduonnet.com/tss/tss2841/stories/20051008002506800. htm.

[47] Berkley, *Vienna and its Jews,* 81; Murray, *World's Game,* 54. There were seven Zionist soccer clubs in Austria, as well as other teams with large Jewish presence like Wiener Austria, which was more of an assimilated squad. See John, "Anti-Semitism in Austrian Sports,"119; Handler, *From the Ghetto to the Games,* 53 (quote), 52, 55, 57, 72, 77. The film *Sunshine* recapitulated the history of sport and assimilation in Hungary. Part of that story is that Jews could never become "real" Hungarian citizens, regardless of their accomplishments or lineage. The protagonist, Adam Sors, is a composite picture of Attila Petschauer, killed by Hungarian prison guards in 1943, and Kabos, who also died during the Holocaust.

[48] Eric Foner, *The History of American Freedom* (New York: W. W. Norton, 1998), 38-39. See also Rogers Brubaker, *Citizenship and Nationhood in France and Germany* (Cambridge: Harvard University Press, 1992); Hans Kohn, *American Nationalism: An Interpretive Essay* (New York: Macmillan, 1957); Milton Gordon, *Assimilation in American Life: The Role of Race, Religion, and National Origins* (New York: Oxford University Press, 1964).

[49] On the history of antisemitism in the United States, see Leonard Dinnerstein, *Anti-Semitism in America* (New York: Oxford University Press, 1994); David Gerber, ed., *Anti-Semitism in American History* (Urbana: University of Illinois Press, 1986). On antisemitism in American sport, see Steven A. Riess, "Sports and the American Jew," in *Sports and the American Jew* (ed. Steven A. Riess; Syracuse: Syracuse University Press, 1998), 40-45; Frederic Cople Jaher, "Antisemitism in American Athletics," *Shofar* 20:1 (Fall 2001): 61-73; Peter Hopsicker, "'No Hebrews Allowed': How the 1932 Lake Placid Winter Olympic Games Survived the 'Restricted' Adirondack Culture, 1877-1932," *Journal of Sport History* 36:2 (Summer 2009): 205-22.

On German Jewish sport, see Hasia Diner, *A Time For Gathering: The Second Migration, 1820-1880,* vol. 2 *of The Jewish People in America* (Baltimore: Johns Hopkins University Press, 1992), 1, 56, 86-87, 162-63, 165; *California Demokrat* (1 January 1867), quoted in Roberta J. Park, "German Associational and Sporting Life in the Greater San Francisco Bay Area: 1850-1900," *Journal of the West* 26:1 (January 1987): 52; Henry Metzner, *A Brief History of the American Turnerbund* (Pittsburgh: National Executive Committee of the American Turnerbund, 1924); Ralf Wagner, "Turner Societies and the Socialist Tradition," in *German Workers' Culture in the United States, 1850 to 1920* (ed. Hartmut Keil; Washington, DC: Smithsonian Institution Press, 1988), 221-40; Horst Ueberhorst, *Turner Unterm Sternenbanner: Der Kampf der Deutsche-Amerikanischen fur Einheit, Freiheit, und Sociale Gerecktigkeit, 1848 bis 1918* (Munich: Moos, 1978); Carl Wittke, *We Who Built America: The Saga of the Immigrant* (New York: Prentice-Hall, 1952), 147-48; Steven A. Riess, *City Games: The Evolution of American Urban Society and the Rise of Sports* (Urbana: University of Illinois Press, 1989), 23, 96-99; Louis J. Swichkow and Lloyd P. Gartner, *The History of the Jews of Milwaukee* (Philadelphia: Jewish Publication Society of America, 1963), 114; Hyman L. Meites, *History of the Jews of Chicago* (Chicago: Jewish Historical Society of Illinois, 1924), 470; Norton M. Kramer and Norton B. Stern, "The Turnverein: A Jewish Experience in Western Jewry," *Western States Jewish Historical Quarterly* 9 (April, 1984): 227-29.

[50] "America's Top Sharpshooter," *Western States Jewish Historical Quarterly* 9 (1976): 43-45; Park, "German Associational and Sporting Life," 11, 14; *EJS*, 32-35, 212-16; Joe D. Willis and Richard G. Wettan, "L.E. Meyers, 'World's Greatest Runner,'" *Journal of Sport History* 2 (Fall 1975), 93-111; Steven A. Riess, *Touching Base: Professional Baseball and American Culture in the Progressive Era* (Urbana: University of Illinois Press, 1999), 56, 67-69, 72-75, 98. There were a number of Jewish owners in the National League in the late nineteenth century and continuously until after World War II; however, there were no Jewish owners in the American League from 1902 until 1946, likely due to antisemitism.

[51] *American Hebrew* (15 November 1880, 6 June 1890, and 20 June 1913), quoted in Naomi Wiener Cohen, *Encounter with Emancipation: The German Jews in the United States, 1830-1914* (Philadelphia: Jewish Publication Society, 1984), 249-50. As in Great Britain, wealthy German American Jews tried to gain acceptance by participating in thoroughbred racing. Rich Jewish racing fans included immigrant financier August Belmont, the first Jew admitted to the New York Yacht Club, who was also the first president of New York's prestigious American Jockey Club, founded in 1865. For a detailed biography of Belmont's personal life and his racing interests, see David Black, *The King of Fifth Avenue: The Fortunes of August Belmont* (New York: Dial, 1981). On Jews and the Jockey Club, see Bernard Livingston, *Their Turf: America's Horsey Set and Its Princely Dynasties* (New York: Arbor House, 1973), 30, 261-67. On the rise of Russian Jews in the turf, see John Hertz, *The Racing Memoirs of John Hertz as Told to John Shipman* (Chicago: n.p., 1954); *EJS*, 313-14, 331; Livingston, *Their Turf*, 267-79. Historian Tony Collins argues that antisemitism played a role in hindering Jewish success in middle-class sports in Great Britain. They were excluded from golf and tennis clubs at the turn of the century, and issues of *Golf Illustrated* often published antisemitic cartoons. Tony Collins, "Jews, Anti-Semitism, and Sports in Britain, 1900-1939," in *Emancipation through Muscles* (ed. Michael Brenner and Gideon Reuveni; Lincoln: University of Nebraska Press, 2006), 146-47, 149-52.

[52] Benjamin Rabinowitz, *The Young Men's Hebrew Association (1854-1913)* (New York: National Jewish Welfare Board, 1948), 11-12, 53, 62, 75, 78, 85; Diner, *Time for Gathering*, 107-08, 163; *EJS*, 143. One of the Y's most attractive features was its outdoors camps. See also William Langfeld, *The Young Men's Hebrew Association of Philadelphia: A 50 Year Chronicle* (Philadelphia: Young Men's and Young Women's Hebrew Association, 1928); Steven Hertzberg, *Strangers Within the Gate City: The Jews of Atlanta, 1845-1915* (Philadelphia: Jewish Publication Society of America, 1978), 118, 123; Howard M. Sachar, *A History of Jews in America* (New York: Knopf, 1992), 157; Dinnerstein, *Anti-Semitism in America*, 52; Digby Baltzell, *Philadelphia Gentlemen: The Making of a National Upper Class* (Glencoe: Free Press, 1959); Stephen Hardy, *How Boston Played: Sport, Recreation and Community, 1865-1915* (Boston: Northeastern University Press, 1982); "The City Athletic Club," *American Hebrew* 84 (20 November 1908): 74; Louis Wirth, *The Ghetto* (Chicago: University of Chicago Press, 1928), 170; Michael Ebner, *Creating Chicago's North Shore: A Suburban History* (Chicago: University of Chicago Press, 1988), 233.

[53] Dinnerstein, *Anti-Semitism in America*, 53-54; Sachar, *Jews in America*, 98-102, 125-26; John Higham, *Strangers in the Land: Patterns of American Nativism, 1860-1925* (Boston: Atheneum, 1963); "Jewish Physique," *American Hebrew* 86 (27 December 1909): 200; *New York Times* (21 December 1907): 1-2 (quote); Edward A. Ross, *The Old World in the*

New: The Significance of Past and Present Immigration to the American People (New York: Century, 1914), 289-90.

[54]For an exception, see Abraham Cahan, *Yekl: A Tale of the Ghetto* (New York: Appleton, 1896), 6; Irving Howe, *World of Our Fathers* (New York: Simon and Schuster, 1976), 182; William C. Smith, *Americans in the Making: The Natural History of the Assimilation of Immigrants* (New York: D. Appleton Century, 1939), 111-16. On manliness and sport in the nineteenth century, see Elliott Gorn, *The Manly Art: Bare-Knuckle Prize Fighting in America* (Ithaca: Cornell University Press, 1986), esp. 140-47.

[55] Rabinowitz, *Young Men's Hebrew Association*, 75; Lillian Wald, *House on Henry Street* (New York: H. Holt, 1915); Allen Davis, *Spearheads for Reform: The Social Settlements and the Progressive Movement, 1890-1914* (New York: Oxford University Press, 1967); Rivka Shpak Lissak, *Pluralism and Progressives: Hull House and the New Immigrants, 1890-1918* (Chicago: University of Chicago Press, 1989); Mina Carson, *Settlement Folk: Social Thought and the American Settlement Movement, 1885-1930* (Chicago: University of Chicago Press, 1990); Cary Goodman, *Choosing Sides: Playground and Street Life on the Lower East Side* (New York: Schocken, 1979), ch. 3, esp. 37-40; George Eisen, "Sport, Recreation and Gender: Jewish Immigrant Women in Turn-of-the-Century America (1880-1920)," *Journal of Sport History* 18 (Spring 1991): 113, 116; Peter Levine, *Ellis Island to Ebbets Field: Sport and the American Jewish Experience* (New York: Oxford University Press, 1995), 14. While Zionism was not an important factor in the United States, it was in Australia. See Anthony Hughes, "Muscular Judaism and the Jewish Rugby League Competition in Sydney, 1924 to 1927," *Sporting Traditions* 13 (November 1996): 63.

[56] Steven A. Riess, "Tough Jews: The Jewish American Boxing Experience, 1890-1950," in Riess, ed., *Sports and the American Jew*, 60-104; Ira Berkow, *Maxwell Street* (New York, 1977), 142.

[57] Pamela Cooper, "Jews and the Making of American Marathoning, 1896-1960," in Riess, ed., *Sports and the American Jew*, 134-35. See also Alan S. Katchen, *Abel Kiviat, National Champion: Twentieth-Century Track & Field and the Melting Pot* (Syracuse: Syracuse University Press, 2009).

[58] Riess, *City Games*, 145-46; Roy Rosenzweig, *Eight Hours for What We Will: Workers and Leisure in an Industrial City, 1870-1920* (Cambridge: Cambridge University Press, 1983), ch. 5; Mark Haller, "Organized Crime in Urban Society: Chicago in the Twentieth Century," *Journal of Social History* 5 (Winter 1971-72): 221-27; Gerald Suttles, *The Social Order of the Slum* (Chicago: University of Chicago Press, 1968), 54-56; Frederick Thrasher, *The Gang: A Study of 1,313 Gangs in Chicago*, abr. ed. (Chicago: University of Chicago Press, 1963), 134-35. On poolrooms, see Michael M. Davis, *The Exploitation of Pleasure: A Study of Commercial Recreation in New York City* (New York, 1911),7-8; Riess, *City Games*, 73-74; Al Hirschberg and Sammy Aaronson, *As High as My Heart: The Sammy Aaronson Story* (New York: Coward-McCann, 1957), 27, 30-32, 34-35, 37, 42-43, 47-50.

The single worst episode of antisemitism in North American sport was the Christie Pits Riot in Toronto, Canada, on August 16, 1933, one of the worst disturbances in Canadian history. It occurred after the second of a three-game series between the St. Peter's team, backed by the Anglo-Canadian, antisemitic Pit Gang, and the visiting, predominantly Jewish Harbord Playground nine, supported by the Jewish-Italian Spadina Avenue Gang.

After St. Peter's won, the Pit Gang arrived at the diamond with a large swastika banner, which set off a melee that went on for six hours between hundreds of youths armed with baseball bats, pipes, and homemade clubs. See Cyril Levitt and William Shaffir, "The Christie Pits Riot: A Case Study in the Dynamics of Ethnic Violence—Toronto, August 16, 1933," *Canadian Jewish Historical Society Journal* 9 (1985): 2-30; Cyril H. Levitt and William Shaffir, *The Riot at Christie Pits* (Toronto: Lester & Orpen Dennys, 1987).

[59] Riess, *Touching Base*, 190; Joseph Gerstein, "Anti-Semitism in Baseball," *Jewish Life* 6 (July, 1952): 21-22.

[60] Eisen, "Jewish History and the Ideology of Sport," 514; Peter Levine, "'Our Crowd' at Play: The Elite Jewish Country Club in the 1920s," in Riess, ed., *Sports and the American Jew*, 179.

[61] Eisen, "Jewish History and the Ideology of Sport," 501-02.

[62] *Sporting News* (9 October 1919): 4, (16 October 1919): 4; Leo Katcher, *The Big Bankroll: The Life and Times of Arnold Rothstein* (New York: Harper, 1958), 148. Abe Attell, a former world champion featherweight and a representative of Rothstein, was approached by the original plotters to try to interest Rothstein. Attell failed to get Rothstein's support, but likely helped finance the fix on his own. On the other side of the table, the White Sox team secretary was Harry Grabiner and Charles Comiskey's attorney was Alfred Austrian, who led the defense team of the Black Sox.

Jews certainly were very involved in sports gambling, going back to Dr. Robert Underwood of New Orleans, said to have been the first person to run auction pools in 1855. There were several prominent Jewish bookmakers on and off the tracks by the late nineteenth century, including Sol Lichtenstein, Abe Levy, and Kid Weller. Rothstein was one of several Jewish protégés of Tammany kingpin "Big Tim" Sullivan, who ran the illegal poolroom syndicate in the early 1900s. On Jewish bookies, see, for example, Michael Alexander, "The Jewish Bookmaker: Gambling, Legitimacy, and the American Political Economy," in Mendelsohn, ed., *Jews and the Sporting Life*, 54-69; Michael Alexander, *Jazz Age Jews* (Princeton: Princeton University Press, 2001); Riess, *City Games*, 191-94; *Spirit of the Times* 136 (12 November 1898): 419, 139 (9 June 1900): 444; Mark Haller, "Bootleggers and American Gambling, 1920-1950," in US Commission on the Review of the National Policy Towards Gambling, *Gambling in America: Final Report of the Commission on the Review of the National Policy Toward Gambling* (Washington, DC: Government Printing Office, 1976), 90-91, 98-99, 101-03, 129-30; Katcher, *Big Bankroll*, 100-03; Christopher Ogden, *Legacy: A Biography of Moses and Walter Annenberg* (Boston: Little, Brown, 1999).

[63] Quoted in David Nathan, "Anti-Semitism and the Black Sox Scandal," *Nine* 4 (December 1995): 97.

[64] Quoted in Arnd Kruger, "'Fair Play for American Athletes': A Study in Anti-Semitism," *Canadian Journal of the History of Sport and Physical Education* 9 (May, 1978): 55.

[65] Roderick Nash, *The Nervous Generation: American Thought, 1917-1930* (Chicago: Rand, McNally, 1970), 130-32; Levine, *Ellis Island*, 116-18; Nathan, "Anti-Semitism," 94-100.

[56] Eisen, "Jewish History and the Ideology of Sport," 506-07.

Cutting the Way into the Nation: Hungarian Jewish Olympians in the Interwar Era

Mihály Kálmán

WAR AND REVOLUTIONS

Hungary lost roughly two-thirds of its territory and population, including nearly half of her Jews, with the Trianon Treaty of 1920.[1] In the ranks of the vanquished Austro-Hungarian Army, the rate of Jews was lower than their share in the population of the monarchy; 300,000 Jews, including 25,000 officers, served in the course of the war. Since many of the Jews of Galicia and northeastern Hungary became refugees, and because Jews were underrepresented in the infantry corps, the rate of Jewish deaths on the battlefield was lower relative to non-Jewish deaths. At the same time, soldiers of Jewish origin featured prominently among decorated veterans.[2]

Jews also played a prominent role in early postwar Hungary, filling eight of the twenty ministerial positions in Count Mihály Károlyi's pacifist-democratic government, which was toppled by the Revolutionary Soviet in March 1919. Thirty of the forty-eight People's Commissars in the short-lived Hungarian Soviet Republic were Jewish, including Béla Kun, the de facto leader, and Tibor Szamuely, the militant ideologue and orchestrator of the Red Terror.[3] If not as markedly as among its leaders and perpetrators, with 7.4% Jews were also overrepresented among the victims of class-based persecution at the hand of Szamuely's "Lenin Boys." Beginning with August 1919, officers of Rear Admiral Miklós Horthy's National Army unleashed a wave of "White Terror." Often assisted by local residents, the death squads murdered hundreds of people identified as Communists, targeting Jews in particular.[4]

In addition to Jewish involvement in the democratic and Communist regimes, Jews were also present at the cradle of the interwar Hungarian Kingdom. While representatives of Hungarian aristocracy established the *Antibolsevista Comité* [Anti-Bolshevik Committee] in Vienna, the main power base of anti-Communist officers was Szeged, a large city near the new Romanian-Yugoslavian border.[5] The Szeged Jewish community warmly supported the government-in-the-making from raising substantial funds to filling high-level bureaucratic positions. On May 7, 1919, Jewish officers in a seventy-two-strong unit of the National Army's officer corps helped disarm the Communist garrison in Szeged, allowing the counterrevolutionary government of Count Gyula Károlyi to relocate from Arad.[6]

The exact number of Jewish officers involved in the disarming became the subject of an early attempt at questioning the role of Jews in the nascent foundation myths and hagiographies of war and counterrevolution, the yardsticks of battle-worthiness and patriotism. A monograph on the history of the Szeged government published by a Jewish news reporter in 1919 claimed that twenty-two Jews partook in the operation in a unit led by a Jewish officer.[7] In response, a commander who had organized the disarming reprimanded the author for inflating the number of Jews from fifteen, falsely claiming that they had been led by a Jewish officer, and exaggerating the importance of the victory.[8] The lower number is confirmed by the *Hungarian Jewish Lexicon*,[9] and according to Kálmán Shvoy, himself a participant of the attack and the foremost organizer of the National Army, no Jewish commander was appointed. As Shvoy pointed out, however, the attack indeed "marked a turning point in the military fortune" of the Szeged government.[10]

Shvoy made no mention of the Jewish officers' role in the disarming in his diary, but he no doubt recalled it in 1933, when addressing leading rabbis and hundreds of attendees in the Szeged Jewish cemetery, at the inauguration of the first Jewish war heroes' memorial, the building of which he had initiated years earlier. Accompanied by a lavish military parade and a variety of Christian leaders, Shvoy spared no compliment to the Jewish community of Szeged, reminding his audience "how many Christians and Jews [had] faced hand in hand the greatest suffering, the greatest bitterness in life: the fear of death."[11] The leaders of the Szeged and Budapest Jewish communities assured Shvoy after the event: "'the future will justify you'. . . 'this statement is bound to receive the warmest welcome from Jews abroad . . . and benefit the cause of Magyarhood abroad.'"[12] Two weeks later, Shvoy was reprimanded by a superior officer for meddling in politics and discharged after an undue and humiliating process.[13] Not only did Shvoy not relent in championing peaceful coexistence or in his fight for the rights of Jewish war heroes, but a few years later he helped codify into law the recognition of the patriotic services of another category of Jews who had advanced the Hungarian cause with their weapons: Jewish Olympians.

The violent succession of the war and three regime changes prepared the scene for the interwar debates on Jewish courage, chivalry, and patriotism—discourses that underlay discussions on Jewish Olympians' achievements. After the exchange on Jewish officers' role in the Szeged disarming, a momentous press trial emerged around the question of Jewish loyalty as expressed by military service and self-sacrifice. In January 1921, Representative Elek Avarffy claimed in an article that the number of Jewish veterans does not exceed 50,000, of whom only 500 died on the battlefield. Lajos Szabolcsi, editor in chief of the preeminent Jewish newspaper, *Egyenlőség* [Equality], immediately refuted the claim and announced that he had compiled an archive of 10,000 Jews killed in action. The parties took the case to court, and the trial dragged on until June 1923. While the government initially refused Szabolcsi's request to publish confessional statistics on war heroes, it did resolve to disclose such data on fraudulent military contractors, commonly believed to have been overwhelmingly Jewish. Finally, war hero statistics were made available and confirmed Szabolcsi's claim.[14] *Egyenlőség* won a major battle against excising the memory of Jewish heroes from the ranks of Hungarian brothers-in-arms.

DUELS

Szabolcsi's *Egyenlőség* became the leading public forum of Hungarian Jewry under his father, Miksa Szabolcsi, who had revived the journal after its single-issue campaign against the Tiszaeszlár blood libel of 1882-1883; he remained editor in chief until his death in 1915. *Egyenlőség* was committed to molding Jews into Hungarian patriots of Jewish persuasion; achieving legal reception, it became the main organ fighting antisemitism.[15] Even in peacetime, this fight in many cases went beyond press insults or legal disputes and took a violent form. The Szabolcsis, both father and son, became staunch supporters of defending Jewish honor in duels—real or reenacted.

In 1892, Szabolcsi attempted to prevent a duel between 1917 Minister of Justice Vilmos Vázsonyi, a gifted Jewish lawyer, and Ferenc Mezey, leader of the Neolog National Office, which had issued a statement questioning Vázsonyi's honor. The editor of *Egyenlőség* published an open letter to the parties, begging the National Office to revoke the communiqué, lest "the Jewish congregation will become a battlefield, the synagogues dueling halls, the rabbinical schools courts of honor, the cantor will fight a pistol duel with the rabbi."[16] Although Szabolcsi despised intra-confessional scandals, he came to be an ardent advocate of dueling. After Theodore Herzl declared in 1893 that "a half dozen duels would very much raise the social position of the Jews,"[17] and when Jewish students came under attack at Hungarian universities in 1895, Szabolcsi echoed his words: "The epidemic of Jew-hatred has to be combated by duels[he wrote in *Egyenlőség*]. Today our Jewish youth will convince the Jew-haters of our right only with the sword. . . . The extremists among the anti-Semites come from the rural areas. They do not yet know that the Jews have learned well the wielding of the sword."[18] Szabolcsi's words resonated well with the broad urbanized, assimilated, and relatively wealthy stratum of Budapest Jews. Indeed, their swordsmanship continued to reign supreme even beyond the Holocaust, although its setting and ascribed meanings had changed remarkably.

If statistics are of any guidance, Jews zealously espoused the practice of dueling. In 1888, Jews represented 13% of those convicted for dueling, and in the interwar period their share was around 50%.[19] The duel fashion among Jews was unquestionably aided by the publicity of a number of high-profile duels of the prewar era that had involved one or more Jews. In 1882, Mór Wahrmann, industrialist and community notable, exchanged shots with Győző Istóczy, founder of the National Antisemitic Party (1883); in the same year, the champion of Szabolcs County challenged and lost to a Jewish lawyer who had blamed county bureaucrats for the exacerbation of the Tiszaeszlár blood libel. Jewish lawyer Dr. Gyula Rosenberg challenged and shot to death Count István Batthyány for the daughter of a wealthy convert, Ilona Schoss-berger, whose secret Jewish marriage to Rosenberg was overruled by a Catholic one to Batthyány, arranged by her father. Rosenberg had to issue a number of open challenges until Batthyány gave in and declared him duel-worthy, a category traditionally reserved for aristocrats, nobles, officers, university graduates, bureaucrats, and wealthy citizens.[20]

As George Eisen put it: "Wielding a weapon satisfied a compensatory reflex, part of an attempt by the emerging Jewish community to identify itself with, and be accepted by, the ruling classes by engaging in a pursuit that was associated with virility, masculinity, and honor in many European societies."[21] Following the German-Austrian tradition, dueling became a significant litmus test of Jewish honor in Hungary in the Era of Dualism (1867-1918), an important quasi-legal step on the path toward complete emancipation and assimilation. By engaging in performing the manners and customs of the loosely defined *úri* "gentlemanly" class, dueling Jewish individuals reaffirmed their equality to it; participating in a duel demonstrated that the duelist was worthy of gentlemanly fight. At times, this classification was subject to written duel codes, as it happened both in the army and on the second most turbulent scene of dueling: duel societies at the universities.[22]

In 1897, a Jewish law student invited criticism from Herzl's *Die Welt* by rejecting the idea of a Jewish duel society in *Egyenlőség*, and no such society appears to have existed in the interwar period.[23] Nevertheless, universities became the hotbed of swordfights in Hungary as well. After an election to the body representing university students, the number of student duels soared in 1896-1897 and were followed closely in *Egyenlőség*. As many of the Jewish law students did not vote, out of fear or disinterest, an antisemitic president was elected, and a number of Jewish students were insulted by their peers. However, the proportion of Jewish students was a reputable 30% among those preparing for legal professions, and thus the Budapest law school became a fertile soil for the duel epidemics that characterized the year following the election.[24] Considering the high number of lawyers and law students among Jewish duelists, it is perhaps not surprising that the first Hungarian Olympic champion in fencing was a young Jewish law student from Budapest, Jenő Fuchs (1882-1955).

JEWISH SPORTS

Fuchs was not the first in the row of Hungarian Jewish Olympians. Alfréd Hajós (1878-1955), the young architecture student dubbed "the Hungarian dolphin," defeated waves and cold, and he won two gold medals in 100-meter and 1200-meter freestyle at the Athens Games of 1896.[25] There were no Jewish sportsmen on the Hungarian teams of the 1900 and 1904 Olympics, but in London two young Jewish men from Budapest carried the day. Richárd Weisz (1879-1945), the colossal weightlifting and wrestling champion, won the first gold medal—in heavyweight wrestling—out of Hungary's three. Even greater praise was won by Fuchs, who led the six-member sabre team to victory and came in first at the individual competition.[26] The Hungarian sabre team included three additional Jewish sportsmen living in Budapest: another lawyer, Oszkár Gerde (1883-1944), Dezső Földes (1880-1950), and Lajos Werkner (1883-1943), a dentist and an engineer, respectively.[27] Four years later, all four Jewish sabre fencers repeated their achievements, again winning two out of three Hungarian gold medals. In 1908, seven, and in 1912, six of the eight sabre finalists were Hungarian, while four out of six and four out of eight of the Hungarian team members were Jewish.[28] At the eleven Olympics that featured a Hungarian team between 1908-1964, Hungarian sabre fencers won all of the individual, and nine of the team championships. Only one among the best Jewish fencers hailed from the "Jewish" *Magyar Testgyakorlók Köre (MTK)* or "Zionist" *Vívó és Atlétikai Club (VAC)*. Instead of Jewish clubs, the most stellar and contentious moments of Hungarian Jewish fencers on the preeminent scene of interwar sports nationalism were the result of universal sports education, Jewish involvement in the Budapest sports scene, and the work of Italian fencing masters.

While the Trianon treaty strictly curtailed the strength of the Hungarian Army, the state was invested in improving the physical fitness of its potential draft pool. Most notably, a physical education system was created (*levente-*

mozgalom, Levente Movement), in order to prepare boys under twenty-one years of age for military service.[29] Schools of all types and levels put emphasis on physical education, and Jewish students soon excelled at national competitions.[30] There was usually no lack of help for talented, young Jewish sportsmen. Even a cursory glance at the Hungarian sports scene through the career paths of Jewish Olympians reveals the ways in which their successes were embedded in a densely interconnected microcosm of Jewish sports enthusiasts, athletes, trainers, managers, and benefactors.

The victories of the three Jewish fencers came at a juncture of the soon-to-be-extinct duel tradition as well as the increasing Jewish interest and involvement in sports. Fuchs was reclusive, trained and competed without being member of a club, and never participated in national championships. He did, however, partake in at least two duels: one against his teammate, Gerde, in 1910, and a second against a Jewish member of Parliament in the 1920s.[31] Gerde and Werkner, on the other hand, were members of prestigious sport clubs, and Werkner won national titles in team and individual sabre in 1913 and 1914.[32] It is symptomatic of the transition from the pursuit of traditional aristocratic pastimes such as hunting and dueling to sports that nearly the entire first cohort of Hungarian Jewish Olympians became involved in organizing sports life in the country.[33] In late Dualist Hungary, the Jewish community welcomed and enriched Hungarian sports in a multitude of ways—and would so with renewed commitment after World War I. Hajós became the head coach of the Hungarian soccer team in 1905-1906, after playing for it twice; Werkner was elected president of his club in 1909; Weisz began training wrestlers in his club in 1908; and even the loner Fuchs agreed to serve as the head fencing trainer of the same club, although he stepped down two years later.[34]

The humanist pacifist pedagogue and physical educator Ferenc Kemény was member of the founding group of the modern Olympic Games, a close companion of Baron Coubertin and the harbinger of international sports to Hungary and her Jewish community.[35] In Hungary, the club of which Weisz and Fuchs were members was established in 1888 by Jewish merchants, in response to a ban on Jewish membership in two of the largest sports clubs of Budapest. Although the club's organizers and membership were overwhelmingly Jewish, it never identified as such and aimed to be accepted as a full-fledged Hungarian club. Its name, *Magyar Testgyakorlók Köre* [*MTK,* Circle of Hungarian Physical Educationists], prominently featured the word "Magyar" and a novel Magyarization of the German *körperliche Erziehung.*[36] *MTK* evolved into a major sports club under the industrialist Alfréd Brüll (1876-1944), its president between 1905 and 1940. Beyond important positions in Hungarian sports, Brüll was also the president of the International Wrestling Federation in 1924 and 1928, and a close companion of the wrestling champion Richárd Weisz. After his victory in London, Brüll provided Weisz a substantial loan to purchase a large coffee house in Budapest, and Weisz continued to train wrestlers in *MTK* until the end of his life.[37]

The closest thing Hungary had to a Zionist sports club was the *VAC*, Established in 1906 with the assistance of the founder of the Hungarian Kadima scout and the Keren Kayemet organzations, Lajos Dömény-Deutsch, the club boasted more than 1,500 members by 1928.[38] Unlike most Zionist sports clubs in Eastern Europe, however, the *VAC* did not allude in its name to the contemporary vocabulary of Jewish power and heroism, and its members did not sport blue-white outfits; rather, the emblem of the club was an inventive representation of the club's name as a Star of David. Although *VAC* adopted an assimilationist stance, in particular after the war, its initially slightly Zionist orientation already rendered it more Jewish in the eyes of the public than *MTK*.[39] As a telling, if not trustworthy, account went, fans at an *MTK-VAC* soccer game encouraged their teams by shouting "Go, Hungarians!" and "Forward, Israel," respectively[40] [Fig. 1].

The only Hungarian Jewish Olympian of the interwar era to have been a member of a "Jewish" club was Endre Kabos, *VAC* member between 1926 and 1930.[41] In his first year there, *VAC* won the national championship. The team also included Zoltán Dückstein, who had reorganized *VAC* in 1920, became its overseer, was the trainer and jury of the Hungarian gymnastics team at the Los Angeles and Berlin Games, and head of physical education at the Budapest Jewish Gymnasium.[42] For most of its history, however, *VAC* only had mediocre fencers relative to the Hungarian swordmasters of the era and even closed down its fencing department for some time after World War I.[43]

Figure 1. *Vívó és Atlétikai Club* silver badge, 1924. Courtesy of Árpád Németh (www.nefeco.hu).

One of the most popular fencing halls in Budapest, the scene of numerous duels, was opened in 1885 by Károly Fodor (Mózes Freyberger), a Jewish fencing master.[44] Attila Petschauer (1904-1943) trained in this hall between the ages of eight and twenty, winning four national youth championships and becoming team sabre Olympic champion in 1928, as member of the *Nemzeti Vívó Club* [*NVC*, National Fencing Club].[45] *NVC* was established by Marcell Hajdú, an early Zionist lawyer from Budapest who had studied in Heidelberg and in 1912 trained the victorious sabre team.[46] *NVC* also counted among its members Sándor Gombos (1895-1968); its captain was János Garay (1889-1945), team sabre Olympic champions in 1928. Both Garay and Gombos were for years members of the *István Tisza Fencing Club* (*TIVC*),[47] established by Gombos in 1925, when Jewish fencers left the oldest, most prestigious, and increasingly hostile Hungarian club, *Magyar Athlétikai Club* [*MAC*, Hungarian Athletics Club]. Endre Kabos was also a member of *TIVC* from 1930 until 1934, became team sabre Olympic champion in 1932, and won individually as well as with the team in Berlin, as a member of the *Újpesti Torna Egylet* [*UTE*, Neu-Pest Athletics Association].[48]

UTE was financed by Lipót Aschner, director of the Tungsram lightbulb factory. After the war, Aschner commissioned the building of the *UTE* stadium to Hajós, the first Hungarian Olympic champion, who also won a silver medal (no gold was awarded) with his plan of the Budapest swimming stadium in 1924.[49] In the mid-1920s, Aschner gave a job at Tungsram to Károly Kárpáti, an emerging wrestler just out of metallurgical school, who went on to win seven national championships, a silver medal in Los Angeles, and a gold in Berlin. In 1934, Aschner stepped down from the leadership of *UTE*, but in the same year hired for Tungsram the new *UTE* member, Endre Kabos, who had struggled to make ends meet even after his first Olympic gold.[50] Apart from *UTE*, another locally embedded team with prominent Jewish involvement was *III. Ker. TVE* [3rd District (Alt-Ofen) Athletics and Fencing Association],[51] which had three Jewish Olympic champions—two goalkeepers, a key player.[52] It was trained by a former player and war veteran Béla Komjádi (1892-1933), coach of the national water polo team from 1926.[53]

Finally, one has to acknowledge the role played by Italian fencing masters. Földes was trained by Angelo Toricelli and became Olympic champion with the team in London and Stockholm. He emigrated after 1912, becoming the only Hungarian Jewish Olympic champion to leave the country before World War II.[54] Even more significant was the role of Italo Santelli, who trained generations of fencers in Fodor's fencing hall, from Földes's teammate, Gerde, to Petschauer, Gombos, Garay, and Kabos.[55] With Santelli's help,

- Well, Mr. Kohn, what do you want
your son to be?
- I will first enroll him to fencing
school, then to university.

Figure 2. Cartoon from the Jewish comic, *Ojság*, November 13, 1927. Courtesy of the Metropolitan Ervin Szabó Library, Budapest.

the sabre team defeated Italy three times before World War II, avenging the defeats in the Olympic final of 1924 and in the World War I. Incidentally, Santelli was also the trainer of Regent Horthy.[56]

It was this multilayered web of motley sports enthusiasts concentrated in Budapest that made possible the tour de force of Hungarian Jewish Olympians between the two world wars. Beginning with the 1920s, dueling became a rare phenomenon,[57] and in the relative peace leading up to another catastrophic war, Jewish masculinity, heroism, and patriotism were primarily expressed by keeping the memory of Jewish war heroes alive. However, the victories of Jewish Olympians presented another opportunity for the Jewish community to prove its virtues to the Hungarian public [Fig. 2].

THE FIRST GENERATION

The contours of the debate on Hungarian Jewish Olympians began to emerge already before the war, as *Egyenlőség* eloquently celebrated the triumph of Weisz and Fuchs with an article entitled "The Ethnic/Racial Magyars."[58] According to the author, their victories "benefited the popularization of Hungarian independence abroad; more than seventy-two books and journals were published with state subvention. . . . This triumph will fill in the hiatus of Hungarian diplomatic representation for a few years." The author denounced the Hungarian press for its silence about the origins of the gold medalists, while it had praised ethnic Magyars who as much as got into the finals. Quite the contrary, *Egyenlőség* wrote, the Jewish champions, who just days before their victory were written off as "the sportsmen from [the wealthy Jewish district of] Újlipótváros, Jewish youngsters," were now celebrated as "representatives of thousand-year-old ethnic Magyar virtues, physical agility and power" by the Hungarian press, although they were "four-thousand-year-old men, even if often dated for yesterday. Yesterday, when they not so much came but intruded to eat up the bread of those who had been residing here for a millennium."[59] *Egyenlőség* decried that while wild-cat bankers and coat thieves were always explicitly identified as Jews, Jewish Olympians were not and could join the team only thanks to the efforts of the "meddlesome [president of the *MTK*] Alfréd Brüll, hailing from Újlipótváros."[60]

Four years later, *Egyenlőség* bitterly condemned the absence of state officials from the reception of the victorious Fuchs at the Western Railway Station. Only children and sports-loving youngsters came to greet Fuchs on the station, and the only body represented was a Jewish rowing club, although "when [Fuchs] himself won, and when he assisted the Hungarian sabre team in its victory . . . the Hungarian flag ran up the pole of the stadium. The flag of Hungarians, not that of the Fuchses, the Pest lawyers, not even that of Jewish settlements in Palestine."[61]

In 1915, Miksa Szabolcsi died and passed on the editorship of *Egyenlőség* to his son, Lajos. After the war, and under Lajos Szabolcsi, *Egyenlőség* became the chief medium of restoring Jewish honor by forcing the state to acknowledge the patriotism of Jewish war heroes. From 1928, *Egyenlőség* had the lion's share in the consequential controversies on Jewish Olympians, which dwarfed the short exchanges following the London and Stockholm Games. The experience and results of war and revolutions, the waning tradition of dueling, and the rise of Jewish sports combined with the discourses of Great Hungarian, Hungarian Jewish, and ethnic Magyar nationalisms to form the background of the debates. As Hungary headed into a collision course in domestic politics and foreign policy, it became a great power in sports, mobilizing and winning the acclaim of millions of fans, including the officialdom of the Hungarian Kingdom, the Jewish leadership, and at times even racist ideologues.

CONSOLIDATION

The Trianon Treaty set the stage for the national and international *Kulturkampf* [culture struggle] waged by the dishonored Hungarian Kingdom against her Jews and the Little Entente, or the Successor States, as Romania, Czechoslovakia, and Yugoslavia were called. Domestically, the "dismembering of Hungary" eradicated the need for Jews as cultural allies and modernizing capitalists by rendering Hungary a virtually homogenous nation-state.[62] As Vera Ranki wrote, "The source of all problems, economic and social was simply put down to two causes: the Entente powers were blamed for all the outside ills and the Jews for internal problems."[63]

After their emancipation in 1867, Hungarian Jewry, particularly in the ethnolinguistic heartlands that were to remain part of Hungary, underwent a process of more rapid and pervasive acculturation toward the ruling Magyars than most, if not all, Eastern European Jewish communities. Jewish acculturation was also significantly more complete than that of other nationalities in Hungary. Magyarizing of names became the norm, intermarriage and conversion rates were high, particularly in times of crises. Nevertheless, the level of integration of Jews into society remained relatively low. Jews were prominent in economic and cultural life and were heavily urbanized relative to the large Magyar peasant-gentry society. In 1868, the religious community split into Orthodox, Status Quo, and moderate reformer, Neolog, denominations. Neolog Judaism, an important channel of assimilation, was strongest in urban areas, particularly in Budapest. The capital also comprised the largest concentration of Jewish industrialists, bankers, businessman, intellectuals, and professionals—this helped Budapest become a Jewish and Hungarian sports scene of national and international significance.[64]

The already unrivaled influence of the capital on Hungarian life, and on acculturated urban Jewry, steeply increased following the annexations of Hungarian land by the Little Entente. In demographic terms, Budapest Jews constituted 22.4% of the Jewish population of the country in 1910; this rate grew to 45.5% by 1920, following the annexations. The Jewish share in the city's population remained about 23.1-23.2%.[65] At the same time, the narrow ethnic majority of Magyars in Hungary increased from a mere 54.5% in 1910 to 92.1% in 1920. Although this number included Jews, who were not officially considered a minority, the Jewish share in the population of the so-called Dismembered Hungary remained approximately 4.5%. As this, Jews comprised the second largest ethnic minority; the proportion of Germans (Danube Swabians) was about 5%.[66] With the ethnic balance tilted decisively in favor of Magyars, Hungarian Jews became a minority competing with them for resources in a mutilated economy.[67] To curb Jewish competition, particularly in light of Magyar immigration from the Successor States, a Numerus Clausus was introduced in 1920. The law limited the proportion of minority students at their share in the population, limiting the rate of Jewish university students to 6%. The law's use of the term "racial and confessional minorities" signaled a change toward the perception of Jews as a race rather than a confessional group, codified by the Law of Reception in 1895.[68] The Numerus Clausus was enforced rather laxly, yet Jewish enrollment in universities gradually decreased from 28.4% before the war to 14.1% and 8.3% in 1931-1932 and 1936-1937, respectively.[69]

After the war, antisemitism exploded with unheard-of pogroms and spread at an alarming rate. Jews were accused of disloyalty, profiteering, and unheroic conduct, while Jewish involvement in Béla Kun's Communist regime and the Red Terror provided further ground for antisemitism.[70] Apart from scattered terror attacks, Jews were also threatened by the emergence of a "Christian course," in which Christian in most cases meant not only non-Jewish, but anti-Jewish.[71] According to Vera Ranki, "The main trends of Hungarian political thought met on the common platform of antisemitism and nationalism," and the former, apart from being a "default" attitude of the narrow Christian middle class, "had an enormous appeal to students and to clerks, to officers and to workers, to grocers and to gentry."[72] The Swabian minority, which played a substantial role in the army, was an important catalyst of antisemitic tendencies.[73] Extremist organizations mushroomed in the 1920s and built strong ties with Hitler's Nazi Party very early on. Radical racism and antisemitism, espousing a pseudoscientific notion of an organic nation, emphasized the innate, primordial attributes of authentic Magyars. Although its thrust developed in a variety of ways, a common denominator of rightist Hungarian political thought was the idealization of the Magyar race, of Christians versus Jews, and of the peasantry versus urban dwellers.[74] As we shall see, these trends in the development of political orientations, and of the perception of Jews, were interwoven into the political rhetoric of the interwar period and increasingly migrated to the legal plane as well.

However, Jews enjoyed a period of relative tranquility after the White Terror. In 1921, the wealthy Transylvanian aristocrat István Bethlen was sworn in as prime minister and served in this position under Regent Horthy until 1931. Bethlen was devoted to the consolidation of Hungary and sought the goodwill of the Entente powers; thus, in Wilsonian Europe, the treatment of the country's Jewish minority acquired particular significance. Concerned about the tarnishing of the country's image by the White Terror, Bethlen played an important role in putting an end to violence.[75] He not only sought to appease the victorious powers by warranting the protection of the Jewish minority, but also counted on Jews to attract and manage domestic and foreign investments, participating in the rebuilding of the country. In 1925, Bethlen announced that the Numerus Clausus had been a temporary measure, and in the next few years he restored Jewish representation in the Upper House and the regional bureaucracies. Nevertheless, Jews were increasingly squeezed out from the bureaucracy, intended to be filled with Magyar gentry, and the officer corps, which contained a strong Swabian contingent.[76] The lack of available jobs, combined with antisemitic attacks, might have also contributed to the turn to sports; as Kramer remarked, "For prospective Jewish tertiary students of this period, street muscle had greater deterrent value than government fiat."[77]

The Jewish community was receptive to Hungarian Jewish rapprochement, though this mainly materialized itself in symbolic pronouncements of mutual loyalty. The "old, nondemocratic Jewish leadership, largely drawn from the Neolog community of Budapest" preserved its position as the sole representative of Hungarian Jewry and was wary of implicating Hungarian authorities in the mistreatment of Jews or antisemitism by having recourse to outside help.[78] Just after the White Terror, Hungarian Zionists attempted to seek redress by mobilizing world opinion, but they were condemned by the official leadership for "betraying the Magyar fatherland." The same isolationism characterized the leadership regarding the issue of the Numerus Clausus. In 1921, 1925, and 1930, representatives of American, French, and Anglo-Jewry, notably the Board of Deputies of British Jews and the Alliance Israélite Universelle, offered help with defending Hungarian Jewish interests in the League of Nations, but the offer was refused by Hungarian Jewish leaders.[79] Indeed, until 1931, Hungarian Jewry did not have substantial contacts with international Jewish organizations;[80] instead, another beacon of its patriotism became its relationship with Hungarian Jews across the new borders.

In the Dualist Era, Magyarized Hungarian Jews were eager and significant allies of Magyars in the borderlands. During and after the Trianon deliberations, their self-identification as Magyars was a key element of Hungarian foreign policy based on border revisionism or irredentism. Despite Hungarian and Jewish protest, Jews in Romania were registered as a minority differentiated from Magyars from 1920, and in Czechoslovakia from 1933.[81] Although Jews in the Successor States were encouraged to become patriots of their new countries, or even Zionists, to a large part they remained dedicated Hungarians. In addition to reiterating stories of Jewish heroism in war and counter-revolutions or of Jewish contributions to economic and cultural development, revisionism as a common denominator and basic tenet of Hungarian and Hungarian Jewish foreign policy became a means of combating mounting attacks against Jews.[82] Whether guided by desperation, optimism, or both, in the interwar period the "ostrich politics" of imperial nostalgia continued to characterize Hungarian Jewish politics, as well as Hungarian domestic and foreign policy.[83] As Mendelsohn noted, "Jewish well-being continued to be firmly linked to the preservation of conservative (or even reactionary) order. . . . This was not a happy position for Hungarian Jewry to find itself in but it is difficult to see what other choice it had."[84] Relentless Jewish eagerness to cooperate with and be of service to the state helped safeguard Jews against bloodthirsty antisemites who were gaining increasing influence in the 1930s. Even so, the Jewish leadership, seen as acquiescent and ineffective, was often portrayed on East European Jewish political fora as cowards, or backward *shtadlones*.[85] Indeed, as Mendelsohn wrote, "Of all the lands of East Central Europe, Hungary was the most unfavorable environment for the emergence of modern Jewish politics."[86] There were no Jewish parties, a markedly Jewish cultural orientation and education were substantially less widespread than among other East European Jewries, and there were no large Jewish organizations apart from the communal leadership.[87] Communism was not a viable option after 1919, and while Jewish representatives were to be found in a variety of parties, their appeals on behalf of the Jewish citizens and community of the state were most often ignored. At the same time, the quest for a new Jew, and a Jewish state, was no less fruitless in Hungary.

As Herzl wrote already in 1903, referring to the Hungarian tricolor, "Hungarian Zionism can primarily be red-white-green."[88] Indeed, Zionism was unappealing and hence marginal in Hungary; its relative unsubstantiality remained essentially unchanged until the Holocaust. The membership of Zionist organizations hardly ever rose above 1% of the Jewish population, or a few thousand people.[89] Hungarian Jewry desired reinclusion into Hungarian society on an equal footing, rather than seeking to build a society for themselves in Palestine or elsewhere. The number of *aliyot* remained diminutive in the interwar period, and the Hungarian Zionist Association (HZA) repeatedly declared its Hungarian patriotic sentiments.[90] As a poet put it: "I am a Zionist in body, heart, and soul, [but] Jewish and Hungarian pain strikes my heart equally. . . . I love and adore my father, Palestine, the land of our ancestors, and my mother country is our sweet homeland, Hungary."[91] Despite a multitude of similar expressions of Hungarian patriotism, the religious community and assimilated Jews looked upon Zionism as a potential threat to Hungarian Jewish relations. As in the case of international appeals against persecution, community leaders took a strong stand against Zionists in favor of the Hungarian state. Thus, for instance, the Neolog National Office played a major role in preventing the Ministry of Interior from recognizing the HZA.[92] Unsurprisingly, when the HZA set up a Betar organization providing sports and military education for Jewish youth, it became the target of numerous attacks on the part of the Jewish as well as the Hungarian leadership during its short-lived history.[93]

FROM AMSTERDAM TO LOS ANGELES

The main vehicle for articulating Hungarian Jewish patriotism in the interwar era remained the press, particularly that of Budapest, where Jewish journalists and periodicals wielded significant influence.[94] In addition to the reports on cross-border Hungarian Jewish patriotism, *Egyenlőség* also ran a series titled "What has Jewry Done for Hungarianhood?," which listed Jewish scientific and artistic contributions to the Hungarian cause. More importantly, the journal also published regularly on the Jewish heroes of the Revolution of 1848.[95] Beginning with 1928, the victories of Jewish Olympians provided ample material for *Egyenlőség* to reassert its attitude to the "Jewish Question." Considering the widely varying audiences, Olympic victories catered to at least three major political aims. For Hungarian Jewry, and its leadership in particular, Jewish Olympians proved the continued Jewish loyalty to Hungary and illustrated the validity of this oft-decried relationship to Jews abroad. For the Hungarian state, Olympics provided the foremost international scene to showcase its talents and demonstrate to the world its indigenous vitality and its superiority in comparison with the Little Entente.

As Jack Kugelmass has noted, male international sports competitions are particularly conducive for catering to nationalism.[96] Indeed, the Olympics had the potential to line up the nation behind its sportsmen, unlike the more divisive national sports competitions, and became an important tool of Hungarian interwar soft power diplomacy. In addition to serving as an international and even playing ground of states, on the national level the Olympics became a point of reference of Jewish patriotism, serving as an even field for Jews vis-à-vis Magyars, just as it had served as such for Hungary vis-à-vis other countries. Unlike Jewish achievements in culture, politics, or economic life, sports successes were viewed as a result of a fundamentally objective, fair, and gentlemanly competition. Thus, it acquired paramount value for Jews anxious to prove their patriotism to their compatriots. In addition, the Olympics were one of the few international scenes where Hungarian Jewry as a group was represented. Indeed, sports, and fencing in particular, became the foremost means of demonstrating "an ability of Jews . . . to hijack the ultimate symbols of a dominating culture, and, in so doing, reassur[e] themselves collectively in their physical potential."[97]

With two gold, three silver, and four bronze medals, Hungary ranked thirteenth at the 1924 Olympics—its all-time worst until 2008. Among the Jewish athletes, Hajós and Dezső Lauber (1879-1966), two renaissance men of sports, won a silver medal for architectural design (no gold medal was awarded), while János Garay finished third in individual and second in team sabre. After the relative failure of the Paris team, Hungary held its breath for two weeks, waiting for the coveted gold medal, in 1928. Finally, the Hungarian anthem was played in honor of Dr. Ferenc Mező, a Jewish teacher, winner of the art competition with his work on the history of the Olympic Games.[98]

The liberal Zionist *Országos Egyetértés* [National Concord], a longtime rival of Szabolcsi's *Egyenlőség,* was the first Jewish periodical to greet Mező's achievement, noting "with great joy that with his spiritual victory the high school teacher of Jewish origin from Budapest rushed to the help of the Hungarian team of athletes, who had been competing not in their best shape."[99] Two days later, *Egyenlőség* published a series of articles, opening a long succession of press debates, in which the overjoyous tone of Jewish pride interfused with that of Hungarian patriotism and clashed with a disoriented Magyar nationalism and racism.[100] Under the headline "Hungarian Jewry and the Olympics," which was to reappear often on the columns of *Egyenlőség,* the subtitle declaimed the success of the unemployed teacher, Mező, "a scion of the Grünfeld family from Zalamegye."[101] The heading went:

> The gleaming ray of Hungarian glory, Hungarian power and talent illuminates some of our excellent young Jewish coreligionists, who with all their might contributed to the lustrous triumph of their homeland and nation. Far be it from us to distinguish between Hungarian sportsmen of equal merits but . . . let us recount the names of the Hungarian champions of Jewish faith who fought so proudly and triumphantly abroad for the greatness and triumph of Hungary.[102]

The article went on to elevate Mező to the pedestal of assimilation, loyalty, and service to his fatherland in war and peacetime. Mező's grandfather was a bibliophile merchant, as was his father, one of eleven brothers, "all faithful Jews and genuine Hungarians."[103] Mező served as a lieutenant in the World War, spending fourteen months on the Russian and eighteen on the Italian front; he was wounded twice, got typhus, malaria, and tuberculosis—and was decorated five times. As the author proudly noted, *Egyenlőség* had already recorded in the Jewish War Heroes' Archive that sixteen members of the Grünfeld family fought in the war, and five of them perished on the battlefield. According to the article, Mező refused to accept employment under Communist rule, sympathized with the counterrevolution, and eventually secured a position as a teacher of Latin and Greek in a Budapest school following the recommendation of the National Association of Veteran Teachers. Mező, the report concluded, was "a professing and self-respecting Hungarian Jew" and had now become "the pride of the whole Hungarian Jewry at the same time bringing glory to his Hungarian nation."[104]

Mező humbly thanked the praise in his letter in the same issue, adding, "I did not fulfill my duty at Nida, Isonzo and Piavena *in the hope of receiving decorations*. It fills me with great pleasure that I *brought glory upon my homeland, faith*, and my silver-headed father." He recalled his years in the Piarist Gymnasium in Nagykanizsa, a city he considered home, even after moving to Budapest, and his work as a sports and literature educator.[105] As Imre Blankenberg, the Jewish director of the local branch of the National Commerce Association later remarked, here was "proof that the small shop and the counter may also be the milieu from which world-famous successes burst out."[106] Mező's life story contested a number of ingrained stereotypes about Hungarian Jews. The son of a religious merchant, coming from a mid-sized urban center now near the Yugoslav border, Mező had already had an impressive oeuvre as a soldier and pedagogue. He was a highly decorated war hero; his honors included the prestigious Signum Laudis and the Iron Cross Third Class.[107] Not less importantly, Mező had been successful as a sportsman and had already written three books on Hungarian literature and politics.[108] In sum, he had every right to be portrayed as an impeccable patriot in war and an exemplary citizen of the state in peace.

Egyenlőség also interviewed Mrs. Berger, the mother of the silver medalist water polo goalie, István Barta. She duly told the reporter that her son had been an excellent student at the Technical University, served as a volunteer in the war, and was a POW in Italy, while his two brothers were POWs in Russia. Upon his return, he quit the university and began working in the textile business. Mrs. Berger also noted that there had been no hostilities between her son and non-Jewish team members.[109] Finally, *Egyenlőség* provided an overview of former Jewish Olympians and praised the achievements of the substitute water polo goalie György Bródy, and of the epée fencer István Hajdú, son of the National Fencing Club's founder.[110] By rehearsing the family histories of the Grünfelds and Bergers, Jewish journals showcased the internationally acclaimed heroes' rise from typical, modest, Magyarized, and productivized Jewish backgrounds to their victories, which enabled Hungary to assert its vigorousness to the world and become a great power in sports, if not in geopolitics.

The majestic victories in other sports notwithstanding, the importance ascribed to sabre fencing overshadowed other Olympic achievements, and it was this sport that fully mobilized the Jewish and non-Jewish public. As the first series of articles appeared in *Egyenlőség*, the Hungarian sabre team, including three Jews, a Greek Hungarian bank clerk, and two high-ranking Hungarian army officers, narrowly won against Italy in the final.[111] *National*

Concord immediately praised Attila Petschauer, who had had a major role in the victory. The article squarely established Petschauer's achievement within the context of masculinity, patriotism, and imperial nostalgia. The title page read:

> The sword is a particular Hungarian sport, the esthetically pleasing tradition of the knightly middle ages, in the nurturing of which the Hungarian noble derring-do has a lion's share. . . . our joy and pride is twofold that Jewish boys also stand their ground in this most Hungarian sport and forcefully demonstrate that the Hungarian Jewish youth can stand its ground not only with respect to spiritual but also physical power on the Olympiad of physical ability. . . . In the World War . . . we sacrificed tens of thousands of crippled and tens of thousands of dead to the homeland . . . , persecution and hatred did not break our steadfast patriotism and our devotion to our faith. . . . And the result? Even the world fame and world position of the most characteristic Hungarian national sport was fought out with the help of Jews.

With the spiritual victory of Mező fresh on his mind, the author went on to praise Hungarian Jewish intellect, along with body: "Film and arts, which captivate the masses, herald not only the unbeatable superiority of Jews in general, but the victory of the spirit of Hungarian Jews in particular." The article mocked the lack of attention devoted to Jewish talent and achievements by the Hungarian public, while "The sword of Hungarian fencers, the gleaming blade of Ferenc Molnár's spirit radiates all around, forcing by its spark and forces the numerous enemies of Hungarians abroad to respect [them]."[112] Having conflated Hungarian Jewish accomplishments on the front, the Olympiad, and in the cultural sphere, the article related the victory to the topical, and recurring, problem of bath resort antisemitism, expressing hope that the "overwhelming majority of the Christian society does not sympathize with such lowly insults."[113]

As in the case of Fuchs in 1908 and 1912, *Egyenlőség* again picked up on the reception of the champion in Budapest and on a report published in a Christian nationalist newspaper. After Petschauer won the gold medal with the sabre team, and lost to a Hungarian officer in the individual final, *Egyenlőség* published an article titled simply "Attila," in clear reference to the Hun ruler and purported ancestor of Hungarians. It described the cheering crowds at the train station and quoted the Catholic conservative *Nemzeti Újság* [National Newspaper], which had reported on the victory thus: "The Hungarian sabre did not jag, did not shake in the hands of the Hungarian youth. The rays of sunshine were dancing on the blade of this sabre, when the troops of Árpád swept to the Hungarian Plain under gleaming lances, with swords in their hands"[114] The author also added "this Hungarian sabre gleamed triumphantly in the hands of Attila Petschauer, a 23-year-old Hungarian Jewish kid, and this sabre gleamed equally in the hands of Vitéz Ödön Terstyánszky, Lt.-Col. of the Hungarian Royal Army when . . . they beat in sabre every other nation." The author appealed to the officials of the Ministry of Culture, under whose auspices education and sports belonged, to reconsider the Numerus Clausus, seeing as they did how eminently Jewish youth had fulfilled "their duty in the sacred service of the Hungarian national idea."[115] Finally, the weekly published Petschauer's letter, in which he reassured Hungarian Jews that there is no real antisemitism in the country and expressed his joy over winning the "fight which is essentially the war of nations in peacetime; the good God to whom I have always prayed helped me and allowed me to win the first Olympic championship to Hungary."[116]

In the same issue, an author voiced doubts about the value of sports in countering antisemitism, noting, however, that Jewish Olympic victories, combined with the fact that many of the winners were also well-educated, is a powerful argument against the delusion of eugenics.[117] To drive this point home with regard to Hungary, he wrote, "where Dr. Ferenc Mező, Barta, Petschauer, Hajdu and others were cheered and applauded, *there Hungarian heroism, masculinity, physical and spiritual culture was celebrated.*" To reinforce the article's claims, *Egyenlőség* again published the ever-growing list of Hungarian Jewish Olympians.[118]

Új Nemzedék [New Generation], one of the largest Christian-conservative dailies of the interwar era along with *Nemzeti Élet* [National Life], was the first to attack the Jewish press for their celebration of Olympians. In a letter to the editor, one Dr. J. M. protested against *Egyenlőség*'s article on Petschauer, claiming that the journal "had made a confessional question from a Hungarian victory" to keep the Jewish Question on the agenda.[119] A few days later, *New Generation* followed up with an article that decried in a similar vein: "Who are those who raise the Jewish question time and again, if not those who grab every opportunity to parade their perception that the Petschauers will always remain Jewish and that they are celebrated by the Jews of Hungary not on account of the glory of the Hungarian but that of the Jewish crest?"[120] While *Egyenlőség* did not relent, *National Concord* soon distanced itself from its congratulatory article, arguing that Jewish successes will not help fight antisemitism and announcing that they did not "consider the triumph of Jewish champions in Amsterdam to be a particular Jewish victory . . . despite all our respect we do not consider these results to be of such importance as to merit shofar-blowing them all over the world."[121]

Even more remarkable was the tragicomic volte-face of *Nemzeti Élet*, the national socialist-Hungarist weekly edited by László Budavári, a militant Hungarist and former representative. At first, it cheered the sabre team in good irredentist spirit thus: "The triumphantly sparkling Hungarian sabre shows us the way of duty to the four trampled country-parts [lost after Trianon]! . . . This victory means the ancient force of our Hungarianhood over all: not the superiority of nothings, swaggerers and the cultured, not the consolidation of cowards, but the superiority of force and courage!"[122] After the articles in *Egyenlőség* and *Egyetértés*, however, László Levatich, the most active contributor of fiercely antisemitic articles in *Nemzeti Élet*, made clear that what was at stake for the extreme right here was not a confessional question, as *Egyenlőség* and even *Új Nemzedék* had written. Levatich wrote: "If we treat the Jewish question in the only correct context, the racial one . . . we should not have allowed Jewish sportsmen to represent Hungary abroad, since foreigners might deduce the consequence that Magyars cannot even put together a decent water polo or sabre team without Jews." Further, the author condemned *Egyenlőség* for its articles on Jewish sportsmen and champions, noting, however, that "*Egyenlőség* is right this time, regarding this question. We Magyars cannot strut in borrowed plumes and cannot misappropriate the success of the representatives of the Jewish race for Hungarianhood." Finally, Levatich proposed that Jews be excluded from the Hungarian team, admitting that this might mean worse results, and suggested that Jews form a separate team at the Olympics, in the hope that *Egyenlőség* will agree.[123] Interestingly enough, at this point *Egyenlőség* chose to ignore the attacks. It merely published an overview of international Jewish Olympians, noting that Petschauer was praised as the best sabre fencer of the world by a German sports newspaper and providing another sketch of the history of Jewish sports.[124]

The state's attitude, or rather the lack thereof, to the question was evident from the articles of the national military-sports youth education system's journal, *Levente*, where any reference to the Jewishness of the Olympians was conspicuously lacking. Throughout several issues in September, *Levente* stressed the importance of the international spotlight on exemplary Hungarians, the quintessential forces of building the organic nation. And an article went: "Since the war, every Hungarian instinctively senses that our sons must fight at the Olympics not only for victory, but for Hungarian honor, and the peace of every Hungarian. Each and every Olympic point obtained is a particle of Hungarian vitality. These, aligned with force-particles cultivated and obtained on other spaces of Hungarian life, multiplied, and grown in power, content, and value assure the fulfillment of our desires and hopes."[125]

The journal of Catholic youth, *Az Erő* [Force], applauded all categories of winners, praising Mező's victory and also establishing the status of the sabre as a national sport: "It is not a coincidence that Hungarian power has shined in the masculine sports of self-defense and assault, in the competitions of sabre fencing, wrestling, and boxing."[126] The reaction of the journal of the National Physical Education Department of the Ministry of Culture was not less laudatory regarding Ferenc Mező's success, described as a Davidic victory, in which "the work, written in the Hungarian language of limited spread, defeated those edited in large world languages."[127] In Mező's life, however, the Hungarian language had defeated German nearly a generation ago, as the champion changed his name from Grünfeld.

Perhaps in order to avoid arousing sentiments again, following the Los Angeles Games in 1932, *Egyenlőség* published only a reserved article after the victory of the water polo team, in which the two goalkeepers and one player were Jewish. The team was trained by Béla Komjádi (1892-1933), a Jewish veteran, former member of the *MTK* and later the *TVE*—the club where all three Jewish players trained.[128] The article merely enumerated other Hungarian Jewish Olympians, but even this was sufficient to cause a minor uproar. Moreover, this time *Egyenlőség* remained alone on the piste. Two weeks later, *National Concord* published a rebuttal of the *Egyenlőség* article, pointing out that Attila Petschauer did not win the team sabre alone in 1928 and that András Székely is not the best swimmer in Europe. As the author wrote, perhaps with excessive optimism, "the article of *Egyenlőség* ['equality'] lacks equality. It was not Christians and Jews who went to the Olympics but Hungarian amateur sportsmen . . . the swimsuit, the athlete shirt makes everyone equal."[129] He also praised the policy of sports newspapers, who anxiously eschewed referring to the Jewish origins of the Olympians. Indeed, sports newspapers, most importantly *Nemzeti Sport* [National Sports], established by the fencing hall owner Károly Fodor, continued to follow this practice throughout the interwar era.[130]

Once again, however, the most grandiloquent, if unintentional, praise of Jewish Olympians' physical abilities and of their role at the helm of Hungary's symbolic war came from somewhat unlikely sources. Ferenc Herczeg, head of the Revisionist League and prominent conservative writer, dramatist, and journalist, provided a lucid interpretation of the success in a conservative daily:

> In the world of gas bombs and tanks the sword is not a military weapon any more but something else: a great sports tool that allows its master to validate his individual excellence, which manifests itself in real life as masculinity and chivalry. If a nation, like ours, produces

a crowd of phenomenally skillful fencers, one can infer the physical and intellectual excellence of the race . . . Our boys, along with the Olympic laurel bring home a truth: that a nation, the youth of which are the best fencers in the world, cannot be the servant and slave of nations that cannot match it in the artworks of war or peace.[131]

The journal of Regent Horthy's order of chivalry [*Vitézi Rend*] praised Olympians for helping Hungary finish sixth in the "great competition of nations" and confidently declared that "they had proven that they are not of a moribund nation condemned to death, but are the battle-trained sons of a nation charging ahead, and possessing a bright future."[132] The Levente Movement's monthly applauded the Magyar race, as one of the Turanian nations, the largely imaginary race of the Japanese, Turks, Magyars, and even Finns.[133] Yet again, it also emphasized the significance of the sabre as the "weapon which to us, Magyars, had brought the most success on the battlefield and in sports, which is the symbol of Magyar courage, chivalry, and masculinity."[134] With an overstretch of the Turanian category, *Levente* applauded in particular the wrestling match between two "Turanians," the Japanese Suzuki and Károly Kárpáti, the young Jewish lightweight wrestler, an employee at Ascnher's lightbulb factory.[135]

Kárpáti finished second in lightweight freestyle wrestling, and three Jewish water polo players won gold medals with the Hungarian team. Although these achievements were also cheered on the pages of the press, the most attention was devoted to the sabre team, and in particular to the young and dashing Endre Kabos (1906-1944). Described as "modest and simple, even austere in his appearance and manners," Kabos regularly reported to an evening paper from Los Angeles and had a major role in the victory of the team.[136] After the Olympics, he announced his retirement due to the lack of sponsors and opened a fruit business. However, he returned to fencing a year later and actively partook in developing a new fencing hall for the *UTE* team and in convincing the master Santelli to train them.[137] Much to his chagrin, Kabos became the focal point of the rapidly exacerbating press debates after 1935.

TO BERLIN

In October 1932, the former paramilitary warlord and Defense Minister Gyula Gömbös was appointed prime minister. Formerly a militant antisemite, Gömbös publicly revoked his antisemitic views when he came to power, mentioning prominently the patriotic services of Jewish soldiers in the World War I.[138] However, Gömbös reinforced Hungarian ties with Italy and the Reich; Gömbös was the first official visitor to Hitler after the latter came to power in 1933. Moreover, Gömbös's slight turn toward the center further catalyzed the strengthening of extreme right.[139] However, Gömbös also feared opinions more extreme than his and thus provided a measure of protection to Jewish interests. As Mendelsohn put it, "So far as the Jewish leadership was con-concerned, the devil they knew was far better than the devil they did not know, all the more so since Gömbös turned out to be not nearly so bad as they had feared."[140] Although in the Gömbös era, Hungarian Jewry was weakened by economic crisis, concerns about the disintegration of the community, and a pervasive sense of fear, it nevertheless remained committed to the government, this increasingly reluctant defender of their rights.[141]

Kabos won European championships both individually and with the sabre team in 1933 and 1934, yet in March 1935, he was not selected to represent Hungary in Naples at a friendly match against Italy. Responding to rumors of discrimination, Lieutenant Colonel Ferenc Filótás, president of the Hungarian Fencing Association, explained that Olympic champions were not welcome by the organizers of the competition. As he assured the public, "no Hungarian fencer may suffer injury."[142] In the same month, just before the Second Maccabiah, the weekly of the Hungarian Zionist Organization reported that *VAC* requested permission for their fencing team, as well as Kabos and János Hajdú, to participate. Although Filótás gave permission, he condemned the "race- and not confession-based" event, adding that the participants "would cause immeasurable harm not only to themselves but to the entirety of patriotically-minded Hungarians of Jewish faith."[143] According to an account, Kabos visited Filótás personally to announce that he had changed his mind, "considers himself, above all, Hungarian . . . and only the spirit of competition urged him to go to Tel Aviv."[144] As another source reported, Kabos had been asked to participate at a fencing academy to which "hundred percent Aryan" fencers were also invited, but instead chose to travel to a competition in Italy.[145] With the Maccabiah already in full swing, the Zionists' weekly finally reported that *VAC* withdrew due to financial reasons. In his report from Tel Aviv, the correspondent gloomily noted that although the Hungarian flag was there, the team was lacking.[146] Another Zionist weekly, edited by the former editor of *National Concord,* claimed that the Neolog leadership had prevented *VAC* from competing, in order to defend them "from the fatal danger of being regarded as Jews."[147] Although we may never know whether *VAC* withdrew due to pressure from the government, the Fencing Association, or the Neolog leadership, the fact that all these were perceived by the contemporary Jewish public as possible explanations speaks volumes of the isolation of the Zionist enterprise on the Hungarian scene.

After the Maccabiah case, Kabos joined the sabre team to the first World Fencing Championship two months later, in June 1935, and won a gold medal. Later that summer, he wrote a piece on "The Mentality of the Contestant" to the journal of the Sports Department.[148] He began with the words, "many of us are made lovers of the saber by the obligatory power of tradition, that is, a historical cause, and even more by the thousand-year-old decrease of the Hungarian race invoked in curses, the tendency to separate."[149] After this description of the "Turanian Curse," he gave a detailed discussion of the art of sabre and its effect in shaping human character. As Kabos summarized, "the Hungarian is a defiant fighter, this shows the fate of his race: a thousand against one."[150] The expression of fear from the dispersal and atomization of the nation and the determination to revive it by restoring the ancient homeland against all odds no doubt struck a chord with Hungarian nationalists and most Hungarian Jews, including Zionists.

While Kabos and his fellow Jewish sportsmen prepared for the Führer's Olympics in the summer of 1936, *Egyenlőség* at first remained carefully neutral on the Olympic boycott movement, publishing an article on "Sports and Honor," perhaps to probe public opinion. Amongst short notes on the disqualification of the Austrian Judith Deutsch and the punishments meted out to pro-boycott Zionist clubs in Czechoslovakia, the article included a short survey of the boycott movement in the international press. It also published, without comments, a letter to the editor, which scorned Hungarian Jewish Olympians, who "having secured their mandate, forgot everything they are obliged to do for Jewry."[151] Despite, or rather because of, the gravity of the situation, however, soon the whole range of the Jewish public lined up behind the mighty column of Hungarian Jewish Olympians, if not behind *Egyenlőség*.

Days before the Olympics, *Egyenlőség* resolutely declared that, despite allegations on the part of "swastika-bearers" to the contrary, there was no boycott movement in Hungary. The author cited in length from the newspaper of the Arrow Cross Party, *Nemzet Szava* [Word of the Nation], established in 1932 by the staunch Hitlerist and Hungarist Zoltán Meskó, founder of the first Arrow Cross Party in 1932. *Nemzet Szava* demanded that Jewish sportsmen be denied the right to represent Hungary, "in the interests of judging rightly the value of the Hungarian race by foreigners." While in 1928 *National Life* was somewhat realistic about the chances of the Hungarian team without Jewish athletes, *Nemzet Szava's* wishful racial thinking was blind to any and all Jewish merits. As the author declared, "there are hardly any excellent Jewish athletes. For the sake of those one or two . . . we should not make this fight of racial importance worthless and meaningless." In its response *Egyenlőség*

Figure 3. Kabos on the cover of the *Radio Magazine* on the opening day of the Berlin Olympics. Courtesy of the Archive of the Hungarian Sports Museum (*Magyar Sportmúzeum Levéltára*), Kabos Heritage Collection.

praised the Jews of the Berlin Team, predicting victory for Kárpáti and Kabos, "the pride of Hungarians and in particular Jewish Hungarians."[152] Even this safe prediction did not prevent *Nemzet Szava* from misfiring a few weeks later [Fig. 3].

Kabos, the standard-bearer of the Hungarian team, was fully conscious of the symbolism of competing in the capital of the Third Reich. As he made clear to *Egyenlőség*, "Jewish athletes, including myself, have a psychological handicap . . . we will go to a place to demonstrate our strength and ability where our Jewish brothers are considered another race, not humans created by God, even harmful, and they get a treatment according to this painful perception." However, Kabos criticized the boycotters; in his view, the appropriate defiance of racism was not to be absent from Berlin, but rather to win. This time, he explained, "we will fight not only for universal Hungarian nationhood, Hungarian pride in Berlin but we, Jewish sportsmen, must and want to show the image of Jewish power and virtue." These thoughts were likely on the mind of most of Kabos's Jewish teammates and the Hungarian Jewish sports world in general. To demonstrate the attitude of the "Zionist" team, Zoltán Dückstein, sports director of the *VAC*, expressed hope in *Egyenlőség* that the gymnast István Sárkány (1913-2009), trained by him in the Budapest Jewish Gymnasium and *VAC*, would do well. As *Egyenlőség* concluded, these facts should have been sufficient to quiet those who had not known excellent Jewish sportsmen.[153]

Instead of denial, the extreme right resolved a new strategy. In response to the *Egyenlőség* articles on Jewish Olympians and the lack of boycotts, *Nemzet Szava* complained that the team is "swarming with Jews. Even the majority of the leaders are Jewish. . . . The Jewish press lies about hoped-for successes, but the whole ado is about having more Jews sent to Berlin on state funds." *Egyenlőség* responded with a list of Jewish champions and the words of the weightlifter Pál Garai, who denied that any of his teammates would capitalize on their Jewishness. He reasserted that a boycott would dishonor the nation and explained that a Jewish sportsman "thinks not about how proud his core-ligionist will be if he wins, but in front of his eyes darkening from the fever of the fight appear the uplifting three colors of the Hungarian tricolor . . . As long ago on the battlefields, so in peacetime at the international competitions only the tearful love of the Hungarian homeland did and will provide inspiration."[154]

In a refined act of disagreement, *Zsidó Szemle* [Jewish Review], the Zionist Association's weekly, published an article on low-cost mass sports, disparaging the Budapest Community's youth organization members who "play unionism and bring with themselves the smoky air of the cafes to gatherings of the youth." Advocating a return to the nation, the author concluded that "it is not books but sports that is destined to move today's Jewish youth. Jewish sports, in which it ceases to be a paper-Jew and . . . the ghetto Jew disappears."[155] *Uj Magyarság* [New Hungarianhood], formerly the mouthpiece of Gömbös and the daily of the Christian "gentlemanly" [*úri*] middle class, prepared the ground for discussions of racial theories by warning that the "Black danger" posed by African Americans in the "battle of races and nations" is relevant in Hungary more than ever, as "a culture that does not strive to rejuvenate will soften, its gentlemanly virtues will decay."[156] Finally, *Zsidó Élet* [Jewish Life], established by a former *Egyenlőség* editor,[157] warned that the journal should not engage in racist debates or celebrate champions as Jews, since they were "firstly Hungarians, secondly Hungarians and even thirdly Hungarians."[158] Kabos's straightforward stance in support of German and, implicitly, Hungarian Jews seemed to have remained ignored.

Just three days into the Games, Károly Kárpáti won the freestyle wrestling in lightweight, defeating the German Wolfgang Ehrl in the Deutschland-halle, with Hitler present.[159] *Egyenlőség* enthusiastically celebrated Kárpáti for achieving "glory for all his *coreligionists* of our ancient faith" and was anxious to emphasize the religious affiliation of his family, the Kellners. Describing his background, the article noted that Mr. and Mrs. Kellner "celebrate Jewish holidays with devotion and have a Torah at home" and that they had "raised their son, Károly, to become a real Hungarian and a real Jew."[160] The first secretary of *VAC*, where Kárpáti was a wrestling coach, extolled him as a sportsmen with "a Jewish heart and a Hungarian will"; a fencing coach praised his religious father, "a gentleman of the most Hungarian flavor" and Kárpáti himself as "the most modest, taciturn sportsman."[161] The articles did not fail to mention his outstanding academic achievements. When a reporter of *Egyenlőség* visited the

Kellners, "sweating toilers of the Hungarian land," the parents boasted with the high school report of Kárpáti, which described him as "modest, service-able, well-mannered, and conscious."[162] Emphasizing the generational divide, the reporter pointed out that the parents had been "in their heart people devoted to the tradition," while their champion son was fully Hungarian and his brother "did not at all resemble a Jew," riding on horseback on the road to his parents.[163]

Although supportive of Jewish sportsmen's participation, the tone of the Zionist *Jewish Review* was sobering and chilling. Remarking upon the excel-lence of African American and Japanese athletes, "peoples closer to nature," the author called into doubt the impact of the Olympics on antisemitism. As evidence for the ungratefulness of the state, the author pointed out that although Jewish Olympians often were in need of financial assistance, state institutions and companies were not eager to employ them—Kárpáti, for instance, had taken up a job at the Debrecen Jewish Gymnasium. From a legal standpoint, the author argued, the state was to blame for the unequal affection and allegiance between it and her Jews. While talented Jews were obligated to serve their country, the state had undone emancipation by the Numerus Clau-sus. Thus, the *Jewish Review* concluded, Hungarian Jews "need not only Jewish world champions but also champions of the Jewish world."[164] The magazine also compared Jesse Owens' victory to that of the new Hungarian foil cham-pion Ilona Elek (1907-1988), whose father was Jewish. In the final, Elek defeated the champions of Amsterdam and Los Angeles, the German Helene Mayer, and the Austrian Ellen Preis, both of whom were Jewish. "Can fencing be called an Aryan sport?" *Jewish Review* asked. With a measure of satisfaction, it noted how fencing took over the role of dueling, "the only struggle in life where the Jews faces only one enemy and also the sole struggle where there is no string-pulling."[165] Finally, in response to the Zionist Telegraphic Agency's disparaging comments on the lack of boycotts and "Jewish solidarity with the Hungarian government," an article remarked that there were three paths of Jewish Olympic participation: some were forced to go, others boycotted the Games, and yet another category participated and won "since Jews can also have the same muscles as those of Aryans."[166]

As with earlier Olympics, the men's sabre events were awaited with the greatest excitement and evoked the fiercest debates. After the victory of the team, *New Hungarianhood* continued to trumpet its racial tirades and exuber-antly venerated the team fighting with "the ancient weapon, the Hungarian sabre," which "demonstrated to the world even more emphatically how much elemental power, how much vitality there is in this long-suffering Hungarian race, squeezed into the narrow borders of its mutilated country!"[167] Having provided an overview of his conception of Hungarian history, the editor-in-chief, István Milotay, explained the Olympic fever in Hungary by declaring that the Games are a unique moment that unite and give much-needed hope to the nation. As he argued, the victories were all the more important since "our great national ills in the past twenty years had attacked the basic conditions of power, manly resistance, and competitiveness vis-à-vis other nations." Now, Milotay wrote, the Olympians had "provided proof of vitality and competitiveness, which demonstrates the nearly limitless racial tenacity of the Hungarian nation."[168]

Rejoicing over the uplifting victories, *New Hungarianhood* cited the words of Minister of Interior Kozma: "our achievements in Berlin are the best Hungarian propaganda . . . the result of our national and racial talents."[169] Finally, Ferenc Rajniss, Gömbös's former comrade and Minister of Religion and Education of the Szálasi regime, lauded the champions as

> our dear sons who had covered the Hungarian flag and crest torn by the storm of history with Olympic wreaths. . . . There is no Trianon today! The gaps and the dashed lines on the mournful map are covered by the mellow layer of wreaths achieved by iron muscles. . . . In the Danube valley indestructible biological facilities and capabilities demand right, justice and sunshine for Hungarians Nothing has changed in the last 1000 years in Hungarian biological facilities.[170]

A few days later, in another "race defender" journal, Lieutenant Colonel Gyula Máté-Törek celebrated the overall third place behind Germany and the United States that Hungary achieved, acclaiming it as "the Westernmost tip of the Turanian sword." The officer likely spoke for many of his comrades as he honored the sabre fencers, asserting that:

> the ancient Hungarian sword is the main and eternal sacrament of our nation, in the midst of our fetteredness it sparkles into the eyes of the world unchipped, and is frightfully sharp. The 1936 Olympics is the mirror of our physical and intellectual vivaciousness, and at the same time a military victory preaching the belief of our national resurrection, and the sacred token of our eternal life.[171]

Although *Egyenlőség* came under fire from all sides for giving voice to the Jewish community's pride in its Olympians, individual sportsmen were at first not insulted. However, while most rightist periodicals satisfied their readers with racist rhetoric, glossing over the origins of the Olympians, *Nemzet Szava* ferociously confronted *Egyenlőség* and did not refrain from ad hominem attacks. Responding to the articles in *Egyenlőség* that had extolled Kárpáti, his victory, and his family, *Nemzet Szava* claimed that it had thought Kárpáti to be a "brother," since "he bears such a fine Hungarian name."[172] The article decried that *Egyenlőség* "had made a racial question out of this," appropriating the victory as the "racial joy" of Hungarian Jews and thereby—unbeknownst to Kárpáti—"the Budapest ghetto impropriated him to itself."[173] The main target of attacks in *Nemzet Szava*, however, became Kabos, who lead the team to victory and won the individual championship defeating the Italian Marzi.[174]

Following Kabos's victory, a former Jewish representative published the programmatic article of *Egyenlőség*'s attitude toward Hungarian Jewish distinctions, and the journal again came under a salvo from multiple sides. The essay, titled "Our Sons," described the feelings of Géza Dési while listening to the broadcast of the sabre final. Dési recalled his "prayer sanctified in blood, sweat and indescribable suffering . . . —Avinu Malkenu—to guide the sword of *David* while he fights against the *Goliath* of the entire world."[175] At this elevated moment, Dési wrote, he was convinced that "our protector, the protector of our son, the heavenly patron of the Hungarian-Jewish Endre Kabos *'shall neither slumber, nor sleep.'"* [176] He also explained Kabos's victory in the context of the sword's militaristic symbol system, so central to Hungarian nationalism:

> You poor little *Trianon Hungary*—he exclaimed—, you disdained, plundered, dismembered, dear Hungarian nation of ours. Your glory, your honor, your retaliation, the faith and consolation of Your resurrection symbolically sticks to *the sword* with which our Hungarian-Jewish brother fights. Our Merciful God, guide his sword *against the whole world, to Hungarian victory.*

As Dési explained, the sword was also the appropriate tool of both polishing character and defending honor; as he wrote, "from ancient times, the sword is the manifestation of chivalry, the weapon of truth and honor . . . *the sword ennobles,* makes thought noble and acts chivalrous."[177]

After his prayer for Kabos's victory, Dési wrote, he sang with no less feeling his homeland's "sacred prayer," the anthem of Hungary, as well as the Hungarian Creed and the *Shehecheyanu* [a Jewish prayer recited to celebrate special occasions].[178] By recounting the central festive and melancholic texts of Hungarians and Jews, Dési reaffirmed his dual national identity and went on to demonstrate the inextricable tie between Jewish and Hungarian fates. As he wrote,

> this world famous, glorious triumph showing the *superiority of the Hungarian genius* will at the same time *illuminate the* dim *consciousness of the world*, and they will be ashamed, and it will rectify that they had made servants to lords over us in the robbed parts of the country. . . . Within the narrow borders of Trianon the Hungarian sun will rise and with its light will chase back to their dens the monsters that ventured out, and will melt together with its warmth the interdependents of one-fate, the sons of our one Homeland, the children of one Nation.[179]

As per its usual strategy, *Egyenlőség* also interviewed Kabos's family; his father, who "had always been a man of deep Jewish sentiments," revealed that he had written on the "Hungarian Question" in the Successor States and expressed sadness over the Numerus Clausus that led his son not to apply to university. "This is the Hungarian Jewish father!" *Egyenlőség* exclaimed.

In addition to racist ideologues, many of the Jewish journalists and periodicals found the emphasis of *Egyenlőség* on Jewish Olympians exaggerated and regarded it as harmful to Hungarian Jewry as a whole. When, for instance, *Nemzet Szava* criticized the sports leadership for allowing Kabos to carry the standard of the Hungarian team, a paper of a Jewish editor denounced the attack, yet it advised *Egyenlőség* to refrain from initiating interfaith debates, by "religious chest-beating that could not only hurt the sensibilities of people of other faiths but also undermine the united Hungarian national thought."[180] *Egyenlőség* refused the attempts of the press to teach them a lesson in representing Jewry, pointing out that their commitment to write in depth on Jewish Olympians dates back to 1928 and comparing the assaults to the ungrounded accusations questioning the number of Jewish war heroes in the early 1920s.[181]

Another attack against Kabos appeared in the extreme rightist newspaper *Magyar Jövő* [Hungarian Future]. The paper remarked in its report on the Olympics that "The triumphal haze is somewhat bitter, since, of all people, Kabos won, but still better than an Italian victory."[182] *Társadalmunk* [Our Society], a journal edited by an influential centrist journalist of Jewish origins, reproached the slanderous sentence, warning that "This is not indiscreetness or tastelessness anymore but, in our view, an assassination . . . committed against the unity of the nation. This is a Balkanic, un-Hungarian voice and we refuse this in order to draw the attention of the Hungarian world to the evildoings of well-poisoners!"[183] Eventually, Kabos himself replied in a newspaper, swearing to mar those few who sympathize with the statements of the author who had dishonored him.[184]

The journal of Ede Kurländer, a wealthy Jewish lawyer and belletrist, also joined the debate. In a series of articles, it developed the argument that Hungarian Jewish Olympians did not represent "members of the Jewish faith," but won as Hungarians, and hence recounting their names was unnecessary, since Jews' "shield and sword is the *Bible* of our ancestors."[185] Not only interfaith relations were considered irrelevant in the Olympic context, but the results also entirely disproved racial theories; neither religious nor ethnic affiliation was accepted as a category of analysis; the sole context of the Olympics was the nation.[186] After *Egyenlőség* was criticized by so many Jewish journals, it is hardly surprising that in the interpretation of *Nemzet Szava*, their attack on

Egyenlőség was justified by the fact that "Jewish newspaper-relatives also rushed to haul *Egyenlőség* over the coal."[187]

As for the official press, the journal of the Levente Movement republished the article of Horthy's Guardist celebrating "the most skillful, most triumphant nation of the great ancient Turanian race," and praised the disproportionate success of its representatives.[188] The xenophobic edge of verbal and written ovations of Hungarian race was only blunted by the Regent's symbolic hand-shakes. In late September 1936, Horthy decorated every Olympic champion with the newly established Toldi Memorial Prize, regardless of confession or ethnicity; six of them were Jewish.[189] The warm words about the Hungarian race addressed to the champions of the last Olympics before the war were an eerie foreboding of the fate of one of them. At the event, the head of the Min-istry of Culture's Sports Department applauded the fact that

> even the people of the Hungarian steppe, formerly disinterested in sports, noticed. . . . that by these victories we overtook other enor-mous and large nations. The national importance of sports came to the foreground, the suffering nation of our dismembered little country welcomed the news of Hungarian victories as the breaking of dawn after a hopelessly long night. . . . Lo, our race is not fallible! Our people is not among the last![190]

Between 1896 and 1936, out of the fifty-eight Hungarian Olympic champions sixteen were Jewish. Hungarian champions brought home eighty gold medals overall, of which the sixteen Jewish athletes claimed twenty-seven, while their forty-two non-Jewish counterparts won fifty-three. Out of twenty-seven indi-vidual gold medals won by Hungarians, Jewish sportsmen received nine, and they were also prominently involved in every team championship—those of five sabre and two water polo teams. The figures indicating Hungarian Jewish sportsmen's significance in the context of Jewish sports are no less impressive: forty-two Jewish sportsmen won at the Olympics where Hungary participated, that is, excluding the 1920 Olympics. More than a third of them, sixteen, were Hungarian. At these nine Olympics, Jewish sportsmen won twenty-two indi-vidual and thirty-six team medals. About half of these were won by Hungarian Jews—nine and nineteen, respectively[191] [Fig. 4].

THE AFTERLIFE OF SUCCESS

After the First Jewish Law came to force in 1938, *Egyenlőség* was discontin-ued, along with numerous other of Jewish-owned journals. The balance of the debate tilted toward the Parliament, and the Jewish Olympians' achievements gained significance in the context of the fight for civil rights. The economic aspects of the Olympics were discussed in the Parliament a number of times

Figure 4. Kabos, third from left, at a competition celebrating the fiftieth anniversary of his club in 1935. Courtesy of the Archive of the Hungarian Sports Museum (*Magyar Sportmúzeum Levéltára*), Kabos Heritage Collection.

before 1936. In this context, Gyula Gömbös spoke up against sending too many sportsmen to the Olympics in 1924. He ridiculed the controversies surrounding the selection of athletes to the sabre team, and the presence of players on the soccer team who were "representatives of the Magyar race; gentlemen, who had been members of Maccabi Brno." Instead of elevating professional sportsmen, Gömbös suggested "drawing from the deep well of talents" in the countryside, and promoting mass sports.[192] After the Amsterdam Games, the editor of *Nemzet Szava,* Representative Meskó, criticized Hungarian cultural and sports luminaries who had not Magyarized their names, mentioning prominently the fencers: Fuchs, Petschauer, and the Greek Glykais.[193]

Since participation at the Los Angeles Games looked exceedingly costly for Hungarian athletes, a number of representatives encouraged the government to finance the Olympic team. Tivadar Homonnay, the Christian socialist president of the National Swimming Association, portrayed the Games as the only opportunity to revive respect for the impoverished but noble Hungarian state, and hence a matter of "national interest." As he put it,

> we can indeed prove that this nation is destined to success, has vitality and ability. . . . the most opportune way to do so is through sports. The most opportune; indeed, unfortunately, under the present conditions Olympics is almost the only one. . . . Hungary is a great power in European sports. In addition, Hungarian sportsmen enjoy popularity everywhere, thanks to their splendid and gentlemanly style. . . . during

the Olympic competitions in Europe, not only in sports newspapers, but also in political ones, the headlines described the high degree of development of Hungarian sports, and thus the aptitude, vitality, and stamina of Hungarian power and the Magyar race, in sports as well as in other respects.[194]

A few months later Kálmán Shvoy, the former army officer from Szeged, whose reverence for Jewish war heroes already cost him his career, also advocated financing the team, so that "it can bear the criticism of the whole civilized world."[195] Although sixth place of Hungary at the Los Angeles Games was certainly an overachievement, the Hungarian Olympic Team rose highest in Berlin, and the response was not long in coming.

In November 1936, János Vázsonyi—son of the Jewish Representative Vilmos Vázsonyi, whose duel *Egyenlőség* likely prevented in 1892—appealed to the government regarding the issue of the construction of the national stadium. Apart from advocating the development of sports for the sake of demonstrating Hungarian vitality, he alluded to the role sports played in enabling Jews to demonstrate their patriotism. Vázsonyi reminded his audience in the House of Representatives of "the results of the [Hungarian Olympians'] fight in Berlin. . . . [which] not only are the successes of physical education and sports, but are also the universal successes of the Hungarian nation, and foreign policy successes, which have made the name of Hungarians more popular and achieved for it more glory than years of diplomacy, in the bygone days as much as in the recent past."[196] Vázsonyi cautiously outlined the asymmetrical warfare effect of Hungarian foreign policy, thereby evoking the relation between Jews and non-Jews:

> The achievements of a small country are always of more significance [Vázsonyi observed] each and every achievement on the international level, in my view, worth more and has more impact on the future and the present of the country than a hundred malicious articles, a thousand instigating posters, a thousand inflammatory speeches, fly-bills or other combustibles of Hungarian public life.[197]

Vászonyi demanded the conclusions of the recent Olympics be drawn, most importantly, that "no one should desire to incite hatred in this country between countryside and city," since the "Budapest boys" had cleansed the name of "sinful Budapest." Finally, he also insisted that there should be no "confessional discrimination" against Olympians and called for its eradication in other walks of life, particularly in light of recent fights at universities. Lastly, Vázsonyi again recalled the moments of victory, a dignified opportunity for "saying to ourselves the national prayer, the first verse of which ends with 'This nation has expiated for past and future.'"[198] The overlapping Hungarian and

Jewish plights in Vázsonyi's words and the desire to overcome the dual humiliation through gentlemanly fight were unmistakable.

In December 1936, news appeared in the Basel newspaper *National Zeitung* that the names of Kárpáti and Kabos would not be inscribed in the *Olympiastadion* [Berlin, Germany's Olympic Stadium]. Kabos refused to comment, but Kárpáti disputed the rumor.[199] In July, Kabos was again left out of the team traveling to the Paris World Championship, which immediately invited speculations, although the president of the National Fencing Association rushed to refute allegations.[200] However, when Petschauer, by now a journalist, interviewed Kabos, the latter complained that he should have been invited, despite his absence from the national competition; Kabos also spoke discreetly of certain insults, but defiantly declared, referring to the Arrow Cross party, that "insult-arrows cannot shoot the sabre out of my hand."[201] The Centrist *Társadalmunk* [Our Society] extoled the elegance with which Kabos brushed off the provocateurs and promised that the "Fuchses, Petschauers and Kaboses of the future will be there on the piste as well, whenever in any part of the world the nations of the world will have to be submitted to the Hungarian sabre!"[202]

A lengthy parliamentary debate took place between April and May 1938 on the First Jewish Law, titled "For a More Efficient Safeguard of Equilibrium in Social and Economic Life," which limited Jewish participation in a number of professions to 20%.[203] At least partly, Hungarian Jews seemed to have acquiesced to the lesser evil, as the government promised to curb the violence of the extreme right and as seemingly even harsher antisemitic measures, governments, and popular opinions gained power in Romania, Austria, and former Czechoslovakia. The Jewish leadership directed its attention to the Hungarian government. They petitioned the Houses, appealed to public opinion by publishing pamphlets and statistics on the role of Jews in building Hungary, and set up a Committee of War Veterans. At the same time, they refused help from the British Foreign Office, and the AIU, which later unilaterally arranged a meeting with the Hungarian ambassador to Paris to express their objections.[204] Again, it was Jewish Olympians who were spotlighted as the chief international representatives of both Hungarian Jewry and Hungary.

Referring to two press articles by Petschauer, Vázsonyi again eulogized Jewish Olympians in the House, rebuking representatives and the government for, supposedly, meticulously surveying statistics on some Jews, but not putting forth statistics on Olympians. As he observed, while the older generation of Jewish Olympians will be exempt from the Jewish Law on account of their service on the front, the younger Jewish Olympians "could not have been front soldiers, and nevertheless achieved pomp, fame, and glory for the Hungarian nation."[205] Vázsonyi then went on to recall the Jewish victims of the Red Terror and demonstrated the Jewish role in the development of Hungary through his illustrious family history. On the same day, Representative Hugó Payr, a former national champion wrestler with *MTK* in 1905, and an Olympian in London with his teammate, the champion Weisz, provided the statistics. According to Payr, thirty-one of the eighty-three Hungarian Olympic gold medals were won by nineteen Jewish sportsmen. Recalling that they had been decorated by Horthy and celebrated "regardless of rank, position, social standing, confession, and race," he declared the Bill to be an act of "ingratitude, not worthy of the Hungarian nation."[206] The law was adopted three weeks later, and Olympians were not exempt.[207] However, the First Jewish Law exempted Jewish front soldiers, their widows and orphans, as well as those who had converted before August 1919, the beginning of White Terror, and their direct descendants who did not return to Judaism. The Second Jewish Law was based on racial grounds to an even larger extent, but again recognized high watermarks of Hungarian patriotism and rootedness.

Nearly a year later, in late February 1939, the House of Representatives began debating the bill "On the Restriction of Jewish Conquest of Space in Public and Economic Life," which became known as the Second Jewish Law from May 1939. Béla Imrédy, prime minister from May 1938, declared that due to the reannexation of territories from Slovakia and Subcarpathia, further anti-Jewish restrictions were necessary.[208] Despite fears that it would serve German interests, and the political crisis it caused, the bill eventually passed, decreasing the acceptable rate of Jews in numerous professions to 6%.[209] According to the first category of exemptions, only those were exempt who had converted before the White Terror and whose direct ancestors had been born in Hungary no later than the end of the 1848 revolution, January 1849. Most importantly, the law restricted the circle of service-related exemptions: only decorated front soldiers, those killed on duty, counterrevolutionaries, and their families were exempt; the hundreds of thousands of Jewish veterans without decorations were not. The Jewish Committee of War Veterans, including the distinguished champion of art and the art of war, Mező, signaled its protest, but the national Alliance of Front Soldiers supported the proposal, which later turned into law.[210] However, while service-related exemptions were restricted, Jewish Olympians' services to the homeland were recognized by the Second Jewish Law.

A week into the debate in the House of Representatives, Károly Peyer, the leader of the Social Democratic Party, praised Hajós and Fuchs for becoming champions at a time when professional sports did not yet exist in Hungary.[211] Two days later the independent Jenő Dulin appealed to reason, referring to himself as a "veteran sportsman." Speaking of Olympic champions as the perfect example of assimilated Jews, he said: "Once we say about someone that he had testified to his Hungarianhood, we have to accept him as a full-fledged member of our nation. . . . we cannot say that such a man is a not sufficiently assimilated Hungarian with regard to his behavior and mentality, can we?"[212] Dulin recalled the joyous moments of the sabre final, which he had shared with not quite Judaophile army officers, who all cheered when Kabos won. Finally, he asked, "Was there anyone then who would have believed that these people, whom we cheered until we barked ourselves hoarse, whom we greeted with tears in our eyes, will be excluded from the community of the nation?"[213]

Following Dulin's speech, it was the demoted Szeged officer, Kálmán Shvoy, who first officially proposed a modification to the bill to provide exemption to Jewish Olympians and require that the House honor Jewish Olympic champions "in grateful recognition for fighting at the Olympic Games with the same ardor and will as their Hungarian fellows, for achieving recognition and glory to their homeland, and because in faraway lands the Hungarian prayer intoned and the sacred Hungarian flag ran up the pole after their victories."[214] Vázsonyi followed up three days later, again pointing out that the Olympians were decorated by Horthy himself.[215]

On March 13, Payr again rose to speak on the issue of Olympians; in a desperate tone, he exclaimed, "It is impossible that we ostracize the people who had achieved glory for the Hungarian name."[216] Nonetheless, at the first vote three days later, the majority of the House refused providing exemption to Olympians. When the House reconvened on March 16, Minister of Justice András Tasnádi Nagy asked the House to refuse Shvoy's modification, promising that an exemption for Olympians will be included in a report of a joint commission, to be confirmed in days.[217] Indeed, the commission confirmed the exemption of Olympians on the next day.[218] On March 21, Payr retold the story of Helene Mayer in the House and asked the Minister of Justice why he wanted to "surpass the nationalism and racial sentiment of Hitler [by persecuting Olympians]?"[219] Finally, welcoming the decision of the minister to provide exemption for Olympians, Payr criticized him for ignoring the possibility that Jews may become Olympic champions in the future, leaving no room for such an option in the law. Despite the tragedy that befell Hungarian Jewry, Payr was justified in his optimism.

EPILOGUE

Ilona Elek was trained by István Fodor, son of the fencing hall founder Károly Fodor, and faced numerous difficulties due to the lack of interest in women's sports.[220] She and her sister survived the war and began training just as the dust of Budapest settled around them in the spring of 1945.[221] Elek went on to win twelve world championship medals, finishing first five times. Repeating her achievement in Berlin, she again became Olympic champion in individual foil in London and came in second in Helsinki.[222] Her sister, Margit, also won numerous European and world titles, placed sixth in London, and also fenced in Helsinki.

Five Jewish Olympic champions did not survive the war. Lajos Werkner died in Budapest in November 1943, at the age of sixty.[223] Gerde died in the Budapest ghetto in October 1944.[224] Garay was deported and murdered in Mauthausen.[225] Regardless of his Signum Laudis medals received from Horthy for his Olympic victories, Petschauer was called up for labor service in 1942. The labor service laws exempted only those Jews who had received this medal or other high decorations for their heroism during World War I, or risked their freedom and lives in 1918-1919.[226] Petschauer was captured near the Don Bend in January 1943, and he died in the same month.[227] Out of 214 Jews in the labor service company in which Petschauer served, only 24 survived. According to some sources, including István Szabó's movie *Sunshine*, he was tortured brutally before his death by an army officer who had himself been an Olympian in horse racing.[228]

The wrestler Weisz survived the war and began to reorganize his beloved club of half a century in his apartment immediately after the war. He died in December 1945.[229] The water polo goalkeeper Barta passed away in Budapest in 1948.[230] Földes, the only champion who had left Hungary before World War II, died in Cleveland in 1950.[231] Many of the Jewish champions continued to work for the benefit of Hungary, sports, or both. The first champion, Hajós, worked for the Agricultural Planning Institute until his death in 1955.[232] Bródy spent two years in labor service, became an official of the Hungarian Swimming Association in 1945, then commercial attaché to the Netherlands, and in 1948 he immigrated to South Africa, where he ran a textile business until his death in 1967.[233] Gombos was head physician in Budapest for more than two decades; he died in 1968.[234] Kárpáti worked as a physical education teacher in Budapest; he later coached the Army's team and the Helsinki Olympics team. He was a member of the Hungarian Olympic Committee (HOC) and passed away at the age of ninety in 1996.[235] Sárkány was also ninety years old when he died in Vienna in 1998. After the war, he was the coach of the *UTE*, moved to the West Germany in 1958, and coached the national team there in 1969-1973.[236] Mező was the principal of a prestigious school in Budapest from 1945, was granted membership in the HOC in 1946, and replaced Regent Horthy as member of the IOC in 1948. However, he was denounced as a class alien, expelled from the HOC in March 1948, and his pension was revoked in 1950. He died in 1961.[237]

Kabos also suffered a tragic fate. According to the testimony of the infamously ruthless Jewish labor service base commander Lipót Muray, one day in 1942 he noticed a Jew with a "figure of classical sculpture-like beauty," who had been sent to the recruitment center under his supervision.[238] It was Kabos, who had also received the Signum Laudis from Horthy, for the first time together with Petschauer in 1932. By his own account, Muray traveled to Budapest twice and convinced his superiors to release Kabos, lest he fell into the hands of the Soviets, who could hold him up as an example of Hungarian brutality. Kabos was probably indeed released from labor service. He died on the Margit Bridge of Budapest, blown up by the Arrow Cross in November 1944.[239] Perhaps the most tragic fate befell the great veteran of sabre fencing, Jenő Fuchs. Fuchs was already thirty when he won his last Olympic championship in 1912; he was of the generation that first proved its devotion to their homeland in sports halls, not the battlefield. When he was called up, he was sixty years old. In late 1942, he served as a sapper in a labor service brigade, when he was awarded the Iron Cross for his heroic help to his battalion. Horthy allowed him to wear the decoration and ordered him back to the hinterland. When Hungary was defeated, Fuchs was imprisoned by the Soviet Army; he died a decade later.[240]

The fates of the most important non-Jewish defenders of Jewish champion's rights were tragically similar. Shvoy was arrested by the Arrow Cross, then cleared by a Soviet court, but demoted and deprived of his pension; he died in 1971.[241] Peyer, the leader of the Social Democratic Party, was arrested on the day of the Nazi takeover; he survived Mauthausen, fled to Austria in 1947, and was convicted at a show trial in absentia in 1948 for conspiring against the democratic order. He died in New York listening to the news of the Hungarian Revolution in October 1956.[242] After the takeover in March 1944, Alajos Béldy, leader of the Levente Movement, was visited by a delegation of eight Jewish Olympians, including his childhood friend, Hajós. He allowed them to not wear the yellow star, but the Minister of Justice refused to give official permission. Béldy was arrested after the Arrow Cross takeover in October 1944; he escaped from the Gestapo's prison and went into hiding until the triumph of the Soviets, who imprisoned him without delay. He died in prison in 1946.[243]

Vilmos E., a Hungarian Holocaust survivor interviewed in 2004, remarked that "when someone wins an Olympic medal, s/he's Hungarian, and when s/he is taken away, s/he isn't anymore."[244] Ironically enough, even the second statement of his sentence did not prove to be universally true; at the same time as the first statement was becoming ever more contentious, its treatment shed light on the increasingly tense demarcation lines between Jewish and Magyar identities, crystallizing the discontents of Jewish assimilation and exclusion. The loyalty of Hungarian Jews, saturated with Magyar patriotism, a longing for the bygone days of Dualism, and the hope of remedying their age-old grief and recent losses, found expression in the praise of Jewish Olympians. Even though this novel and dynamically evolving experience of modern Jewish heroism, masculinity, and patriotism could not but have failed to save Hungarian Jews, as the cases of the exemption from the Second Jewish Law and that of Kabos saved from labor service demonstrate, the idea that Jewish Olympians were exemplary Hungarians possessing enormous international significance gained currency, even at some of the lowest points of the country's history. Despite its emphasis on demonstrating the achievements of the Magyar race, Hungarian officialdom did not exclude Jews from the Olympic team, although it was equally unprepared to grant even the least measure of recognition to the champions as Jews. Nevertheless, thanks to the early development of Hungarian fencing from an aristocratic pastime to a modern sport, and the fact that sabre teams regularly included army officers, Jewish Olympians certainly won the respect of a number of good-hearted officers. Most notably, Kálmán Shvoy made self-effacing attempts to alleviate the plight of Jewish champions, as well as Hungarian Jewry as a whole.

To be sure, one might question the efficacy with which the Hungarian Jewish leadership exploited the political potential of Jewish Olympic victories; still, as the debates surrounding these amply demonstrate, Hungarian Jews were not lacking particularly Jewish political inclinations, causes, and possibilities to influence Hungarian policies, at home and abroad. Although the opportunities of self-professed Hungarian Jewish patriots for navigating the hostile Hungarian political scene were increasingly harshly constrained, Hungarian officialdom was unable to eschew joining the celebration of the ornament of interwar Hungarian Jewry: Jewish Olympians.

ACKNOWLEDGMENTS

I would like to thank Lajos Szabó, the director of the Hungarian Sports Museum, for his guidance and permission to peruse images from the Kabos Collection. My thanks are also due to Árpád Németh, who allowed me to use images of his fencing collection (www.nefeco.hu). I also thank László Karsai for directing me to the Metropolitan Ervin Szabó Library, which generously scanned and permitted use of an image from their collection. Finally, my thanks are due to Dr. George Eisen, who provided valuable feedback on a draft of this paper.

NOTES

[1] Gyula Zeke, "Statisztikai melléklet," in *Hét évtized a hazai zsidóság életében* (ed. L. Ferenc Lendvai, Anikó Sohár, and Pál Horváth; *Vallástudományi tanulmányok;* Budapest: MTA Filozófiai Intézet, 1990), 187 [Statistical appendices].

[2] István Deák, *Jewish Soldiers in Austro-Hungarian Society,* vol. 34, (Leo Baeck Memorial Lecture New York: Leo Baeck Institute, 1990), 4, 10, 21-22; ———, *Beyond Nationalism: A Social and Political History of the Habsburg Officer Corps, 1848-1918* (Oxford: Oxford University Press, 1990), 195-98.

[3] William O. McCagg Jr., "Jews in Revolutions: The Hungarian Experience," *Journal of Social History* 6, no. 1 (1972): 78.

[4] László Csorba, "Zsidó szellemi élet a húszas-harmincas évek Magyarországán," in *Hét évtized a hazai zsidóság életében* (ed. L. Ferenc Lendvai, Anikó Sohár, and Pál Horváth; *Vallástudományi tanulmányok*; Budapest: MTA Filozófiai Intézet, 1990), 200 (Jewish Intellectual Life in Hungary in the 1920s-1930s).

[5] Vera Ranki, *The Politics of Inclusion and Exclusion: Jews and Nationalism in Hungary* (St. Leonards: Allen & Unwin, 1999), 88.

[6] T. D. Kramer, *From Emancipation to Catastrophe: The Rise and Holocaust of Hungarian Jewry* (Lanham: University Press of America, 2000), 49; Lajos Szabolcsi, *Két emberöltő: Az Egyenlőség évtizedei (1881-1931):* Géza Komoróczy, ed., *Emlékezések, dokumentumok* (Hungaria Judaica; Budapest: MTA Judaisztikai Kutatócsoport, 1993), 282-83 [Two Generations: The Decades of Egyenlőség (1881-1931): Memories, Documents]; Csorba, "Zsidó szellemi élet," 200-01.

[7] Jób Paál, *A száz napos szegedi kormány: Az ellenforradalom története* (Budapest: Bíró Miklós, 1919), 28-34 (The Hundred-Day Old Szeged Government: A History of the Counterrevolution).

[8] Béla Kelemen, ed., *Adatok a szegedi ellenforradalom és a szegedi kormány történetéhez (1919)* (Szeged: Author's publication, 1923), 115-17 [Data on the History of the Szeged Counterrevolution and the Szeged Government (1919)]. Lajos Szabolcsi also presents Paál's account: Szabolcsi, *Két emberöltő,* 282-83.

[9] "Ellenforradalom," *Magyar Zsidó Lexikon (MZSL)* 1:220-21 [Hungarian Jewish Lexicon]. Online: http://mek.niif.hu/04000/04093/html/.

[10] Kálmán Shvoy, *Shvoy Kálmán titkos naplója és emlékirata,* eds. Mihály Perneki (Budapest: Kossuth, 1983), 46-47 [The Secret Diary and Memoirs of Kálmán Shvoy].

[11] "Lélekemelően szép ünnepségen avatták fel a zsidó hősi emlékművet," *Szegedi Napló* (31 October 1933) [Jewish Heroes' Memorial Inaugurated with Sublime Celebration]; "Lélekemelő katonai ünnepség keretében avatta fel vitéz dr. Shvoy Kálmán altábornagy a zsidó hősök emlékművét," *Délmagyarország* (31 October 1933) [Lt.-Gen. Kálmán Shvoy

Inaugurated the Jewish Heroes' Memorial with Sublime Celebration]. Online: http://www.bibl.u-szeged.hu/shvoy/dokumentumok/index.html.

[12] Shvoy, *Napló*, 119. In Hungarian, "magyar" means both "Magyar" and "Hungarian." I will use Magyar in the ethnic sense and translate "magyarság" as "Magyarhood" without such distinction.

[13] Ibid., 121-28.

[14] Szabolcsi, *Két emberöltő*, 316-26.

[15] Imre Monostori, "A zsidókérdés változatai a magyar folyóiratokban a húszas évektől a zsidótörvényekig (I. rész)," *Kortárs* 47, no. 9 (2003): 76 [Variations of the Jewish Question in Hungarian Periodicals from the 1920s to the Jewish Laws (First Part)]; Tsvi Zehavi, *Toldot ha-tsiyonut be-Hungariyah*, vol. 2 (Mi-hitbolelut le-tsiyonut-meqor tsiyonuto shel Hertsl Jerusalem: Ha-sifriyah ha-tsiyonit, 1972), 384 [The History of Zionism in Hungary]; Csorba, "Zsidó szellemi élet," 214. After the emancipation of Jews in 1867, Judaism was made a recognized religion in 1895.

[16] Raphael Patai, *The Jews of Hungary: History, Culture, Psychology* (Detroit: Wayne State University Press, 1996), 382.

[17] George Eisen, "Jewish History and the Ideology of Modern Sport: Approaches and Interpretations," *Journal of Sport History* 25, no. 3 (1998): 509.

[18] Patai, *The Jews of Hungary*, 383; Avigdor Löwenheim, "Zsidók és a párbaj," *Múlt és Jövő*, no. 4 (1992): 88 [Jews and Dueling].

[19] Patai, *The Jews of Hungary*, 379; Eisen, "Jewish History," 509; Löwenheim, "Zsidók és a párbaj," 87; Béla Novák, "A párbajozó úriember" (Ph.D., Eötvös Loránd Tudományegyetem, 2008), 182 [The Dueling Gentleman].

[20] Szabolcsi, *Két emberöltő*, 41; Patai, *The Jews of Hungary*, 379-81; Löwenheim, "Zsidók és a párbaj," 83, 85-86.

[21] Eisen, "Jewish History," 508.

[22] Löwenheim, "Zsidók és a párbaj," 83; Tamás Eszes, *Híres bajvívások, hírhedt párbajok* (Budapest: Népszava, 1988), 131-32 [Famous Duels, Infamous Fights]; Patai, *The Jews of Hungary*, 379, 384; Arnd Krüger, "'Once the Olympics are Through, We'll Beat Up the Jew': German Jewish Sport 1898-1938 and the Anti-Semitic Discourse," *Journal of Sport History* 26, no. 2 (1999): 366; Eisen, "Jewish History," 501, 504-05; Deák, *Jewish Soldiers in Austro-Hungarian Society*, 19-21.

[23] Löwenheim, "Zsidók és a párbaj," 90-92; Bernard Klein, "Anti-Jewish Demonstrations in Hungarian Universities, 1932-1936: István Bethlen vs Gyula Gömbös," *Jewish Social Studies* 44, no. 2 (Spring 1982): 113-24.

[24] Löwenheim, "Zsidók és a párbaj," 88-90.

[25] "Hajós Alfréd," *Magyar olimpiai lexikon 1896-2008* (*MOL*) 1:118-19 [Hungarian Olympic Lexicon, 1896-2008]. Andrew Handler, *From the Ghetto to the Games: Jewish Athletes in Hungary* (East European Monographs 192; New York: Columbia University Press, 1985), 18-19.

[26] Ibid., 21-24.

[27] "Gerde Oszkár," *MOL* 1:101; "Dezső Földes," *MOL* 1:92; "Werkner Lajos," *MOL* 1:364.

[28] Handler, *From the Ghetto to the Games*, 28-30.

[29] Alajos Béldy, *Az IHNETOV Munkanaplója vitéz Béldy Alajos vezérezredes Hadtörténelmi Levéltárban* őrzött *irataiból,* 1941-1943, (ed. Róbert Blasszauer; Budapest: Petit Real, 2002) [The Journal of the National Leader of Youth Military and Sports Education, Alajos Béldy, from His Papers in the Military History Archive]. Online: http://mek.niif. hu/04900/04982/html.

[30] Elek Klein, "A magyar tornászok dicsősége Dückstein Zoltán." *Egyenlőség* 52, no. 44 (27 August 1932): 3; Aron Moskovits, *Jewish Education in Hungary (1848-1948)* (New York: Bloch, 1964), 226-29; László Felkai, *Zsidó iskolázás Magyarországon (1780-1990)* (Budapest: Országos Pedagógiai Könyvtár és Múzeum, 1998), 91, 98-105 [Jewish Education in Hungary (1780-1990)].

[31] "Gerde Oszkár," *MOL* 1:101; Eisen, "Jewish History," 509.

[32] "Gerde Oszkár," *MOL* 1:101; "Werkner Lajos," *MOL* 1:364.

[33] Doros György, "A sportmozgalom társadalmi lélektana," *Testnevelés* 5, nos. 8-10 (August-October 1932): 641-42 [The Social Psychology of the Sports Movement]; Miklós Hadas, "Football and Social Identity: The Case of Hungary in the 20th Century," *The Sports Historian* 20, no. 2 (November 2000): 45; ———, "Gymnastic Exercises, or Work Wrapped in the Gown of Youthful Joy: Masculinities and the Civilizing Process in 19th Century Hungary," *Journal of Social History* 41, no. 1 (Fall 2007): 162.

[34] "Hajós Alfréd," *MOL* 1:118-19; "Werkner Lajos," *MOL* 1:364; Handler, *From the Ghetto to the Games*, 31, 38.

[35] "Kemény Ferenc," *MZSL* 1:461; Ibid., 16.

[36] "Torna," *MZSL 1:907* [Gymnastics]; Hadas, "Football and Social Identity," 46; Péter Szegedi, "A cionizmustól a futballgazdaságig: A Makkabi Brno az első világháború után," *Múlt és Jövő* 1(2006): 69-70 [From Zionism to the Economy of Football. Maccabi Brno after the First World War]; Viktor Karády and Miklós Hadas, "Soccer and Antisemitism in Hungary," in *Emancipation Through Muscles: Jews and Sports in Europe* (ed. Michael Brenner and Gideon Reuveni; Lincoln: University of Nebraska Press, 2006), 213-14.

[37] Handler, *From the Ghetto to the Games*, 21-25; Gyula Zeke, "A nagyvárosi kultúra új formái és a zsidóság," *Budapesti Negyed: Lap a Városról* 3, no. 2 (8) (1995): 95 [New Forms of Metropolitan Culture and the Jews].

[38] "Vívó és Atlétikai Club," *MZSL* 1:955; Zehavi, *Toldot ha-tsiyonut be-Hungariyah*, 338.

[39] Péter Szegedi, "Pozíciók és oppozíciók: a futballmező kialakulása, struktúrája és dinamikája: Az 1945 előtti debreceni labdarúgás történetszociológiai elemzése" (Budapesti Corvinus Egyetem, 2005), 26-27 [Positions and Oppositions: The Emergence, Structure and Dynamics of the Football Field: A Historical-Sociological Analysis of the Pre-1945 Football Scene of Debrecen]; Szegedi, "A cionizmustól a futballgazdaságig," 69-70; Handler, *From the Ghetto to the Games*, 42-43, 99.

[40] Szegedi, "A cionizmustól a futballgazdaságig," 70.

[41] "Kabos Endre," *MOL* 1:148-49.

[42] "Vívó és Atlétikai Club," *MZSL* 1:955; "Dückstein Zoltán," *Magyar Életrajzi Lexikon* [Zoltán Dückstein]. Online: http://mek.niif.hu/00300/00355/html/ABC03014/03603. htm; Moskovits, *Jewish Education in Hungary (1848-1948)*, 227.

[43] Handler, *From the Ghetto to the Games*, 37-38.

[44] Zeke, "A nagyvárosi kultúra," 95.

[45] "Petschauer Attila," *MOL* 1:265-66.

[46] "Hajdu Marcell," *MZSL* 1:337; Handler, *From the Ghetto to the Games*, 37.

[47] Count István Tisza was Prime Minister in 1903-1905 and 1913-1917.

[48] "Gombos Sándor," *MOL* 1:105-06; "Garay János," *MOL* 1:96-97; "Kabos Endre," *MOL* 1:148-49.

[49] "Hajós Alfréd," *MOL* 1:118-19.

[50] "Kárpáti Károly," *MOL* 1:154-55; "Kabos Endre," *MOL* 1:148-49.

[51] Szegedi, "Pozíciók és oppozíciók," 44, 217; ———, "A cionizmustól a futballgazdaságig," 70. The 3rd District had only a relatively small Jewish population, see Gyula Zeke, "A budapesti zsidóság lakóhelyi szegregációja a tőkés modernizáció korszakában (1867-1941)," in *Hét évtized a hazai zsidóság életében* (ed. L. Ferenc Lendvai, Anikó Sohár, and Pál Horváth; *Vallástudományi tanulmányok*; Budapest: MTA Filozófiai Intézet, 1990: 182) [The Residential Segregation of Budapest Jewry in the Era of Capitalist Modernization (1867-1941)].

[52] "Barta István," *MOL* 1:29; "Bródy György," *MOL* 1:48; "Sárkány Miklós," *MOL* 1:291.

[53] "Magyar zsidók az olimpiászon," *Egyenlőség* 52, no. 43 (13 August 1932): 1.

[54] "Dezső Földes," *MOL* 1:92.

[55] "Gerde Oszkár," *MOL* 1:101; "Petschauer Attila," *MOL* 1:265-66; "Gombos Sándor," *MOL* 1:105-06; "Garay János," *MOL* 1:96-97; "Kabos Endre," *MOL* 1:148-49; Rónai, "'Pengeélen'—sportélet az UTE vívótermében," *Terézváros* (January 2006): 20 [On a Blade—Sport Life in the UTE Fencing Hall].

[56] Ferenc Zöld, *Tűnődés egy arckép előtt* (Cleveland: Magyar Sporthíradó, 1971), 34 [Pondering in Front of a Portrait]; András Kő, *Pengevilág: A Magyar Vívó Szövetség megalakulásának 90. évfordulójára* (Budapest: Magyar Vívó Szövetség, 2004), 57 [Blade World: To the 90th Jubilee of the Establishment of the Hungarian Fencing Association].

[57] Hadas, "Gymnastic Exercises," 164.

[58] "Fuchs és Weisz vagy a fajmagyarok," *Egyenlőség* 27, no. 2 (2 August 1908): 3-4 [Fuchs and Weisz, or the Ethnic Magyars].

[59] Ibid., 3; on the percentage of the Jewish population in Újlipótváros (Neu-Leopoldstadt), see Zeke, "A budapesti zsidóság," 174, 182.

[60] "Fuchs és Weisz," 3-4, citation from p. 3.

[61] "A világbajnok" *Egyenlőség* 31, no. 31 (4 August 1912): 7-8 [The World Champion]; citation from p. 8.

[62] Randolph L. Braham, *The Politics of Genocide: The Holocaust in Hungary*, 2 vols., vol. 1 (New York: Columbia University Press, 1981), 23.

[63] Ranki, *The Politics of Inclusion and Exclusion*, 94.

[64] Victor Karady, "Antisemitism in Twentieth-Century Hungary: A Socio-historical Overview," *Patterns of Prejudice* 27, no. 1 (1993): 71-92; Viktor Karády, "Asszimiláció és társadalmi krízis: A magyar-zsidó társadalomtörténet konjukturális vizsgálatához," *Világosság* 34, no. 3 (1993): 33-60 [Assimilation and Social Crisis: A Conjunctural Analysis of Hungarian-Jewish Social History]; Ezra Mendelsohn, *The Jews of Eastern Europe between the World Wars* (Bloomington: Indiana University Press, 1983), 87-95.

[65] Zeke, "A budapesti zsidóság," 163.

[66] Braham, *The Politics of Genocide*, 26-28; G. C. Paikert, "Hungary's National Minority Policies, 1920-1945," *American Slavic and East European Review* 12, no. 2 (1953): 202, 206, 217; Mendelsohn, *The Jews of Eastern Europe*, 99-102.

[67] Ranki, *The Politics of Inclusion and Exclusion*, 86; Karady, "Antisemitism in Twentieth-Century Hungary," 80-83; Csorba, "Zsidó szellemi élet," 246-47; Mendelsohn, *The Jews of Eastern Europe*, 95.

[68] Mendelsohn, *The Jews of Eastern Europe*, 105; Kramer, *From Emancipation to Catastrophe*, 53-54; Nathaniel Katzburg, *Hungary and the Jews: Policy and Legislation, 1920-1943* (Jerusalem: Bar-Ilan University Press, 1981), 155-56.

[69] Mendelsohn, *The Jews of Eastern Europe*, 105-06; Kramer, *From Emancipation to Catastrophe*, 53-55; Katzburg, *Hungary and the Jews*, 60-79.

[70] Karady, "Antisemitism in Twentieth-Century Hungary," 83.

[71] Katzburg, *Hungary and the Jews*, 81-84, 90-91; Ranki, *The Politics of Inclusion and Exclusion*, 110.

[72] Ranki, *The Politics of Inclusion and Exclusion*, 86, 98-99.

[73] Mendelsohn, *The Jews of Eastern Europe*, 113; Katzburg, *Hungary and the Jews*, 87-88.

[74] Ranki, *The Politics of Inclusion and Exclusion*, 97-103.

[75] Kramer, *From Emancipation to Catastrophe*, 49-50.

[76] Katzburg, *Hungary and the Jews*, 84-85; Kramer, *From Emancipation to Catastrophe*, 57-58; Mendelsohn, *The Jews of Eastern Europe*, 106.

[77] Kramer, *From Emancipation to Catastrophe*, 55.

[78] Mendelsohn, *The Jews of Eastern Europe*, 108.

[79] Kramer, *From Emancipation to Catastrophe*, 49-50, 56, quote from 50.

[80] Csorba, "Zsidó szellemi élet," 243.

[81] Ibid., 238-39.

[82] Ranki, *The Politics of Inclusion and Exclusion*, 122-24; Mendelsohn, *The Jews of Eastern Europe*, 105; Csorba, "Zsidó szellemi élet," 238-43.

[83] Csorba, "Zsidó szellemi élet," 247.

[84] Mendelsohn, *The Jews of Eastern Europe*, 104.

[85] Ibid., 110.

[86] Ibid., 107.

[87] Ibid., 111; Kramer, *From Emancipation to Catastrophe*, 109.

[88] Attila Novák, "Cionizmus a két világháború közti Magyarországon," in *Hágár országa: A magyarországi zsidóság— történelem, közösség, kultúra*(ed. Anna Szalai; Budapest: Antall József Alapítvány—Kossuth Kiadó, 2009), 133 [Zionism in Interwar Hungary].

[89] Ibid., 133-40; Zehavi, *Toldot ha-tsiyonut be-Hungariyah*, 383-86; Mendelsohn, *The Jews of Eastern Europe*, 107-08.

[90] Novák, "Cionizmus a két világháború közti Magyarországon," 133.

[91] Csorba, "Zsidó szellemi élet," 255, quote from 263; Novák, "Cionizmus a két világháború közti Magyarországon," 134.

[92] Ranki, *The Politics of Inclusion and Exclusion*, 129-30; Csorba, "Zsidó szellemi élet," 248, 255-57.

[93] Novák, "Cionizmus a két világháború közti Magyarországon," 139-140; Yitzhaq 'Eizdorfer, "Yisud tnu`at betar," in *Yad le-betar hungaryah, 1928/1948* (ed. Natan Ben-

Chayim; n.p.: Netzivut betar hungaryah, 1988), 24 [The Establishment of the Betar Movement].

[94] Mendelsohn, *The Jews of Eastern Europe*, 87-94; Karády, "Asszimiláció és társadalmi krízis," 33-60; Zeke, "A budapesti zsidóság," 163.

[95] Csorba, "Zsidó szellemi élet," 228-29.

[96] Jack Kugelmass, "Why Sports?," in *Jews, Sports, and the Rites of Citizenship* (ed. Jack Kugelmass; Urbana: University of Illinois Press, 2007), 11.

[97] Ibid., 25. See also: Doros, "A sportmozgalom," 641-42; Paul Taylor, *Jews and the Olympic Games: The Clash between Sport and Politics: With a Complete Review of Jewish Olympic Medallists* (Brighton: Sussex Academic Press, 2004), 19-20.

[98] Handler, *From the Ghetto to the Games*, 76-77.

[99] "Hirek: Zsidó tanár, az olimpiai szellemi bajnokság győztese," *Országos Egyetértés* 3, no. 31 (9 August 1928): 10 [News: Jewish Teacher Wins the Spiritual Olympics]. The word *szellemi* [spiritual, "intellectual"] was used in the name of the art competitions.

[100] On Hungarian Jewish newspapers, see: "Budapest," *MZSL* 1:152; Csorba, "Zsidó szellemi élet," 114-15. A report to the Prague Zionist Congress from the Budapest Group in 1933 likely overstates the Zionist sympathies: Zehavi, *Toldot ha-tsiyonut be-Hungariyah*, 384.

[101] Mező [field in Hungarian] is a Magyarized version of Grünfeld.

[102] "A magyar zsidóság és az olimpiász: Mező Ferenc dr., a zalamegyei Grünfeld-család sarja: a szellemi olimpiász győztese," *Egyenlőség* (11 August 1928): 1 [Hungarian Jewry and the Olympics: Dr. Ferenc Mező, scion of the Grünfeld Family from Zalemegyer, Wins the Spiritual Olympics].

[103] Ibid.

[104] "A magyar zsidóság és az olimpiász," 2. According to other sources, Mező was member of the City Soviet in Nagykanizsa: "Mező Ferenc," *MOL* 1:226-27.

[105] Mező Ferenc, "A világbajnok levele az Egyenlőséghez," *Egyenlőség* 48, no. 31 (11 August 1928): 2 [The World Champion's Letter to *Egyenlőség*]. All italics are in the original, unless otherwise noted.

[106] "Mező Ferenc dr. ünneplése Nagykanizsán," *Egyenlőség* 48, no. 32 (18 August 1928): 4 [Celebrating Ferenc Mező in Nagykanizsa].

[107] "Hány zsidóvallású Magyar nyerte eddig meg az olimpiászt?," *Egyenlőség* 48, no. 31 (11 August 1928): 3 [How Many Hungarians of the Jewish Faith have Won the Olympics?].

[108] Mező Ferenc, "A világbajnok levele az Egyenlőséghez," 2.

[109] "Barta István, a nagy magyar kapus," *Egyenlőség* 48, no. 31 (11 August 1928): 3 [István Barta, the Great Hungarian Goalie]; "Látogatás Berger néninél," *Egyenlőség* 48, no. 31 (11 August 1928): 3 [Visiting Mrs. Berger].

[110] "Hány zsidóvallású Magyar nyerte eddig meg az olimpiászt?," 3; "Hajdu János és Bródy György," *Egyenlőség* 48, no. 31 (11 August 1928): 3 [János Hajdu and György Bródy].

[111] See, "Garay," 96-97; "Gombos," 105-06; "Petschauer," 265-66; "Glykais Gyula," *MOL* 1:104-05; "Rády József," *MOL* 1:275-76 "Terstyánszky Ödön," *MOL* 1:329.

[112] Ibid.; Ferenc Molnár was a celebrated Hungarian Jewish writer and dramatist. In 1939, he immigrated from Hungary to the United States, where his plays achieved success both on Broadway and in Hollywood.

[113] Ibid., 1-2.

[114] Zoltán Klár, "Attila," *Egyenlőség* 48, no. 32 (18 August 1928): 3 [Attila]. Árpád (845-907) was the Second Grand Prince of Hungarians, under whom the *honfoglalás* [conquest of the homeland] took place in 896.

[115] Ibid.

[116] Attila Petschauer, "A jó Isten, akihez mindig imádkoztam, megsegitett," *Egyenlőség* 48, no. 32 (18 August 1928): 9 [The Good God, to Whom I Had Always Prayed, Helped Me].

[117] C. B., "Miss Rosenfeld Kanadából," *Egyenlőség* 48, no. 32 (18 August 1928): 9-10 [Miss Rosenfeld from Canada].

[118] "Zsidó atléták az olimpiászon," *Egyenlőség* 48, no. 32 (18 August 1928): 12 [Jewish Athletes at the Olympics].

[119] "Kinek köszönjük: Santellinek, Terstyánszkynak vagy - 'Attilának': Két levél a magyar kard dicsőségéről," *Uj Nemzedék* (18 August 1928) [Whom to Thank: Santelli, Terstyánszky, or "Attila": Two Letters on the Triumph of the Hungarian Sword].

[120] "Petschauer a mogendoviddal vagy: kik csinálják az antiszmitizmust?," *Uj Nemzedék* (23 August 1928) [Petschuer with the Mogen Dovid, or who Generates Anti-Semitism].

[121] "Színfoltok a napisajtóban: a kardcsapatbajnokság és az 'Uj Nemzedék'," *Országos Egyetértés* 3, no. 33 (23 August 1928): 7 [Curiosities in the Daily Press: The Sabre Team Victory and *Uj Nemzedék*].

[122] "Testedzés," *Nemzeti Élet* 8, no. 33 (19 August 1928): 267 [Physical Education].

[123] László Nagykálnai Levatich, "A zsidók és az olimpiász," *Nemzeti Élet* 8, no. 34 (26 August 1928): 271 [Jews and the Olympics].

[124] "'Petschauer a világ legjobb kardvívója'—írja egy német sportújság: Az olimpiász győzelmes zsidó bajnokai," *Egyenlőség* 48, no. 33 (25 August 1928): 2 ['Petschauer is the World's Best Sabre Fencers'—Writes a German Sports Newspaper]; "A sport és a zsidók," *Egyenlőség* 48, no. 34 (1 September 1928): 17 [Sports and Jews].

[125] "Fel az új olimpiádra!," *Levente* 7, nos. 17-18 (2 September 1928): 3 [Up, to the New Olypics!]. For similar, if less eloquent discussion of sports as a public diplomacy, see: Leventebarát, "Az amsterdami olimpiád után . . . ," *Levente* 7, nos. 17-18 (2 September 1928): 3 [After the Amsterdam Olympics . . .]; Egy leventebarát, " Az amsterdami olimpiai versenyek," *Levente* 7, no. 19 (2 October 1928): 5-6 [The Amsterdam Olympic Games].

[126] "Szentlélek temploma: A mi sportunk: Nemzetek vetélkedése," *Az erő* 12, no. 2 (October 1928): 22 [The Temple of the Holy Spirit: Our Sports: Competition of Nations].

[127] "Olympiai ügyek: Általános jelentés az amsterdami Olympián szereplésünkről," *Testnevelés* 1, no. 12 (December 1928): 795-810 [Olympic Affairs: General Report on Our Participation in the Amsterdam Olympics].

[128] "Magyar zsidók az olimpiászon," *Egyenlőség* 52, no. 43 (13 August 1932): 1 [Hungarian Jews at the Olympics].

[129] László Krausz, "Olimpikonok vallási viszonyai," *Országos Egyetértés* 8, nos. 34-35 (26 August 1932): 2 [Confessional Affiliations of Olympians].

[130] For a digest of fencing-related news in sports newspapers between 1928 and 1936, see: Kő, *Pengevilág*, 57-79.

[131] "A magyar kard," *Pesti Hirlap* (August 14, 1932) [The Hungarian Sword].

[132] "Magyar győzelmek az olimpiászon," *Vitézek és gazdák lapja* 10, no. 31 (20 August 1932): 2 [Hungarian Victories at the Olympics].

[133] Tornay, "Egy nemzetnél sem vagyunk alávalóbbak," *Levente* 11, Nos. 14-16 (15 September 1932): 202-203 [We are Not Inferior to Any Nation].

[134] Holly, "A losangelesi olimpia eredményei," *Levente* 11, nos. 17-18 (15 October 1932): 249 [The Results of the Los Angeles Olympics].

[135] Holly, "A losangelesi olimpia eredményei," *Levente* 11, nos. 19-20 (15 November 1932): 283 [The Results of the Los Angeles Olympics].

[136] "Kabos Endre, akit az olaszok nem szeretnek . . . ," *Esti Kurir* (March 25, 1932) [Endre Kabos, Whom Italians Don't Like].

[137] "'Pengeélen,'" 20; "Kabos Endre, az olimpiai kardvívó-bajnokcsapat kiváló tagja nem indul több vívóversenyen," *Sporthirlap* (October 27, 1932) [Endre Kabos, the Excellent Member of the Olympic Champion Sabre Team, Will Retire from Further Competitions]; "Kabos elindul az Európa-bajnokságon," *Esti* Kurir (14 April 1933) [Kabos to Participate at the European Championship].

[138] Katzburg, *Hungary and the Jews*, 85-87; Kramer, *From Emancipation to Catastrophe*, 59-60; Mendelsohn, *The Jews of Eastern Europe*, 114; Csorba, "Zsidó szellemi élet," 207.

[139] Kramer, *From Emancipation to Catastrophe*, 62-63; Mendelsohn, *The Jews of Eastern Europe*, 114.

[140] Mendelsohn, *The Jews of Eastern Europe*, 115.

[141] Csorba, "Zsidó szellemi élet," 219-22.

[142] "Miért nem indul Kabos is," *8 Órai Ujság* (2 March 1935) [Why does Kabos not Participate?].

[143] "1000 külföldi sportolót várnak a tel-avivi Makkabiahra: A Vívószövetség és a VAC," *Zsidó Szemle* 30, no. 12, (28 March 1935): 8 [Thousand Sportsmen from All Over the World Expected at the Tel Aviv Maccabiah: The Fencing Association and the VAC]. On *Zsidó Szemle* [Jewish Review], see, Monostori, "A zsidókérdés változatai (I. rész)," 76; Novák, "Cionizmus a két világháború közti Magyarországon," 138-39; Zehavi, *Toldot ha-tsiyonut be-Hungariyah*, 384.

[144] "Kabos: Semmiesetre sem megyek Tel-Avivba," *8 Órai Ujság* (March 28, 1935) [Kabos: I Will by No Means Go to Tel Aviv].

[145] "Bemutatóra hívták Kabost—de lemondott", *Esti Kurír* (March 29, 1935) [Kabos was Invited to a Sparring Demonstration but He Refused].

[146] "Megkezdődtek Tel Avivban a II. Makkabiah versenyei," *Zsidó Szemle* 30, no. 13 (5 April 1935): 8 [The Second Maccabiah Games Begins in Tel Aviv]; Ottó Reiner, "A telavivi Makkabia," *Zsidó Szemle* 30, nos. 14-15 (16 April 1935): 37-38 [The Tel Aviv Maccabiah].

[147] Anna Szalai, "Assimilation and Zionism in the Journal Entitled Új Út—Világvándor (New World—World Wanderer), 1931-1939," in *Previously Unexplored Sources on the Holocaust in Hungary: A Selection from Jewish Periodicals, 1930-1944*, (ed. Anna Szalai, Rita Horvath, and Gabor Balazs; Jerusalem: Yad Vashem, 2007), 65-66.

[148] Endre Kabos, "A versenyző lelkivilága," *Testnevelés* 8, nos. 7-8 (July-August 1935): 676-89 [The Mentality of the Contestant].

[149] Ibid., 676.

[150] Ibid., 688.

[151] "Deutsch Judit esete: Sport és becsület," *Egyenlőség* 56, no. 29 (16 July 1936): 4 [The Case of Judith Deutsch: Sports and Honor].

[152] "Magyar zsidók a berlini olimpiászon," *Egyenlőség* 56, no. 30 (23 July 1936): 1 [Hungarian Jews at the Berlin Olympics].

[153] Ibid., 2.

[154] "Az olimpiász körül," *Egyenlőség* 56, no. 31 (30 July 1936): 5 [Around the Olympics].

[155] Ch. Bar. Goldmark, "Filléres sportot a zsidóság szolgálatában," *Zsidó Szemle* 31, no. 30-31 (31 July 1936): 10 [Sports for Pennies in Service of Jewry]. Predictably, the grassroots Zionist sports club of Keszthely the article chose as an example of fencing equipment was among the first pieces of equipment purchased.

[156] "Fekete veszedelem az olimpiászon? A fehér faj fizikai erejének hanyatlása?," *Uj Magyarság* (5 August 1936): 2.

[157] "Kecskeméti Vilmos," *MZSL* 1:459.

[158] "A berlini olimpiász," *Zsidó Élet* 4, nos. 27-28 (1 August 1936): 1 [The Berlin Olympics].

[159] Handler, *From the Ghetto to the Games*, 82.

[160] "Kárpáti Károly diadala," *Egyenlőség* 56, no. 32 (6 August 1936): 1 [The Triumph of Károly Kárpáti].

[161] "Az olimpiász körül," *Egyenlőség* 56, no. 32 (6 August 1936): 3 [Around the Olympics].

[162] "Az olimpiász körül," *Egyenlőség* 56, no. 33 (13 August 1936): 4 [Around the Olympics].

[163] Ibid.; see also, John Hoberman, "'How Fiercely That Gentile Rides!': Jews, Horses, and Equestrian Style," in *Jews, Sports, and the Rites of Citizenship*, (ed. Jack Kugelmass; Urbana: University of Illinois Press, 2007), 31-50.

[164] "Zsidó bajnokok és a zsidóság bajnokai," *Zsidó Szemle* 31, no. 32-33 (14 August 1936): 1-2 [Jewish Champions and the Champions of Jewry].

[165] "Helene és Ilona: Elek Ilona olimpiai győzelmére," *Zsidó Szemle* 31, no. 32-33 (14 August 1936): 11 [Helene and Ilona: On the Olympic Championship of Ilona Elek].

[166] "Olvasás közben Budapest, 31 July (Z. T. A.)," *Zsidó Szemle* 31, no. 32-33 (14 August 1936): 7 [Reading the News: Budapest, 31 July (Z. T. A.)]; "Olvasás közben: Az Olimpiász zsidó hősei," *Zsidó Szemle* 31, no. 32-33 (14 August 1936): 7-8 [Reading the News: the Jewish Heroes of the Olympics].

[167] "A magyar kardvívócsapat veretlenül, nagyszerű győzelmekkel nyerte meg az olimpiai bajnokságot," *Uj Magyarság* (14 August 1936): 7-8 [The Hungarian Sabre Team Won the Olympic Championship Unbeaten, With Magnificient Victories].

[168] "Olimpiai láz," *Uj Magyarság* 3, no. 187 (15 August 1936): 1-2 [Olympic Fever].

[169] "Kozma Miklós belügyminiszter: Berlini szereplésünk a legjobb magyar propaganda," *Uj Magyarság* 3, no. 188 (16 August 1936): 7-9, quote from p. 8 [Minister of Interior Miklós Kozma: Our Achievements in Berlin are the Best Hungarian Propaganda].

[170] "Üdvözlet a bajnokoknak," *Uj Magyarság* 3, no. 188 (16 August 1936): 1 [Welcome, Champions].

[171] "Olimpiai győzelmünk értékelése," *Nemzeti Figyelő* (23 August 1936): 4 [The Evaluation of Our Olympic Victory].

[172] "Zsidó izléstelenség," *Nemzeti Élet* 16, nos. 32-33 (16 August 1936): 4 [Jewish Tastelessness]. "Kárpáti" means "Carpathian."

[173] Ibid.

[174] Leni Riefenstahl's *Olympia* shows Kabos fencing against Marzi, see: https://www.youtube.com/watch?v=79EsZgZFZqA.

[175] Géza Dési, "A mi fiaink," *Egyenlőség* 56, no. 34 (19 August 1936): 1 [Our Sons].

[176] Ibid.; see Psalms 121:4.

[177] Ibid.

[178] The revisionist "Hungarian Creed" went: "I believe in in One God, in one country/I believe in eternal divine truth/I believe in the resurrection of Hungary. Amen."

[179] Ibid., 1-2.

[180] "Mi fáj a Nemzet Szavának? Miért vitte Kabos Berlinben a magyar lobogót?" *Uj Magyarország* (August 24, 1936) [What Hurts *Word of the Nation?* Why did Kabos Carry the Hungarian Flag in Berlin?].

[181] "Vihar az Egyenlőség egy cikke körül: Szörnyű nagy bűnt követtünk el . . . ," *Egyenlőség* 56, no. 35 (27 August 1936): 3-4 [Tempest Around an Article of *Egyenlőség:* We have Committed a Grave Crime . . .].

[182] "Gyalázatos támadás Kabos Endre kardvilágbajnok ellen," *Társadalmunk* (August 28, 1936) [Atrocious Attack Against Endre Kabos Sabre World Champion].

[183] Ibid.

[184] "Kabos Endre levele a 'Miskolc'-hoz," *Miskolc* (September 7, 1936) [The Letter of Endre Kabos to *Miskolc*].

[185] Ede Kenéz-Kurländer, "Nem irunk," *Szombat* 9, no. 20 (29 August 1936): 3 [We Do Not Write].

[186] Ibid., 3-4; "A fajelmélet csődöt mondott Berlinben," *Szombat* 9, no. 20 (29 August 1936): 12 [Race Theory Failed in Berlin].

[187] "'Nem csak jogunk, de kötelességünk felekezetieskedni'—írja az Egyenlőség," *Nemzet Szava* 10, no. 36 (6 September 1936): 3 ['It is not Only Our Right But Obligation to Engage in Confessional Debates'—Writes *Egyenlőség*].

[188] Gyula Máté-Törék, "Olimpiai győzelmünk értékelése," *Levente* 15, no. 9 (15 September 1936): 203-04 [The Evaluation of Our Olympic Victory]; Holly, "A folyó évi olimpia magyar hősei és leventevonatkozásai," *Levente* 15, no. 9 (15 September 1936): 201-07 [The Hungarian Heroes of This Year's Olympics and their Levente Affiliations]; Vitéz Károly Nagy-Megyeri Nagy, "Olimpiai sikereink levente szempontból," *Levente*, Vol. 15, Nos. 9 (15 September 1936): 211-14 [Our Olympic Achievements from a Levente Point of View].

[189] "Olimpiai kitüntetések," *Testnevelés* 9, nos. 8-9 (August-September 1936): 605-08 [Olympic Decorations].

[190] Gedényi Mihály, "A Toldi emlékérem átadása," *Testnevelés* 9. nos. 10-11 (October-November 1936): 748 [The Award Ceremony of the Toldi Memorial Prize].

[191] Joseph Siegman, *Jewish Sports Legends: The International Jewish Sports Hall of Fame* (Washington, DC: Potomac Books, 2005), 273-78. I included in the statistics Ilona Elek, whose father was Jewish and hence was perceived to be a Jew by the Jewish, and likely the non-Jewish Hungarian public.

[192] *Nemzetgyűlési napló*, vol. 24 (31 May 1924): 259 [Minutes of the National Assembly]. The reference regarding the sabre team is to Fuchs, who refused to compete; see, "Vívás," *MZSL* 1:955; Taylor, *Jews and the Olympic Games*, 21. All state documents are accessed online at http://mpgy.ogyk.hu/.

[193] *Képviselőházi napló (KN)*, vol. 20 (15 May 1929): 288 [Minutes of the House of Representatives].

[194] *KN*, vol. 4 (14 January 1932): 4.

[195] *KN*, vol. 7 (6 May 1936): 208.

[196] *KN*, vol. 10 (18 November 1936): 180-81.

[197] Ibid., 181.

[198] Ibid.

[199] "Kabos Endre és Kárpáti Károly neve kimarad?," *Egyenlőség* 56, no. 51 (December 17, 1936): 2.

[200] "Szilaveczky vívóelnök perdöntő nyilatkozata: 'Kabos-ügyet nem ismer a Szövetség, Bandi kardjára a jövőben is számítunk!'" *Hétfői Napló* (18 July 1937) [Conclusive Declaration of Szilaveczky fencing president: 'The Association Knows of no Kabos-Affair, We Count on Bandi's Sword in the Future'].

[201] "Beszéljünk őszintén Kabossal mellőzéséről," *Az Est*, (21 July 1937) [Let Us Speak Openly with Kabos about His Neglect].

[202] "Pengecsattogás Kabos Endre körül," *Társadalmunk* (23 July 1937) [Blade Clatter around Endre Kabos].

[203] Katzburg, *Hungary and the Jews*, 100-04.

[204] Ibid., 104-12.

[205] *KN*, vol. 18 (9 May 1938): 359.

[206] *KN*, vol. 18 (9 May 1938): 383. On Payr, see László Lengyel and Gyula Vidor, eds., *Magyar országgyülési almanach: Ötszáz magyar élet 1931-1936* (Budapest: s.n.,1931), 229 [Hungarian Parliamentary Almanac: Five Hundred Hungarian Lives, 1931-1936].

[207] Katzburg, *Hungary and the Jews*, 100-04.

[208] Ibid., 114-17.

[209] Ibid., 117-38.

[210] Ibid., 140-41. "A magyar zsidó hadviseltek emlékirata,", *A magyar zsidók lapja* 1, no. 4 (February 3, 1939): 7 [Memorandum of Jewish War Veterans].

[211] *KN*, vol. 22 (1 March 1939): 64.

[212] *KN*, vol. 22 (3 March 1939): 155.

[213] Ibid.

[214] *KN*, vol. 22 (7 March 1939): 176.

[215] *KN*, vol. 22 (10 March 1939): 315.

[216] *KN*, vol. 22 (13 March 1939): 363.

[217] *KN*, vol. 22 (16 March 1939): 394.

[218] *Képviselőházi irományok (KI)*, vol. 13 (17 March 1939): 85-86, 95 [Documents of the House of Representatives]; see also *Felsőházi irományok (FI)*, vol. 9 (27 March 1939): 289.

[219] *KN*, vol. 22 (21 March 1939): 429.

[220] Ilona Elek and Margit Elek, *Így vívtunk mi* (Budapest: Sport, 1968), 13-14 [We Fenced Thus].

[221] Ibid., 59-60.

[222] "Elek Ilona," *MOL* 1:76-77.

[223] "Lajos Werkner," *MOL* 1:364.

[224] "Gerde Oszkár," *MOL* 1:101.

[225] "Garay János," *MOL* 1:97.

[226] Katzburg, *Hungary and the Jews*, 201-05.

[227] "Petschauer Attila," *MOL* 1:267. According to the death certificate in possession of Dr. George Eisen, Kabos, "being unable to march further due to cardiac decompensation," became prisoner of war on January 14, and died on January 30, 1943.

[228] Taylor, *Jews and the Olympic Games*, 32-33; Judit Pihurik, *Naplók és memoárok a Donkanyarból, 1942-1943* (Budapest: Napvilág, 2007), 158 [Diaries and Memoirs from the Don Bend 1942-1943]; Szabolcs Szita, "A magyarországi zsidó munkaszolgálat," in *The Holocaust in Hungary: Fifty Years Later* (ed. Randolph L. Braham and Attila Pok; East European Monographs; New York: Columbia University Press, 1997), 335-36 [The Hungarian Jewish Labor Service System].

[229] "Weisz Richárd," *MOL* 1:364.

[230] "Barta István," *MOL* 1:29.

[231] "Földes Dezső," *MOL* 1:92.

[232] "Hajós Alfréd," *MOL* 1:119.

[233] "Bródy György," *MOL* 1:48.

[234] "Gombos Sándor," *MOL* 1:106.

[235] "Kárpáti Károly," *MOL* 1:155.

[236] "Sárkány Miklós," *MOL* 1:291

[237] "Mező Ferenc," *MOL* 1:227

[238] "Muray Lipótnak, a nagykátai bevonulási központ parancsnokának írásbeli memoranduma nagykátai 'működéséről' (1941 November-1942), in *Fegyvertelen álltak az aknamezőkön: Dokumentumok a munkaszolgálat történetéhez Magyarországon,1939 március-1942 május*, vol. 1, ed. Elek Karsai, (Budapest: Magyar Izraeliták Országos Képviselete, 1962), 160 [Written Memorandum of Lipót Muray, Commander of the Nagykáta Recruitment Center, on his "Operations" in Nagykáta (November 1941-1942)].

[239] "Kabos Endre," *MOL* 1:148.

[240] "Fuchs Jenő," *MOL* 1:95.

[241] http://www.bibl.u-szeged.hu/shvoy/shvoy/index.html; Shvoy, *Napló*, 19.

[242] József Marelyn Kiss and István Vida, eds., *Országgyűlés almanachja: 1947. szeptember 17.-1949. április 12.* (Budapest: s.n.,2005), 319-321 [Parliamentary Almanac: 17 September 1947-12 April 1949].

[243] Alajos Béldy, *Az IHNETOV Munkanaplója.*

[244] Réka Kis, interview with Vilmos E., February-June 2004, accessed at http://hu.centropa.org/?nID=1.

Grappling with Ghosts:
Jewish Wrestlers and Antisemitism

William Kornblum, Erin Sodmiak, and Phil Oberlander

This paper traces the influence of Jewish wrestlers on their sport from the late 1920s to the present. Using methods of memoir, historical reconstruction, and archival research, we focus on the careers of four Jewish wrestlers who gained prominence in wrestling in the twentieth century: Fred Oberlander wrestled for the Hakoah, in Vienna, during the period of National Socialist takeover; Henry Wittenberg, the most accomplished amateur wrestler in United States history (Olympic gold medalist and nine times United States light heavyweight champion in freestyle); Phillip Oberlander, who represented Canada in two Olympic Games; and Stephen Friedman, former CEO of Goldman Sachs and champion collegiate wrestler, who donated a major wrestling facility to Cornell University, putting that institution once again at the center of the nation's collegiate wrestling scene. As their sporting careers and personal lives became interrelated, the wrestlers influenced each other and their sport over the past half century, creating a unique story of the sport and Jewish identity.

From Genesis 32:28-29:

And he said to him, "What is your name?" And he said, "Jacob." Then he said, "Your name shall no longer be called Jacob, but Israel, for you have striven with God and with men, and have prevailed."

From Rilke:

Every angel is terrifying and would come more fiercely to interrogate you,
and rush to seize you like a blazing star,
and bend you as if trying to create you,
and break you open, out of who you are.

Jacob famously wrestled with God and won the name Israel, meaning "he who struggles." Jews continue to wrestle among themselves and their neighbors over their birthright and their identity in the modern world, but the sport of wrestling itself did not become associated with this historic struggle until the bloody twentieth century. Faced with the rise of murderous antisemitism, "Muscular Jews" fought their antagonists in the streets of Vienna and Budapest and Berlin, and in athletic tournaments where they sought victory over the racist stereotypes that portrayed Jews as bookish, weak, and genetically inferior beings. During the second half of the twentieth century, Jews have confronted more subtle forms of antisemitism in the United States. As they moved in increasing numbers from inner city immigrant neighborhoods that were perceived as Jewish ghettos to the newly built suburbs, where they would be an ethnic religious minority, athletic competition often became a way of asserting their rights to fully belong in the broader society. In some of these suburban communities, wrestling, like football and basketball, became sports where young Jewish athletes could prove their mettle in contests with their Christian schoolmates.

The lives and careers of the four Jewish wrestlers on whom we will focus—Fred Oberlander, Henry Wittenberg, Steve Friedman, and Philip Oberlander—span important, historic phases of antisemitism in the twentieth century. Oberlander, of Vienna's famous Hakoah sports club, followed in the footsteps of Mickey Hirschel, another famous Jewish wrestler from the same city. Like Hirschel, Oberlander became a European champion in his weight class before escaping the Holocaust to live in England; then, after the war, he moved his family and business to Canada. He met his close friend, Henry Wittenberg, some ten years his junior, on a trip to New York City prior to the 1948 London Olympics. At those historic games, the first after the war, Wittenberg won a gold medal in the light heavyweight freestyle class. At the Helsinki Olympic Games four years later, Wittenberg won a silver medal and went on to become the most accomplished amateur wrestler that the United States has ever produced.

As a coach at Yeshiva University and the City College of New York (CCNY), Wittenberg mentored generations of Jewish and non-Jewish New Yorkers in wrestling, fitness, and life. He died in 2010 after a long illness. During much of his illness he was regularly visited by a former wrestling protégé Philip Oberlander, the son of Wittenberg's close friend Fred. The younger Oberlander, through his accounts of experiences with his father and the other wrestlers discussed here, provides much of the narrative detail in this paper. Philip wrestled at Cornell in the early 1960s and became Canadian champion during that decade. He represented Canada in wrestling at two Olympic Games, Rome (1960) and Tokyo (1964). His senior teammate on the Cornell wrestling squad, Steven Friedman, compiled a notable record of victories during his collegiate years, including an Eastern Championship, before going on to law school and to an illustrious career in business and finance. He served as economic advisor to President George W. Bush during the early phases of the economic "bailout" of 2008. Friedman recently endowed a major wrestling and fitness facility at Cornell.

All four distinguished athletes were practicing Jews whose Jewish identities and public personae were formed, in part, through their experiences with different manifestations of the antisemitism they experienced during their early careers. Through wrestling, their lives were closely intertwined and they influenced each other profoundly. Their stories exemplify the ever-changing nature of the Jewish struggle to compete on an equal footing among athletes who represent their nations and societies; however, their personal challenges and achievements also highlight aspects of each athlete's character and background as Jews and as men of their world and time.

PRE-WORLD WAR II EUROPE AND THE GATHERING STORM OF ANTISEMITISM

As his son Phil recalls, Fred Oberlander started wrestling in Vienna, Austria, where he was born and grew up:

> His life was filled with problems dealing with antisemitism. He was very combative. He was a very large, boisterous kind of guy, and he was proud of his background. He was a cosmopolitan Viennese man with a thick German accent in English. He spoke fluent French and could speak several other European languages. He would tell us how he belonged to these sports clubs that were Jewish sports clubs and they would go out and they would compete but were always berated for being Jews. If there was a wrestling meet in the morning, the wrestlers would go to see the water polo match in the afternoon, and then they would go see the soccer games in the evening. They were all members of this great club in Vienna called Hakoah, which won the European championships. They had an outstanding soccer team and a championship women's swim team. But they were like lightning rods. They would draw reproach and get into fights.

Oberlander Sr., like other elite Jewish athletes of the interwar period, would never hide the fact that he was Jewish. In Vienna this often led to confrontations with Austrian antisemites and fascists. After frequent fights and trouble with the authorities in Vienna, his father decided that it would be best that Fred leave Vienna and take up residence in Paris. There he worked for the furrier Marcus Landesman, whose son, Robert, was also an accomplished wrestler who represented France in the 1948 Olympics. As Phil remembers the family histories, they had strong Jewish identities but were also proud of their citizenship in a world of accomplished secular Europeans. He continues:

> My father's father was in paper and packaging of various products. He was religious, although by no means orthodox, but I remember he did teach me to lay *tefillin* [that is, put on phylacteries]. His connection with the Landesmans might have come through the fact that he traveled extensively in Europe for business and was also a mason. Marcus's

son, Robert, was a fireman, so he belonged not to a Jewish sports club, but one affiliated with Les Pompiers de Paris.

Although Oberlander was living and working out in France, before the 1936 Olympics, the head of the sports authority in Austria, a high-ranking member of the National Socialist Party, asked him to return to Vienna to train and to represent Austria at the 1936 Olympics. It might have been an extremely fortuitous moment for his wrestling career, because he defeated the reigning Olympic champion, a French heavyweight, in two recent European tournaments. 1936 would have been his best opportunity to compete for Olympic gold, but many Jewish athletes at that time boycotted the games. Fred Oberlander stood proudly among them, although he missed his chance at an Olympic championship.

As elite athletes who traveled widely throughout Europe for tournaments and meets, the Hakoah athletes often heard stories about persecution of Jews, as the Nazis consolidated their reign later in the 1930s. Friends on the swim team, for example, found their way before the war to New York, where the Wertheimers, Hedie and Fritz, continued careers in aquatic sports on Manhattan's West Side. Fred, however, returned to Vienna shortly before the Anschluss, in March 1938, to bring out his grandfather and complete the immigration of the family to London, where they passed the war and part of the 1950s, and where young Phil learned more about defending his Jewish identity:

> During the war my father set us up in England where he was a young businessman and a celebrity among the expatriate Austrian Jews. In his heart he remained a rough and ready street fighter. And he tried to impart that to us as kids. He said always be proud of the fact you're Jewish and stand up for it. If someone calls you a "dirty Jew," you go up to them and tell them to take it back. So even at an early age I learned to fight back against antisemitism from other kids.

Fred and his Parisian wife, Alice, who had converted to Judaism, lived in relative affluence due to the family's business successes. As Phil recalls:

> We lived in this big home, we had cars, we had a chauffeur . . . it was a privileged life. And in the summers we went a couple of times to France. And I think part of that was probably why when his firstborn was a son he started grooming me to be an athlete. They sent us to an Orthodox Jewish day school, but we were also rather secular in many ways. I felt like, when I look back in retrospect, I was sort of a circus performer because it was in the family. I learned how to circle my brother, who was two years younger than I was, when I was four or five; we would push away the chairs and the coffee tables and the Ori-

ental rug was our wrestling mat. And we would start making the moves
of people we had seen, watching my father wrestle at competitions.

Their comfortable home became a gathering place for the Viennese intel-
ligentsia residing in London during and after the war. One of Fred's closest
friends was Pierre Guildsgame, whom the Oberlander children called "Uncle
Pierre." A passionate sports fan and ardent Zionist, Guildsgame enlisted Fred
in efforts to promote Jewish participation in sports and especially in creating
what became the modern Maccabiah Games in Israel. Another frequent visitor to the Oberlander family's London home was the philosopher Karl Popper,
author of *The Open Society and Its Enemies*, and a harsh critic of authoritarian
politics of the right and the left.

On a trip to New York in 1947, while he was still British heavyweight
champion, Fred worked out in the gym where Henry Wittenberg, a young
and extremely gifted United States national champion, was training. This
encounter would lead to a lifelong friendship. Wittenberg would also become
Phil Oberlander's coach for the Olympics of the 1960s; however, in 1947 both
Fred and Wittenberg were preparing to represent their nations in the London
Olympics of 1948, the first games to be held after the war. As athletes, Wittenberg was just reaching his prime, while Fred, brash and flamboyant as ever,
was relying more on savvy and guts than on his waning strength and speed.
The two wrestled in different weight classes, however, so Fred's admiration of
Wittenberg's immense talent would not be tinged with envy. At the 1948 Lon-
don Olympics, Fred finished out of the medal rounds, but Wittenberg won a
gold medal in the light-heavyweight class, the first ever Olympic gold for an
American wrestler.

HENRY WITTENBERG AND POSTWAR NEW YORK JEWISH IDENTITY

Henry Wittenberg went on from his victory at the London Olympics to com-
pile one of the longest winning streaks in sports history—over 300 consecutive
matches before losing in the gold medal round in the 1952 Olympics, where
he took the silver. In fact, by the time he won his Olympic medals, Wittenberg
was somewhat beyond his prime, which would have been at the 1940 and
1944 games, cancelled because of the war. After winning eight national AAU
championships, his last in 1952, he was inducted into the National Wrestling
Hall of Fame in Stillwater, Oklahoma, in 1957. While working full-time as
a New York City police officer, Wittenberg coached wrestling at Yeshiva University and CCNY, and he was the coach of the United States Greco-Roman
wrestling team at the 1968 Mexico City Olympics.

If Fred Oberlander personifies the cosmopolitan lifestyle of the inter-war Viennese Jewish haute bourgeoisie, Henry Wittenberg can be viewed as almost the quintessential New York Jewish hero of the postwar decades. The choices he made about his life's course—from a lifelong marriage to Edith, a former champion fencer and early female officer in the NYPD, to his deci-sion to remain in New York and coach local wrestlers in nationally unranked programs—exemplify a pattern of choices that established him as a New York Jewish leader of a special standing.

As a freshman at City College in Harlem, the no-tuition, educational mecca for eager children of the city's immigrant generations, Wittenberg was primarily interested in schoolwork, chess, and swimming, but he was having trouble mastering the racing turns. As Wittenberg told the *New York Times* in a later interview, "The swimming coach said: 'Kid, forget it. You'll never be a swimmer. You've got no intestinal fortitude. You know what that means? You've got no guts.'" But Wittenberg was hardly discouraged. While standing on a course registration line at City College, he was approached by the school's wrestling coach, who told him to come out for the team because he had "a wrestler's build." He soon became a protégé of Joe Sapora, the wrestling coach and a former NCAA champion at the University of Illinois. Wittenberg, it turned out, had no lack of stamina or guts and soon became a collegiate star. After graduating in 1940, he dominated national and international freestyle wrestling in his weight group and became a leading contender for United States Olympic gold.

As he rose to the level of internationally ranked elite athletes, his need to find the best training partners and training facilities brought him into contact with numerous antisemitic sports institutions, such as the New York Athletic Club. That most elite and well-equipped athletic club in Manhattan did not permit Jews among its members, but that was also where elite wrestlers worked out. They accepted Wittenberg as an athlete trying to make the United States Olympic squad, but that was as far as the welcome would extend. Out in the American hinterland, the antisemitism he encountered was often more blatant. Wittenberg told Phil Oberlander years later that when he wrestled in competi-tions in the Midwest or Southwest, "if you were a New York Jew, you had to win with a pin, because if it was a close match, the judges would invariably vote for the non-Jew." That experience helps explain why Wittenberg always chose to remain in New York and to coach local prospects, novices like he had once been. When he was offered coaching positions at major Big Ten wrestling universities like Iowa, Michigan, or Oklahoma, he chose to coach at CCNY and Yeshiva University.

Jews of the post-World War II period were pushing back with peaceful force against the mores and institutions that supported America antisemitism. If before the war it was acceptable among Gentile elites in business and politics to voice antisemitic sentiments and practice discrimination, it was fast becoming less so. Jewish Americans, many of them veterans, challenged restricted covenants and quotas of all kinds, especially in business and education. Science and engineering, which flourished at CCNY and other public universities, were more meritocratic fields. So was sports. Wittenberg believed that Jewish young men and women were just as capable of stunning success in sports as those of any other group, another reason he devoted so much of his life to coaching youth of his native city.

He visited Jerusalem before the 1972 Munich Olympics, giving pointers to the Israeli wrestling team. On the night of September 4, 1972, Wittenberg and his wife, Edith, spent time at a Munich hotel with their friend Yosef Gutfreund, an Israeli wrestling referee. The next day, Gutfreund and ten fellow Israelis—athletes and coaches—were killed when Palestinian terrorists invaded the Olympic village. "The whole concept of the Games was turned upside down," Wittenberg told *Newsday* twenty years later. "It was murder for political reasons. People go to war and get killed, all right. The Olympics were fun."

During his own active career, Wittenberg had become a pioneer in the use of weight training. Coaches often worried that weight lifting would tighten and bulk muscles to the athlete's disadvantage, but Wittenberg was the first American wrestler to fully embrace the practice in his training. Indeed, throughout his lifetime as an athlete, as a coach, and then as a celebrated strongman on the beach at Fire Island where his family had a summer home (in the largely Jewish enclave of Seaview), Wittenberg was always in training, always using his body and reveling in its strength. He was one of the earliest advocates of isometric exercise, about which he wrote a very successful book.

At a memorial service in 2010, a few months after his death at age ninety-one, middle-aged men who had trained under his tutelage gave emotional testimony to his dedication and ability to make them believe in themselves as athletes and as individuals. It is also the case that no one, including Yeshiva and CCNY former wrestlers, claimed that his efforts were to better the status of Jews. That was not necessary, nor was it Wittenberg's goal. As a coach, a police officer, and a neighbor, his love was for the people of his city—Jews, Gentiles, Muslims, Buddhists, atheists, black, white, and brown. Thus throughout his lifetime, Wittenberg worked tirelessly to maintain and build the underfunded wrestling programs at Yeshiva and CCNY, work that included the difficult tasks of fund-raising. One of Henry's most stalwart supporters in these efforts was the financier Stephen Friedman, a former wrestling star who had also trained with Wittenberg in his active sports years.

STEPHEN FRIEDMAN: MUSCULAR JEWS IN SUBURBIA AND HIGH FINANCE

One of the stars of Cornell University's nationally ranked wrestling team in the late 1950s was a wiry middleweight from suburban Long Island. Stephen Friedman had wrestled with distinction in the tough local high school wrestling circuit, where he was one of a number of talented Jewish wrestlers to be recruited by top collegiate programs. At Cornell he helped his team gain national rankings in 1958 and 1959, and he won an Eastern Collegiate Wrestling Association championship in 1959. He also was the Amateur Athletic Union national champion at 160 pounds in 1961 and won a gold medal at the Maccabiah Games in Israel that year. Law school ended his athletic career, but his loyalties to the sport, and the people and intuitions that support it, endure. Friedman went into finance, becoming the CEO of Goldman Sachs, and later he was named Presidential Economic Advisor by President George W. Bush at a moment of grave national crisis, when he was asked to take leadership in developing the first phase of the nation's controversial fiscal emergency program in 2008.

Always a quiet but extremely effective champion of Cornell wrestling, Friedman and his spouse took the lead in creating the university's new wrestling gym, one of the first in the nation devoted solely to that sport. At the same time, they also were major funders of a separate fitness facility open to all athletes and students. Nor was his philanthropic generosity limited to Cornell. Henry Wittenberg mentioned to Phil Oberlander on numerous occasions that he had received generous gifts from Friedman for the CCNY and Yeshiva wrestling teams. While none of this philanthropy has an explicitly Jewish aspect, there is ample evidence in Friedman's public activities—from his background growing up in Rockville Centre his membership in a "Jewish fraternity" while an undergraduate at Cornell, his success at Goldman Sachs in the highly competitive world of Wall Street financial firms, and his loyalties to mentors like Henry Wittenberg—that his particular experiences as a Jewish American coming of age in the 1950s and 1960s continues to shape his worldview and his passions.

Rockville Centre in Long Island's Nassau County is one of a number of classic "bedroom suburbs" of New York City that experienced explosive population growth after World War II. According to the town's own website, it is more than a conveniently located suburb. It is a village of houses of worship.

In addition to St. Agnes Cathedral, the seat of the Roman Catholic Diocese of Rockville Centre, churches of many denominations and synagogues abound. The village is also home to Molloy College and Mercy Medical Center. Doris Kearns Goodwin, one of the community's eminent native daughters, extols its virtues as a place to raise children in her memoir, *Wait Till Next Year*. Kearns writes with great warmth about the community's excellent schools and the fact that so many of the graduates in her time (she is a contemporary of Friedman's) went on to enroll in the best universities and colleges in America. But as the town's official website indicates, it is also a community where religious institutions have a strong part in defining who belongs and where. In the 1950s, as more Jewish families were moving into what had been a predominantly Roman Catholic enclave, competition in sports, among other activities, brought young men and women of differing religious and ethnic backgrounds into new peer relations not defined by the older, parental demarcations of appropriate friendships. Wrestling, in this heterogeneous milieu, was an appealing sport in which boys could test their strength and agility, and they could develop the skills of self-defense. Even smaller athletes could show on the wrestling mat that people of their background had guts and could fight. For these reasons and due to the presence of some outstanding coaches at the high school level, Long Island wrestlers began to be recruited in the 1950s, like boys from Nebraska farm towns and the Pennsylvania coal belt, to top wrestling schools, Cornell among them.

Despite its secular origins and it status as both an Ivy League and a land-grant university, social life at Cornell in the 1950s reflected the racial and religious segregation of the era. African Americans were admitted in small numbers, but Jewish students, especially in engineering and the sciences, but also in quantitative fields like economics, were breaking older quotas and entering by the score. After their freshman year, when all students lived together in newly built cinder block dorms, most male students and a high proportion of the females joined fraternities and sororities. Alternatives in Ithaca's private housing market were far more problematic, and the Greek system entirely dominated the university's social life. Freshmen learned, however, that there were "white" and "Jewish" fraternities and sororities, in the crude terminology of the time. These were not official designations, but they produced an ecology of student residential life at the time that was highly segregated by religion. Friedman, like other Jewish students, eventually joined a Jewish fraternity, Tau Delta Phi, where his fraternity brothers were predominantly boys like him from New York City and its suburban communities. Phil Oberlander, a Canadian two years Friedman's junior, became his steady training partner at

Cornell and, not surprisingly, also joined the same fraternity. At home meets their "brothers" came out in full force to cheer them on, shouting loud acclaim for their victories and taking an explicit but more quiet pride in the fact that they were Jews.

As noted earlier, Friedman wrestled for a short time following his time at Cornell, but after completing a law degree at Columbia, he went into business and eventually found his competitive niche on Wall Street at Goldman Sachs. He joined Goldman Sachs in 1966 and became a partner in 1973. He rose to vice chairman and co-chief operating officer in 1987, and to chairman in 1990. He retired as chairman in 1997. Most recently, he was a senior principal of Marsh & McLennan. Throughout his career he has served on important boards and public commissions, and he and his wife have maintained a staunch loyalty to Cornell, as this passage from a Cornell alumni website attests:

> Friedman and his wife, Barbara Benioff Friedman, also Cornell Class of 1959, have been active and supportive alumni of the university, serving on the Cornell University Council and other key Cornell advisory groups. A long-time university trustee, Barbara Friedman currently serves as co-vice chair of the Cornell Board of Trustees. On campus, both the Friedman Strength and Conditioning Center and the Friedman Wrestling Center have been named in recognition of significant gifts the two have made during campaigns for those facilities

Well before making these highly generous and visible gifts, however, stories circulated about his strength and abilities that made him something of a legend among his wide network of friends and acquaintances. Some of these date back to college. A fraternity brother, Harry Ptechesky, remembers an incident in a Rockville Centre bar, where one of the locals made an antisemitic crack when he and Friedman walked in. Apparently, Friedman threw off his coat and challenged anyone there to say something to his face. When no one did so, the two walked out of the crowded bar; or there was the time Friedman made a bully wince just by grabbing his arm and squeezing; or, best of all, the story of the Henry Paulson challenge. As the legend goes, on a company retreat, Henry Paulson, also a high executive in the company, heard it said that Friedman had been a wrestler in college. A *New York Times* story reported "an oft-told tale of how Paulson, also a former wrestler as well as football player but unaware of Friedman's wrestling prowess, challenged him to a match during a Goldman Sachs executive retreat and was quickly defeated by him."

The symbolism of Friedman grappling with Paulson, regardless of its legendary aspect, hardly needs to be drawn out. Nor does the significance of the

Friedman Fitness Center and the Friedman Wrestling Center. They are new buildings on the Cornell campus, firmly planted among those with names like Sage, Goldywn Smith, Noyes, and Johnson. And one must mention the Uris Library, a gift of the Uris family, also Jews from New York City, to add balance to the cultural symbolism of the important gifts by the Friedman family. Nor is it conceivable that Friedman was directly motivated by his Jewish identity in any of this philanthropy. Instead, what seems particularly the case is that these gifts speak to deeply felt beliefs about the value of sport and physical training that we see running through the lives and examples of each of the four wrestlers considered in this paper.

While each wrestler strongly felt his Jewish identity, their Jewish fans invariably made them champions of a far larger cause. The responsibility for representing his people fell with most weight on Fred Oberlander, who wrestled in Europe at a time when Jewish athletes had to compete as Jews if they wanted to gain athletic renown at all. After World War II, when American Jewish wrestlers participated in university and nationally sponsored teams, few of their Jewish peers could resist imagining them grappling with specters of the Holocaust, fighting against images of the weak or defenseless Jew. Strong and vigorous men, they found pleasure in a sport they loved and excelled at, and they did not make public statements about the larger significance of their successes. The political messages in their victories would be for others to decipher. Each athlete was so touched by his wrestling experience that a large part of life became devoted to the democracy of sport, to the art and science of wrestling, to the meritocracy of sweat and strain, and to coaching others as a path to self-knowledge. One could argue that Fred Oberlander and his generation of pioneering Jewish athletes on the international scene made it possible for those who came after them to compete for their nations rather than for the Jewish people. It is also true that the personal and professional lives of these elite wrestlers became closely intertwined largely because of their Jewish backgrounds and that each in his own way has contributed to the development of what it means to be a Jewish athlete in the contemporary world.

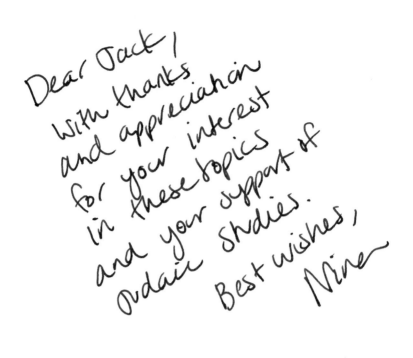

Dear Jack,
With thanks
and appreciation
for your interest
in these topics
and your support of
Ordain Studies.
    Best wishes,
        Nina

Sporting a Nation:
The Origins of Athleticism in Modern Israel

Nina S. Spiegel

Annually, in celebration of Israel's Independence Day, a poster is selected to symbolize the country. The widely disseminated choice addresses different themes and topics each year. In 2004, the Independence Day poster in honor of Israel's fifty-sixth year of statehood was dedicated to sports with the byline: "Israel salutes the competitive and recreational sports." Filled with bright colors, the images include Olympic rings, soccer balls, a gymnast or dancer, and sailboats alongside national symbols such as flags and the country's emblem.

It is not surprising that a twenty-first-century Independence Day poster was devoted entirely to sports, as athletic activities and physical prowess hold an important place in contemporary Israeli society. Sports are a popular pastime; the country has produced prominent athletes and established a variety of sports associations. Israelis regularly participate in the Olympic Games, and the country houses the Wingate Institute for Physical Education and Sports, an educational, academic, and athletic center established in 1957. In addition, every four years, Israel hosts the Maccabiah Games or "Jewish Olympics," an international sports competition drawing Jewish participants from around the world.

Physical fitness and agility are also promoted in a variety of other arenas. Hiking around the country is both an important pastime and a component of the educational experience.[1] Dance activities are also prevalent. For a small nation, Israel possesses numerous theatrical dance companies and independent choreographers. Israeli folk dance is likewise a popular activity; Israelis and international visitors alike flock to an annual folk dance festival in the northern development town of Karmiel. In addition, Israeli folk dance events take place around the country every night of the week, and this form is taught in schools and performed at national events and celebrations.

The significant value placed on athletic ability in contemporary Israeli society originated before the establishment of the State. Consolidated during the British Mandate in Palestine, this goal was integrally connected to the nation-building process. From their conquest in 1917 during World War I, until the establishment of the State of Israel in 1948, the British controlled the territory of Palestine, ultimately under a Mandate granted by the newly formed League of Nations; it was ratified in 1922.

Jews immigrating to Palestine in these years, referring to their community as the *Yishuv* [settlement], aimed to build a new life and to create a model of a new Jewish society. Zionist theory, broadly defined, called for the creation of a Jewish homeland in the ancient land of Israel. While there were several different competing strains of this theory within *Yishuv* society, a central element of Zionist theory that divergent Zionist groups shared was the rejection of Jewish life in the Diaspora. Jews in Palestine sought to create a "new Jew," seeking to transform Jews in every way—how they looked, acted, thought, and spoke. All agreed on the need to build a "new Jew" in a "new Jewish body." The lifestyle and image of Diaspora Jews, no matter their origin, was to be overturned, a component of Zionist thought referred to as *shelilat ha-gola* [negation of the Diaspora].

Viewing Diaspora Jewry as passive and weak, Jews in Palestine rejected not only Jewish life in the Diaspora, but also images of the Diaspora Jewish body. Although Jews were actively involved in sports activities in Europe at the time, Zionists internalized negative stereotypes of Jews in European society that depicted Jewish men, in particular, as weak and emasculated.[2] Considering the Diaspora Jewish body as shackled, helpless, and effeminate, Zionists aimed to create a physique that was the opposite, seeking to, in Judith Butler's terms, "perform" a male identity.[3] This emphasis on masculinity was not only part of the gymnastics groups in Europe, but also of the Jewish and later Zionist youth movements in Europe and Palestine.[4]

The idea of recreating the Jewish body originated from European circles and was espoused in particular by the ideologist Max Nordau. In 1898 at the Second Zionist Congress in Basel, Nordau called for the creation of a "Muscular Jewry." In order for Jews to disprove the image of being weak and feminized and to refashion themselves, he claimed that they needed to become physically strong, a quality that was associated with, and promoted, a masculine image. These notions had their origin in the German Physical Culture Movement [*Turnen* or *Körperkultur*] that began in the early nineteenth century and placed an emphasis on the connection between the body and the mind. A healthy body, in this view, was intimately linked to a healthy spirit.[5]

Physical activities were thus integrally connected to the national project. In the early twentieth century as Zionism was developing, Jewish sports presentations became a component of the Zionist Congresses held in Europe. Gymnastics displays in particular were quite popular, with performances commencing in 1903, when the Jewish Gymnastics Federation was established. At the Sixth Zionist Congress in Basel that year, there was an international "Jewish Gymnastics Day."[6] As Todd Presner describes, "In front of the delegates and distinguished guests at the Sixth Zionist Congress, including Nordau, Herzl, Bodenheimer, and Mandelstamm, several dozen young Jews performed various gymnastics feats 'with agility' and 'ease,' according to the report published in *Die Judische Turnzeitung*."[7]

In Palestine, a dynamic physical culture movement developed with the aim of fostering a "new Jewish body." Sports and dance served this goal directly, and physical activities were nurtured and encouraged; it was a fervent period in both areas. While the sports and dance arenas developed separately, there was also fluidity between them because they were both working toward the same national goal of the cultivation of the physique.

Significant developments in the sports arena in the Jewish community in Palestine in this era included the first *Eretz Yisrael* [land of Israel] sports day in Jerusalem in 1923; the foundation of Hapoel, the workers' sports association, in 1925; the formation of the Physical Education Teachers Association in 1927; the first and second congress of Hapoel in 1928 and 1930, respectively; the first Maccabiah Games and the third Hapoel Congress, both in 1932; the second Maccabiah Games and the Fourth Hapoel Congress in 1935; the formation of the Association of Private Teachers for Physical Culture in Palestine in Tel Aviv in 1938; and the foundation of Elitzur, the religious sports association, in 1939.[8]

Important developments in dance also characterized this era. Both theatrical and folk dance forms were cultivated during the Mandate. The National Dance Competition was held in Tel Aviv in 1937, designed to solidify a space for theatrical dance, and the Dalia Dance Festivals in the 1940s at Kibbutz Dalia were created to consolidate an Israeli folk dance form.[9] In 1929 and 1931, two folk dance festivals took place at Ben Shemen, a youth village, organized by Gurit Kadman, considered the "mother" of Israeli folk dance and the organizer of the Dalia Dance Festivals as well. The arrival of a prominent modern dancer named Gertrud Kraus, from Vienna in 1935, alongside additional dancers and choreographers escaping Germany in the 1930s, was also influential, and several dance studios were established in these years.[10] Further important institutional developments took place in folk dance, particularly by the 1940s, such as Gurit Kadman's organization of the first leadership course for folk dance teachers in Tel Aviv in 1945.

Although they developed separately, the arenas of dance and sports were at the same time interconnected. A number of dance instructors were deeply involved in the foundation of the Association for Private Physical Teachers.

Indeed, many concert dancers and dance activists served as physical education teachers in the schools. As of 1935, concert dancers such as Yehudit Ornstein and Yardena Cohen, as well as dance teacher and organizer Gurit Kadman, were enrolled in the Physical Education Teachers Association. They, along with other dancers and educators, participated actively in the physical education activities of the time. Furthermore, in 1945, Kadman taught Israeli folk dances at the course for physical education teachers, thereby incorporating folk dance into the physical education curriculum.

In both the sports and dance arenas, the aim of cultivating a strong and upright body played a central role as members of the *Yishuv* sought to prove to themselves and the world that Jews could indeed be tough and thereby were capable of building a nation. While there was a multitude of physical activity in this era, this analysis focuses on two examples: from the sports arena, the first Maccabiah Games in 1932; and from the folk dance domain, the prevalence of the hora dance. Both of these illustrations became national symbols and have continued to possess a symbolic effect in the State through contemporary times.

The first Maccabiah Games, a nine-day international athletic competition and sports festival, were held in Tel Aviv in March 1932. The Games were organized by the Maccabi sports association, an international organization whose center was in Berlin with branches throughout Europe, Palestine, and the United States. Modeled after the modern Olympic Games, the Maccabiah included the usual diversity of Olympic sports competitions for men and women. Jewish athletes from approximately twenty-seven nations participated in the Games, designed to show off the achievements of Jewish life in Palestine, to foster Jewish sports activity, and to bring Jewish athletes to the country in the hopes that they would remain as permanent residents. The Games included the following competitions for men and women: track and field, gymnastics, hockey, track races, soccer, basketball, tennis, rugby, handball, wrestling, fencing, indoor events, swimming (in Haifa),[11] and boxing (in Haifa).

The first Maccabiah was viewed as a great achievement and became a model for subsequent sports competitions. With 2009 marking the eighteenth Maccabiah, the Games have endured in contemporary Israeli society.

The hora, a Rumanian peasant dance brought to Palestine by Jewish immigrants, was considered to be the emerging national dance already by the 1930s. While European Jews arrived with many dances, including the krakoviak and the polka from Poland and the tcherkessia from Russia, the hora quickly became the most popular. It was danced in a variety of locations and events: at festivals throughout the country, in urban environments, and, most legendary in the lore of the time, in the *kibbutzim*, the collective agricultural settlements. Numerous accounts from the era describe festive hora dancing in the *kibbutzim* at night, after long days of work in the fields.[12]

The hora was also integrated into the sports arena: it was prevalent in the activities and publications of the sports associations as well as at the first Maccabiah Games. Evening hora dancing in the streets added to the festive atmosphere at the first Maccabiah and was also a celebration of the successful completion of the Games.[13]

In addition, in films and advertisements of this period, the hora was viewed as an emblem of Jewish life in Palestine. It remains a force in contemporary Israeli folk dance as well as in national and religious celebrations, both in Israel and in Jewish communities around the world. The hora endures as a symbol for Israeli society.

Both the Maccabiah Games and the hora promoted an image of a tough Jewish body. The first Maccabiah Games were viewed as a testimony to the health and virility of the Jews in Palestine. The athletic bodies were young, strong, straight, and flexible, standing in direct contrast to impressions of the European Jewish physique. A journalist in the *Palestine Bulletin* described the reaction of English tourists to the "new Jewish body" as represented in the closing display: "Behind me sat a group of English tourists. They were as surprised at everything they saw. What struck them most was the splendid health and physique of the Palestinian Maccabees. 'Look!' said Tourist A to Tourist B, as thousands of young Maccabees filed by, 'How healthy they look! Every one of them.'"[14]

The strength and physicality of the "new Jew" were also represented in posters and pamphlets associated with the Games. While women participated actively in the first Maccabiah, only men were featured in advertisements and posters. Women's involvement was not represented in these venues in order to promote a male, macho, virile image. Published in October 1931, the booklet titled *Haitztadion* [The Stadium] aimed to prepare the *Yishuv* for the upcoming event, containing information about the impending Maccabiah as well as updates on different sports in Palestine. The front cover featured a sketch of a man running forward, with his head raised high. This figure was wearing only shorts and sneakers in order to emphasize his muscular body. His right arm was crossed in front of his body to emphasize the upward gaze. The image, which evoked pride, epitomized the desired new Jewish character.[15]

These notions were also featured in a 1934 advertisement in the aftermath of the first Maccabiah. Appearing in preparation for the second Maccabiah in 1935, the advertisement presented a picture of a Maccabi athlete holding up a car.[16] The figure was male, strong, and muscular; the athlete portrayed attributes akin to Superman as he was capable of lifting the vehicle. Dressed in shorts and a tank top with a Jewish star in the middle, he donned the typical outfit of a Maccabi athlete. His head was raised high, exhibiting his pride.

The depiction of the strong Maccabi athlete portrayed as the herald of an emerging nation also appeared in a variety of forms beyond visual images. For instance, the Hebrew writer Avigdor Hameiri wrote a song for the event titled, "Hymn for the Maccabees," with the following refrain:

> Maccabi, Maccabi
> Strengthen your muscles and make the blood courageous!
> Maccabi, Maccabi
> Be the leader for the glory of the nation![17]

This chorus represented the notion that the health of the nation was dependent upon the cultivation of the body. Through lyrics, it advocated the same message as the visual representations.

As with the Maccabiah Games, the hora dance also promoted and represented a strong and tough image. This circle dance featured fast movements, including jumping and running steps. Typically danced by a large number of people, it was often performed in concentric circles. With men and women dancing the same movements side by side and locking their arms in a tight embrace shoulder to shoulder, the hora promoted an ideal of gender equality in the *Yishuv*. Gurit Kadman advocated this value in the 1940s: "this Horra is exactly suited to the social mood of the pioneers with their strong feelings about equal rights for all men and women alike."[18] Although gender equality was not achieved in this era, the dance personified this ideological objective.[19]

Standing in direct contrast to impressions of a weak and passive European Jew, the dancing bodies performing the hora were upright, vigorous, and proud. Even though both men and women danced the hora, the gender identity performed in the dance was distinctively masculine: a central feature of the hora was that it both felt and appeared macho and virile. In her 1938 article titled "Folk Dance," Kadman reflected on the reasons and the process through which the hora was becoming a national dance:

> And the matter is strange: what is our general dance here today. . . .
> A Rumanian village dance: hora! It's very strange and very understandable! A people that returns to its land and to nature—needs an unproblematic dance, simple, strong, healthy. There isn't anything like this among the original Jewish Diaspora dances. They took from the villagers of a different nation, and this foreign dance was turned into an expression—not original, but true--of our existence. It is certain that this dance has changed with us,it acclimated, and got used to our character and to our temperament and to the character of the land.[20]

By emphasizing the hora's robust and vigorous qualities, Kadman directly linked the importance placed on toughness in the *Yishuv* to the hora's attainment of a central role in the emerging nation.

In addition to its active prevalence in a variety of locations and settings in the *Yishuv*, the hora also acquired a symbolic standing in this era. Appearing in print media of the time, for instance, the hora's tough qualities were represented in a cartoon in the cultural weekly *Tesha Ba'erev* in November 1937.[21] The sketch commences with the following statement: "When tourists come to our country, they immediately request to see how we dance the 'hora' here." In the illustration in the first panel, the tourists are portrayed calmly watching the people dancing happily and pleasantly together. By the second section, the tourists become surprised as the hora becomes more fierce and stormy. In the third panel, the tourists are injured and running away as the hora has become somewhat violent even: it has turned into something of a brawl. On the one hand, this cartoon comments on the character of *Yishuv* society, implying— and critiquing—that it is aggressive and argumentative. The cartoonist may have had this concept in mind, but on another level, the cartoon emphasizes the tough and strong quality of the hora and the ways in which that characteristic was translated into the symbolic realm of the *Yishuv*.

Both the hora and the Maccabiah Games in this era represent the process of reimagining the Jewish physique—and promoting its strength. With the shared goal of fashioning and displaying a "new Jewish body," they demonstrate the intersection and nexus of the sports and dance arenas. As the 2004 Israeli Independence Day poster vividly encapsulates in a visual format, this commitment to cultivating the physique has maintained its place into the contemporary era in Israeli society.

NOTES

[1] For a discussion of the role of *tiyulim* [hikes] in contemporary Israeli society, see Orit Ben-David, "Tiyul (Hike) as an Act of Consecration of Space," in *Space and Place in Contemporary Israeli Discourse and Experience* (ed. E. Ben-Ari and Y. Bilu; Albany: State University of New York Press, 1997); and Tamar Katriel, "Trips and Hiking as Secular Rituals in Israeli Culture," *Jewish Folklore and Ethnology Review* 17 (1995): 6-13.

[2] Sander Gilman, *The Jew's Body* (New York: Routledge Press, 1991). For a discussion of the relationship between Jews and sports in Europe, see, for instance, Michael Brenner and Gideon Reuveni, eds., *Emancipation Through Muscles: Jews and Sports in Europe* (Lincoln: University of Nebraska Press 2006).

[3] Judith Butler, "Performative Acts and Gender Constitution: An Essay in Phenomenology and Feminist Theory," in *Performing Feminisms: Feminist Critical Theory and Theatre* (ed. Sue-Ellen Case; Baltimore: Johns Hopkins University Press, 1990), 270-82.

[4] Tamar Mayer, "From Zero to Hero: Masculinity in Jewish Nationalism," in *Israeli Women's Studies: A Reader* (ed. Esther Fuchs; New Brunswick: Rutgers University Press, 2005), 99.

[5] Michael Krüger, "Body Culture and Nation Building: The History of Gymnastics in Germany in the Period of its Foundation as a Nation-State," *The International Journal of the History of Sport* 13 (December 1996); Todd Samuel Presner, *Muscle Judaism: The Jewish Body and the Politics of Regeneration* (New York: Routledge, 2007); Michael Stanislawski, *Zionism and the Fin de Siècle: Cosmpolitanism and Nationalism from Nordau to Jabotinsky* (Berkeley: University of California Press, 2001).

[6] Presner, *Muscle Judaism*, 122.

[7] Ibid. (JTZ, 1903, no. 11:89).

[8] For a description of the politicization of sports in the *Yishuv*, see Anat Helman, "Zionism, Politics, Hedonism: Sports in Interwar Tel Aviv," in *Jews, Sports, and the Rites of Citizenship* (ed. J. Kugelmass; Urbana: University of Illinois Press, 2007); and Haim Kaufman, "Jewish Sports in the Diaspora, Yishuv, and Israel: Between Nationalism and Politics," *Israel Studies* 10.2 (Summer 2005): 147-67.

[9] Nina S. Spiegel, "Cultural Production in Tel Aviv: Yardena Cohen and the National Dance Competition of 1937," in *Seeing Israeli and Jewish Dance* (ed. J.B. Ingber; Detroit: Wayne State University Press, 2011); Nina S. Spiegel, "New Israeli Rituals: Inventing a Folk Dance Tradition," in *Jewish Cultural Studies* (ed. S. J. Bronner; Oxford: Littman Library of Jewish Civilization 2011).

[10] Ruth Eshel, "Concert Dance in Israel," *Dance Research Journal* 35 (2003): 61-80; Ruth Eshel, *Lirkod Im Ha-halom: Reshit ha-mahol ha-omanuti be-Erets Yisrael 1920-1964* [Dancing with the Dream: The Development of Artistic Dance in Israel,1920-1964] (Tel Aviv: Dance Library of Israel, 1991); Anat Helman, *Young Tel Aviv: A Tale of Two Cities* (Waltham: Brandeis University Press, 2010), 108-09.

[11] A pool had not yet been built in Haifa. It was built for the Second Maccabiah in 1935.

[12] See, for instance, Oz Almog, *The Sabra: The Creation of the New Jew* (trans. Haim Watzman; Berkeley: University of California Press, 2000); and Zvi Friedhaber, *Hava Netze B'meholot: Lekorot Rikudei Am B'Yisrael* (Tel Aviv: Mercaz Letarbut u-le'hinuh, Histadrut, 1994).

[13] *Davar* (1 April 1932): 5.

[14] *Palestine Bulletin* (3 April 1932): 3.

[15] *Haitztadion*, October 1931. Wingate Institute 4.01/30.

[16] Jewish National and University Library, V1985/3.

[17] Avigdor Hameiri, "Hymn of the Maccabees," *First Maccabiah Song Book*. Wingate Institute 4.01/29.

[18] Gurit Kadman, *Horra*. Palestine Folk Dance Series No. 4 recorded by Gert Kaufmann (Gurit Kadman's name before she changed it), Tel Aviv. Wingate Institute, 1.17/4.

[19] See, for instance, Deborah Bernstein, *Pioneers and Homemakers: Jewish Women in Pre-State Israel* (Albany: State University of New York, 1992); and Esther Fuchs, ed., *Israeli Women's Studies: A Reader* (New Brunswick: Rutgers University Press, 2005).

[20] *Omer* (5 August 1938): 4.

[21] *Tesha Ba'erev* (4 November 1937): 15.

Gyms and the Academy: Professional and Personal Reflections on Stepping Up to the Scholarly Plate

Jeffrey S. Gurock

The serious study of the Jewish sports experience in the United States had great difficulties getting out of its starting blocks. Historiographical traditions of apologetics and self-congratulation weighed down scholarly considerations of the Jews in the American gym. Emblematic of why Jews wrote so defensively about their comrades of strong arms and legs, a predominant trend that had to be surmounted, was Harold U. Ribalow's implicit explanation of what was behind his chronicle, *The Jew in American Sports,* composed in 1948. Clearly as late as the post-World War II period, Jews, in his view, had something to prove to those around them about their manliness–only male athletes were profiled–Americanization, and ultimately their patriotism. "When a Jewish fighter wins a title," he observed, "it means to sports fans that Jews can fight. They don't need lengthy, scientific treatises to show that Jews have guts; they don't need long histories revealing that Jews have an admirable war record to prove it." Similarly, when sports fans see "a Jewish baseball catcher stand up to flying spikes . . . they know that it is a lie to call Jews cowards."[1]

Interestingly, in a subsequent edition, Ribalow, intent on continuing to put only the Jews' best sneakered foot forward, cagily decided to remove an interview with legendary City College of New York (CCNY) basketball coach Nat Holman from the volume. He was "omitted because of the tragically unsavory conclusion of his glorious coaching career." Ribalow's editorial discomfit arose out of the infamous 1951 point-shaving scandal that rocked Holman's college and implicated several of his Jewish and African American star athletes. Ribalow was quick to proclaim that "no stigma attached to Holman personally" and the debacle did not end the coach's career, even if CCNY's basketball heyday came to a crashing conclusion. Still, the author allowed—and the apologetic mode remained apparent—that "it became impossible to judge fairly the teams under his command when a basketball scandal broke and revealed that some of his finest players succumbed to gamblers."[2]

Other books had a more benign, celebratory mission. For example, Robert Slater's *Great Jews in Sports,* the quintessential bar-/bat-mitzvah gift that first appeared in 1983, was simply "designed to entertain and enlighten by telling some of the most heartwarming and fascinating stories of the best

Jewish athletes ever." It profiled mostly American men and women players, coaches, announcers, and team and league executives. By his time, endemic Jewish defensiveness in an accepting America was largely a problem of the past. There are hints in the work that Slater understood how Jewish sports history could be taken to a higher level. He noted in passing that star performers were often "rebels from the traditional Jewish pursuits," that these athlete's activities "reflect the change in the social and economic roles played by Jews in society in general," and that "some Jewish sports stars have been caught up in the history of their times," including the challenges of antisemitism. But he did not address comprehensively these complex and intriguing historical dilemmas and difficulties. Rather, Slater retained the hope, from edition to edition, as *Great Jews in Sports* continued to sell strongly in updated versions, that his work will "bring joy and satisfaction" to his readers.[3]

In 2001, the American Jewish Historical Society inaugurated a digital "Jews in Sports" archive to relate "the largely underappreciated story of Jewish athletes, from the famous to the unknown," recording "the proud legacy of Jewish athletes, and how each one's accomplishments in the world of sports reflected on his or her particular society and era." Here, beyond a chronicling impulse, lay a communal continuity concern. The belief was that in this era of extensive disaffection from Judaism in America, if Jewish youngsters would become aware of their sports heroes, it would lead to feeling a greater sense of pride in their ancestral background. This rationale was not explicitly noted in the Society's sports group mission statements, but was frequently articulated to me as I then served as associate editor of *American Jewish History,* its scholarly academic journal. Subsequently, in 2008, when I returned to the Society's boardroom for a second term as chair of its Academic Council, I heard comparable arguments even if the online archive was no longer part of its website. To give them their sympathetic due, their motivations were laudable. But their efforts did not advance the serious study of Jews, Judaism, and sports in America.[4]

In many ways these tendencies toward defensiveness, celebration, and even the quest for affirming Jewish identity through history paralleled both the long-term struggles of American Jewish historiography in general to reach academic respectability and its continuing challenges to retain its hardearned place within the world of scholarship. Actually, when Ribalow wrote his apologetic volume, the field was just beginning to free itself from threequarters of a century of writing that incessantly hallowed American Jewish military heroes and extolled beyond proportion Jewish contributions to the growth of America. These early, passionate writers upheld a communal agenda that German American Jewish leader Oscar S. Straus had first set late in the nineteenth century. When this defender of Jewish status in America engaged a historian to prove Columbus' Jewish ancestry—to publicly emphasize how his group "founded" the New World—Straus argued that if the explorer and key members of his crew were Jews and coreligionists had backed the voyage, "this fact would be an answer for all time to come to antisemitic tendencies in this country." Such sorts of writing were sure to stay clear of even hints of criticism of poor Jewish behavior on these shores while ignoring what would intrigue dispassionate scholars most: the nuances of the social processes that Jewish newcomers faced in adjusting to free American environments.[5]

Straus also more than hinted at the internal value of telling the American Jewish saga toward securing future Jewish identification. In 1908, in commemorating the Society's first quarter century of patriotic writing—a full three quarters of a century before its sports group set off on its quixotic identity quests—Straus averred that "I have never met a Jew who was familiar with the history of his people, who ever was ashamed of being a Jew. It is only those," he continued, "who are not acquainted with the heroic history . . . it is only those whose minds are closed to that history, who *apologize* [emphasis mine] for Judaism." For him, personal embarrassment about Jewish identity, and not literary defensiveness, defined unwarranted apologetics.[6]

American Jewish historiography moved beyond Straus' motives in the late 1940s to early 1950s. Some credit the sparks of interest generated by the communal commemoration of the tercentenary of Jewish life on the North American continent as spurring a new sophisticated style of writing. I would prefer to acknowledge the impact the imprimaturs given by the great Jewish historian Salo W. Baron and the renowned American immigration scholar Oscar Handlin—not to mention the yeoman work of Jacob Rader Marcus, who dug up so much of the basic source material requisite for the field—as having made all of the difference. Over the succeeding two generations (1950s-1990s), the discipline did much to actualize a vision that was only dreamed of when Straus and his allies set the tone of writing. Back in the first decade of the last century, Dr. Cyrus Adler, a longtime president of the Society, took off time from his major scholarly pursuits and his myriad of communal occupations to think imaginatively of an academic future for American Jewish historical writing. (Adler was a distinguished Orientalist, a key figure in the Jewish Publication Society and the American Jewish Committee, and would soon head up the Jewish Theological Seminary and Dropsie College to name only a few of his large-scale involvements.) He envisioned a time when "the professional student" would be enticed to become "engaged in the study of our history" and perhaps ultimately teach within an American university or, at least, offer a systematic course of lectures. Adler likewise surmised that if the field became properly sophisticated, "scientifically-trained students" in other fields—like statisticians and economists—would provide their expertise "since so much of the history of the people is bound up with economic science."[7]

However, while the field of American Jewish history in the 1950s through 1990s did achieve many of Adler's dreams, and, of course, Baron's and Handlin's goals, the study of American Jewry and sports remained largely outside the lines. Even as insightful social historians argued that it is imperative to describe how Jews learned to speak, dress, eat, act, and think as Americans to fully interpret their adjustment to a new society, little consideration was given to how they came to play or recreate like those around them and what that new sports identity meant to community life.

To be sure, Moses Rischin, one of the most illustrious historians of that generation, who set an agenda for what "valuable" works had to inform the field, noted in 1954 the importance of the "study of the transformation of the 'pale ghetto Jew' into the sportsman, athlete, 'sport,' and genuine sports enthusiast." He also asked the trenchant question of "how closely did the 'golden age' of American sports coincide with the Maccabean [sic] emphasis in immigrant life." And in his classic work on New York Jewish history, *The Promised City*, Rischin paused three times to enumerate athleticism's impact on Lower East Side life. Settlement House physical fitness programs that were "slighted by serious youngsters" were promoted by downtown settlement houses. In 1909, the Socialist Yiddish daily, *The Forward*, printed a diagram of the Polo Grounds' baseball diamond as its renowned editor Abraham Cahan attempted to bridge cultural gaps between generations. And the Yiddish nationalist press trumpeted heroic Jewish boxers as modern day Gideons and Samsons. Still notwithstanding his and a few others' salutes to sports, as scholars like Rischin attained their academic majorities, the athletic context remained largely unexplored.[8]

Comprehensive consideration of American Jewry and sports long remained out of bounds because of a palpable sense among American Jewish historians—particularly younger, untenured members of academic faculties—that work in their field, for all of its advances, had yet to garner the unqualified respect of scholars in the cognate fields of American and Jewish history. One of the leading contemporary American Jewish historians has recalled that when he contemplated work in the field in the 1970s, "a scholar at a distinguished rabbinical seminary . . . was absolutely appalled" at his career choice. For this critic, American Jewish history could be simply summarized as "Jews come to America, they abandoned their faith, they began to live like *goyim* [Gentiles], and after a generation or two they intermarried and disappeared." His advice was "don't waste your time. Go and study Talmud." I can relate that at approximately that same time the word around Columbia University, where I earned my doctoral degree, was that the chief doyen of the department had uncharitably characterized a serious study of outer-borough New York Jewish social life as an examination of "breweries in Brooklyn." To the extent that this dismissive attitude toward the entire field was regnant, it had a chilling impact on anyone considering writing on a topic that seemingly was déclassé as American Jews and sports.[9]

While American Jewish historians remained on the sidelines, cadres of intrepid social historians made the case for the value of sports historiography overcoming academic prejudices. Actually, the beginnings of serious sports study of athleticism date back to the 1950s at the same that works on Jews were starting to come of age. Still, the founding of the North American Society for Sport History was a turning point. At that society's first convention in 1973, David Q. Voigt of Albright College strongly asserted that "sporting history [had] come into its own as part of a burgeoning social history movement." Sounding, as it were, like a Baron, Handlin, or Marcus talked about their own field, he declared in no uncertain terms that "the growing recognition of sports, along with other ignored areas of human behavior, is ending a long era of snobbery characterized by a fallacious attitude on the part of those historians who held politics, economics, and intellectual pursuits to be the only proper avenues for historical inquiry." Believing that "the primary and secondary materials on sports like baseball offer a rich vein for exploitation by students that point to excellent insights into American culture," he challenged "faint-hearted students" to be fearless in pursuing their academic interests and to not "steal away silently to labor at one of the 'proper' subjects of history." Voigt's passionate address was considered "to be of such caliber" by inspired attendees that it was published as the lead article in the inaugural edition of the *Journal of Sport History* that appeared in the spring of 1974. In subsequent issues, those devoted to sports history showed their gumption as they explored more than just activities on the North American continent, but looked at athletics' impact upon civilizations worldwide and throughout history. However, in the first decade of its publication, the American Jewish sporting experience received very little attention.[10]

Given short shrift, when noted, the references in the *Journal of Sport History* were tangential points hardly addressing Jewish issues. For example, a study of a mid-late-nineteenth-century sprint champion suggested that he "may be descended from Myer Myers," a colonial Jewish silversmith from New York. But no other ethnic or religious connection in that runner's biography was discussed. In writing about the genres of groups that were invited in and those who were excluded from metropolitan area athletic clubs from the end of the Civil War until World War I, the focuses were on class discrimination, and to a lesser extent on gender restrictions. As evidence, a leader of the Metropolitan Athletic Club is quoted as allowing that "I have no aspersions to cast on men who work for a living with their hands, but they are not exactly desirable members for a club which wants to establish itself on the plane of social clubdom." Similarly, a policy of the University Athletic Club was analyzed that required a college or university degree of all applicants. In passing, the study indicated that in the 1890s, several new "*exclusive* [emphasis mine] athletic clubs patterned after the old model were formed. The most notable was the City Athletic Club. Although not limited to those of the Jewish faith, a large portion of the membership was Jewish. Wealthy families included the Baruch, Gimbel, Guggenheim, Knopf and Rothschild family." The emphasis there was on how Jewish elites emulated the class consciousness of Gentile associations. There is no discussion of the old clubs' possible religious discriminatory clauses that caused Jews to build their own sports groups—an important Jewish theme. The only essay in that journal's first decade where Jews were front and center was a 1976 contribution on "issues of racism," which described the battles within American circles and between Jewish defense organizations and the United States Olympic Committee over whether to boycott the 1936 Olympic Games in Nazi Berlin.[11]

The lack of interest in the Jewish story among serious sports scholars went beyond the journal. When ten years into that society and its publication's tenure Melvin Adelman surveyed the state of that field's "progress," he could enumerate, in a paragraph identifying emerging studies of immigrants and sports, only four that dealt with Jews. Only two of the four were readily identifiable as such by their titles. The most intriguing piece was an examination of the impact that in 1926 a visiting Austrian all-Jewish soccer team, Hakoah of Vienna, made upon New York Jews, providing this American Jewish community "with a hitherto unknown sense of pride and self-esteem." The other very impressive article, albeit of the genre where the Jewish story was subsumed under immigrant sports historiography, was Steven A. Riess' work on race and ethnicity in American baseball in the early twentieth century. He argued that during the Progressive era, newcomers from Eastern Europe neither participated in professional baseball nor attended the games of the national pastime even if the rhetoric of the times bespoke a sense that the game attracted folks from all backgrounds.[12]

In the years that followed, however, Riess would become far more explicit in his interest in Jews and athletics, and perhaps became the central figure in the integration of sports and American Jewish history. Riess came initially to the story of American athleticism out of his examination of Progressive attempts to control immigrant behavior. He has been credited with being "the first American historian to apply the new literature on social control to the study of sports."[13] Jews were obviously part of the political and cultural mix that intrigued him. Emerging as a central figure among scholarly writers on sports with his selection in 1985 as the editor of *Journal of Sport History*, he was, especially for Professor Marc Lee Raphael, who was my senior colleague as editor of *American Jewish History*, the now highly-regarded organ of the American Jewish Historical Society, the ideal person to bring sports and American Jewish scholars into communication with each other.

As guest editor in 1985 of our journal's first foray into the world of scholarship of American athleticism, Riess brought across the field a distinguished lineup of sports historians to speak directly to Jewish issues. He would return ten years later for a complementary issue. Many of the essays from the 1985 effort would be republished in 1998 as *Sports and the American Jew* by Syracuse University Press.[14]

It remained for Peter Levine, in 1992, to synthesize the growing body of materials on American Jews and sports into *Ellis Island to Ebbets Field: Sport and the American Jewish Experience,* the first scholarly monograph on the subject. Like Riess, whom he assisted in conceptualizing the *American Jewish History* issues, Levine, too, came to the sports discipline out of the study of the Progressive movement as he understood and wrote about how social reformers viewed sports "as a way of controlling certain tendencies that threatened to undermine the virtues and values of the American republic." Eventually, he directed his wide focus on the immigrant Jewish experience.[15]

While all of this academic activity was going on, I remained on the sidelines. Several years ago, I reflected publicly on my sedentary stance and admitted to the "faint-heartedness" that Voigt critiqued, which had characterized my non-productivity as I made my way as an American Jewish historian through the obstacle courses of tenure and promotion. Concerned with "being tarred through being associated with such a low brow subject as sports" that "would marginalize me in the academic marketplace," I put work on hold that was ironically not only "close to my heart," but that could also elevate sports historiography while further contextualizing my home field.[16]

When I eventually found the moment to enter the lists—and I am grateful that sports historians have accepted me as their colleagues—one of the
sensitivities that I brought to my contribution was impressed upon me by a
distinguished African American historian. While a graduate student, thinking
ahead toward the possibility of writing a dissertation on black-Jewish relations—that idea eventually morphed into my first book *When Harlem was
Jewish, 1870-1930*—I took classes with the late Professor Nathan I. Huggins,
then at Columbia University, author of the award-winning cultural history
Harlem Renaissance. One of Huggins' oft-repeated themes in his classes about
his group's experience was that for minorities in America, wars and sports
were "community-defining" situations. The degree to which blacks were
allowed to fight for America as well as whether they were permitted to uphold
a local or national club's sports standards were effective gauges of acceptance
levels in majority white society. Fittingly and not surprisingly, Huggins had
in mind the day in April 1947 when Jackie Robinson broke the color barrier
in Major League Baseball, our national pastime, as a turning point moment
in American history. He and other historians have posited that Robinson's
sports admission—two years before President Truman fully desegregated the
nation's armed forces—constituted the beginning of the modern civil rights
movement. Princeton's Eric F. Goldman heartily concurred as he characterized
the second baseman as "this revolutionist in a baseball suit . . . the flashing
symbol of an era in the national life when . . . the social and economic walls
were coming tumbling down."[17]

Huggins' thesis and Goldman's assertion resonated with me as a Jewish
historian, and I saw its applicability to the experience that I chose to study.
Although Jews in America never faced the levels of prejudice and discrimination that African Americans endured, there were times historically where
exclusion from, or pressures on, Jews from within the playing realm underscored their larger marginality. Such was the case with two iconic moments
involving two legendary American Jewish athletes in the 1930s—episodes that
attracted much scholarly and popular attention, but which I believed still war-
ranted reconsideration.

In 1934, Hank Greenberg, the star first baseman for the Detroit Tigers,
was the most outstanding American Jewish athlete of the time. In the midst of
a heated pennant race against the New York Yankees, the question arose—and
became a point of public debate—over whether he would play for his home
team on or absent himself during the approaching Jewish High Holidays of
late September. Then, as now, the race for the league title and Judaism's holiest days coincided or were in conflict. Although hardly an observant Jew,

Greenberg sensed that he should not violate a basic faith tradition. But his owner and his manager pressured him to play. Field boss Mickey Cochrane and Tigers owners Frank and Charles Nevins asserted that he had nothing less than a "civic duty" to his community to play—not the Jewish community, but the secular sports community. The metaphor of sports defining community is readily apparent here as was the opinion of local Rabbi Leo Franklin. While not instructing Greenberg as to what road to take, this Reform rabbi contextualized his advice in community-directed terms. He suggested that "it might be argued quite consistently, that his taking part in the game would mean something not only to himself but to his fellow players, and in fact at this time, to the community of Detroit." Greenberg played during the two days of the Jewish New Year. A week or so later, with the pennant almost secured, Greenberg stayed away from the stadium. When he turned up at a local synagogue in Detroit, he received a tumultuous ovation. Others have reflected glowingly on how his staying out of the line-up on Yom Kippur was such a prideful statement. I was more intrigued by how the pressures placed on the sports star that caused him to play on Rosh Hashanah were emblematic of the stresses upon Jews in this Midwestern city. In the 1930s, Detroit, home to infamous Jew-haters Henry Ford and Father Charles Coughlin, not to mention its legacy a decade earlier of support for the Ku Klux Klan, was one of the most antisemitic towns in pre-World War II America. For clear and troubling vistas into how Jews were doing during the intolerant 1930s, Greenberg's dilemmas were worthy of examination.[18]

Two years later, in 1936, Jews were defined as outside the world community through sports when at the Berlin Olympics sprinters Sam Stoller and Marty Glickman were taken off the American Olympic relay race team by United States officials so as not to embarrass Adolf Hitler by having Jews stand on the victory stand at the close of one of the signature events at the Berlin Games. Elsewhere I noted that " the willingness of our country's . . . Olympic officials to kowtow to Nazi demands . . . has been cast as anticipating our government's later, and far more horrible, acquiescence toward Hitler's murderous policies during the Second World War." Suffice it to reiterate that, for me, to see how tenuous Jewish status was both in America and abroad as the Holocaust period approached, one might do well to look at the experience of sports. Like the young American Jewish sprinters, in subsequent years, their people worldwide would find that they had few allies to whom they could turn.[19]

Alternatively, the change in Jewish status in a more tolerant postwar America was witnessed in what I would call Judaism's most honored baseball moment when in 1965 Sandy Koufax decided not to pitch the first game of the World Series on Yom Kippur. This iconic moment continues to be noteworthy not only for the player's assertion of pride in his faith, but for the understanding that his teammates, team owners, and sports fans showed a Jew desiring to respect his holiest day, the same way a Christian might feel about Christmas eve.[20] In even more recent times, American Jewry's sense of belonging and even of entitlement in this country has been evidenced by assertions that critical games not take place at all on the High Holidays. For example, in 1986 Jewish fans of the New York Mets had the chutzpah to protest to the lords of baseball about the scheduling of a National League Championship game on Yom Kippur. There were no Jewish players on the Mets or their opponents, the Houston Astros, although some of the Mets owners were Jewish. Still as loyal fans, and perhaps as important as longtime ticket holders, Jewish supporters demanded religious considerations. The disaffected immediately found an ally in *New York Times* columnist George Vecsey, who in an op-ed piece prophesized, only semi-tongue in check, that God would intercede. "It is going to rain," wrote the scribe, "for 24 solid hours, children. A storm is blowin' in the wind, untrackable on any human-built radarscope. Television and baseball have defied the fates by scheduling not one but two baseball games within 24 hours in the city that has the most Jewish residents of any city in the world. . . . Public officials are advised to prepare arks."[21]

At that point, the proprietors of the national pastime did not fold to Jewish complaints. But a quarter century later, an even more empowered community, faithfully devoted to their sports, had its wishes accommodated. Twice in the spring and then in the late summer of 2009, big-time professional leagues quickly backtracked under a torrent of criticism. First, the National Football League initially scheduled the New York Jets for a 4 p.m. tilt on the eve of Yom Kippur. The game would have concluded after the fast day began, inconveniencing seat-holders who observe the holiday. And then, similarly, in September 2009, ESPN prevailed over Major League Baseball to move the start of a Yankee-Red Sox Game to 8 p.m., at the time when so many Jews were attending Kol Nidre services. In both cases, Jewish communal leaders, rabbis, and fans upbraided those who were so thoughtless or insensitive, and the offenders hastily retreated. In the latter case, the surrender took place scant hours after the first cries were heard, but not before I had a chance to weigh in with my own protest. Approached by Yeshiva University's public affairs office to speak my piece, I quickly wrote that Jews "are so much part of this country that all concerned must take cognizance of that minority group's inviolable, if particular, religious clock and calendar." Though, in fact, my essay, which appeared only on my school's website, had no real impact on the favorable resolution of this outcry, I did accept high-five congratulations from the few colleagues and students who saw the article online.[22]

This willingness of American Jews to assert their equality in this sports arena and the respect they are accorded are not limited to New York Jews nor is it a function of their big league purchasing power. In September 2006, Ben Fuller, a high school football player at Des Moines, Iowa's Roosevelt High School, with the help of his Rabbi David Kaufman of Temple B'nai Jeshurun, requested that his local school board reschedule a Friday night game that conflicted with the start of Rosh Hashanah. A year earlier, "the senior receiver," the *Register* reported, "sat out a game . . . that conflicted with one of the most sacred days in the Jewish religion." A new date, the young man told school officials, would permit him to play and then to pray without conflict. Friday night football is a community defining moment in that state as it is in so many parts of the United States. In acquiescing to Fuller's request and moving some six local games, seemingly to accommodate both this vocal and other quiet Jewish players, the school board defined their neighbors as within the civic culture of their city. This decision also provided the *Register* with a teaching moment for its readership. In a sidebar piece, the newspaper explained to Iowans what the Jewish High Holidays, "a period of solemn reflection on the past year and resolutions for the coming year," were all about.[23]

But if sports tell the tale of American Jewish comfort and security today, it also underscores how tenuous Jewish life is for Israel as it continues to be counted out in many quarters as a full member of the family of nations. In 1972, the Jewish State acutely felt not only the pain of having Palestinian terrorists murder eleven of its athletes at the Munich Olympics, but also suffered from the reaction of international sports' officialdom. After but one day of mourning for slain Jewish sportsmen, it was decreed that the competitions would resume. A year later, Israel would hear more about how the world community felt about its presence and survival when another international organization that has been less than favorable toward it, the United Nations, equated Zionism with racism.[24]

The ostracism and lack of acceptance of Israel that continue to the present day are seen over and again in international sports competitions. Though situated in Asia Minor, FIFA (the world governing organization of football-soccer) has since 1948 defined Israel as a European team because Arab countries refuse to play against the athletes of a state they do not recognize. Noteworthy here from a purely athletic perspective, this placement in the tough European bracket—as opposed to the weaker Asian or African groupings—has undermined Israel's possibilities of qualifying for the World Cup, that quadrennial gathering of sporting nations. Not that FIFA has been neutral when it comes to sports and Middle East politics. In 2006, for example, reportedly "it condemned Israel for an air strike on an empty soccer field in the Gaza Strip that was used for training exercises by Islamic Jihad and the al-Aqsa Martyrs Brigade. This strike did not cause any injuries. But at the same time FIFA has refused to condemn a Palestinian rocket attack on an Israeli soccer field . . . which did cause injuries." Iran also made clear where it stood against Israel and Zionism within the playing venue when in 2004, it rewarded one of its judo competitors $115,000 in prize money for refusing to fight an Israeli opponent. Arash Miresmaeli, who carried his country's flag at the opening ceremonies in Athens, was treated back home as if he had won a gold medal. Thus, through sports we are reminded of the differing fates and statuses of secure American Jews as opposed to their endangered Israeli brethren.[25]

Ultimately, however, for me as a historian with a primary interest in religious life and identity, it was the intersection of sports with Judaism in America that was most intriguing and of consummate concern. It was a way of exploring how a foreign cultural influence—largely unknown among those of East European origins—entered in the lives of immigrants and their children and the conflicts that arose as that "open, alternative *community* of athletes" posed a "variety of strictures, commitments and obligations that challenged ancestral faith and practice." At the very outset of my *Judaism's Encounter with American Sports,* I argued that

> sports, in many ways, is a competing secular religion, complete with
> its own book of rules and holy in its own right. It possesses traditions
> to be followed, a lifestyle to be adhered to, central historical figures
> to be emulated, holidays . . . and even a belief system that speaks
> reverently about personal salvation at the end of days, the quest for
> immortality through victory at the finish line.

Upon positing that thesis, I was pleased to find that some eighty years ago, an immigrant Jewish writer felt the same way. Upon encountering big-time sports, Marcus E. Ravage observed that "it was a highly developed cult, sprung out of the soil and the native spirit, and possessed of all the distinguishing characteristics of its type. It had a hierarchy and ritual of its own . . . with all the solemnity and all the fervor and color of a religious service." Such ideas were worthy of book-length examination.[26]

This perspective has not only brought sports into conversations on the past, present, and future of American Judaism, but also has equipped me to add an additional dimension to the serious study of athleticism. Back in 1976,

Benjamin Horowitz portrayed the pride and excitement that Hakoah Vienna generated in New York in 1926 when this soccer club played exhibition games in famous American stadiums. Unquestionably, there was a story to be told of a Jewish team being welcomed at the White House by President Coolidge—taciturn Calvin met with few folks during his tenure—at a time when anti-semitism limited Jewish social status and political access in this country. But with the eyes that I possess, I saw a complementary Jewish religious element to the visit, worthy of close examination. During Hakoah's appearance at sports venues in New York, Philadelphia, Boston, Chicago, and St. Louis, four of its eleven games were played on Saturday, the Jewish Sabbath. This scheduling conflict, which the soccer team refused to counter, led to its censure not only by the immigrant Orthodox rabbinate in several cities, but by the newly-formed Synagogue Council of America, a national combine of rabbis and lay leaders from most American Jewish denominations. The latter organization "protested against this desecration of the Sabbath and called upon Hakoah as an all Jewish team to maintain the traditional sanctity of the day." One local rabbi in St. Louis went even further when he declared that if the visitors were "a national entity seeking in its activities to be a role model for our youth, then it certainly is a national crime to desecrate the Sabbath."

As interesting was the reaction of Jewish fans that clearly were in a different place than their religious leaders. They basically ignored the remonstrations and calls for boycotts, so proud were they of these athletes. In the popular view, nothing was to abridge Hakoah's successful tour. This episode bespoke issues of communal pride and priorities and also underscored two realities of American Jewish life in the 1920s. First, this era was a period of massive decline in religious observance among second generation American Jews. Thus, it is no surprise that tens of thousands of fans turned out for the matches. Finally, the lack of affirmative response from Hakoah and its sponsors—particularly the Zionist Organization of America—suggests a lack of sensitivity to Jewish observance within the Zionist movement of interwar America. Thus, in offering this more nuanced story of Hakoah, I was able to achieve a long-standing academic objective of contributing to American Jewish sports history while standing well within the lines of the larger issues that affected Judaism and Jewish nationalism in the United States.[27]

NOTES

[1] Harold U. Ribalow, *The Jew in American Sports: Revised Edition* (New York: Bloch Publishing Company, 1955), 3.

[2] Ibid, xviii.

[3]Robert Slater, *Great Jews in Sports* (New York: Jonathan David Publishers, Inc., 1983, rev. editions, 2000, 2003), 3-5.

[4] On the inauguration of the online archive, see jewsinsports.org.

[5] Naomi W. Cohen, *A Dual Heritage: The Public Career of Oscar S. Straus* (Philadelphia: Jewish Publication Society, 1969), 71.

[6] "The Reception by the Judaeans," *Publications of the American Jewish Historical Society* 26 (1918): xviii-xix

[7] Jeffrey S. Gurock, "From *Publications* to *American Jewish History*: The Journal of the American Jewish Historical Society and the Writing of American Jewish History," *American Jewish History* (Winter 1993-1994): 175-79, 212-25.

[8] Moses Rischin, *An Inventory of American Jewish History* (Cambridge: Harvard College, 1954), 50-51; idem, *The Promised City: New York's Jews, 1870-1914* (Cambridge and London: Harvard University Press, 1962), 102, 127, 263-64.

[9] Jonathan D. Sarna, *American Judaism: A History* (New Haven: Yale University Press, 2004), xiii.

[10] David Q. Voigt, "Reflections on Diamonds: American Baseball and American Culture," *Journal of Sport History* 1.1 (Spring, 1974): 3-5. See also, "Editorial": 1

[11] Joe D. Willis and Richard G. Wettan, "L. E. Myers: 'World's Greatest Runner,'" *Journal of Sport History* 2.2 (Fall 1975): 93-111; idem, "Social Stratification in New York City Athletic Clubs, 1865-1915," *Journal of Sport History* 3.1 (Spring 1976): 45-64; D. A. Kass, "The Issue of Racism at the 1936 Olympics," *Journal of Sport History* 3.3 (Fall 1976): 223-35.

[12] Melvin L. Adelman, "Academicians and American Athletics: A Decade of Progress," *Journal of Sports History* 10.1 (Spring, 1985): 95. See also, Benjamin Horowitz, "Hakoah in New York (1926-1932)," *Judaism* 25 (Summer, 1976): 375-82, and Steven A. Riess, "Race and Ethnicity in American Baseball, 1900-1919," *Journal of Ethnic Studies* 4 (Winter, 1977): 39-55, noted and described by Adelman, "Academicians," 95.

[13] Adelman, "Academicians," 95.

[14] See on the recruitment of Steven A. Riess, "Acknowledgement," in *Sports and the American Jew* (ed. Steven A. Riess; Syracuse: Syracuse University Press, 1998), xi.

[15] On Peter Levine's background, see Adelman, "Academicians," 84: Peter Levine, *Ellis Island to Ebbets Field: Sport and the American Jewish Experience* (New York: Oxford University Press, 1992).

[16] Jeffrey S. Gurock, *Judaism's Encounter with American Sports* (Bloomington: Indiana University Press, 2005), 2.

[17] Eric F. Goldman, *The Crucial Decade: America, 1945-1955* (New York Alfred A. Knopf, 1956), 52.

[18] William M. Simons, "Hank Greenberg: The Jewish American Sports Hero," in Riess, *Sports,* 194-95. On the Klan in Detroit, see Kenneth T. Jackson, *The Ku Klux Klan in the City, 1915-1930* (New York: Oxford University Press, 1967), 127-43.

[19] Gurock, *Judaism's Encounter,* 4; on viewing the 1936 Olympics as a forerunner to the Holocaust, see the early work on America, American Jews, and the Holocaust, Arthur D. Morse, *While Six Million Died: A Chronicle of American Apathy* (New York: Random House, 1968).

[20] Jane Leavey, "The Chosen One," *Sports Illustrated* (September 6, 2002): 64-65.

[21] George Vescey," Sports of the Times: Mets Forecast, A Deluge," *New York Times* (1 October 1986): B13.

[22] "NFL honors Jets' request to alter Week 3 kickoff time for Yom Kippur," www.nfl.com; "Game moved back to 1 p.m.," espn.com. "Dr. Jeffrey S Gurock Calls Foul on ESPN," www.yu.org.

[23] Mike Malloy, "Football Schedules Now Consider Jewish Holidays," *Des Moines Register* (September 21, 2006): online edition.

[24] For criticism of the Munich Olympic Games' decision to resume play after the murder of the Israeli athletes, see the editorial "Munich, 1972 . . ." *New York Times* (7 September 1972): 42. See also Paul Hoffman, "U.N. Votes, 72-35 to term Zionism Form of Racism," *New York Times* (11 November 1975): 65.

[25] Tom Gross, "Football Killing Fields: Outrage and Disbelief as World Soccer Body Condemns Israel, Not Hamas." *National Review* (11 April 2006): online edition; "Israel and FIFA World Cup Soccer" http://blogsofzion.com/blog; "Iranian Judo Champion Refuses to Face Israeli," *New York Times* (14 August 2004): D2.

[26] Gurock, *Judaism's Encounter*, 8-9. See also, M. E. Ravage, *An American in the Making: The Life Story of an Immigrant* (New York: Harper and Brothers, 1917), 216-17.

[27] Jeffrey S. Gurock, "Pride and Priorities: American Jewry's Response to Hakoah Vienna's U.S. Tour of 1926," *Studies in Contemporary Jewry* 23 (2008): 77-83.

Jewish Women in the American Gym: Basketball, Ethnicity, and Gender in the Early Twentieth Century

Linda J. Borish

INTRODUCTION

Basketball for Jewish women, generally neglected by historians of American sport and women, and Jewish sport history scholars, represents a topic of considerable importance in understanding historical experiences of Jews in the gym. In the early twentieth century Jewish women played basketball at settlement houses, ladies auxiliaries of Young Men's Hebrew Associations, where women faced gender constraints on the male spaces of sporting facilities, and at Young Women's Hebrew Associations, before YM-YWHAs merged, and then early Jewish Community Centers (JCCs). Mrs. Bella Unterberg, founder and president of the Young Women's Hebrew Association (YWHA) in New York City established in 1902, advised her fellow YWHA workers, "It is the finest thing a Young Women's Society can start with, with the gymnasium and the basket-ball teams for your recreational work."[1] In various regions of the United States Jewish American female immigrants played basketball as part of "Americanizing" and gaining physical health, and formed Jewish teams; some Jewish women competed against other Jewish women for ethnic pride and charity fundraising, while at some Jewish institutions Jewish women played against intercity teams and Christian Ys for larger championships.

Gender and ethnicity shaped aspects of Jewish women's involvement in basketball. The founder of women's basketball, Senda Berenson, born in a shtetl in Vilna, Lithuania, as Senda Valvrojenski, came to Boston, Massachusetts, at age seven with her immigrant Jewish family. She used her training from the Boston Normal School of Gymnastics to develop women's basketball at Smith College. In 1892, Berenson became the director of physical training at Smith College, Northampton, Massachusetts, at the new Alumnae Gymnasium. Berenson observed Dr. James Naismith's new game of basketball at Springfield College and then organized the first women's basketball game in 1892 at Smith College. Known as the "Mother of Women's Basketball," Berenson remarked in her speech, "Basketball for Women," that "in January, 1892—Smith College introduced it," and from "that day to this it has been by far the most popular game in that college." The first official game pitted the

Smith sophomores against the freshmen at Alumnae Gymnasium on March 22, 1893. To avoid the roughness of the men's game, Berenson adapted the rules for women with specific gender guidelines to modify the men's game: dividing the court into zones, prohibiting snatching the ball from another player, allowing five to ten players on a team, and emphasizing teamwork. Berenson authored the official rules and edited *Spalding's Athletic Library Basket Ball for Women* in 1901, explaining the women's game avoided "undue physical exertion."[2] American Jewish women in the gym played the popular game of basketball; at times some wanted to play in a more vigorous competitive game in the early twentieth century and displayed athletic skills on teams of Jewish cultural institutions and other American teams.

JEWISH WOMEN AND BASKETBALL AT JEWISH SETTLEMENTS

Jewish immigrant young women often learned basketball at Jewish settlement houses in cities with growing numbers of immigrant Jews. The settlements served to orient Jewish women to their new culture in American life and to teach them English, domestic and vocational skills, and gender-appropriate physical activities and sport. For example, the Jewish Institute in Detroit housed a large gymnasium and other facilities. Jewish girls and boys participated in sporting activities in the gymnasium at the Institute. The popular sport of basketball took place in the gymnasium with Hannah Schloss's women's team playing other teams. The Institute was relocated in 1924 and serves as the forerunner of the Jewish Community Center of Metropolitan Detroit, which opened in 1933.[3]

The Irene Kauffmann Settlement founded in Pittsburgh in 1895 incorporated "many social, civic, health, recreational and educational activities." Known as the "IKS," the settlement conducted "Gym Work for Girls." The house organ, the *I.K.S. Neighbors*, in 1923 on "Gym Work for Girls" stated that, "Many of our girls have asked for the use of the gymnasium and their requests have been granted." For girls of various age levels classes were held in "dancing, gymnasium, and swimming" and "basketball."[4] In keeping with gender conventions about the female body, this settlement, sponsored sports deemed suitable for girls similar to sports encouraged for Gentile females. The *I.K.S. Neighbors* advocated that "every girl may be as slender as the fashion demands if she will take advantage" of gym, swimming, and basketball. And if the girls needed the appropriate gym costume, that might also be part of their domestic training: "Dig up your bloomers and middies and c'mon! If you want to make new bloomers, you can do it in the sewing class," the I.K.S. commentator urged in 1923.[5]

The Chicago Hebrew Institute (CHI), described as "another outstanding organization promoting Americanization activities" for Eastern European
Jewish immigrants, offered men and women a comprehensive range of classes
in citizenship, English, commerce, domestic science, Jewish culture, literature,
art, physical culture, drama, and music. The CHI, located on the Lower West
Side of Chicago, organized in 1903 by a group of young men, promoted
the moral, physical, religious, and civic welfare of Jewish immigrants and
residents.[6] Jewish philanthropist and businessman Julius Rosenwald helped
secure property for the CHI. President Jacob M. Loeb, elected in 1912, and
Dr. Philip L. Seman, general director of the CHI (1913-1945), guided the
expansion and programs to create a thriving Jewish institution, the forerunner
of today's Jewish Community Centers. General Director Seman explained,
"The Institute is frankly Jewish and staunchly American." In 1922, the CHI
changed its name to the Jewish People's Institute (JPI) and later moved into a
new building in Lawndale in 1927.[7]

Throughout its history, the CHI underscored the importance of physical well-being for all of participants, males and females. "'Good, Clean Sport,'
Motto of the C.H.I.," an article highlighted the physical and moral aims of
the physical culture department directed by Harry Berkman. "The Chicago
Hebrew Institute was founded on the idea that athletics are a good thing and
dedicated to the idea that mind, body and morals should be developed at one
and the same time" for the 500 boys and girls who belonged to the gymnasium. Berkman explained the physical work: "We train the boys and girls to be
self-reliant, independent, and on the square in everything." In a 1914 article in
The Sentinel, "The Temple of the Body, How the Hebrew Institute is Laboring
to Make Jews Physically Fit," journalist Bertha A. Loeb acknowledged the prevailing conception about Jews, sport, and physical health in the early twentieth
century [Fig.1]. Loeb asserted, "The undersized, anaemic 'Jewish weakling'
will soon be a recollection of by-gone days." Thus, the CHI aimed to establish
that "one of the first activities to be set into being was a gymnasium for the
youth of both sexes."[8]

A new gymnasium and swimming pool opened in June 1915 reveals
a debate on gender and how much money should be devoted to women's
physical culture. At first the physical pursuits of girls and women received little
focus in the building plans. But President Jacob M. Loeb wanted to serve the
needs of Jews of both sexes, and he battled to construct equal athletic facilities
for men and women. Loeb and James Davis, the athletic committee chairman,
believed separate gyms and swimming pools should be included in the new
facility.[9] Over time Loeb raised the necessary funds, and he addressed the CHI

Figure 1. "The Temple of the Body, How the Hebrew Institute is Laboring to Make Jews Physically Fit," in *The Sentinel,* May 1914. Image courtesy of the Jacob Rader Marcus Center of the American Jewish Archives, Cincinnati, Ohio.

on March 31, 1914, applauding the sport sites accessible to both genders: "Our demands were different than any Y.M.C.A. or social center building in as much as we wished to accommodate all of our people, namely boys and girls, men and women" and to achieve this "it was necessary to draw plans for practically two gymnasiums."[10] Superintendent Seman affirmed the new gymnasium started a "new epoch in our Athletic Work" with "equal facilities for men and women, therefore, having a separate Gymnasium, Swimming Tanks, Locker Rooms, Shower Baths . . ." One journalist even declared the gym "Is Boon for Women. . . . In a city where the women have as little athletic opportunity as Chicago this is a great step forward. It is only another instance of the aggressiveness that has placed the Hebrew Institute where it is on the athletic map."[11]

Using the new gymnasium, the CHI girls enhanced their basketball skills and competitive team spirit playing Jewish and non-Jewish teams [Fig. 2]. For example, in 1917 the CHI girls' basketball team "was successful in winning 13 games out of a total of 15, having competed with some of the strongest teams in and out of the city." The 1921 season showed that "The Girls' Basketball Team has played 26 games and has not a single defeat against its name." The CHI girls won the Central Amateur Athletic Union (AAU) Girls' Basketball Championship with their first-rate play. In 1922, the team again played for the Central AAU Championship, but they "were beaten by the 'Uptown Brownies,'" the only team that defeated them in the past two years.[12]

A standout of the CHI girls' basketball team, Rose Rodkin, became captain and helped the team win. The *Chicago Tribune* in 1922 showed her photograph with the caption, "Salute the New Captain of the Chicago Hebrew

Figure 2. Chicago Hebrew Institute, girls in gymnasium uniforms in front of the building, ca. 1915. Image courtesy of the Spertus Institute, Chicago.

Institute girls' basketball team" [Fig. 3]. Of note, Rodkin starred on the "Institute's five" rather than a team with girls' rules requiring more players per team.[13] Rodkin's athletic talent extended beyond the basketball court as she also was a terrific sprinter on the CHI track team. On the basketball team, Rodkin lead the girls to victories in citywide contests in Chicago. In fact, the first girls' basketball game to be played under men's rules, which took place December 3, 1916, was played at the CHI between the Institute and the Hull House girls' team

Figure 3. "Salute the New Captain of the Chicago Hebrew Institute Girls' Basketball Team, Miss Rose Rodkin," *Chicago Tribune*, January 8, 1922, B.22.

(consisting of some Jewish girls). In "Boys' Rules Speed Girls' Basket Games," *Tribune* reporter Harland Rohm noted that before this game at the CHI, girls' basketball "had been the cream puff brand of the days when girls celebrated their transition from girlhood to womanhood by donning a variation of a knights steel cuirass and no lady played anything more strenuous than croquet. That girls game," Rohm explained, in which each girl plays in a certain section of the floor like an animated checker, still survives," but he supported the more strenuous and fast game played by the CHI girls. Rodkin initiated playing a more athletic basketball game for the CHI girls. Rodkin, now in 1926 serving as manager of the Institute's girls' basketball team, went to watch a Hull House boys' basketball game. "She became so fired with the game" that with the aid of the assistant director of the CHI, Louis Berger, she organized "a girls' team to play under the 'rough' boys' rules." In addition to this CHI girls' basketball team, Hull House, the Illinois Athletic Club, Christ Church, and Sinai Social Center (featuring Jewish female athletes) organized teams to compete against the CHI. Rodkin and her CHI hoopsters earned victory in the first game, beating Hull House 25 to 15.[14]

For Jewish and Gentile girls, the JPI girls' team "has been directly responsible for the popularity of basketball among the girls of Chicago and the towns close by." In keeping with the CHI's goal of preparing Jewish youth with proper values, "Everywhere the girls went they were well received, and the teams always asked to be allowed to play at the Institute." Girls' basketball team members "displayed the best sportsmanship." JPI girls' basketball teams continued to excel—"Girl Cagers Look Impressive in Victory" and hosted large crowds.[15]

JEWISH WOMEN'S BASKETBALL AND ETHNIC IDENTITY AT YOUNG WOMEN'S AND YOUNG MEN'S HEBREW ASSOCIATIONS AND EARLY JEWISH COMMUNITY CENTERS

Jewish young women participated in the Young Women's Hebrew Athletic League and competed against other YWHAs and YWCAs as members of the New York City YWHA. Given the appeal of the game, no wonder the New York City YWHA promotion for girls' classes asserted that in "Basketball— Enjoy a weekly work-out playing the greatest of all indoor games."[16]

Most YWHAs, however, had neither their own funding nor female staff trained in physical education and sports, with a different history of women's basketball and sport than New York City's YWHA. During the early twentieth century, most YWHAs were affiliated with YMHAs, and YMHA athletic spaces usually remained the male domain. Over time, however, with the aid of National Jewish Welfare Board (JWB), several YM-YWHAs in various communities provided more athletic spaces for women. The JWB, organized in 1921, became the national governing body for YM-YWHAs, actively promoted the merger of YM-YWHAs, and sought to develop them into JCCs by the mid-twentieth century. As one of the first researchers to use these JWB records about the development of YM-YWHAs in an initial effort to examine these huge collections, although still unprocessed and in storage, I published "'An Interest in Physical Well-Being Among the Feminine Membership': Sporting Activities for Women at Young Men's and Young Women's Hebrew Associations" (*American Jewish History,* March 1999, 61-93).

Most situations explored by the JWB revealed that women wanted to partake of physical culture classes and sports, but women faced gender tension over use of the gym; male personnel often limited women's use of popular athletic facilities. The national Field Secretary for Women's Work Emily Solis-Cohen recorded hardships Jewish women confronted in the YWHA, as noted in my publication when first using these unprocessed JWB records in discussing the early YWHAs, "Women, Sports, and American Jewish Identity in the Late Nineteenth and Early Twentieth Centuries," a chapter that appeared in *With God on their Side: Sport in the Service of Religion* (Magdalinksi and Chandler, 2002, 71-98). In South Brooklyn, New York, plans to merge the YWHA with the YMHA in November 1923 were presided over by Solis-Cohen as the YWHA voted to reorganize and merge with the YMHA. On January 8, 1924, Solis-Cohen reported, "The girls also said they had no use of the gymnasium and therefore were not holding their members and had difficulty in collecting their dues." In fact, Mr. Harris, executive secretary of this YMHA, informed the YWHA, "The gymnasium schedule is full, for evenings, being given to the boys, and Monday evenings to lectures. Consequently, for this season the women cannot have the gymnasium." Yet the YWHA members wanted to use the gym; Solis-Cohen asserted in her correspondence that she and Samuel Leff, a JWB worker, "would take up the matter of the women's gymnasium" in communicating with Harris.[17] Solis-Cohen explained in her report, "It is apparent that there is a feeling among some of the members that the building is man's building and the association a man's association." Even JWB Field Secretary Leff uttered that the YWHA president seemed concerned about losing members. He noted that Harris "promised to let the YWHA have as much space in the building as it could use," however, once again "with the exception of the gymnasium" in the report for October 1924 of this Brooklyn YM-YWHA. Therefore, Jewish women wanting to play basketball needed another space due to meager access to this YM-YWHA for sports.[18]

As the national organization of Jewish Ys, the JWB met with women in YWHAs about finding places to pursue their athletic interests. In 1927, Solis-Cohen attended a meeting at the YWHA-110th street about the "Young Women's Hebrew Association Athletic League" consisting of "21 representatives for six associations in the Metropolitan League." At this meeting and others, the representatives discussed rules of "basket ball tournament, volley ball tournament and similar matters."[19]

As YWHAs procured space for members' use, they offered basketball and other athletics. The Hartford YWHA was founded in 1915 by a group of young Jewish women. The leadership of Marion Scharr, executive secretary, enabled the Hartford YWHA to administer a full range of programs, and the athletic department became a success even though the girls lacked "proper quarters." *The Connecticut Hebrew Record* commented on the Hartford YWHA: "There was good and enthusiastic material for several basket ball teams," but not until the Brown School gymnasium "was procured, and then for but once a week." Despite this handicap, the YWHA team was good enough to play the YWCA, and the 1920 Hartford YWHA basketball team wore uniforms with "YW" to identify their squad[20] [Fig. 4].

In fact, athletics expanded with the female autonomy of this association. The Hartford YWHA boasted in 1920 that "there are two basket ball teams and the girls have picked out the five best players and challenge any team in the State." These Jewish girls wanted to play and win. Other Connecticut YWHAs preferred "playing with Y.W.H.A. organizations," and a game with great significance between rival Ys occurred. "December 14 will establish a new precedent in the history of the Y.W.H.A.'s of this State," a journalist explained, "when two associations will meet in battle on the basketball court," the Hartford team representing "the State Capitol" and the New Haven team

Figure 4. Young Women's Hebrew Association Basketball Team, 1920. Image courtesy of the Jewish Historical Society of Greater Hartford.

representing the "City of Elms. As both Hartford and New Haven are confident of winning, the contents will afford many thrills to spectators." While admission to the game cost fifty cents, Jewish charities benefited: "the entire net proceeds will be divided equally and contributed to the Jewish Home for Orphans and the Home for the Aged." In this contest, described as "a snappy game complete with thrills from start to finish," the press noted, "the Y.W.H.A. of New Haven emerged the victor over the Y.W.H.A. of Hartford," with a score of 11 to 2. The contest proved a success for players and spectators alike, as a report claimed, "An audience as large as ever turned out for any men's basketball game witnessed the match." The loss in no way dampened the athletic spirit of the Hartford YWHA team members.[21]

By 1921, these YWHA girls practiced twice a week, still using Hartford-area school gyms. But playing keen competition appealed to the basketball players of this YWHA, and "the association expects to join the basketball leagues comprising the Travelers Insurance Company, the Aetna Fire, the Simsbury Independents, the New Departure of Bristol and the Y.W.C.A." Teams of working-class and ethnic young women participated in basketball to showcase their sporting ability and to earn pride for the organization they represented in the contests. These YWHA hoopsters played in the Hartford

Figure 5. Captain Dot Gilman of the Young Women's Hebrew Association Basketball Team, ca. 1920s. Image courtesy of the Jewish Historical Society of Greater Hartford.

County Basketball Girls League, led by the "clever shooting on the part of Dot Gilman, captain of the YWHA five" in a victory over the Aetna Life Girls.[22] Captain Dot Gilman led the Jewish women on the court to several wins [Fig. 5]. The athletic prowess of the Hartford YWHA team continued when the YWHA team, coached by Morris N. Cohen, won the State Championship in 1930 and 1931. Although without their own building, the Hartford YWHA achieved its mission of "developing Jewish young women morally, intellectually, socially, and physically."[23]

The need for adequate material culture of basketball courts, gym uniforms, and locker spaces for women continued to be a point of contention in budgeting for expanded YM and YWHAs. When the St. Louis YMHA moved to a new location in the early 1920s, men remained in control of the athletic spaces. An anniversary bulletin of the YMHA-YWHA stated, "The 'W' part of the 'Y' had little or no activity with the Physical Department being strictly male territory."[24] Generally, progress occurred slowly once the JWB prompted local Jewish Y officials to implement renovations of programs and buildings to accommodate female members. In St. Louis, the JWB aided in the plans for the new YM-YWHA building in 1923 located on Union Avenue and exercised sway to encourage women and girls to use the facility. "A campaign was launched under the auspices of the National Jewish Welfare Board and under the inspiring leadership of Dr. Philip R. Goldstein $500,000 was procured to erect a modern center." This new structure included a "gymnasium, swimming pool, exercise room, massage room, locker rooms, and a roof garden." The YMHA president emphasized the scope of the Y to invite "the Conservative and Reform Jew, the Zionist and Anti-Zionist . . . the American and the aspirant toward Americanism . . . boys and girls, young men and women, fathers and mothers."[25] A description about athletic facilities in the building explicitly mentioned women: "In order to accommodate the girls and women, a women's gymnasium has been planned that will be adequate in every respect."[26]

Yet when the new St. Louis YM-YWHA opened in 1927, the women's gymnasium was not built due to the need for additional funds. Men and women shared the one gymnasium, with men allotted more time than women in the gym schedule. Then in the mid-1930s, Mark C. Steinberg, a member of the board of directors, donated $100,000 and the Y expansion led to building the second gymnasium for women. On the tenth anniversary of the YM-YWHA in 1937, the "Physical Department" directed by Blanche Bronstein improved its sport offerings to women. In basketball the "girls varsity sextet . . . is anxiously looking forward to their annual tussle with the Jewish Hospital Nurses' team." The Jewish Y girls' team trained hard in their time using the gym and participated in other sports like volleyball, badminton, swimming, tennis, and softball. Indeed, "Beatrice" wrote in her "Fair Facts" column in *The Y Journal* that when she saw "what big things are being done in the girls' physical department I was very anxious to relay this information to you lucky people who will receive all the benefits from this tremendous program."[27]

Girls at the St. Louis YM-YWHA in the 1930s showed enthusiasm in heeding the call of Bronstein to sign up for instruction and enjoy playing basketball at various levels: "The time to get into condition is now, whether one is out for the big time on the girls' varsity squad, or else set to participate in the inter-club circuit."[28] The girls' varsity basketball team in 1936-1937 was coached by George Rickels and assisted by "the willing and capable Mollie Becker, former varsity star." The girls' basketball team won their opening game, "showing the results of hard and strenuous training" defeating the Jewish Hospital Nurses by the score 20-18.[29] They played the strong WPA [Works Progress Administration] College basketball team; in this contest "the 'Y' lassies sprung a startling surprise in turning back their rivals, 31-10," led by the scoring of Rose Schneider.[30]

Other Jewish Ys pursued keen competition between interleague YWHA teams, games against YWCAs or industrial teams. The Philadelphia YM-YWHA in its periodical, *The Review*, urged members to go see "the strong Y.W. sextet attempt to repel the stellar Trade School aggregation." Another time the journal remarked, "Our Girls' Basketball Team sports a winning streak, having won every game except the first."[31]

At the Pittsburgh YM-YWHA, "Girls' Basketball Practice Arranged," a *Y Weekly* headline in November 1926 appeared; not only beginner's classes, but regular games were held in order to "choose material to compete against the leading girls' teams of the district" as these girls played hard and competed for victories. Manager Evelyn Dunn of the girls' varsity basketball team started to book games against other city teams and scheduled regular team practices. The game attracted women, old and young: "A challenge to play basketball with the single girls of the 'Y' has been issued by the married women." To assure a game took place, the reporter noted, "In case there are not enough married dames spry enough to handle the ball, an 'old timers' single girls' game will played." Some of these married women played on college teams, and "are anxious to star on the basketball court" again.[32]

The Pittsburgh Jewish Y women's basketball team exhibited ethnic and gender pride in achieving victories. In winter 1927, the girls' basketball team continued to "set a torrid pace" in its first year in league competition: "The girls include among their victims so far" some of the "best sextets in Western Pennsylvania and stand an excellent chance of winning the championship." Talented players included captain and guard Sylvia Wechsler, who was "playing a game that stamps her as one of the finest amateur basketball players in this section of the state," and Bee Tolochko, sharpshooter of the team. Coach Edith Lazarus guided the team with only one loss in eight victories, vying against teams of Christian Ys, first Presbyterian Church, Owl Girls, Northside Community House, Kingsley House, among others, and only losing to the McKees Rocks Tumblers, comprised of teachers of that high school, by two points. The photo of the YWHA girls' basketball team in April 1927 hails their "first season on the floor."[33]

This Jewish Y team continued to excel, and in the 1927-1928 season, they played in the Pioneer Press team against other top teams. Girls' varsity basketball leagues at YM-YWHAs, sponsored by newspapers, community, or commercial establishments, prompted Jewish women to practice the sport in Jewish athletic facilities and public spaces to express their passion for the game. Physical education leaders and women's gym directors organized new sports classes and competitions to meet the demand of women and girls seeking sporting experiences. The 1927-1928 varsity team compiled another impressive record against teams like the Philadelphia Company, National Union Fire Insurance, the Goldenson's Vanities, and YWCAs [Fig. 6]. In some events at YM-YWHAs, women showed both athletic and female gender form with a dance following a girls' basketball game. For a January 5, 1928 evening, "A small admission will be charged and the entire Jewish community is invited." Such sporting events and hard work of democracy on the court yielded some profits to enable young women to then further the athletic participation and

Figure 6. Pittsburgh Young Men's-Young Women's Hebrew Association Women's Basketball Team, 1927-1928. Image courtesy of the Jewish Community Center of Greater Pittsburgh Photographs, Rauh Jewish Archives at the Senator John Heinz History Center, Pittsburgh, Pennsylvania.

show Jewish identity. The YW team beat the champion McKees Rocks Tumblers, handing the Tumblers their first loss, to tie them in the city league in the "close and hotly contested" game; impressively, the "loyal rooters" of the YW team attended this contest on the Tumbler's home floor and "cheered them on to the most important triumph of the current campaign" (the first lost in 24 games for the Tumblers). In the quest for the championship, the Pittsburgh Y squad lost a tough contest to these Tumblers in the playoffs.[34] The *Pittsburgh Sun-Telegraph* on December 30, 1928, featured the headline "Star Floor Squad of YWHA" with a photo; these Jewish athletes embarked on their new season with "one of the best girls' basketball teams in the district, and its prospects are for an even more successful squad this season."[35]

Important to promote their team and to secure profits to further the YWHA victories, in the 1929-1930 season in the Press-Treeman King Basketball League, sponsored by one of Pittsburgh's sporting goods houses, the girls' varsity team hosted the University of Pittsburgh alumnae team. During this event, the "proceeds of the game are to be used toward the trip the 'Y' squad is planning to Washington, D. C." in March, where they hope to "defeat Capitols Institution. The admission charge to the game will be twenty-five cents." Other fund-raisers the girls pursued included sponsoring a dance, selling candy at the boys' games, and admission to another of their games; these hoopsters hoped to take a squad of thirteen girls and two managers on the trip to Washington, DC. These sportswomen achieved their goal: the "'Y' girls collected a sufficient amount of money to defray all the expenses of the trip." The Y players earned a narrow victory on court and enjoyed the sights of the city.[36]

Other Jewish Ys endorsing women's basketball recalled the place of the game in their history. For example, at the twenty-fifth anniversary of the Bronx YM-YWHA (1934) a commentator observed, "Even in basketball, the girls have demonstrated that the knack of tossing an inflated leather spheroid into an iron hoop was not confined to the boys." Using a gendered description, this basketball enthusiast noted that in the 1930s the Bronx YM-YWHA "produced a squad of court queens that was a sight for sore eyes," and this "girls' team occupies a position of prominence in gymnastic activities second only to the men's varsity."[37] The YWHA of Yonkers, too, participated in Inter-Y basketball. The *Dedication Week Program of Yonkers, New York Jewish Community Center* in April 1929 announced on "Athletic Night" the "Yonkers Y.W.H.A. vs. Mt. Vernon YWHA" basketball game, preceding the men's basketball game, and listed the lineups of both women's squads. The Mt. Vernon YWHA in 1914 praised the senior girls who played basketball in the evening: "the team won laurels playing other Westchester Y's."[38]

At the Jewish Community Center of Washington, DC, Ruth Green, director of women's physical education, endorsed basketball for working women and organized the city basketball league. Many talented basketball players competed at the JCC of Washington, DC, in the 1930s. The JCC sponsored a basketball league, and teams pursued spirited play. In the *Washington Post's* sponsored AAU basketball tournament in 1930 for the District of Columbia, the JCC girls' team was considered among the best in the city. The *National Jewish Ledger* of DC reported that women enjoyed a successful season, advancing to the finals of the AAU tournament. The JCC women's team continued its strong play. In March 1932, the *Jewish Ledger* reported, "The Center will be represented by two teams in the women's division of the current AAU basketball tournament. The senior team is expected be a strong contender for the title." The senior team consisted of Pauletta Banner, Bessie Dicken, Louise Fishman, Ethel Hertz, Betty Kronman (manager), Yetta Morgenstern, Alta Schnitzer, Leah Shofnos (captain), Ruth Stein, and Frances Teplitz. The

JCC players participated in a Community Center League of working-class women, pitting their dexterity against teams of Bell Telephone, United Typewriters, Gallinger Hospital Nurses, of government workers from agriculture, general accounting, and other teams.[39] JCC players like Lillian Rosenbloth, a forward on the "Blue Star" team, appeared in photos of the *Washington Times* [Fig. 7]. So, too, other JCC teammates displaying their uniforms with the Star of David and the JCC logo on their shirts appeared in a press image: "Not Reaching for the Moon, But the Jewish Community Center girls' basketball players are reaching for the ball in one of their mad practice sessions"[40] [Fig.8].

At the JCC of Washington, DC, Ruth Green wanted girls to maintain propriety and not be concerned about the score of basketball games, though the girls themselves wanted to compete and win. Green stated the goal of the league: "The board does not seek large attendance at games, and neither does it lay emphasis on scores and competition. It is the game for the sake of recreation." Green remarked that, "games are essentially a neighborhood affair . . . rather than playing for a championship." She reiterated, "'Off the bleachers and on the field' is one of the slogans of the national associations . . . which the local board is carrying out in practice" in athletics for DC-area girls. Keeping with gender conventions for Jewish and Gentile working women, and the emphasis on physical fitness and a slender body, Green created a flyer for the JCC Women's Physical Education Department to attract women to participate in bodily exercise. Green addressed JCC women: "Hi Gals! Seen the Gym lately? Now's the time to check your chassis for Salesgirls' slouch, Government Spread, Housewives' Hips. We've got a cure for all so come and get it," recommending young women partake of calisthenics, paddle tennis, volleyball, and other exercises.[41] Green promoted a fundraising event for the Women's Physical Education Department featuring the girls' basketball team; the girls' basketball boosters' slogan for the evening was "Hustle Your Bustle to the Gym." In promoting the event, Green announced, "The basketball team is playing hostess as well as a game in costume according to the oldest rules available." Playing in a bustle fit the theme of the Gay Nineties, and such gender-appropriate conventions for the gym activity demonstrated the women's game of the past.[42] The JCC girls' basketball team, however, asserted their athletic ability in training for games in the 1930s as captured in a newspaper piece [Fig.9].

Some Jewish women wanted more competitive athletic experiences, and basketball became a forum for them. In 1926-1927, Lee Shofnos (mentioned above on the JCC team) as a twenty-year-old played for the Washington, DC team the "Arcadians." The "Arcadians" was DC's only professional girls' basket-

A BLUE STAR OF GIRLS' BASKETBALL

HERE'S Lillian Rosenbloth, forward of the Blue Stars of the girls' basketball league at the Jewish Community Center. Games are played every Tuesday and Thursday nights. Times Staff Photo.

Social to Launch Jewish Program

Meeting Tomorrow Opens Season for Center.

An open meeting in the form of a social will begin the 1934 program tomorrow night at 8:30 o'clock for the Jewish Community Center. The program for the next four months will bring to the center many authorities on local, National and International topics. Rabbi Stephen S. Wise will be heard later in the year.

Entertainment tomorrow will be furnished by the "Three Aces."

This evening Rabbi Solomon Metz will resume classes in the study of Bible. These classes will continue each Tuesday.

The first theatrical presentation of the coming season will be given Monday.

Figure 7. Lillian Rosenbloth, a forward on the "Blue Star" team, of the Jewish Community Center, Washington, DC, ca. 1930s, photograph in the *Washington Times*. Image courtesy of the Jewish Historical Society of Greater Washington.

Figure 8. "Not Reaching for the Moon," Jewish Community Center Girls' Basketball Team, Washington, DC, newspaper photograph, ca. 1930s. Image courtesy of the Jewish Historical Society of Greater Washington.

Figure 9. Jewish Community Center Girls' Basketball Team practicing, Washington, DC. *Washington Times,* December 16, 1933, newspaper clipping. Image courtesy of the Jewish Historical Society of Greater Washington.

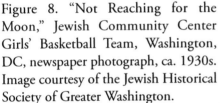

ball team, and Shofnos, who later became Lee Weinberg, recollected her days on the basketball court. She worked for a department store and in her spare time, she played basketball in the "girls' leagues sponsored by the Jewish Community Center downtown." This professional team featured six women who played by the men's rules against men in basketball, in exhibition type games, lasting one season. Weinberg recalled, "They played against high school boys, mostly, and rarely-if ever-won. . . . and she was paid $10—the equivalent of an entire week's salary at Kann's" where she worked. The roughness of the games drew criticism as well as the fact that these women challenged the physical educators' views on women's athletics in the early twentieth century. Weinberg left the JCC team to play for the Arcadians in December 1926 and remembered some of her JCC teammates "didn't think women should play with boys."[43] Although playing professional women's basketball certainly appeared unusual at this time, still some Jewish female players participated in competitive games against other women.

Several Jewish women played on collegiate teams as opportunities for women to attend colleges increased. Claire Strassman played forward on the

New York University Varsity Girls' Basketball Team in 1924. Of note, Strassman and her teammates were granted varsity status by a recent ruling, entitling the members the privilege of wearing the New York University letters. Additionally, Strassman played on the team the following year. The *American Hebrew* included Strassman in its "Personalities in Sports" column in 1924.[44]

For Jewish women of various ages, Jewish sport leaders encouraged them to play basketball. In Nashville in the *YMHA News*, a section about the YWHA for February 1927 presented a new spots club: "B.A.G. may just spell bag to most people in this world, but to a certain group of business and athletic girls" it means the "Business-Athletic Girls Club, and it also means they are going to 'bag' everything good that brings sportsmanship and understanding of things essential to a better developed life." The "B.A.G.s" increased their membership, and the director of the girls' work at the YWHA considered this group the heart of the YWHA. They shared with their mothers their sporting interests at their annual mother and daughter supper, displaying fashions for golf, tennis, basketball, and swimming. The Nashville Jewish weekly paper, the *Observer,* reported in January 16, 1936, a basketball game to be played "Matrons vs. Business Girls" as the first of a series played at the YM-YWHA.[45]

CONCLUSION

Whether Jewish women played basketball in games at Jewish Ys or competed on a girls' Y varsity team against other teams in city leagues, basketball permeated the athletic landscape of Jewish women in the American gym. Long after the earlier days of the modified rules, Jewish women basketball players in the twentieth century displayed their ethnic identity and athletic prowess in this popular sport in American culture. The Nashville JCC featured the outstanding women's team of the "Pepettes" in winning a championship[46] [Fig. 10]. These young Jewish women playing basketball followed the success of the Jewish young men's team, the "Peps," the well-known Nashville team that started in the early twentieth century for the Jewish Y and achieved victories against top-notch basketball team [Fig.11]. The tremendous play of the "Pepettes" basketball team demonstrated that Jewish women did excel in the gymnasium at different places and times in the record of Jews in sport in the United States. American Jewish women played a key role in the history of sport, gender, and Jews in the gym.

ACKNOWLEDGMENTS

I thank Leonard Greenspoon for his generous support of my participation in the Symposium and for his enthusiasm for my research for this paper. At

Figure 10. "Nashville Pepettes" Jewish Community Center Women's Basketball Team, 1949. Image courtesy of the Annette Levy Ratkin Jewish Community Archives funded by the Jewish Federation of Nashville and Middle Tennessee.

Figure 11. "Nashville Peps," Young Men's Hebrew Association Basketball Team, 1920. Image courtesy of the Annette Levy Ratkin Jewish Community Archives funded by the Jewish Federation of Nashville and Middle Tennessee.

Western Michigan University, I am grateful to the Department of History for the support from the Burnham-Macmillan History Endowment Grant, for funding for travel to previous conferences related to my work and to acquire archival materials for this research. I deeply appreciate the ongoing interest in my historical research on Jewish women and American sport and suggestions on my work offered by Jeffrey Gurock and Steven Riess as I seek to add Jewish women's experiences to materials about Jews in sports.

I want to thank the archivists and librarians who have provided expert assistance in my seeking the appropriate images I include in this essay from their historical collections. Images used are from: the Jacob Rader Marcus Center of the American Jewish Archives, Cincinnati; Spertus Institute of Jewish Studies, Chicago; the Jewish Community Center of Greater Pittsburgh Photographs, Rauh Jewish Archives at the Senator John Heinz History Center, Pittsburgh; Jewish Historical Society of Greater Washington, Washington, DC; the Annette Levy Ratkin Jewish Community Archives funded by the Jewish Federation of Nashville and Middle Tennessee; and the Jewish Historical Society of Greater Hartford, Hartford.

NOTES

[1] "Second Triennial Convention. Conference: Girls' and Women's Work," *Publication of the Council of YMHA and Kindred Associations,* November 1916.

[2] Linda J. Borish, "Senda Berenson Abbott," in *Encyclopedia of Ethnicity and Sports in the United States* (ed. G. B. Kirsch, et al.; Westport: Greenwood Press, 2000), 63; Linda J. Borish, "'Athletic Activities of Various Kinds': Physical Health and Sport Programs for Jewish American Women," *Journal of Sport History* 26 (Summer 1999): 240-70; Ralph Melnick, *Senda Berenson: The Unlikely Founder of Women's Basketball* (Amherst: University of Massachusetts Press, 2007). On Berenson and women's basketball, see essays in Joan Hult and Marianna Trekell, eds., *A Century of Women's Basketball: From Frailty to Final Four* (Reston: American Alliance for Health, Physical Education, Recreation, and Dance, 1991). See also material and archival footage of Jewish women's basketball in different time periods in the documentary film, *Jewish Women in American Sport: Settlement Houses to the Olympics,* Linda J. Borish, executive producer, researcher, historian, working with Producer and Director Filmmaker Shuli Eshel, Eshel Productions, 2007 copyright, in conjunction with Maccabi USA/Sports for Israel.

While scholars in Jewish studies and sport history have focused on men in basketball, little scholarly research has been done on Jewish women in basketball. On Jewish men in basketball, see, for example, Steven A. Riess, ed., *Sports and the American Jew* (Syracuse: Syracuse University Press, 1998); Jeffrey Gurock, *Judaism's Encounter with American Sports* (Bloomington: Indiana University Press, 2005); Peter Levine, *Ellis Island to Ebbets Field: Sport and the American Jewish Experience* (New York: Oxford University Press, 1992). Historical studies on women's basketball, too, have neglected the role of Jewish women in basketball except for some information on the founder, Senda Berenson. Studies on women's history, sport history, and basketball that contain slim material on Jewish women in basketball include Pamela Grundy and Susan Shachkelford, *Shattering the*

Glass: The Remarkable History of Women's Basketball (New York: The New Press, 2005). Beyond the entry on Berenson, little material occurs about Jewish women and basketball in *Encyclopedia of Ethnicity and Sports in the United States* (eds. George B. Kirsch, et al.; Westport: Greenwood Press, 2000). On the need for additional scholarly work on Jews and sport, see Steven A. Riess, "Sport and the American Jew: A Second Look," *American Jewish History* 83 (March 1995).

³ Linda J. Borish and Elizabeth A. Zanoni, "Michigan Jewish Women, Physical Culture and Sport During the Early Decades of the Twentieth Century," *Michigan Jewish History* 46 (Fall 2006): 28-40.

⁴ "1895-GREETINGS-1925; A Brief History of the Irene Kaufmann Settlement" *Irene Kaufmann Settlement Neighbors* 3 (15 January 1925): 1-3; "Gym Work for Girls," *I.K.S. Neighbors* 1 (1 April 1923): 4; "Dancing! Gymnasium! Swimming!" *I.K.S. Neighbors* 1 (25 October 1923): 4.

⁵ "Dancing! Gymnasium! Swimming!" *I.K.S. Neighbors* 1 (25 October 1923): 4; "Girls, Use the Shower Baths and Swimming Pool!" *I.K.S. Neighbors* 3 (15 February 1925): 23; "The Water is Fine on Mondays," *I.K.S. Neighbors* 5 (13 March 1927): 34.

⁶ Charles S. Bernheimer, "Jewish Americanization Agencies," *American Jewish Year Book 5682,* 23: 3 Oct. 1921-22 Sept. 1922 (Philadelphia: Jewish Publication Society, 1922), 90-1; Linda J. Borish, "The Chicago Hebrew Institute," in *Chicago History Encyclopedia* (ed. J. R. Grossman, et al.; University of Chicago Press, 2004), 113. For additional information on some of the sport programs at Jewish settlement houses, see Linda J. Borish, "Place, Identity, Physical Culture and Sport for Women in Jewish Americanization Organizations," *STADION: Internationale Zeitschrift für Geschichte des Sports/ International Journal of the History of Sport/ Revue International d' Histoire du Sport,* "Sport and Religion," Special Issue, 35 (2009, published 2011): 87-108, and Borish and Eshel's documentary film, *Jewish Women in American Sport: Settlement Houses to the Olympics.*

⁷ Hyman L. Meites, *History of the Jews of Chicago* (Chicago: Jewish Historical Society of Illinois, 1927); Philip L. Seman, "Democracy in Action," *Chicago Jewish Forum,* 1943: 49-54, Philip L. Seman Collection, Scrapbooks, the Jacob Rader Marcus Center of the American Jewish Archives, Cincinnati, OH (hereafter AJA); Irving Cutler, *The Jews of Chicago From Shetl to Suburb* (Urbana: University of Illinois Press, 1996); Gerald R. Gems, "Sport and the Forging of a Jewish-American Culture: The Chicago Hebrew Institute," *American Jewish History* 83 (March 1995): 15-26; Gerald R. Gems, "Sports and Identity in Chicago," in *Sports and Chicago* (ed. E. J. Gorn; Urbana and Chicago: University of Illinois Press, 2008), 1-18 on ethnic sports in Chicago; Samuel L. Levine, "The Jewish Community Center Movement," *The Sentinel's History of Chicago Jewry, 1911-1961* (Chicago: Sentinel Publishing Co., n.d.), 184-86.

⁸ "'Good, Clean Sport,' Motto of C.H.I.," Philip L. Seman Collection, Scrapbook, Vol. I, 1910-1916; Bertha Loeb, "The Temple of the Body: How the Hebrew Institute is Laboring to Make Jews Physically Fit," *The Sentinel* (1 May 1914), Jacob M. Loeb Collection, Chicago Hebrew Institute (hereafter cited as CHI), AJA.

⁹ For information on this case and the petition to Jewish philanthropist Julius Rosenwald to contribute more funding for the CHI gymnasium to assist women, see Linda J. Borish, "Jewish Women, Sport, and Chicago History," in *Sports in Chicago,* 67-8.

[10] Jacob M. Loeb, Address, 31 March 1914, Chicago Hebrew Institute; "Break Ground for New Gymnasium at Hebrew Institute," *Chicago Israelite* (15 August 1914), Jacob M. Loeb Collection, CHI, AJA; Philip L. Seman, *Chicago Hebrew Institute, Superintendent's Report, 1915-1916,* no page nos., Chicago Jewish Archives/Spertus Institute of Jewish Studies, Chicago; see Borish, "'Athletic Activities of Various Kinds': Physical Health and Sport Programs for Jewish American Women," for information about the June 1915 dedication of the CHI new gymnasium.

[11] "Hebrew Institute Dedication is the Result of Hard Work and Optimism," ca. June 1915, Jacob M. Loeb Collection, CHI, AJA.

[12] Seman, *Chicago Hebrew Institute, Superintendent's Report, 1917-1918,* 45; *C.H.I. General Director's Report, 1921,* 56-7, *J.P.I. General Director's Report, 1922,* 80.

[13] "Salute the New Captain of the Chicago Hebrew Institute girls' basketball team, Miss Rose Rodkin," *Chicago Tribune* (8 January 1922): B3; for discussion of the CHI girls' basketball team and ethnic identity in other sports played, and coverage by the Anglo American and American Jewish press, see Linda J. Borish, "Jewish Girls, Gender and Sport at the Chicago Hebrew Institute: Athletic Identity in Jewish and Cultural Spaces," unpublished paper presented at the Association for Jewish Studies Annual Conference, 18 December 2005, Washington, DC.

[14] Harland Rohm, "Boys' Rules Speed Girls' Basket Games," *Chicago Tribune* (27 December 1926): 24.

[15] Newspaper Clippings, "Girl Cagers Look Impressive in Victory; Team is Host to Large Crowd at Dance," *Observer* (13 December 1934), Philip L. Seman Collection, Scrapbook, AJA; see Borish, "Jewish Women, Sports, and Chicago History," about sports teams CHI girls' played.

[16] Young Women's Hebrew Association Printed Materials of Class Activities, February 1934, YWHA Records, 92nd Street YM-YWHA Archives. 92nd Street Y, New York (hereafter 92nd Street YM-YWHA Archives).

[17] "Report Young Women's Hebrew Association, South Brooklyn, N.Y.," 8 November 1923, 1-2, and 8 January 1924, 1-3, Brooklyn YM-YWHA, Jewish Welfare Board Archives, American Jewish Historical Society Library, Waltham and New York (hereafter JWB Archives).

[18] "Report Young Women's Hebrew Association, Brooklyn, N.Y.," 15 April 1924, 1; "Report of Brooklyn YM-YWHA" 9 October 1924, JWB Archives.

[19] "Summary Field Work, Jewish Welfare Board," January, February, and March 1927, 14, 27; "Summary Field Work, Jewish Welfare Board," April 1927, JWB Reports, JWB Archives.

[20] "History of Hartford Y.W.H.A.," *Connecticut Hebrew Record* 1 (21 May 1920): 1, 3, 5, Jewish Historical Society of Greater Hartford, Hartford (hereafter JHSGH); Sander Hartwell Becker and Ralph L. Pearson, "The Jewish Community of Hartford, Connecticut, 1880-1929," *American Jewish Archives* 31 (November 1979): 184-214; for information on Hartford YWHA basketball teams and success in leagues and against other teams, see Linda J. Borish, "'An Interest in Physical Well-Being Among the Feminine Membership': Sporting Activities for Women at Young Men's and Young Women's Hebrew Associations," *American Jewish History* 87 (March 1999): 61-93; for historical material about the Hartford YWHA programs, see Linda J. Borish, "The Young Women's Hebrew

Association in Hartford, Connecticut and Affiliations with Immigrant Aid Associations Supporting Jewish Young Women in American Sporting Activities," American Studies Association Annual Conference, Hartford, October 2003.

[21] "Hartford Y.W.H.A. Challenges Teams," 13; "New Haven," *Connecticut Hebrew Record* 2 (10 December 1920): 12; "New Haven Y.W.H.A.," *Connecticut Hebrew Record* 2 (24 December 1920): 13, JHSGH.

[22] "Hartford Y.W.H.A.," *Connecticut Hebrew Record* 4 (30 September 1921): 18; "Hartford Y.W.H.A. Athletics," *Connecticut Hebrew Record* 4 (25 November 1921): 19; "Y.W.H.A. Girls Victorious," *Connecticut Hebrew Record* 4 (9 December 1921): 16, JHSGH.

[23] Morris Silverman, *Hartford Jews, 1659-1970* (Hartford: Connecticut Historical Society, 1970), 90; Marion Scharr, "Annual Report of the Young Women's Hebrew Association, Hartford, Connecticut," 30 June 1922, 3-5, YM-YWHA Collections, JHSGH.

[24] "Cornerstone of New Building to be Laid October 25th at 2:00 P.M.," *The Y Journal* 8 (23 October 1925), 4, St. Louis YM-YWHA Collections, Box 1, American Jewish Historical Society, Waltham and New York (hereafter cited as AJHS); "Physical Department Increases its Facilities," *The Y Journal, Silver Jubilee, 1927-1952* (16 May 1952): 10, Philadelphia Jewish Archives Center, The Balch Institute for Ethnic Studies, Philadelphia.

[25] "Cornerstone of New Building to be Laid October 25th at 2:00 P.M.," 4, St. Louis YM-YWHA Collections, AJHS.

[26] "The New Y.M.H.A. Building—A Description," *The Y Journal* 6 (25 April 1924): 4, St. Louis YM-YWHA Collections, AJHS.

[27] Beatrice, "Beatrice's Fair Facts," *The Y Journal* 20 (3 September 1937): 3, St. Louis YM-YWHA Collections, AJHS.

[28] "Instructions Given to Girls On Basketball," *The Y Journal* (16 October 1936): 2; "Youngsters To Bolster Girls' Basketball Team," *The Y Journal* (6 November 1936): 2, St. Louis YM-YWHA Collections, AJHS.

[29] "Girls Varsity Secure New Basketball Coach," *The Y Journal* 20 (23 October 1936): 1; "Girls' Varsity Is Victorious Over Nurses, 20 to 18," *The Y Journal* 20 (22 January 1937): 2, St. Louis YM-YWHA Collections, AJHS.

[30] "Varsity Girls Find Hard Schedule in Forthcoming Meets," *The Y Journal* 20 (19 February 1937): 2; "Girls Beat W.P.A. and Lose to Webster Five," *The Y Journal* 20 (5 March 1937): 2, St. Louis YM-YWHA Collections, AJHS.

[31] "Girl Basketballers in Benefit Game," *The Review* 14 (12 February 1932): 1; "Gym Gems," *The Review* 17 (22 March 1935): 1, see also "Girl Basketballers Forge Ahead," *The Review* 15 (6 January 1933): 1, AJHSL. See William R. Langfeld, *The Young Men's Hebrew Association of Philadelphia: A Fifty-Year Chronicle* (Philadelphia: The Young Men's and Young Women's Hebrew Association of Philadelphia, 1928), on the early years of women's activities in the YMHA.

[32] "Sports" section—"Married Women Get Basketball Challenge," and "Girls' Basketball Practice Arranged," *Y.M.-Y.W.H.A. Weekly* 1: 11 (12 November 1926): 3, "Girls Basketball Team Organized," *Y.M.-Y.W.H.A. Weekly* 1: 12 (19 November 1926): 4, Rauh Jewish Archives at the Senator John Heinz History Center, Pittsburgh (hereafter Rauh Jewish Archives).

[33] "Kingsely House Girls Lose to 'Y' Sextet in Slow Game, 77-3," *Y.M.-Y.W.H.A. Weekly* 1: 22 (28 January 1927): 3; "Sports Chats" and "Girls' Sextet Downs Wilmerding 'Y,'

36-10," *Y.M.-Y.W.H.A. Weekly* 1: 26 (25 February 1927): 3; "'Y' Girls' Continue Pace, Defeating Community House," *Y.M.-Y.W.H.A. Weekly* 1: 27 (4 March 1927): 3; "Girls Close Cage Year with Eight Wins, One Loss," *Y.M.-Y.W.H.A. Weekly* 1: 26 (11 March 1927): 3, and other related articles; photograph *Y.M.-Y.W.H.A. Weekly* 1: 33 (15 April 1927): 3, Rauh Jewish Archives.

[34] "Cage Stars from 1907-1918 'Y' Squad Fives Will See Action—Girls' Sextet Scheduled to Play in Preliminary Encounter," *Y.M.-Y.W.H.A. Weekly* 2:14 (28 December 1927): 7; "Basketball Games and Dance Carded for Gym February 8" and "Sport Chats," *Y.M.-Y.W.H.A. Weekly* 12: 18 (27 January 1928): 3; "Goldenson Girls-Johnston Y Game and Dance February 8," *Y.M.-Y.W.H.A. Weekly* 2: 19 (3 February 1928): 3; "Girls' Sextet Defeats M. Lebanon Loefflers—Go Into Tie with Tumblers for First Place in City League," *Y.M.-Y.W.H.A. Weekly* 2: 22 (2 March 1928): 3; "Varsity Sextet Defeats Tumblers in Upset Game," *Y.M.-Y.W.H.A. Weekly* 2: 25 (23 March 1928): 3; "Varsity Sextet Finishes Card in Second Place," *Y.M.-Y.W.H.A. Weekly* 2: 27 (30 March 1928): 3, and Photograph "Girls Basket Ball Team," 1927-1928 YM &YWHA, MSP# 389, JCC, Rauh Jewish Archives.

[35] "Floor Squad of Y.W.H.A.," *Pittsburgh Sun-Telegraph* (30 December 1928), YM &YWHA, Pittsburgh, PA, MSS #271, and photograph of YWHA Girls' Varsity Basketball Team, 1928-1929, Jewish Sports Hall of Fame, MSP#308, Rauh Jewish Archives.

[36] See various articles such as "Enter Girls' Sextet in New Cage League," *Y.M.-Y.W.H.A. Weekly* 4: 15 (20 December 1929): 3; "'Y' Girls' Basketball Team Triumphs, 22-11," *Y.M.-Y.W.H.A. Weekly* 4: 17 (10 January 1930): 3; "Girls' Sextet wins First Half Crown," *Y.M.-Y.W.H.A. Weekly* 4: 20 (31 January 1930): 3; "Pitt Alumnae Play Girls' Sextet Here This Saturday," *Y.M.-Y.W.H.A. Weekly* 4: 23 (21 February 1930): 3; "Girls' Sextet Meets Coraopolis Here Sat.," *Y.M.-Y.W.H.A. Weekly* 4: 4 (28 February 1930: 3; "Capital Institution Bows Before Girls," *Y.M.-Y.W.H.A. Weekly* 4: 26 (13 March 1930): 3, Rauh Jewish Archives.

[37] *The YM-YWHA Observer* (20 April 1934): 31-2, JWB Archives, AJHSL.

[38] *Jewish Community Center, Dedication Week Program, Yonkers, N.Y.*, 14-21 April 1929; *YMHA-YWHA, 1909-1934, Twenty-Fifth Anniversary, Mount Vernon, N.Y.*, 16-24 March 1934, JWB Archives, AJHSL.

[39] Jewish Community Center of Washington, DC, Scrapbooks, 1930s Jewish Historical Society of Greater Washington, (hereafter JHSGW); *Washington Post* (11 January 1930): 12; (27 February 1936): 16; (2 March 1936): 18; (21 November 1937): SP8.

[40] Jewish Community Center of Washington, DC, Scrapbooks, 1930s JHSGW.

[41] "Leaders Plan Sport Event for D.C. Girls," *Washington Post* (14 December 1937); Ruth Green, "D.C. Women in Athletics," *Washington Post* (19 December 1937); Flyer, Women's Physical Education Department, November 1938, Jewish Community Center of DC, Scrapbook, JHSGW.

[42] "Leaders Plan Sport Event for D.C. Girls," *Washington Post* (14 December 1937); "Center Gym Scene of 'Gay Nineties' Party, January 20," *National Jewish Ledger* (14 January 1938), Jewish Community Center of Washington, DC, Scrapbook, JHSGW.

[43] Jennifer Frey, "In Women's Basketball, She's an Old Pro," *Washington Post* (23 February 1997): D1, D6.

[44] "Personalities in Sports," *American Hebrew* 115 (6 June 1924): 126.

45 "Y.W.H.A. Notes," *The Nashville Y.M.H.A. News* 2 (October 1916): 9; "Y.W.H.A. Notes," *The Nashville Y.M.H.A. News* 3 (May 1917): 9, the Annette Levy Ratkin Jewish Community Archives, Nashville; "Matrons vs. Business Girls in Basketball Game," *Observer* (16 January 1936): 7.

46 "Pepettes Champs," *Observer* (27 January 1950), the Annette Levy Ratkin Jewish Community Archives, Nashville.

From Benny Leonard to Abi Olajuwon: Jews, Muslims, Evangelicals, and the Evolving Religious Challenges of Being an American Athlete

Ori Z Soltes

It is a truism of the immigration process into the United States in the early twentieth century that successful participation in sports presented itself as a way into the American mainstream. Not only was the American passion for sports surging toward an obsessive popularity that has continued until our own time, but sports at its most morally accomplished could offer an even · playing field, uninflected by religion and ethnicity, with respect to success. Where myriad businesses, emerging country clubs—and even institutions of higher learning that taught otherwise—most often remained laden with stated and unstated exclusivity clauses and promotion ceilings, athletic competition offered genuine opportunities to fulfill dreams. Sports offered itself as a genuine version of the melting pot ideal, where the combination of skill, sweat, and occasional good luck could yield success regardless of ethnicity and religion.[1]

JEWS, BOXING, AND BASEBALL IN THE GOLDEN AGE

For Jewish immigrants and their offspring (among others), sports in America offered a chance to fight one's way out of the ghetto—literally, in the case of boxing. One can easily enough understand how natural it could and would have been for someone who grew up in a tough city neighborhood in New York City or Chicago (or elsewhere), honing his fighting skills on the street, to be drawn to pugilism as a profession. Street skills developed on the lower rungs of society's ladder offered opportunities for their possessor to be recast as an athletic genius who could command the admiration and even the adulation of those dominating the upper rungs.

It is arguable that for some Jews in particular, boxing would have been attractive not only as a means, first, of protecting one's self on the street, and second, of leaving those mean streets behind. This in spite of centuries and centuries that had emphasized the intellectual and the spiritual rather than the physical as a means of Jewish survival.

But the entire idea of "scientific" boxing—of boxing with speed and technique, so that it was not a given that the bigger and stronger man prevailed—

had been shaped by an English Jew, Daniel "Battling" Mendoza, back at the end of the eighteenth century.[2] Moreover, by the late nineteenth and early twentieth centuries there were also broader movements afoot in different parts of Europe encouraging Jews toward a more physical approach to functioning in the world. A concept of "Muscular Judaism" and perhaps its most significant offshoot, "Muscular Zionism," were taking shape during this period. The American immigrant context offered a more intense setting in which to pursue new, physical goals.

Benjamin Leiner, aka Benny Leonard (1896-1947), the "Ghetto Wizard," certainly reflects this layered context. He grew up in the Jewish immigrant "ghetto" on the Lower East Side of New York City, and his primary training grounds were the streets. He later commented that "you had to fight or stay in the house when the Italian and Irish kids came through on their way to the baths."[3] But he developed as a first-rate tactician in the ring, combining speed and timing with his strength. He "moved with the grace of a ballet dancer"[4] and was also a powerhouse: "[Jack] Britton came back to the corner once in a fight with Benny and said, 'Nobody ever lived as strong as this guy.'"[5]

The beginning of Leonard's ring career is of interest from a Jewish perspective, in two ways. One, because it came against the backdrop of his mother's anguish that he should wish to go in that direction at all—"Is that a life for a respectable man? For a Jew?"—and as a consequence he changed his name from Leiner to Leonard.[6] Once he was out of that closet, his parents were in fact very supportive—and he never fought on Jewish holidays, in order to adhere at least somewhat to their sensibilities. Two, because it oddly and obliquely recalls the oft-told tale of how Hillel the Elder began on the road to his outstanding role as father of the rabbinic tradition.[7] The fifteen-year-old Leonard could not afford to buy a ticket to watch the fights, and one night he climbed up to a skylight of the club where they were taking place. He lost his balance, fell through the window, breaking the glass—and to pay for it, offered to take the place of a fighter who had not shown up for his bout.

He fought Mickey Finnegan (September 1911)—and lost, when the fight was stopped in the third round because of his bloody nose.[8] Of the next nine fights, he won six by knockouts, three were no-decisions. He lost once again in March 1912 and again in May 1912. He lost only once again in the next twenty years—on a technical disqualification.[9] Leonard fought 209 times as a professional, amassing a record of 204-5, and, as world lightweight champion, he successfully defended his title 88 times.[10] He held onto his title for a time stretch of more than seven and a half years, retiring in 1925. He would come out of retirement after losing all of his money in the stock market crash

and won either 19 or 23 more fights before encountering Jimmy McLarnin—
a future champion coming into his prime—who scored a TKO in the sixth
round against Leonard on October 7, 1932.[11]

More to the point of this narrative, Leonard inspired a generation of
young Jewish boys from the ghetto to take up the sport. As sportswriter Al
Lurie put it, as the champ, Leonard was "the most famous Jew in America—
beloved by thin-faced little Jewish boys, who, in their poverty, dreamed of
themselves as champions of the world."[12] If boxing experts argue whether he
was the greatest or merely the second greatest lightweight champion of all time
and where he fits among the greatest fighters in history in any and all weight
divisions, Jewish sports and culture aficionados argue whether he was the
greatest Jewish sports figure of all time.

Certainly his role as an instrument in fighting antisemitism is clear:
"When Leonard was accepted and admired by the entire fair-minded American community, the Jews of America felt that they themselves were being
accepted and admired."[13] As a practical matter he may be viewed as a double
starting point for Jewish engagement in professional sports in America. One,
in that he inspired so many others to follow in his footsteps—and succeed;
over the course of the 1920s and 1930s roughly 30 percent of professional boxers were Jews, with some 27 champions in various weight categories between
1910 and 1940.[14] Two, in that he represents the beginning of the question:
can one be both a Jew and a professional athlete in this country? What are
the lines that are crossable and what lines are not crossable? Leonard's decision
regarding fighting (which is to say, not to fight) on Jewish holidays (in part to
please his parents) was and is an important symbol of his consciousness of his
responsibilities as a Jew and not just as an individual with a talent for fisticuffs.
Whether he kept kosher we don't know.

Barney Ross (1909-67), born Beryl (or: Dov Ber) Rasofsky, was among
those who might be said to have picked up where Benny Leonard left off,
in a number of obvious ways, from his street-to-ring rise to his position as a
symbol of Jews to the non-Jewish world, to his engagement of his Judaism and
the role model he came to offer to other Jews, both those who were aspiring
fighters and those who were not. He was born on the Lower East Side of New
York City, but by the time he was two years old his family had moved to the
Maxwell Street "ghetto" in Chicago, where his father took over running a small
grocery store. Growing up, Ross was a student of Torah and Talmud whose
ambition—as that of his family for him—was to become a Hebrew school
teacher or a rabbi.

In 1923, his scholarly father—who had been a Hebrew teacher in the old country (Belarus) from which the family fled in the wake of state-sanctioned pogroms, in 1903, and who told his son that fighting was the wrong direction for a Jewish boy: "Let the *goyim* [non-Jews] be the fighters, the trumbleniks, the murderers; we are the scholars"—was gunned down during a botched robbery of his grocery store. This heartbreaking moment—perhaps enhanced by the inspiration that the shadow of Benny Leonard cast across the American Jewish landscape—effected a transformation in the young Ross. From being a formally religious fourteen-year-old, he angrily turned his back on the Orthodoxy lived and touted by the father, who is said by later tradition to have died in his arms.

He became a street-tough and street-smart kid who brawled and stole and ran money for the likes of Al Capone. His mother suffered a grief-induced nervous breakdown. His younger brothers and sister were put into an orphanage while Ross and his two older brothers were left pretty much on their own. His ambition was to earn enough money to buy a home where he could reunite the family; seeing boxing as a vehicle to accomplish that ambition, he began to train with his buddy, another Jewish ghetto kid, Jack Ruby.[15] He began to win amateur bouts and would pawn the prizes, saving the money for that family home he hoped to gain.

Because of his desire not to use his father's name in a profession of which his father so thoroughly disapproved and because he did not want his mother to find out that he was thus engaged—and perhaps also because of the not uncommon tendency among Jewish immigrants to shorten and Americanize their names—he began to call himself Barney Ross, with which name he became a Golden Gloves champ by 1929, soon thereafter turning pro and achieving that rarest of outcomes: he became a champion in three different weight divisions—lightweight, junior welterweight, and welterweight—the first pugilist to accomplish that feat.

Along the way he fought a number of notable opponents, including three epic bouts with Jimmy McLarnin in 1934—two years after McLarnin had defeated Benny Leonard in Leonard's last fight. Over his entire career, as an amateur and as a pro, he is said to have fought 329 fights—seventy-nine times in the professional ranks, winning seventy-two fights, losing four times, and fighting three times to a draw. His last fight, on May 31, 1938, was a losing effort to fellow three-division world champion Henry Armstrong. Armstrong pounded Ross severely, but, against the importuning of his trainers, Ross refused to quit and couldn't be taken down: he lost in fifteen rounds by decision. Boxing aficionados typically refer to that performance as among the most courageous in boxing history. Indeed, some have expressed the view that his refusal to go down resulted from his consciousness of his responsibility as a symbol of and for Jews: not only fighting back, but not going down.

From the perspective of this discussion, this last issue intersects the significance of when he didn't fight as opposed to when he did. In an era—the 1930s—marked by the rise of Nazism in Germany and increasingly vocal antisemitism in the United States, he took his position as a Jewish symbol to both a personal and a public level. In part to satisfy his mother, who came to accept and perhaps even to appreciate the fighter that he became, he refused fights scheduled on Saturdays, and while willing to fight on Friday evenings, he only fought within walking distance of his mother's home, so that he could walk her there after the bout.[16]

At his peak Ross was one of the two most visible and admired Jews across the country. The other was "Hammerin' Hank" Greenberg (1911-86), the consummate Jewish athlete in the consummate American sport. By the 1920s and 1930s, the era of Babe Ruth, baseball was in its Golden Age as America's pastime par excellence, and Hammerin' Hank was the second player (Jimmy Foxx was the first, in 1931) over a decade after the Babe's remarkable year of sixty home runs (1927) who seemed poised to outdo that number, in the summer of 1938.[17] By then Greenberg had won the first (1935) of his two major league MVP awards (the second came in 1940) and was in the midst of a spectacular all-star, Hall-of-Fame career.

If many a Jewish lad—particularly those living in the inner cities of America with their Jewish-Italian-Irish and other ghettos—admired Benny Leonard and Barney Ross and would have loved to accomplish what they had, one could multiply that number exponentially with regard to the dream of being the next Babe Ruth, until Hank Greenberg came along to offer a specifically Jewish star-focus. Baseball was the absolute ultimate, and dreamers like to dream of absolute ultimates.

As memorable as were his skills as a player and his role in bringing the Detroit Tigers to the top of the American League again and again and to the World Series, Greenberg is best remembered for the game he chose not to play. The year was 1934—a year after Hitler had come to power—during which the Detroit in which he lived and for whose Tigers he played was a center of American Nazi sympathy and antisemitism. Its epicenter was Father Charles Coughlin, a Catholic priest whose hatred of Jews was notorious and who expressed himself to that effect on a weekly radio program spewed across the air waves every Sunday.

That September—Greenberg's second full Major League season,[18] the Tigers were in the throes of a tight pennant drive against the New York

Yankees—they had not made it to the World Series in twenty-five years and the previous year had ended up in fifth place, twenty-five games out of first place—and Greenberg announced that he would not be playing on Rosh Hashanah (September 10) or on Yom Kippur (September 19). The fans were more than a bit disgruntled—after all, some said, Rosh Hashanah comes ever year but winning the pennant hasn't happened for the Tigers since 1909. The story has it that any number of Detroit rabbis were consulted. Greenberg's own rabbi is said, in the star's autobiography, to have referenced a passage in the Talmud in which "the start of a new year was supposed to be happy. He found that Jews in history played games on that day."[19]

Moreover, the rabbi argued that the importance of Greenberg's playing to his teammates and to the community of Detroit at such a time outweighed his potential personal need to sit the game out. The compromise was this: Greenberg showed up at his synagogue—Shaarey Zedek—that Rosh Hashanah morning and went directly from services to the stadium, did not take batting practice, but played in the game. Dramatically enough, he hit two home runs, as the Tigers beat the Boston Red Sox, 2-1. But he drew the line at Yom Kippur. He sat out the game—and remarkably, when he entered the synagogue, the congregation stood up and broke into spontaneous and sustained applause.[20] The Tigers were playing the Yankees that day and lost without Greenberg, 5-2, but they did go on to win the pennant with him—if not the World Series.[21] The following year the Tigers won the World Series, and Greenberg won his first MVP award.

More to the point, Greenberg's decision not to play on Yom Kippur caught the imagination of Detroit and the entire nation in the midst of the Father McCoughlin era. Detroit poet Edgar Guest was inspired to write (in part):

> Come Yom Kippur—holy fast day worldwide over to the Jew—
> And Hank Greenberg to his teaching
> > and the old tradition true
> Spent the day among his people and he didn't come to play.
> Said Murphy to Mulrooney, "We shall lose the game today!
> We shall miss him in the infield
> > and shall miss him at the bat,
> But he's true to his religion—and I honor him for that!"

The issue that most distinctly connects Ross and Greenberg as sports star contemporaries is that their decisions were based not simply on their own needs and desires, but in part on the responsibility that they both felt as Jews and the question they addressed internally as to how, as bigger than life public figures, to serve both as models for other Jews and as statements regarding Jews to the non-Jewish majority. In Ross's case, he commented in his autobiography on how, particularly when he fought McLarnin in Madison Square Garden before an audience of 50,000 fans, he felt as if he had the entire Jewish world on his shoulders. Every punch he threw was being thrown at Hitler and his venomous antisemitic rants. When in his last fight he refused to go down and wouldn't allow his corner to throw in the towel although he was being pummeled badly, at least part of his reason pertained to a sense of who he was as a symbol of Jewry. Conversely, his decisions not to fight on Saturdays pertained to his strong sense of the responsibility that came with his combined Jewish/boxing star identity.

In Greenberg's case, he was not only literally bigger than life—as a 6'4" athlete he towered over the congregation in which, according to the awestruck recollections of one of its members, most of the men were about 5'5" or 5'6"—but in the era of Hitler and Father Coughlin, he was viewed as a messianic figure: a secular messiah. That sense of Hammerin' Hank is literalized in a series of paintings done in the early 1990s by Detroit-born folk-style painter Malcah Zeldis, in which she depicts herself as a child together with her family sitting in their small living room in a house on a street of carefully kept houses, gathered around the radio from which a Tigers game is being broadcast. Rising, as it were, up out of the radio is a stadium, and within it, virtually filling the picture plane of the stadium, from home plate to scoreboard, and towering in significant perspective over the houses and their inhabitants, is an enormous Hank Greenberg, baseball bat over his shoulder.

Zeldis has commented on how, for her and Detroit Jews in general, the messianic, Moses-like Greenberg was leading the Jewish community through the Red Sea of Father McCoughlin's virulent tirades into the paradise and promised land of acceptance in America through his exploits in America's national sport.[22]

From a ground-level perspective, one may recognize of figures like Greenberg and Ross and Leonard that, as they present an attractive face of Jewry to a sports-obsessed Christian America, they also present a model for the hundreds and thousands of young Jewish boys who not only may aspire to become the next Leonard or Ross or Greenberg, but who, along the way, on a more limited plane, will also surely find it necessary to make some of the same decisions with respect to how to balance the obligations of their Judaism with those of their sports-playing hopes and desires.

That is: the challenges facing the Jewish athlete—whether playing on an elementary school baseball team or the Detroit Tigers—in a secular United States, which is also subtly and at times emphatically Christian, cover a range of issues and ideas. These extend from the question of how exactly or how firmly to keep the Sabbath or which festivals require changes in playing availability—some or all of the holidays, to what degree?—to the question of how to maintain *kashrut* as one moves from place to place to compete in locations where kosher food is not readily accessible to large-scale moral and ethical issues (how are issues like cheating or giving up under adverse pressure informed by one's Judaism?).

One might consider this layered issue by reference to the sort of comments made by Barney Ross's father regarding Jewish "values"—to wit, that fighting is for non-Jews, and studying is for Jews. The same sort of sentiment was effectively expressed by Benny Leonard's mother. If baseball presented a somewhat less objectionable goal for an aspiring young Jew—and if on the one hand, the legacy of "Battling" Mendoza could still be felt more than a century and a quarter after he was gone from the scene, and on the other, the idea of "Muscular Judaism," especially allied with nascent Zionism, had brought a new attitude toward physical accomplishment to many Jews in Europe—nonetheless, as George Eisen has put it:

> In the hierarchy of Jewish religious values, feats of physical prowess were invariably relegated to the "secular" and the "mundane." There has always been a strong aversion in Jewish culture and tradition toward violent or blood sports that often were the hallmarks of neighboring tribes, societies and cultures.[23]

Thus, fundamentally, any Jewish American athlete was making a choice with regard to how to define himself as a Jew and, should he succeed, with regard to what sort of responsibility that implied as a Jew. If there was no time in modern history when a Jew could outrun his identity, however assimilated he might become—and in many cases, even if he converted out of the faith[24]—certainly the 1930s in general and the situation in Detroit in particular accentuated the issue of Jewish identity for public figures.

FROM PLAYING FIELD TO BATTLEFIELD TO OTHER BATTLES

Not surprisingly, this sensibility extended beyond the playing field and the decision not to fight on the Sabbath or not to play ball on Yom Kippur, particularly given the era. As the 1930s yielded to the 1940s and the era of the Great Depression, the rise of Hitler and other fascist leaders gave way to war. Mid-career, Hank Greenberg was the first Major League star to elect to give up baseball for battle, asserting the primacy of responsibility to his country over his personal baseball ambitions. In fact, when he was initially classified 4-F due to flat feet, tradition has it that he bribed the enlistment board to re-test him. When after having missed most of the 1941 season he was honorably discharged (the army was discharging everyone over age twenty-eight), he re-enlisted after Pearl Harbor—the first pro baseball player to do so.

He stayed in uniform, active in the South Pacific (as opposed to doing his service in a domestic army camp where he could have played baseball) until the end of the war—by far the longest service of any Major League baseball player. The first day back, with no spring training, he homered—and he brought the Tigers back to the World Series with a grand slam on the last day of the season and to a World Series victory over the Chicago Cubs in seven games with two homers that fall.

Similarly, Benny Leonard had served in World War I and served again in the maritime service during World War II. Barney Ross, after his career was already over and he was also well beyond the standard age of military enlistment, pushed himself into the arena of conflict. In the South Pacific his bravery achieved legendary status. At Guadalcanal, he and three comrades were pinned down by enemy fire. His fellow marines badly wounded, he spent all night, using up each of their weapons in turn, fighting against some two dozen Japanese soldiers, killing them all by morning. At dawn, with two comrades dead, he carried his fellow survivor—who outweighed him by ninety pounds—to safety. His bravery earned him a Silver Star and a Presidential Citation.

In this appositional context—the heroic Jewish fighter as a singular symbol of his people to others—one might consider a related lens through which to perceive the position of star Jewish athletes in the United States of the 1930s. That lens is offered up by the Orthodox theologian Rabbi Joseph B. Soloveitchik in his essay on "The Lonely Man of Faith."[25] Soloveitchik uses the two contexts in Genesis in which Adam is presented—the first, in Genesis 1, where Adam is created together with Eve ("male and female He created them") and in which he is commanded to "fill the earth and subdue it"; and the second, in Genesis 2, where Adam is created and then Eve is created from his rib—to suggest two kinds of human beings. The first—Adam I—is the "majestic man," who uses his creative abilities to master the world around him; the second—Adam II—is "covenantal man," who surrenders himself to God's will and seeks an intimate relationship with the world around him and the God who made it all.

The latter is part of a covenantal community of redemption-seeking faith. The self-aware messianic contexts of these sports figures, however secularized, can be translated easily enough into Soloveitchik's terms: each of them might be understood as "lonely men of faith" and each may be defined as such in part through being "covenantal men," who submitted humbly to God's will and recognized their talents as a consequence of that will. Each saw himself as part of a Jewish community of redemption-seeking faith. Each saw himself as having a noncontradictory dual responsibility to his country and to his faith.

One might apply the question of defining that faith—of understanding the relationship between the Judaism of athletes like Leonard, Ross, and Greenberg and the sports in which they participated—not only in terms of grand and heroic gestures, such as serving in the American army or sitting out a Yom Kippur game, but also of small, daily decisions. Among those daily decisions was whether or not to maintain *kashrut* in places (this would be more obvious for a baseball player than for a boxer) where such food was not readily available. There were also decisions regarding the keeping of a Jewish holiday that might inherently conflict with athletic performance. As with *kashrut*, the conditions for a boxer and a baseball player would not be identical. An accomplished fighter could choose with some ease to avoid a match on Yom Kippur, or even on Shabbat, due to relative flexibility in scheduling that involved himself, his opponent, the necessary officials, and their respective entourages; but a professional baseball player cannot control the schedule that juggles dozens of games each week in the course of more than half a year for an entire league of teams; and his individual decision to play or not to play on a given day can affect his entire team.

But the Soloveitchikean "Lonely Man of Faith" is about more than that. It encompasses what, particularly in the era when these Jewish athletes were in their prime, every action that specifically identified them as Jewish athletes and not merely as athletes, because of their fame, drew the attention of both the Jewish and the larger non-Jewish world. If Ross articulated it overtly— that in every fight he felt a particular and peculiar sense of responsibility; that every fight became a fight against Hitler and a statement about Jewish grit—Greenberg understood just as clearly the ramifications of his decision to play under modified conditions on Rosh Hashanah, and not to play at all on Yom Kippur.

Each of these athletes, who exhibited the traits of "majestic man" by subduing the world of his sport, also transcended that self-focused mode of being in the world and became an example of "covenantal man." Each submitted humbly to the transcendent reality beyond him and sought an intimate relationship with the world around him, reaching out to serve it as part of a redemptive—messianic, however secularized—process. For each, that Jewish sensibility was uniquely intertwined with—and challenged by—their American sensibilities.

Most obviously, beyond the arena of their sports accomplishments, their respective senses of Jewish American and American Jewish responsibility as public figures were articulated in their decisions with respect to the military. Greenberg chose to sacrifice the best years of his playing career and not to take the cushy domestic position away from the fire that was offered to him as someone who felt a responsibility to serve, combining his American with his Jewish sensibilities. Ross fought to get into uniform even though he was beyond standard military service age. And his wartime heroism vied with his accomplishments in the ring as a stunning statement not only of his own quality of character, but also of Jewish physical and psychological grit.

A small incident, the conditions of which are in a sense antithetical to those of his physical bravery, offers yet another angle from which to recognize subtle cultural elements within Ross's Jewish consciousness: that consciousness extended from the boxing ring to the battlefield by way of music. At Guadalcanal, he became good friends with the well-known Catholic chaplain Father Frederic Gehring, who asked him to participate in a Christmas Eve gathering before he (Ross) and his fellow Marines would be going into battle. Ross was the only one who could play the organ located on the island, and Father Gehring asked him to play some Christmas songs for the troops, after which Gehring asked him to play a Jewish song. Ross chose "My Yiddishe Momma"—which the troops would all recognize as the tune that was always played as Barney entered the boxing ring. But this was the first time they heard the lyrics, which speak of a child's love for his self-sacrificing Jewish mother. The soldiers are said to have teared up substantially.

* * *

So what does it mean to be a Jew? What are the ways and the challenges to expressing one's Jewishness on the playing field? It may be said to be comprised of small gestures and large statements. It would not come as a surprise that when Jackie Robinson broke the color line as the first African American player in the Major Leagues, Hank Greenberg was the first star—perhaps the first Major-Leaguer—who greeted him warmly and encouragingly at the time of their first encounter. It's not that other, non-Jewish players couldn't have done the same based on the ethical codes of their own traditions—but they didn't and he did. Was this because of his Judaism or because of his family upbringing or because of the personality makeup of Hank Greenberg as an individual, or was it perhaps through a combination of such factors? It is impossible to know for sure.

Be that as it may, the times and the world and the demographic shape of the United States all continued to evolve in different directions as the 1940s yielded to the 1950s and 1960s. Jews began to move on, from the ghettoized cities to the burgeoning suburbs, from the immigrant and child-of-immigrant fringe to the mainstream within American socioeconomics, culture, even politics, and, by and large, their numbers shrank within the boxing ranks and in general in professional sports, as athletes.[26]

One might suppose, in reflecting on the America that was beginning to rebel against narrower aspects of itself by the mid-1960s, that sports would be at the forefront of the process of rebellion: after all, Jackie Robinson was already a star and Major League Baseball significantly integrated well before schools in the American South were. So when the Los Angeles Dodgers—the former Brooklyn Dodgers, long-suffering serial victims to the New York Yankees (as the Tigers, among others, had been), now on the West Coast and experiencing a new lease on baseball life—were about to go up against the Minnesota Twins in the 1965 World Series and the peerless Jewish Dodger pitcher, Sandy Koufax (b. 1935), elected to sit out the first game because it fell on Yom Kippur, the headlines were rampant.

More than thirty years had passed since Hank Greenberg's grand gesture, and such a decision—facilitated in large part, Koufax would himself comment, by the memory of Greenberg's decision—might be supposed to have been relatively easy to arrive at. But this was, after all, the World Series. The opening game. It proved not to be so simple, as—to Koufax's own amazement—a sports column in the *St. Paul Pioneer Press* appeared the day after the Twins pummeled Don Drysdale and the Dodgers, 8-2, with several unfriendly allusions to the Jewish factor in Koufax's decision not to pitch that day, to which the pitcher responded that he thought that such small-mindedness had disappeared years earlier.[27] The challenges and choices pertinent to being a Jewish athlete in America still presented themselves, even in the era of the emerging Civil Rights, ethnic identity, and feminist movements.

Changes had also reshaped the American Jewish community in both broad and sports-specific ways. In the course of the 1950s and 1960s many Jews, socioeconomically successful or at least aspiring to be so, moved out of the cities and into the new, uniquely American phenomenon of the suburbs. With such demographic shifts, the participation of Jews in sports like boxing—for which so much of the human material came out of the "ghettoes" in the cities—began to all but disappear. On the other hand, in addition to the continuing interest and star-level success in broadly popular "mainstream" professional sports like baseball (e.g., Cleveland Indians' star Al Rosen), football (Sid Luckman), and basketball (Dolph Shayes), there emerged an increasing interest on the part of Jews in "country club" sports endemic to the suburbs, such as tennis (in which Dick Savitt had already starred by the early 1950s), swimming (where by the late 1960s and early 1970s Mark Spitz starred), and even golf.

Moreover, the importance of sports for Jews, particularly immigrants and the children of immigrants, as a mechanism for weaving one's self into the American tapestry would be felt by a succession of other groups, from Italians to African Americans to Hispanics; and similar patterns of participation would follow standout athletes within these groups from the boxing ring to the baseball field and beyond as the country evolved in essential ways from the era of Leonard to that of Ross and Greenberg to the time of Koufax and beyond.

CHALLENGES TO MUSLIM ATHLETES IN A NON-MUSLIM SPORTS WORLD

By the year of Koufax's 1965 Yom Kippur decision, Hakeem Olajuwon was two years old (b. Jan 21 in 1963 in Lagos) and living in Nigeria, where he was born. Like many of the Jews of Leonard's, Greenberg's, and Ross's parents' generation, Olajuwon was an immigrant to the United States, albeit under circumstances that would distinguish him from the Jewish players whom we have discussed and the context in which their families came to the United States. Olajuwon was already viewed as a potential basketball star while still in his country of birth and came to the United States in 1980 as a teenager, separated from the family that he left behind in Africa. He was recruited as a player—brought here to play for the University of Houston, where, under Coach Guy Lewis, he enjoyed a standout career that included three appearances in the NCAA Final Four championship games.

He was the first player drafted into the NBA in the year of his graduation, 1984, and spent a long career starring for the Houston Rockets. Known fondly as "Akeem the Dream" for his graceful demeanor off the court as much as for his grace as a player on it, the 7' player combined with the 7'4" Ralph Sampson to give Houston an extraordinary front court known popularly as the "Twin Towers." Together they led the Rockets to the 1986 NBA playoff finals, where they lost in six games to the Boston Celtics. After Sampson's departure for the Golden State Warriors, Olajuwon emerged as the unquestioned leader of the team and led the Rockets to back-to-back NBA championships, in 1994 and 1995. In the first of those years, he became the only player in NBA history to win the MVP award, the defensive player of the year award, and also the playoff finals MVP award in the same year.

During the early 1990s Olajuwon, raised as a Muslim in Nigeria, but having lived a fairly secular life at least since his arrival in the United States, began to become more focused on his religion—as he put it, not dabbling, but seriously studying the Qur'an every day. This was the context in which he restored the spelling of his name from Akeem to its original form, Hakeem, in

March 1991. More to the point of this discussion, issues that would not have provided a focus for him began to do so. At least two aspects of his faith would provide challenges paralleling issues of potential challenge for Jewish players.

The first is simply and directly gastronomic: as a Jewish player might be concerned about maintaining a certain level of *kashrut*—and one could imagine that this would provide a particular challenge for athletes playing in sports like baseball and basketball, where the team was frequently on the road in places where kosher food might not be readily available—the equivalent of that gastronomic concern in Islam is *hallal*. If these are not the same—an observant Muslim may eat shellfish, for instance, where an observant Jew may not; and an observant Jew may consume alcohol, where an observant Muslim may not—yet both require a divergence from the standard gastronomy across America, in particular where the nonconsumption of pork and the consumption of properly slaughtered beef and lamb are concerned.

There is no documentary evidence that *kashrut* was an issue of concern for Hank Greenberg or Barney Ross or Benny Leonard—nor for any of the Jewish athletes who starred in various American sports through the mid-1970s—nor is there clear documentary evidence that Hakeem Olajuwon followed an insistently *hallal*-guided diet through the course of his career, and should he or other Muslim athletes choose to do so, the requirements, less stringent than those of *kashrut*, would have perhaps made the process less difficult than it would be for their Jewish counterparts. But the point, of course, is that in both cases, Jewish and Muslim players would have to make a decision as to whether and with what precision to observe their respective gastronomic prescriptions, whereas such an issue would rarely if ever cross—would rarely if ever need to cross—the mental and spiritual radar screens of their Christian counterparts, however secularized or observant they might be.

Further, the decisions of a Jewish athlete like Barney Ross or Benny Leonard with regard to not playing on the Sabbath have no genuine comparative context for a Muslim athlete. Arguably, the issue of the Sabbath would have potential implications for Christian athletes, but historically it seems that, in the United States, at least, it rarely if ever did. The evolution of professional sports competition in this country seems to have run on a track parallel to that of widespread secular sensibilities with regard to Sunday Sabbath observance.

On the other hand, one might find parallels in modes of praying that fall outside Sabbath observance. A Jewish athlete wishing to pray in a traditional manner will wrap his right arm and forehead with the phylactery boxes and straps called *t'fillin* during his morning prayers (every day except the Sabbath). Barney Ross recounts that, while training for the rematch scheduled with

Tony Canzoneri in September 1933, "[b]efore I took off for my roadwork, I dug out the bag of *t'fillin* . . . and said my morning prayers." While there is no direct parallel to this ritual act in Islam, the oblique parallel would be the mode of Muslim prayer five times a day. Each set of prayers includes several rakka'as—a bodily process of kneeling on the earth and placing one's forehead to it. Thus each set requires a place somehow apart from the busy world around, where one can lay out some material—be it as simple as newspaper or, more elegantly, a prayer rug specifically designed for this purpose—to create a physical space that separates the devotee engaged in a sacred act from the profane world.

The parallels between Yom Kippur as a twenty-five-hour fast—or at least a day-long complete cessation from the everyday activity of baseball, and the decision not to play on that day, however significant the game—and the Muslim fast of Ramadan are interesting.[28] Ramadan lasts an entire month[28] and requires of Muslims that they refrain from food from sunrise to sunset. Thus on the one hand, whereas the Jewish fast begins before sunset on the eve of the festival and continues until after sunset the following day, the Muslim fast continues daily for an extended period of time, albeit with food consumption once night has fallen on each of those days.

There are obvious concomitants of this. Taking an entire day off for Yom Kippur would (at least in theory) be accompanied, for a Hank Greenberg or a Sandy Koufax, by spending much or all of the day in prayer in the synagogue, surrounded by the Jewish congregation of which he was part—and/or part of it at home, be it alone or as part of the family. Ramadan would require not only the five sets of prayers in which a traditional Muslim engages every day (at sunrise, mid-morning, midday, mid-afternoon, and sunset) of the year, but often additional prayers, for any or all of which there may or may not be an opportunity to be with other Muslims. And each of these sets of prayers involves the bodily process referred to above, which requires the space needs referred to above.

A Muslim is not expected not to go about his business during the entire month of Ramadan, as a Jew is expected to during the entire night and day of Yom Kippur. So the question is: how can a world-class athlete go about his business, engaging in grueling physical activities while not eating all day long? Since the Muslim calendar is lunar, and thus the Muslim year is 355 days long—ten to eleven days shorter than the solar, Gregorian calendar—the month of Ramadan falls at different times during the year. Thus as with Yom Kippur, which might or might not fall on the day of a crucial game, Ramadan might or might not fall during the playing season. But it certainly can and many times has. For Olajuwon, this meant that many times throughout his NBA career he played without eating or drinking for one month at some point during the season. In 1995, for example, Ramadan fell in February—the very month when Olajuwon won the NBA Player of the Month award. His teammates commented then and thereafter that he seemed to play with a particular intensity during Ramadan. So at least in Olajuwon's case, the spiritual focus sharpened by fasting also sharpened, rather than distracting from or weakening, his mental and physical focus.

Other issues further the question of what challenges might be faced by members of a particular religious minority even as the world and the world of sports have moved to the end of the twentieth century and into a new millennium. Hakeem Olajuwon's daughter, Abi Olajuwon (b. California in July 1988), began a successful career as a basketball player in the new millennium. Having starred for her California high school team and gone on as a McDonald's All-American to a splendid college career at the University of Oklahoma, she began her professional career for the WNBA team, the Chicago Sky, in 2010.

On the one hand, it is a function of gradual changes in the American and world sports scene since the 1960s that such a career arc for a woman would be possible. On the other hand, an obvious question that might be raised for Abi Olajuwon as a Muslim woman that would not have needed to cross the radar screen of her father—or of any male Muslim or Jewish athlete—is not gastronomic, but sartorial. The question of female modesty—what parts of the body, or even of the face, should be shown to the world—is a broad one, which can be seen to preoccupy not only Muslim and Jewish, but Christian thought.[29] But to a certain extent the sartorial issue is limited: those who choose to compete in sports, such as basketball, swimming, or track and field, where garments tend to be skimpy, are not likely to be affiliated with the orthodox branches of their traditions.

Indeed, images that record the emergence of basketball as a women's sport in the late nineteenth century show the players covered from neck to toe.[30] But by the time of Abi Olajuwon, and the change in rules of play that have provided the women's game with as much speed and aggressive possibilities as the men's game, such clothing would be more than impractical. So the question of sartorial choices runs parallel to that of keeping the Sabbath or fasting on certain holidays within the larger question of what precisely is required to consider one's self a Jew or a Muslim—or a Christian. Clearly for Olajuwon, the standard skimpiness of a basketball uniform does not affect her sense of herself as a Muslim. And in the United States it would not occur to non-Muslims to judge her otherwise—and those Muslims who might view her negatively are a silent minority with no affect on her personal choice. Certainly it has not occurred to her father, who cheers her on at her games, to judge her negatively because of her basketball uniform.

This last sort of issue, in fact, causes the matter of being part of a religious minority within the sports world of secular Christian America to intersect a related but separate subject, that of gender politics as they have continuously affected the world of sports inside and outside the United States. The sartorial aspect of this issue seems to be unique to parts of the Muslim world. Thus, on the one hand, the dominant Algerian track star Hassiba Boulmerka found it dangerous to return home from the 1992 Olympic games after her gold-medal performance in the 1,500-meter race because a prominent imam in her community in effect offered a death threat to her because of what he regarded as the affront to Islam—that she presented in being skimpily attired (as all her fellow sprinters were) for her event.

On the other hand, eight years earlier, Nawal El Moutawakel of Morocco, the first Muslim woman to earn a gold medal in the Olympics—she won the 400-meter race in Los Angeles—was adulated upon her return, ultimately being appointed to the position of minister of sports in her country. And then again, a growing number of female Muslim athletes have found success in events that require no sartorial compromises. Nassim Hassanpour of Iran, for example, fared quite well in sharpshooting in the 2004 Olympics in Athens, and her event did not require that she be other than fully covered in order to participate. So clearly this issue offers a range of possible and actual responses not only from individual athletes, but also from the specific communities of which they are part in reflecting a reality different from that in American sports.

EVANGELICALS AND EPILOGUES

Thus to date, using Abi Olajuwon as my example, the sartorial modesty issue has not shown itself in the United States. But that does not mean that other issues affecting religious minorities, most obviously Jews and Muslims, have not emerged to greater prominence in the last few decades. The matter of prayer or peer pressure regarding prayer or even conversion, oddly, seems to have been altogether foreign to the eras of Hank Greenberg or Sandy Koufax but not to those of Hakeem or Abi Olajuwon. As early as 1989, the Eleventh Circuit Court in Texas ruled (in *Jager v. Douglas County School District*) that pregame invocation prayers by coaches, officials, or students at high school football games are unconstitutional—this in response to the decidedly

Christological tone of those invocations and the implied exclusion of non-Christians from them or pressure (implicit or explicit) for non-Christians to be part of them.

Six years later (the year of Hakeem Olajuwon's most stunning successes on the basketball court) in the Fifth District US Court of Appeals a ruling argued that informal student-initiated and student-led prayers at sports events are constitutional. Four years after that, a lawsuit was filed in the Santa Fe School District in Galveston, Texas, by a Mormon and Roman Catholic pair of families to challenge that ruling—and the news coverage of the discussion kept the names of those families anonymous in order to protect them from expected reprisals. So the question of whether and where to fit particularized religious sensibilities within the world of American athletic competition—and where to draw lines between participation and coercion—has grown, not shrunk in the past two decades.

Perhaps more astonishingly, as recently as the summer of the Beijing Olympics (2008), a long article in the *New York Times*—beginning on the front page, not the front sports page—reported, regarding Kisik Lee, coach of the US archery team, that he had successfully converted a number of his charges to serious Christianity.[31] The front page lead included a photograph of him baptizing one of them, and within the first few paragraphs he was quoted as saying that, while he would ideally like to treat all of the young athletes committed to his care equally, he cannot honestly treat those who do not share his religious beliefs as warmly as he does those who do.[32]

The coach, who came from Korea to the United States in order to reshape and upgrade the quality of the US Olympic archery team, is himself a born-again Christian with an obviously very strong evangelical sense of his mission as a coach. The question raised by the article is whether he has the right—and should continue to be afforded the opportunity—to mix the shaping of his athletes' physical skills with the shaping of their spiritual direction. And that question, while it is addressed in the article primarily with regard to nonpracticing, secularized Christian youths, can and does extend even more emphatically to Jewish and Muslim (and other non-Christian) athletes as they continue to participate—or desire to participate—in the wide range of team sports, from the school and university level to the Olympic and professional level, in which one's participation can subtly or distinctly be determined by a coach's decision and in which that decision may be informed by one's acquiescence or nonacquiescence to personal faith style—as opposed to one's inherent athletic prowess or effort.[33] We have come full circle to the issue of American sports in America presenting or not presenting an even playing field to all of its players, based on sweat and skill and not on ethnicity, race, or religion.

As an epilogue, one might also return this discussion full circle to the sport with which it began, boxing—an individual, not team sport, as it were—and arrive at Yuri Foreman. Foreman arrived in the United States as an immigrant from Belarus (part of the former Soviet Union) by way of Israel and is popularly known as the "Lion of Zion." In a manner reminiscent of Hakeem Olajuwon, somewhere in the course of his rise to athletic prominence he became more attuned to and interested in his faith. Foreman ultimately became Orthodox as a Jew—in fact he began to study to become a rabbi in 2007. On December 5 of that year he defeated Andrey Tsurkan for the North American Boxing Federation (NABF) super welterweight title.[34] Two years later, in 2009, he became the new WBA super welterweight champ.[35]

Foreman was scheduled to fight a major bout, the first defense of his title, against Miguel Cotto—in Yankee Stadium, no less—and the fight was scheduled for June 5, 2010, which turned out to be a Saturday. He refused to fight unless the fight was scheduled for well after sundown (which, in June, is fairly late in New York City). So the fight was scheduled to begin at 11:30 p.m., after the Sabbath had firmly and clearly ended.

Foreman lost that bout by a TKO, in part, perhaps, due to a previously-sustained injury to his right knee that made it difficult for him to put weight on it. He had surgery on the knee and is back training for his next encounter in the boxing ring, while he continues his rabbinic studies—and continues to observe the Sabbath as a traditional Jew, saving his ring work for the other six days of the week, all of which are legitimate sports days not only for him, but for most of the secular Christian American world of sports.[36]

NOTES

[1] Eventually, that would encompass race and even gender. But one can look at the story of Jack Johnson, the black boxer of this early-twentieth century era, as much as a morality tale of how far even sports were from being color-blind at that time as of how sports opened doors otherwise closed to African Americans.

[2] Mendoza was the English boxing champion in 1792-95. He was the only middleweight ever to win the Heavyweight Championship. After he retired, he opened a school to which Jewish boys particularly flocked and also wrote what became a popular book on the scientific art of boxing.

[3] This is quoted both in Harold U. Ribalow and Meir Z. Ribalow, *The Jew in American Sports (New York: Bloch, 1955), 160;* and in Robert Slater, *Great Jews in Sports,*(New York: Jonathan David, 2005), 132.

[4] Dan Parker (1893-1967), renowned sports writer (four decades for the *New York Daily Mirror* and, toward the end of his career, after the *Mirror* folded, for the *New York Jour-*

nal-American), is quoted by Ribalow and Ribalow, *The Jew in American Sports*, 176, and by Slater, *Great Jews*, 134, from an obituary Parker wrote at the time of Leonard's sudden death at age fifty-one from a brain hemorrhage.

[5] The manager Dan Morgan reports this in discussing the most memorable fight of Britton's career, in which he was knocked down by Leonard in their epic June 26, 1922 fight. See fn. 9.

[6] Mrs. Leiner's rhetorical question is quoted in Ribalow and Ribalow, *The Jew in American Sports*, 157.

[7] The story is told that he was too poor to afford to pay his way into the classroom, so he would sit outside by a window listening. One time when it began to snow, the teacher noticed the boy outside and brought him inside; impressed by the young man's dedication, he offered him a seat in the classroom: one might call Hillel the first scholarship student.

[8] Slater refers to this first bout as a victory, but I believe he is mistaken. Every other source indicates that Leonard lost in the third round. One account even suggests that he was knocked out. Of course, I am assuming that the Finnegan bout was the one that he fought in order to pay for the broken skylight. It may be that the Finnegan fight was the first "official" one for Leonard after he had stepped in, and perhaps that first fight is not recorded in his official record, but then how does Slater know that it was a victory? There is quite a paucity of precise information.

[9] In the midst of holding the lightweight championship, Leonard moved up to challenge Britton for the welterweight title—he had "defeated" Britton in two prior no-decisions—and was winning when, in the thirteenth round, with Britton down on one knee, Leonard inexplicably continued with a blow to his opponent that caused the referee to disqualify him. That seems to have been Leonard's only loss between May 1912 and the last fight of his career, in 1932.

[10] One can find a range of variations in the statistics for Leonard's career. One source, for example, gives his career as having included eighty-five wins (sixty-nine by knockout), five losses, and one draw—and 119 no decisions. Part of this may be explained by the fact that, for much of his career, in order to prevent corrupt skewing of wins and losses, any fight that did not result in a knockout or other decisive win/loss resulted simply in a no-decision outcome. Another source refers to 183 wins, including seventy knockouts, nineteen defeats, eleven draws, and several no-decisions—in a career said to have included 213 fights. For our purposes, aside from the amusing datum that "facts" are hard to come by in this realm (and perhaps the irony, since sports as a medium is so statistic-obsessed), it doesn't matter. Other issues are more important.

[11] Again, one finds varied statistics regarding how many fights he fought between coming out of retirement and his defeat by McLarnin.

[12] Sportswriter Al Lurie made this statement in a 1943 obituary immediately following Leonard's death. It is quoted in the Benny Leonard article in www.Jewsinsport.org.

[13] Ibid.

[14] These statistics are asserted in a number of places, most recently in the texts for the exhibition, "Sting Like a Maccabee: The Golden Age of the American Jewish Boxer," at the National Museum of Jewish American History, in Philadelphia, in 2004.

[15] Yes, the same Jack Ruby would become famous four decades later for shooting Lee Harvey Oswald in the aftermath of the JFK assassination.

[16] The night he first took the lightweight crown from Tony Canzoneri (June 23, 1933) he completely missed the post-fight celebration, since it was a Friday night and he was busy walking his mother home from the stadium.

[17] Like Foxx, Greenberg ended up with fifty-eight home runs. There were many who asserted that he was receiving an inordinately large number of walks—being pitched around—during the last week or two of the season, due to antisemitic prejudice. Greenberg himself consistently disavowed that notion.

[18] He batted .339, led the league in doubles (63; fourth highest all-time), and was third in slugging percentage (.600; behind Jimmie Foxx and Lou Gehrig, but ahead of Babe Ruth) that season.

[19] Sportscaster Dick Schaap would later note that "the rabbi knew that the Talmud really said that it was Roman children who played on Rosh Hashanah. But the rabbi didn't tell Hank that part." (Quoted in Aviva Kempner's article "The Game Came Second: When Hammerin' Hank Greenberg Stayed Home for Yom Kippur," in the *Washington Post*, Sunday, September 18, 1994.) Kempner was working at that time on what has been a well-received documentary film about Greenberg, *The Life and Times of Hank Greenberg*, 1999.

[20] Quoted from his autobiography by Kempner in the same article.

[21] The Tigers would end the season with a seven-game lead over the Yankees and the best record in baseball, but ultimately lost the World Series to the St. Louis Cardinals in seven games.

[22] This in interviews with the artist in spring, summer, and fall 1991. See Ori Z. Soltes, *Symphonies in Color: The Paintings of Malcah Zeldis* (exhibition catalogue, B'nai B'rith Klutznick National Jewish museum, 1994), 8. There are other Jewish American artists for whom baseball became an important image, most obviously R. B. Kitaj, but his work was offered more from the perspective of an American who, having grown up in Ohio, became for many years an expatriate living and working in England, and looking with a certain hard-edged nostalgia at baseball as a symbol of that childhood world of his past, rather than looking through the lens of the Jewish experience. Kitaj reserved the latter issue for another body of work focused mainly on the Holocaust. See Ori Z Soltes, "Center Field of Dreams and Questions: Baseball and Judaism," in *What is Jewish About America's "Favorite Pastime"? Essays and Sermons on Jews, Judaism and Baseball* (ed. Mark Lee Raphael and Judith Z. Abrams; Williamsburg: The College of William and Mary, 2006). Zeldis and Cohen are also discussed in that essay.

[23] He made the comment in the introduction to the volume he co-edited, of selected papers from a 2001 international symposium held on the occasion of the 16th Maccabiah games, *Sport and Physical Education in Jewish History* (Jerusalem: Wingate Institute, 2001). Of course, on the other hand, Leonard himself commented in a 1925 interview in *Palestine Magazine* that "the Jew is especially adapted for the sport of boxing because, in the final analysis, it is the most elemental form of self-defense." We might consider Leonard the Hillel and Eisen the Shammai in this Talmudic discussion . . . or vice versa.

[24] I am thinking most obviously of Felix Mendelssohn and Karl Marx, both of whom were converted to Protestantism while still children, at the behest of socioeconomically

ambitious fathers in Prussia of the early nineteenth century (Mendelssohn was seven in 1816, and Marx was six in 1824, when they were converted). Upon Mendelssohn's death in 1847, an anonymous article excoriated the composer for sullying German music by "judaizing" it—which turned out to have been written by a younger composer whom Mendelssohn had championed: Richard Wagner. In 1871, in the context of a philosophico-political quarrel with Marx, Michael Bakunin wrote that "[a] Jew himself, Marx is surrounded . . . by a crowd of little Jews, more or less intelligent, stirring up intrigue, troublemakers, as is the case with Jews elsewhere." This quote is found in Michel Bakounine, "*Rapports personels avec Marx*," in *Archives Bakounine* (ed. and trans. Arthur Lehning; Leiden: Brill, 1963), Vol 1/2, 124.

[25] This essay and its relevance to athletic competition are discussed at length elsewhere in this volume. See Danny Rosenberg, "The Jewish Athlete of Faith: On the Limits of Sport."

[26] But not in other ways. Their numbers would begin to grow in other directions, from innovative sports journalism to team ownership.

[27] The situation wasn't helped when Koufax pitched and lost the second game. But his pair of shutout victories in games five and seven, which ultimately keyed the Dodgers' World Series victory, offered the perfect complement to his Yom Kippur decision within the process of elevating him from Jewish hero to icon.

[28] Ramadan is the name of a month on the Muslim calendar—the ninth month—and lasts twenty-nine or thirty days, depending on the year.

[29] Ironically enough, most of the legislation within the more orthodox branches of these three traditions (and other religious traditions, as well) pertaining to female clothing and modesty issues stems from male discussions, concerns, and conclusions. But that issue takes us beyond the confines of this narrative.

[30] See the images accompanying the article by Linda J. Borish, "Jewish Women in the American Gym: Basketball, Ethnicity, and Gender in the Early Twentieth Century"—elsewhere in this volume.

[31] The article was by Katie Thomas and appeared on Wednesday, August 20, 2008.

[32] "I don't want to have any favorites," he said. "I would love to be fair for everyone. But sooner or later, if they can see through me God, that's what I want them to try to do."

[33] This issue may be seen from a different angle in the case of the tennis star Dick Savitt. He was clearly the outstanding American tennis player in the early 1950s. In 1951, he won both the Wimbledon and Australian Open singles titles—the first player in thirteen years to accomplish that feat. But the following year he was left off the US Davis Cup team (in favor of a semiretired player well past his prime) by Coach Frank Shields, who could not accept the fact that such a skilled athlete could be a Jew—and who was willing to sacrifice the success of the team and the image of the country to his own religious prejudices.

[34] There are several recognized professional boxing entities, of which NABF is only one. There is also some variation with regard to weight-class terminology; thus the super welterweight class is also known as the light middleweight class.

[35] He defeated Daniel Santos in a twelve-round unanimous decision on November 14.

[36] It is a truism of Jewish history that the beginning of every Jewish community with a particular individual turns out to have had some Jew there before the first one and that

every Jewish community that disappears turns out to have one more Jew remaining after the last one has died or left. In that spirit, two epilogues to this epilogue: one, between the first version of this paper and the present, Foreman fought—and lost—his first bout since his surgery, against Pawel Wolak, retiring after the sixth round, perhaps because his knee was not really yet quite ready. Two, Na'ama Shafir, a basketball player from Israel, starred this year (2010-11) for the University of Toledo, scoring forty points against USC in the WNIT final to earn the tournament MVP award. Shafir is an Orthodox Jew, but her rabbi permits her to compete on Shabbat provided that she maintains all other restrictions—including not only maintaining *kashrut* but walking to every road game arena from the team hotel rather than taking the team bus. She also wears a T-shirt under her uniform for modesty reasons: as an Orthodox Jewish woman, guided by her rabbi, she regards it as immodest to have her shoulders exposed. Religious challenges continue to offer themselves to minority athletes and continue to be met.

Buster Haywood and the Jews of Black Baseball

Rebecca T. Alpert

We wear the mask that grins and lies
It hides our cheeks and shades our eyes
                              Paul Laurence Dunbar[1]

When I began to research Jewish participation in black baseball,[2] I assumed I would be writing primarily about Syd Pollock, Abe Saperstein, and Ed Gottlieb, the white Jewish owners and promoters of Negro League teams, and the Jewish communist sportswriters who fought for baseball's integration. Talking about the research with my colleague Walter Isaac led me to another discovery. He was certain that the Jewish presence in the Negro Leagues went beyond the white owners and sportswriters to include black players as well. I challenged him to find some for me, and he found not only individual players, but an entire team.

Isaac introduced me to Rabbi Curtis Caldwell, whose Temple Beth El community of Hebrew Israelites fielded a baseball team in the 1920s and 1930s. This team, the Belleville Grays, played against the well-known Negro League teams like the Pittsburgh Crawfords and Newark Eagles. They also sent some of their players on to play at the highest professional levels available to blacks in segregated America. The team was a mix of local stars and community members. Of the local men who played for the Grays and went on to Negro League careers, Albert "Buster" Haywood (1910-2000) stood out as a man who had more than casual links to Temple Beth El. I wanted to find out whether Haywood not only played for the Grays, but also identified with the community. As I investigated Haywood's life, I found that he had links, some public and some hidden, to other dimensions of Jewish participation in black baseball beyond the Belleville Grays.

In baseball the catcher crouches behind home plate, creating the target with his body for the pitcher to throw the ball. Catchers wear special equipment to protect themselves: shin guards, chest protectors, masks. Those masks serve not only to protect, but to conceal, especially for black catchers, as Dunbar's poem suggests. Haywood's mask hid a multitude of complex identities and concerns not only about connection to this community of Hebrew Israelites, but also his experiences with the Indianapolis Clowns where he played most of his career. The Clowns were owned by Syd Pollock, one of the white Jewish owners about which I was writing. The team was known best for their controversial practices of clowning in black baseball. Haywood's experiences would have much to reveal about that world. Haywood also played a hidden role in the advancement of baseball's integration through his friendship with Jackie Robinson. Robinson, too, figured prominently in the story of Jews in black baseball. This was true primarily for Jews, including the communist sportswriters, who saw Robinson's groundbreaking entrance into Major League Baseball in 1947 as a model for social justice and the end not only to racism, but to antisemitism in post-World War II America.[3] Haywood's life and baseball career provided an unusual window into multiple dimensions of the world of Jews in black baseball.

The black baseball era began in the 1890s when blacks were barred from playing on white teams. Black baseball was often referred to as "shadow ball" because its existence was not well known outside the African American community, although its quality rivaled that of the (white) major or high-level Minor Leagues. Beginning in 1920, many of the best teams were organized into what are commonly known today as "Negro Leagues." But the league structures were fragile, and most black baseball was played by independent barnstorming teams against a variety of white and black teams. Haywood played on league and barnstorming teams in the last era of black professional baseball, from 1932-1954.

Haywood began his career as an infielder and played second base and shortstop in his youth. But he became a catcher when he had to substitute for another player[4] and played that position for the rest of his career. Sportswriters who followed the games in the black press considered Haywood to be one of the best catchers in the Negro Leagues. He played excellent defense, had a strong throwing arm, an ability to handle pitchers, and baseball intelligence. He was also, at 5'8", one of the shortest players. Although he was an excellent base stealer and runner, he was only an average hitter.

Haywood was born in Whaleysville, Virginia (a small town near Portsmouth) on January 12, 1910, the son of Robert E. Haywood and Mary Goodman. He attended I. C. Norcom High School, which was founded in 1913 as the first high school in the region for black students. According to family members, Haywood's parents did not want him to play baseball as a profession. But in 1932 the name "B. Haywood" began to appear in newspaper box scores as the second baseman for the Grays of the Belleville Industrial School, also known as "the Saints" and later as the Belleville Grays. Haywood played for and traveled with the team from 1932-1939.

The Belleville Grays had an unusual history and background. The team formed in the 1920s under the direction of Bishop William H. Plummer, leader of the Temple Beth El community of Hebrew Israelites. Founded as a religious community that understood themselves as descendents of the lost tribes of Israel, they observed many Jewish laws and customs along with rituals derived from apocalyptic Christian and Masonic traditions.[5] Temple Beth El was a self-sustaining residential community that owned a large plot of land near Portsmouth, called Belleville. The community farmed the land and maintained a lumber mill. Plummer organized the baseball team to provide recreational opportunities for members. Baseball was so central to the life of the community that Plummer built a wooden frame ballpark on the land. The team wore professionally made uniforms, used the best equipment, and played high-caliber baseball.[6]

Bishop William Plummer died in 1932. His son, Howard Z. Plummer, who was only thirty-two years old at the time of his father's death, succeeded him as the leader. Until then H. Z. Plummer had been playing second base on the Belleville Grays, but when Plummer became chief rabbi, Buster Haywood took over his role at second base.[7] Plummer had bigger ambitions for the team than his father had. Under his leadership the Grays held spring training sessions in Florida. Plummer brought in several established players from the Portsmouth area, some of whom would go on to significant professional careers in the Negro Leagues. By 1935, most of the players were no longer community members. Only Mark Hill, Sonnie Jeffries, and Haywood remained from the 1932 team. By 1938, Plummer built the Belleville Grays into the dominant team in Virginia, playing league games against local teams and meeting Negro League teams in exhibition games.[8] The team was most frequently referred to as "the Plummermen" in the newspapers, an indication of Plummer's involvement and powerful influence. Although the team professionalized, they maintained their Israelite character and commitments. In newspaper listings, for example, they made it clear that they would play "any day excepting Friday and Saturday."[9]

It is not clear what Haywood's exact affiliation with the community was. At the very least, evidence suggests that Haywood was in some way a part of this group and abided by community rules that included no smoking or drinking.[10] Like other members of the Belleville community, Buster would have most likely have kept his affiliation as an Israelite hidden both in the context of the league and to nonmembers in general. Temple Beth El maintained a high level of privacy about their identification as Israelites and their unique religious practices, which set them apart from the mainstream of the African American community in the Portsmouth area and from other (white) Jewish groups who tended to be skeptical about their unique religious practices.

Compared to other work available to black men in the South, professional baseball paid well. Haywood was enticed to seek more competitive opportunities, and in 1935 he traveled to Jacksonville to try out for a new professional team that would become part of the Negro National League, the Brooklyn (later Newark) Eagles, owned by Abraham Manley and managed by Hall of Famer Ben Taylor. Haywood played a few games with the team, but ultimately Taylor judged Haywood to "need a little seasoning," so Buster returned to Portsmouth.[11]

From that point on, Buster was the star of the Belleville Grays, and his individual accomplishments (both at bat and behind the plate) during this period were often chronicled in the sports pages of the local African American newspaper, the *Norfolk Journal and Guide*. Haywood frequently garnered headlines for scoring or batting in the winning run. He hit "leadoff" (first in the batting order) because of his speed and ability to run the bases. This was an unusual role for a catcher. Haywood's talents caught the attention of the new manager for the Birmingham Black Barons of the Negro American League, Ben Taylor's brother Candy Jim. The Barons signed Haywood and three other Grays' players—Gentry Jessup, Tommy Sampson, and James Mickey—to play for them in 1940. Haywood played with the Black Barons for only a brief period at the beginning of the 1940 season. Although he was playing at a more competitive level with the Black Barons, the salaries they offered did not compete. In search of better wages, he left the Barons by mid-May to join an independent traveling team, the Ethiopian Clowns.[12]

The Clowns did better financially, but at a price. When Haywood joined the team in 1940, the Clowns played in whiteface, sometimes in grass skirts, and always using invented "African" pseudonyms. Ethiopia was in the news, and the Clowns' owner, Syd Pollock, one of the Jewish businessmen who was involved in the Negro Leagues in the Great Depression era and who figures prominently in the story of Jews in black baseball, thought nothing of exploiting the reference. He seemed indifferent to the anger expressed by other Negro League owners and black sportswriters over the trivialization of this powerful African kingdom that was under siege.[13] To Pollock, he was simply using a place name that would draw attention to the team and mark them as exotic "Africans." Pollock was a genius at creating publicity and drawing crowds. Sportswriters in the black press found his practices disturbing, but they were also grateful to Pollock, who, unlike other owners, sent regular press releases to all the newspapers, often daily. Black newspapers relied on owners to report results as the writers did not have the budget to travel, and Pollock's releases were welcome.

But team owners would not permit the Clowns in the Negro National or American League, not only because of the mockery the team made of Africa, but also because of the controversial type of entertainment the Clowns performed. The Clowns played serious baseball, and the men, like Haywood, that Pollock hired were talented ballplayers whose skill level equaled that of other Negro League teams. But they also clowned.

In his first two years as a Clown, Haywood played under the name "Khora" (a small town in southern Ethiopia) and often hit and ran the bases in his catching equipment.[14] The various stunts and routines that were the trademark of the team were not uncommon among barnstorming teams, both white and black. Some of the routines (such as the pantomime shadow ball and the fast-paced pepper ball) involved a high level of skill. They also did clever verbal humor in the tradition of the dozens that had been part of black baseball from its beginnings.[15] But some of the clowning was low comedy, evoking degrading stereotypes and reminders of minstrelsy that many Negro League owners and sportswriters and some players found most objectionable. [Fig. 1]

Figure 1. The Ethiopian Clowns in costumes from the 1940s. Haywood is kneeling in the first row, second from the right. (3.2)

When questioned, Buster Haywood defended the style of play and the necessity to add comedy to baseball:

> The thing was to draw people. The Negro leagues weren't drawing. . . . But the Clowns outdrew every team in both leagues. We brought money and good baseball into the league, and that was our purpose, and the critics can say whatever they want about that.[16]

For most black men of this era, opportunities for good paying employment were limited. Haywood made a choice to work under conditions that provided the best financial arrangements and also allowed him to use his talents and skills.

Haywood became a popular and solid performer. Pollock's advanced publicity for their appearance in Portsmouth in May 1941 announced that there would be a "Buster Haywood Day" to bring crowds for his hometown appearance.[17] Later that season the Clowns won the *Denver Post* Tournament, a prestigious, semi-professional contest that began accepting black teams beginning in 1934. Haywood was named the 1941 tournament's Most Valuable Player by the *Denver Post* columnists and received a Gruen-Curvex watch as a prize. The *Post* reporter commented, "I'd give Babe Ruth and Ty Cobb in their primes plus $100,000 for Haywood Khora." [18] Negro League owners took notice.

In March of 1942 the *Pittsburgh Courier* reported that Alex Pompez, owner of the Negro League New York Cuban Stars, enticed five of the Clowns' best players to join his team, including Buster Haywood.[19] Haywood played for the Cubans for the 1942 league season, to the pride of local fans in the Portsmouth area. Although he got good notices for his fielding and hitting in the black press that year, Haywood shared the catching with several others and did not get significant playing time or satisfactory wages. The Cubans finished the season with a losing record, 8-14, next to last in the league. For Haywood, the atmosphere in Harlem was unfamiliar. Used to the ways of the South, he may have had trouble accommodating to life in a northern city.

Haywood returned to the Clowns in 1943. Meanwhile, the Clowns had also undergone changes. The Negro League owners permitted the Clowns to join the league and in exchange Pollock agreed to stop using costumes, makeup, and pseudo-African names. The Clowns continued most of the comedy routines however, even the offensive ones. They were now officially the Cincinnati (and then Indianapolis) Clowns, although as was the case with Miami, they rarely played in either place, spending most of their time traveling on the road. The Clowns had another catcher, Lloyd "Pepper" Bassett, who performed his catching duties in a rocking chair, as he had with other Negro League teams.

Haywood was no longer required to be involved in the comedy routines, and his hitting improved dramatically in 1943. He led the team with a .411 batting average in July and hit safely in twenty-seven straight games.[20] In 1944, he was named to the Negro American League's All-Star roster for the East-West game, the most prestigious event of the Negro League season. He was again mentioned by national columnists in the black press as "among the top catchers in the Negro Leagues."[21]

Although Haywood did not generally call attention to himself, he occasionally displayed a temper on the field, manifesting the anger that simmered beneath the surface. In 1945, he struck an umpire at a game in Houston, Texas. Although it was reported that fans were upset and *Chicago Defender* sports editor Fay Young was critical of Haywood for this behavior, no action was taken against him by the league.[22] Black sportswriters were vigilant against the "rowdyism" that tarnished the reputation of the Negro Leagues. But the players' lives traveling under Jim Crow conditions were hard, umpires were not well paid, and maintaining "decorum" was not always possible.

Haywood played throughout the war years because he was already thirty-five when the United States entered World War II, and few blacks were drafted into the segregated units the Army reserved for them.[23] Given the number of Major League ballplayers who were in the armed services and the scarcity of available white players, this would have been a logical time for baseball to integrate. But the Major League owners preferred to employ older players, men with disabilities, and even create the All-American Girls Professional Baseball League to keep baseball profitable. Racial integration of Major League Baseball would wait until the end of the war.

When the war ended Haywood began to play year-round. From 1945-1947, he was the catcher for the California Winter League team, the Kansas City Royals. The California Winter League was made up primarily of minor league-caliber, white, semi-professional teams, but included black teams as early as 1910 and is considered to be the first integrated league in the United States.

Jackie Robinson also played on the Royals in 1945 before signing his Major League contract. That October, Haywood played a hidden (even to Buster himself) role in the plan to bring Robinson into the majors. To bring attention to Robinson in preparation for his major announcement, Branch Rickey commissioned a story in *Look Magazine*. Maurice Terrell was asked to do a photo shoot of Robinson in action to accompany the story. Rickey later decided to hold back the article, and it was more than four decades before the photographs (donated to the Baseball Hall of Fame by *Look Magazine*) and the original essay were discovered by baseball historians. In the photographs, Robinson wore a Kansas City Royals uniform, which is how Haywood came to be identified. The photographs show Robinson batting with Haywood behind home plate. Haywood had no idea at the time that the practice was being photographed or for what reason Robinson asked him to go work out that day.[24]

During the regular season, Buster continued to play baseball for the Clowns. Although baseball researchers date the demise of the Negro Leagues to 1948 when Major League teams slowly began to sign black talent, for Haywood this year marked a new beginning. He assumed the job of player-manager, a role he performed with great success. Under Haywood's leadership, the Clowns won the Negro American League championship three times. His managerial duties also including occasionally driving the Clowns' bus (he had a chauffer's license) and making team travel arrangements.[25] He also had the task of handling the comedy acts, work that required great diplomatic skill dealing with artistic temperaments of the performers.[26] As a manager, Haywood had opportunities to assert himself and step out from behind the mask, although some of his accomplishments would go unnoticed.

In 1952, Haywood had the good fortune to have eighteen-year-old Hank Aaron come to play for the Clowns and thus go down in history as Aaron's first manager. Major League scouts, who were in contact with Negro League owners looking for young talent, quickly noticed Aaron's abilities, and Syd Pollock eagerly sold Aaron's contract to the Boston Braves. Aaron was gone by mid-June, but his appearances in twenty-six games for the Clowns made a lasting impression. Haywood predicted, "Aaron will develop into one of the great shortstops of baseball within a couple of years."[27] Although Pollock is often given credit for discovering Aaron, others reported that Aaron was Haywood's discovery, but Haywood never made such a claim, another case where Haywood's role was hidden from public view.[28]

The year 1953 was Haywood's last as a Clown. Haywood was responsible for scheduling spring training, and this was the year he brought the team to the Portsmouth area where they slept and trained in Belleville at Plummer's place, as Haywood described:

> We stayed at . . . Plummer's about ten miles outside Portsmouth. He was minister at my church. There was an old diamond near his place. I played there . . . as semi-pro back before I joined the Birmingham Black Barons. We trained two days.[29]

This comment was another elusive clue to Haywood's close connection to Temple Beth El. It is likely that he called the community his "church" and Plummer his "minister" because he was using coded language, as part of his (and the community's) tendency to hide their Israelite identity. But at the time, Haywood's issues were not with his former Jewish owner. Rather, he was distraught over another tactic that was being used by his present one, Syd Pollock. Haywood continued describing the season opener:

> We opened against the Norfolk Palms [black team] in Norfolk. Day after that we faced the Portsmouth Merrimacs [a white Minor League team] in Portsmouth. Wish we'd have had more time before Portsmouth. Wish I hadn't had a woman on second for a game like that. Right in my home town, too. [30]

Haywood was quite proud to play in his hometown, especially against the white Piedmont League team the Merrimacs. This was the first time a white Minor League team played a Negro League team in Virginia. Five thousand black and white fans watched the Merrimacs win. The game took place even though the Merrimacs maintained separate seating and entrances for African American fans and a boycott was suggested by the black press.[31] Haywood, inured to negotiating the vagaries of the Jim Crow South, was more concerned with a different problem.

As interest in segregated baseball teams was rapidly diminishing in the face of the integration of the Major Leagues (nine of sixteen teams had integrated at this time), Pollock tried one more publicity stunt to bring customers. He hired Toni Stone, the first woman in professional baseball, to play second base.[32] Haywood had made his peace with whiteface and grass skirts, clowning routines and their high maintenance performers, and the evils and hardships of Jim Crow segregation. But he could not accept the idea that a woman had the ability to play for the team he managed.

What in a contemporary context might look like gender equality was a mark of disrespect to the black ballplayers of the era. Haywood (and eventually others) saw the inclusion of women as an insult to the dignity of the game they were playing. That was the main reason why Haywood decided to leave the Clowns after the 1953 season and ended his baseball career as player-manager of the Memphis Red Sox in 1954.

Haywood enjoyed playing in Southern California in the winters and moved there permanently. He began a job at Hughes Aircraft in El Segundo as a maintenance engineer and worked there until he retired in 1992. He married Theola Haskins and raised her five younger brothers as his own. She was an evangelical Christian, and he was buried alongside her. The minister who performed his funeral claimed not to know what Haywood believed or practiced in his later years, although she observed him to be a quiet man who continued his abstemious behavior.[33]

Haywood played for six owners in his career. His experiences with the four teams for which he played briefly proved unsatisfactory from a financial and personal perspective. The two teams he played for at length had Jewish owners, the Plummers and Syd Pollock. His relationship with the Plummers lasted for many years and was, from every indication, genuine and positive. Syd Pollock was the man who introduced Haywood to the "comedic baseball" that paid the bills. While never publicly critical of Pollock except over the Toni Stone incident, it would not be surprising if Haywood had merely hidden his disgust at some of the conditions and requirements of this painful, if lucrative, career.

Haywood had the chance to reflect on his experiences with the Clowns in a conversation with Syd Pollock's sons, Jerry and Alan, in 1994. The Pollocks flew Haywood to Florida for five days to record his reminiscences for the book Alan was writing about his father. Haywood spoke positively of the playing conditions that Pollock created: a decent salary, a regular schedule, comfortable lodging, and a high-quality bus in which to travel.[34] Buster also revealed his goal for the conversation. He wanted to do this in order

> . . . to bring my race together. We have few blacks at our autograph
> shows, and they don't know what we were. We ought to put the ways
> of the past behind and move on, but to know how to leave them
> behind, we got to understand what the ways of the past are. You can't
> shove back something you don't
> recognize.[35]

Haywood's statement argues for confronting and naming some of the difficult aspects of the Negro Leagues and life under Jim Crow in order finally to make peace with the past and educate the next generation about this proud and painful legacy. [Fig. 2]

Haywood's baseball career was summed up by Syd Pollock's son, Alan, who often traveled with the Clowns as a young man and knew Haywood well. He described Haywood's complicated personality:

> Buster Haywood was a category
> of one. Not all agree he was
> baseball's best catcher, but some
> very knowledgeable baseball
> men thought so. Buster's aggres-

Figure 2. Buster Haywood (right) after his retirement with Chet Brewer, his teammate on the Kansas City Royals of the California Winter League (2.6)

sive, even abrasive, play and his lack of power at the plate may have stunted his reputation. He was quiet and steady and did not always endear himself to those who played against him.[36]

Buster Haywood died on April 19, 2000. Unlike many Southern black men of his era, he made a good living because he was able, with rare exception, to cope with difficult conditions and hide and manage his feelings. He left a legacy that reveals much about the man behind the mask and opens a window on the complex roles that Jews played in black baseball. But he also maintained a level of privacy and silence that would remain impenetrable, and the question of his religious identity an open one.

NOTES

[1] Paul Laurence Dunbar, *The Collected Poetry of Paul Laurence Dunbar* (ed. Joanne M. Braxton; Charlottesville: University Press of Virginia, 1993).

[2] This research resulted in a book, *Out of Left Field: Jews and Black Baseball* (New York: Oxford University Press, 2011).

[3] See Rebecca Alpert, "Jackie Robinson as a Jewish Icon," *Shofar: The Journal of Interdisciplinary Jewish Studies* 26.2 (Winter 2008): 42-59.

[4] George Haskins, Haywood's nephew, telephone conversation with author, October 16, 2008.

[5] For an introduction to Hebrew Israelite religion, see James E. Landing, *Black Judaism: Story of an American Movement* (Durham: Carolina Academic Press, 2002). To understand the group from their own perspective, see their self-published history, Historical Committee, *History of the Church of God and Saints of Christ* (Suffolk: The Church, 1992) and website, www.cogasoc.org.

[6] Hannah Penner, Temple Beth El community member, face-to-face conversation with author, June 20, 2008. I am indebted to Rabbi Curtis Caldwell, a current leader in the Temple Beth El community, for introducing me to the history of the Belleville Grays and to members of this community.

[7] *Norfolk Journal and Guide* (*NJG*) (11 May 1932, 31 May 1932, 23 July 1932). In a game against the YMHA of Patterson, the newspaper report commented, "Plug Haywood also slammed a four sacked [sacker] to swell the scoring." At the time, Haywood was still playing second base as one of Plummer's brothers was doing the catching.

[8] See Darrell J. Howard, *"Sunday Coming": Black Baseball in Virginia* (Jefferson: McFarland, 2002) 26-28.

[9] *NJG* (7 May 1938).

[10] Players thought of him as a religious man who did not engage in the drinking, gambling, and sexual adventures common in the sporting life. He was also not judgmental of others who had different ways. As a manager, he often caught players with women and later remarked that it "wasn't something I would have done, but I can't make my morals theirs" (Pollock, *Barnstorming*, 158).

[11] *Chicago Defender* (*CD*) (20 April 1935).

[12] *Atlanta Daily World* (*ADW*) (28 May 1940); Brent P Kelley, *The Negro Leagues Revisited: Conversations with 66 More Baseball Heroes* (Jefferson: McFarland, 2000), 109. According to Alan Pollock, the Birmingham Black Barons were paying Buster $90 a month when the Ethiopian Clowns came to Birmingham in 1940, and the Clowns' players were averaging $200 to $300 for a game. The players were not on salary, but dividing 60 percent of the gate receipts. From this, they paid their own room and board. *Barnstorming*, 112-113.

[13] Cumberland Posey, "Posey's Points," *Pittsburgh Courier* (*PC*) (28 September 1940). The owner of the Homestead Grays and columnist for the *Pittsburgh Courier*, Posey was particularly vocal in his opposition to Pollock.

[14] *Birmingham World*, (*BW*) (26 August 1941); Pollock, *Barnstorming*, 98.

[15] See James E. Brunson III, "'A Mirthful Spectacle': Race, Blackface Minstrelsy, and Base Ball, 1874-1888," *NINE: A Journal of Baseball History and Culture* 17.2 (2009): 13-30.

[16] Pollock, *Barnstorming*, 97.

[17] *NJG* (17 May 1941).

[18] *Denver Post* (14 August 1941).

[19] *PC* (7 March 1942).

[20] *ADW* (23 July 1943), *BW* (30 July 1943), *NJG* (31 July 1943).

[21] Dan Burley, "Confidentially Yours," *New York Amsterdam News* (*NYAN*) (22 July 1944), *CD* (5 August 1944).

[22] *CD* (11 August 1945).

[23] On September 5, 1942, the *NJG* reported that Haywood was to report to the Army on September 15, having been given a few weeks off to complete his playing season. But there is no record of his military service and the family members I spoke to don't recall this event.

[24] John Thorn and Jules Tygiel, "Jackie Robinson's Signing: The Real, Untold Story," *Mr. Baseball,* http://www.mrbaseball.com/index.php?Itemid=57&id=23&option=com_content&task=view.

[25] Syd Pollock to Effa Manley April 4, 1944, Newark *Eagles Papers,* Newark Public Library, Newark, New Jersey.

[26] Pollock, *Barnstorming*, 65.

[27] *CD* (7 June 1952).

[28] Bob Motley and Brian Motley, *Ruling over Monarchs, Giants & Stars: Umpiring in the Negro Leagues* (Champaign: Sports Pub, 2007), 98-99.

[29] Pollock, *Barnstorming*, 243.

[30] Ibid.

[31] *NJG* (2 May 1953).

[32] Stone's story is told by Tracy Everbach, "Breaking Baseball Barriers: The 1953-1954 Negro League and Expansion of Women's Public Roles," *American Journalism* 22.1 (2005): 13-33.

[33] Program of the "Homegoing Celebration of Albert Buster Haywood" (26 April 2000), Inglewood Cemetery. Retrieved from Buster Haywood's personal scrapbook, courtesy of George Haskins. Reverend America Washington, telephone conversation with the author, 6 February 2009.

[34] Kelley, *Negro Leagues*, 110.

[35] Pollock, *Barnstorming*, 391.

[36] Ibid.

A Global Game: Omri Casspi and
the Future of Jewish Ballers

David J. Leonard

One of the more hyped and media saturated stories of the 2009-2010 NBA season was the arrival of Omri Casspi, a rookie with the Sacramento Kings. Treated like a "rock star"[1] and receiving tremendous fan support throughout the league, Casspi's Israeli/Jewish identity has been placed front and center. While not the first Jew to play or even excel in the NBA, Casspi as the first Israeli to play in the NBA has received ample support from the Jewish American community. According to Andy Altman-Ohr, "Fans in opposing arenas welcomed Casspi with banners and Israeli flags, and even *Sports Illustrated* jumped on the bandwagon, publishing an article titled 'Welcome, The King of Israel.'"[2]

While this paper will examine Casspi's emergence as an international phenomenon, focusing on the ways in which specific teams (through Jewish-theme nights) have commodified his Jewish identity as well as the ways in which media narratives have used his Jewishness as part of telling his unique story, this paper works to situate Casspi's ascendance to the NBA within a broader history of the NBA's globalization into Israel. The success of Maccabi Tel Aviv (Israel's biggest sports club) and the influx of former and future NBA players have made basketball a huge success in Israel, argues Jeremy Fine in his blog post about Israeli athletics. Fine writes, "Young Israeli children are growing up watching these great athletes and wanting to play the game."[3] In other words, the emergence of Omri Casspi as a symbol of Jewish athletic success and the media sensation that surrounds him is not only an outgrowth of the globalization of the NBA in terms of its international popularity, but also a result of the influx of NBA-quality players who have been instrumental in transforming basketball in Israel. This paper examines this phenomenon and offers insight into its broader cultural, social, and racial implications. It seeks to examine how the discourse surrounding Casspi's entry into the NBA was defined by his Jewishness and his kinship with/to his Jewish brethren within the United States.

It additionally examines how food and the meeting/conflict that results from various food cultures coming in contact are imagined as an obstacle to globalization (as defined as the movement of people/culture). It will focus on

275

how globalization is not only constructed as the movement or confluence of peoples and commodities, but culture as well, using the NBA and Casspi's arrival into the league as an example. It also seeks to reflect on how the celebration and identification of Casspi as a pioneer erased the presence of other non-white Jews within American professional basketball. Given the hegemonic idea concerning the inability of "Jews" to play basketball and broader discourse surrounding Jews and sports, it isn't surprising that Omri Casspi has elicited so much celebration, commodification, and interest. Yet, the focus on his Israeliness and the limited attention afforded to black/Jewish players demonstrate the ways in which history is in operation here.

REPRESESENTATIONS AND MARKERS OF IDENTITY

A consistent theme marking Casspi's identity, and the potential difficulties he might find in assimilating into the NBA and American culture at large, has been that of food. Numerous articles, as well as the NBA documentary (*The Promised Land*) that chronicled his first year in the league, focused, if not fixated, on his culinary adjustment. At one level, the focus on food as a cultural gulf, as a point of tension, reflects the hegemony of a narrative that focused on food as a source of difficulty in Casspi's assimilation into the NBA/American culture. Focusing on food and how Casspi can assimilate into America/the NBA "is thus one way to elide larger issues"[4] that he and other Jewish people might face in contemporary America.

Describing his first year in the league, Casspi summarized the experience in the following way: "There are a lot of differences. The food is different, the culture is different, obviously the language. It's hard being away from home, from my family and friends. It's different going to a new team and the NBA. It is a whole new level of basketball."[5] Food, or better said the absence of "authentic hummus," represented one of the biggest hardships that Casspi faced during his initial year in the NBA. At another level, food became the most salient, identifiable, and commodifiable marker of his Jewish-Israeliness. Reducing ethnic and racial identity to taste and food allows one to experience (taste) the other: "what really having to confront what it is that makes" the other "different," argues Anita Mannur; more specifically, it downplays the importance of larger historical and social issues.[6] Food thus operates as authenticator of identity, or as noted by J. A. Brillat-Savarin, "tell me what you *think* you eat, and I will tell you who you *think* you are." More importantly, Warren Belasco takes this a step further, arguing, "If we are what we eat, we are also what we don't eat. . . . To eat is to distinguish and discrimination, include and exclude. Food choices establish boundaries and borders."[7]

In several media accounts, Casspi's love for hummus is noted, so much so that during one road game a family handed him a homemade batch. In cities where the Jewish fans didn't come to the game with hummus in hand, he spent his off time searching for Israeli food.[8] Most indicative of the narrative that imagines food as both the basis of identity and the obstacle to full assimilation was an article in the *New York Times*, titled, "From Israel to the N.B.A., Missing the Hummus":

> The first Israeli in the N.B.A., Omri Casspi, is busily trying to adapt to life in the United States.
>
> For starters, he needs a cellphone with a local number. He just received a $4,500 bill for about two weeks of calls, which is expensive even by N.B.A. standards. He needs new chargers for all his gadgets. But he is struggling most to find comfort food.
>
> "Hummus," Casspi said, with a hard h and a long u, stressing the first syllable in a way that conveyed utter seriousness. "You don't have that here, though."
>
> A reporter insisted that the chickpea spread is widely available in grocery stores in the United States, but Casspi—who was drafted last month by the Sacramento Kings—smiled dismissively.
>
> "Man, I tried it; that's all I can say," he said last week during a break in the Kings' summer league schedule. "I will bring some from Israel, maybe. I'll let you taste it and you tell me."
>
> It seems that a bulk order from the Tel Aviv equivalent of Costco may be necessary.[9]

While erasing the complexities of identity and reducing the personal impact of globalization through imaging the process as a culinary transition, this portion of the discourse represents an effort to reduce Jewish (ethnic and racial in general) identity to foodways. Samantha Kwan describes this process as part of a larger phenomenon where "individuals can vicariously experience another culture and foster cross-cultural understanding." Describing it as a safe cultural exchange, she concludes:

> Whether it is food, fashion, or travel packages, shopping becomes a means to finding one's roots, history, and sense of ethnic self. Identities are not only constructed here; they are literally purchased. In short, in a postmodern consumer society, identities are malleable and food becomes one important vehicle for identity construction. Or as Giddens so eloquently puts it, "food and other basic organic necessities are socially and culturally organized *regimes* that are manifestly, a means of symbolic display, a way of giving external form to narratives of self-identity." [10]

It represents an effort to celebrate and elucidate the signifiers of identities that are easily digestible and profitable, not surprising given the efforts to market

Casspi's NBA arrival as an entry way into the cultural practices of Israelis/ Jews. In the context of the NBA, Casspi's Israeli-Jewish identity, as a marker of whiteness, offered consumers not only exposure of another culture and identity, but one that was clearly not African American. He ate hummus.

COMMODITY CULTURE

Casspi's identity is imagined as not so much a personal sense of self, his background, or his connections to a broader history and community, but rather a commodity that is both interesting and profitable given his uniqueness within the context of the NBA. Building upon the success and popularity of Asianthemed nights that have corresponded with Yao Ming playing in stadiums across the country, opposing teams have used Casspi as the featured "performer" in Jewish-themed heritage nights. For example, in February, the Golden State Warriors hosted a Jewish-themed night that featured a halftime show where members of the Jewish Community High School of the Bay hip-hop dance team performed, which was followed by the "rally Rabb," who didn't yell charge or some other clichéd sports chant, but instead blew his shofar in an effort to pump up the fans. Beyond the halftime show, the Warriors went to great lengths to promote Casspi as the main attraction, marketing the game and the heritage to Jewish organizations throughout the Bay Area. Over 1,000 tickets were sold through Jewish organizations, members of which were out in full force, passing out literature.[11]

Similarly, when the Sacramento Kings visited New Jersey, the Nets orchestrated a Jewish heritage event as well. Describing these events as part of the Casspi road show, Jacob Kamaras described the occasion at the Meaddowlands in the following way:

> NBA teams understand that Casspi is a real source of pride for the Jewish community and puts Jewish fans in the seat. . . . The distribution of Israeli flags and pins as well as the availability of extra kosher food at concessions were among the elements the Consulate [of Israel in New York] pushed for inclusion in "Jewish Family Night". . . . With the playing of Matisyahu's new song "One Day" before the game and "Hava Nagila" when Casspi first checked in the game, a booming "mazel tov" from the loudspeaker after a Nets fast-break dunk, and the flashing of Orthodox Jewish boxer Dmitriy Salita on the JumboTron, the Jewish atmosphere dominated the arena.[12]

In Philadelphia, Matisyahu served as the encore act for Casspi, offering fans a free concert before the Sixers-Kings game. They also were treated to Hebrew Sixers T-shirts, performances by a choir from the Jack M. Barrack Hebrew Academy and from Rabbi Saul Grife (Beth Tikvah B'nai Jeshurun in Erdenheim) and his rock band, brisket sandwiches from Max & David's kosher food stand, and Jewish sports history that appeared on the JumboTron throughout the game.[13]

Of course, the Knicks, who organized Jewish-themed nights before Casspi entered the league, capitalized on Casspi's visit to Madison Square Garden. Fans were offered the opportunity to buy a Hebrew-lettered New York Knicks T-shirt. As with so many of Casspi's away games, American Jewish and Israeli fans not only attended his game in New York, but did so in a way that marked the event and their attendance through their identity with Israeli flags, Hebrew chants, and even the singing of the Israeli national anthem prior to the game.

Writing about Yao Ming, Anna Chow argues that these NBA performances constitute what anthropologist John Ogbu calls "the 4Fs: food, fun, fashion, and festivals."[14] Jared Sexton offers a similarly critical conceptualization of multiculturalism, arguing: "The blanket injunction against situating multiple forms of oppression has become articulated with the neoliberal containment strategies of multiculturalism, wherein diversity is managed as a depoliticized term of experience."[15] Focusing on the broader context and the importance of reflecting on the differences between shifts at the surface and those driven by commodification and performance, and fundamental shifts structurally and culturally, Lisa Lowe challenges those who equate multiculturalism with inclusion and equality:

> The production of multiculturalism as a representation of changing cultural hegemony must, however, be distinguished from shifts in the existing hegemony itself. The synthetic production of multiculturalism unravels and its crises are best seized and contested at the moment when the contradiction between the representational economy of ethnic signifiers, on the one hand, and the material economy of resources and means on the other, becomes unavoidably clear.[16]

These events not only reflect an effort to market to the Jewish community, to expand and grow the NBA fan base, but importantly also embody cultural products that define Jewishness through cultural practices and attributes that can be easily replicated within public performances, all while blurring the lines between Jewishness and Israeliness. Note that while the events are called Jewish-heritage nights, the vast majority of elements—from Israeli flags and the deployment the Hebrew lettering, to the inclusion of recognizable Israeli artists, sports stars, and public figures—erase any identity differences, conflating a Jewish American identity with that of an Israeli Jew.

Although Casspi's initial year in the NBA often represented him as a commodity, as a representative symbol and marketing tool into the Jewish American community, one of the more interesting aspects of the media coverage has been the explanations for his success and his style of play. Historically, reflecting on the successes of Jewish basketball players in the 1930s and 1940s, sports commentators and the Jewish community itself has cited qualities, cultural attributes, and even race-based characteristics as the source for such dominance. For example, in the 1930s, Paul Gallico explained the prominence of Jewish basketball superstars in the following way: "The reason, I suspect, that basketball appeals to the Hebrew with his Oriental background, is that the game places a premium on an alert, scheming mind, flashy trickiness, artful dodging and general smart aleckness."[17] In 1936, a Jewish star at the City College of New York (CCNY) offered a similar assessment of his community's hold on the basketball world: No other sport required "the characteristics inherent in the Jews . . . mental agility, perception . . . imagination and subtly. . . . If the Jew had set out deliberately to invent a game which incorporated those traits indigenous in him . . . he could not have had a happier inspiration than basketball."[18]

Other sports writers cited the gaudy skills of "natural athletes," the advantages that Jewish players had became of their short stature, which resulted in better foot speed and balance, and their "sharp eyes." Reflecting on shared experiences of Jewish and African American basketball players, Jon Entine described the historical continuity as such:

> There are plenty of parallels between the Jewish stars of years past and today's "flashy" black players. The players then and now were subject to sometimes egregious racial stereotyping. The newest showmen of modern basketball, such as Allen Iverson and Kobe Bryant are singled out for their "athleticism" and "natural talents," rather than their well-rounded play. Such stereotypes reflect a long tradition that goes back more than seven decades, when the game emerged from the ghettos of Philadelphia, New York and Baltimore.[19]

The arrival of Casspi has not elicited a recycling of Gallico or any arguments that have put an emphasis on Jewish characteristics or cultural attributes. Yet the media discourse certainly emphasizes his Israeli identity in discussing his talents and his approach on the floor. Focusing on his physical and mental toughness, his discipline, his determination, and his swagger, much of the discourse points to these qualities as (1) why he has become a successful NBA player, and (2) the result of his experiences, life, and cultural upbringing in war-torn Israeli. Whether citing his military service (although as a great basketball player he was assigned to desk duty and refereeing basketball games as part of his military service) or mentality, Casspi shows on the court that his Israeli identity is part of the explanation as to why he is in the NBA.

Focusing on toughness, his edginess, and his gruff exterior, there is a clear link between his basketball prowess and being Israeli. Described as mentally and physically tough, aggressive, and having that swagger, his success is attributed to his personality, demeanor, and attitude rather than his athleticism, skill, or even his talents. For example, one commentator identified his mentality as the reason why he would be a great addition to the Sacramento Kings: "Omri Casspi always plays with a swagger that says, 'I'm better than anyone else on the court.'"[20] Eran Soroka of the *Ma'ariv Sports Newspaper* described Casspi in the following way:

> Casspi is a great guy to deal with, as a start. Smiling, talkative, ambitious. But on the court, he's always driven. He brings energy and intensity in every step on the court. He's a good athlete comparing to some of his European colleagues, he's fast and runs the fast breaks to finish with authority. He hustles for loose balls, moves very well without the ball and have a knack for finding the basket.
>
> The most important thing about Omri, in my humble opinion, is his motivation to improve and his quick learning and execution. When he was told that he needs to improve his outside shooting, he did, and he shot 45% in the Euroleague from downtown last season. He was told to work on his midrange game, and he did improve it. Now he still needs to bulk up, and to improve his passing and shooting mechanics.
>
> Although he's not a massive guy, he's a tough one. In our *Ma'ariv Newspaper* he explained a couple of days ago: "When I went to the workouts, I knew I can be like everyone else and then I can fall between 25th and 40th picks, but I wanted to bring something different to the table. I wanted to bring the toughness, to be competitive and aggressive in every workout. Maybe I wasn't a combat soldier at the Israeli army, but there's something in the Israeli spirit that is injected into you in an early stage of your life. You learn how to fight."[21]

A King's blogger latched onto this description, noting how much the Kings "need fighters."[22]

These qualities in Casspi are not linked to his Israeli identity, but are positioned as reflective of growing up amid violence and turmoil. His mental toughness reflects his "Israeli spirit," one defined by perseverance and durability, surviving war and persecution, which we are told is part of a larger Jewish history.

ERASURE: PART 1

The narrative documenting Omri Casspi's ascendance into the NBA has focused on his Israeli background—the fighter spirit and the disciplinarity required within a war-torn culture—as well as his family's links to basketball (his mother played professionally and his brother also played), thereby ignoring how the globalization of the NBA has sought to produce players like Casspi. At one level, it demonstrates the cultural reach of the NBA. Beginning in 1992 with the Barcelona Olympics and for some 10 to 15 years, the NBA was able to successfully market itself throughout the world, selling the coolness/youth appeal of the game. From Michael Jordan and Allen Iverson, to Kobe Bryant and LeBron James, youth from all parts of the world have long consumed American basketball stars, learning to love the game from these celebrities. Lee Jenkins, in "Welcome, The King of Israel," writes, "Like most NBA players, Casspi grew up watching Michael Jordan—only he had to wake up at 4 a.m. to do it."[23]

The arrival of Casspi reflects the talents and efforts to market these players as well as the concerted focus of NBA Commissioner David Stern on expanding overseas. Casspi is the result of Stern's "Basketball Without Borders initiative [that] has dispatched more than 300 NBA players abroad to work with more than 1,300 young players from at least 100 countries and territories. Stern is responsible for opening an international pipeline that runs in both directions."[24] These institutional efforts and the nature of basketball—its accessibility—has furthered this process. Unlike baseball, football, tennis, or golf, basketball (like American soccer) is easily transported and made available. Casspi's arrival to the NBA is evidence of the globalization at work.

ERASURE: PART 2

Throughout the media coverage there is an effort to blur the lines between Jewishness and Israeliness so that Casspi functions as a symbol and as a representative for both the American Jewish community and the Israeli Diaspora. While clearly functioning at the borderlands and representing both identities, the inability to reflect on the diversity of the Jewish community in using these identities interchangeably is striking. In other words, he is imagined as Jewish because he is Israeli and Israeli because he is Jewish; similarly, white Jewish American fans, whose American and white identities represent fissures and points of rupture with Casspi, are imagined as identical to their new found idol. This reflects a longstanding tension within the American Jewish community in regards to its secured whiteness and what that means to a Jewish/outsider identity. Casspi, as both representative of Jewishness (in a Diasporic sense) and Israeliness, allows for the Jewish American community to celebrate its own difference without comprising its privileged position within the milieu of American Jewish whiteness. This isn't evident only in the ways in which the

American Jewish community has celebrated and commodified Casspi as "one of our own," but also in the erasure of black Jewish NBA players.

At the conclusion of the 2010 season, Amare Stoudemire announced his plans to sign with the New York Knicks. Shortly thereafter, he announced plans for a trip to Israel, hinting at a newly found Jewish identity. *Slam* reported it as such:

> Believe us, we couldn't make this story up. Amar'e tweeted an hour ago that he's already arrived in Jerusalem. From *Haaretz*: U.S. Basketball star Amar'e Stoudemire is apparently on his way to Israel for a voyage of discovery after learning he has Jewish roots. "On the flight to Israel. This is going to be a great trip," announced the power forward, who plays in the NBA for the New York Knicks, via the micro-blogging site Twitter. According to an Army Radio report, Stoudemire plans to spend time in Israel learning Hebrew, having recently learned he has a Jewish mother. "The holy land. Learn about it," wrote, adding "ze ha'halom sheli"—Hebrew for "this is my dream." News of Stoudemire's trip quickly had Israeli basketball fans buzzing with speculation that they might one day see him playing alongside another Jewish NBA star, Israel's Omri Casspi, on the national team.[25]

Part spectacle, part fascination, part shock, and part doubt, the media, bloggers and the online community in general debated the veracity and meaning of his purported Jewishness. His wearing a yarmulke, his Star of David tattoo, his mother's possible Jewishness, his efforts to learn Hebrew, his Hebrew tweets, and countless other invoked signifiers were digested as to whether or not he was indeed Jewish. In the end, his agent announced, "I know there are some reports that he is Jewish, but he is not. He thinks there may be some Jewish blood on his mother's side and he is researching it."[26]

Yet it points to the ways in which Jewishness is defined through whiteness. While representing a sizable portion of the American Jewish population (estimates place the number of black, Latino, Asian, and indigenous Jews at 435,000), the history of Jews in the United States has been a story told through a white imagination. Jews of color are represented and in many ways function as a contradiction in terms, experience, questions, doubts, and alienation. In "Black and Jewish, and Seeing No Contradiction," Trymaine Lee describes the experience of Orthodox black Jews in the following way: "In yeshivas, they are sometimes taunted as 'monkeys' or with the Yiddish epithet for blacks. At synagogues and kosher restaurants, they engender blank stares."[27] The efforts to define Jewishness through whiteness are evident outside the Orthodox community. "Still, black Jews feel there is more that needs to be done. Most of the Jewish textbooks and curricula feature illustrations of only white faces. And black Jews are still asked if they are from Ethiopia or if they converted," writes Donna Halper. "Says Rabbi Funnye, 'I can understand why some black Jews almost prefer to find an all-black congregation—it's not a desire for segregation, but a desire to pray without people staring at you because you look different from everyone else.'"[28]

The power afforded to Casspi and not Amare Stoudemire or Jordan Farmar is understood given the desire to celebrate white Jewish people's success within an athletic context. Farmar, whose mother is Jewish and who grew up with his mom and his Israeli-born Orthodox father, does not embody what is seen/mandated as an authentic Jewish identity. Mixed-raced and non-practicing as an adult (while he was bar mitzvahed, he didn't celebrate Shabbat), his experiences (and the limited identification of his Jewishness) demonstrates the power of whiteness and particular Jewish identities. In a profile of Farmar in the *Jewish Journal,* Brad Greenberg described Farmar and the broader history of Jews in sports in the following way:

> Indeed, a sport once dominated by Jews now counts only one MOT [member of the tribe] at the highest level. And Farmar, who doesn't celebrate Jewish holidays and considers himself spiritual but not religious, is no Sandy Koufax. At the same time, though, Farmar doesn't shy away from his Jewish heritage, from the mixed racial and ethnic identity to which it contributes or from the pride that many Jews take in having their own hoop hero.[29]

Casspi was able to pass or function as an honorary white American, allowing for him to become representative for the white American Jewish community, whereas Stoudemire or Farmar could never represent and embody the Jewish community (there won't be Jordan Farmar heritage nights) given their blackness. Questions regarding what it means to be Jewish and how we define the authentic Jewish identity or community have long been posed within the Jewish community.[30] Linking Jewish identity to shifts in immigration policy and world wars, John Stratton, in *Coming Out Jewish* (2000), chronicles the transformative nature of Jewish identity. He writes, "In being accepted as white, Jews were able to express their Jewishness provided they did so within the bounds of civility."[31] David Biale's discussion of Jewish identity and American multiculturalism is instructive here, although whiteness is additionally central to Jewish identity: "I would argue that only a narrow, religious definition of Jewish culture—'Judaism'—restricts the possibilities for contemporary Jewish identity. Only once this culture is understood as exactly that, a secular culture, can all the possibilities, from Orthodoxy to socialism, be taken as equally legitimate."[32]

CASSPI AND THE MEANING OF JEWISH IDENTITY

Throughout the history of Jews in twentieth century America, popular culture has been instrumental in their assimilation; popular culture has been a fundamental vehicle for the acquisition of whiteness and the privileges associated with this racial identity. From the theater and Hollywood, to the worlds of music and sports, Jewish success in these cultural spaces, especially those traditionally reserved for white American bodies (e.g., sports) contributed to heightened levels of acceptance, decreased levels of antisemitism, and anointment of Jewishness as a cool cultural aesthetic or "spice" of difference. Benny Friedman, an all-American quarterback from Michigan, who also served as the first athletic director at Brandeis University, captured the unique and important place of sports within a history of Jewish Americanization and assimilation: "You know the two greatest things that ever happened in the history of the Jewish people? Well, I'll tell you. There first was when the Jews got up an army and walloped the British and the second was when I made All-American twice from Michigan."[33] Not surprisingly, American Jewish participation in sports and the military, given questions about Jewish masculinity and loyalty to an American project, have been instrumental in the Jews becoming white and fundamentally American within the national landscape.

Yet this acceptance and waning levels of antisemitism also disrupted a longstanding element of Jewish identity. In other words, "To be a Jew no longer brings much trouble, but it takes trouble to practice Judaism."[34] In the twenty-first century, American Jews face virtually no threats of reprisal or discrimination, and in fact, in the context of a rising conservative movement within post 9/11 America, many Jews experience ample praise for acceptance of dominant values concerning family, work, community, and religion. The experiences of Jews, irrespective of class, geography, or religious practice in the twenty-first century, highlights the claims offered by Stephen Whitfield, Bernard Susser, and Charles Liebman:[35] It is easy to be a Jew but hard to practice Judaism. In absence of visible antisemitism individually and institutionally and in the face of Jewish success, Jewish identity (or better said, what it means to be Jewish in the twenty-first century) has become increasingly ambiguous. Jews are "racial insiders,"[36] leading to questions as to what it means to be Jewish. In response:

> Synagogues and Jewish federations scramble for ways to instill group identity in the younger generation and try to stem the tide of intermarriage. And despite their higher level of economic and social integration, Jews discuss, read about, and memorialize the Holocaust with zeal as a means of keeping their sense of difference from non-Jews

alive. Far from having been eliminated by Jews' increasing integration into white America, the tensions and conflicting impulses of American Jewish identity have only been accentuated. . . . Many American Jews want to have it both ways.[37]

In this context, Casspi provides a vehicle to celebrate Jewishness and the identity connections between Jewishness in the twenty-first century and support for Israelis.

At one level, the celebration of Casspi within the American Jewish community reflects an expanded definition of Jewishness. It is defined not just by love, adoration, and connection to Casspi, but it is all about culture—hummus—and an abstract sense of Jewishness. It brings together American Jews and those from Israel as ostensibly members of the same group. Casspi reinforces a notion of identity based on an imagined community founded on a connection to a myriad of cultural practices, folkways, and individuals who simultaneously enact these practices.

Yet at another level, the claiming of Casspi reflects a narrowed definition of Jewishness defined by support for Israel. In inscribing Casspi as an authentic Jewish subject and hummus as authentic Jewish cuisine, the popular discourse here positions Israeliness and Jewishness as interchangeable. As such, Jewish identity is thereby positioned in relationship to a national identity. In wake of the 1960s and the corresponding revival of ethnic identities, "more and more American Jews looked to the Jewish state as a source of ethnic pride."[38] The narrative and representational fields that constituted Casspi as being from the same "tribe" or community as American Jews reflects an effort to depict the Jewish community as ostensibly white yet simultaneously different. Without "the language of race" to express these deep attachments, the power of Casspi rests with cultural arguments and shared allegiance. He reflects a reliance "on the echoes of Jewish racial identity, a discourse of tribalism, which gives voice to the feelings of loss Jews are experiencing in a world resistant to seeing them as a group apart."[39]

The celebration and treatment afforded to Casspi reflect an effort from American Jews to "occupy a liminal position in American society,"[40] to stand between white Christian and racial otherness. Unwilling to renounce the privileges afforded by whiteness, yet uncomfortable with the perceived loss of identity and unique culture, Casspi offers the best of all worlds. As a brother excelling in the NBA, a space defined by its blackness, he represents a perceived challenge to longstanding stereotypes about Jewish masculinity, all the while articulating the unique cultural attributes and experiences that define the Jewish community.

CASSPI V. KARPMAN: DEFEATING BLACKNESS, SAVING JEWISHNESS

In the ninth season of Comedy's Central *South Park*, the lone Jewish character, Kyle, decided to tryout for the all-state team. While giving voice to dominant ideologies regarding black dominance of basketball and stereotypes about the physical superiority of black bodies (evident in the fact that the black players are three times the size of Kyle), the episode brings into focus the presumed incompatibility of whiteness, Jewishness, and athletic success. The truth—(white) "Jews can't play basketball"—is not only evident in Kyle's ineptitude on the court, but in the show's dialogue:

> Stan: Dude, don't be nervous.
> Kyle: How can I not be nervous? Trying out for the all-state team has been my dream for years.
> Stan: You're the best player at our school, dude. You'll make the team for sure.
> Cartman: This is ridiculous. Jews can't play basketball.
> Kyle: I beat out *your* fat ass, Cartman!
> Referee: All students trying out for the all-state team to center court!
> Stan: Good luck.
> Coach: All right boys, now you're all here because you're the best of the best. I know that you've all worked really hard to make it this far, so let's get out there and *show me what you've got!* Uh, uh excuse me, Brof-Broflovski, is it?
> Kyle: Yeah?
> Coach: Can we talk to you for a minute? You uh . . . You're the best player in your school, are ya?
> Kyle: Yep! I love basketball. I wanna play for the Denver Nuggets one day.
> Coach: Yeah. Uh, look, kid, you've got great skills and a great attitude. But you're just not physically . . . built for the game.

Kyle's Jewishness not only thwarts his dreams, but those of Jewish kids throughout the country in search of a basketball hero. Likewise, neither Farmar nor any other black Jewish players are able to challenge Cartman's assertion that Jews can't play basketball given their blackness; on the other hand, Casspi is able to demonstrate the physical talents and skills worthy of celebration. So while Farmar did not and could not function as the "Jewish Jordan," Casspi had the identity credentials that allowed him to emerge as the BOT [the baller of the tribe] and therefore a commodity inside and outside the NBA.

NOTES

[1] Benjamin Hochman, "Jewish Casspi Gets 'Rock Star' Treatment," *Denver Post* (7 February 2010) http://www.denverpost.com/sports/ci_14350571

[2] Andy Altman-Ohr, "Omri Casspi Putting a Charge into Jewish Heritage Night," February 4, 2010, http://www.jweekly.com/article/full/41283/omri-casspi-putting-a-charge-into-jewish-heritage-night/

[3] Jeremy Fine, Israeli (Jewish) Basketball on the Rebound," November 17, 2009,http://www.oychicago.com/blog.aspx?id=4670

[4] Anita Mannur, "Model Minorities Can Cook: Fusion Cuisine in Asian America," in *East Main Street: Asian American Popular Culture* (ed. Shilpa Dave, et al.; New York: New York University Press, 2005), 87.

[5] Josh Sayles, "Israeli Rookie Makes Immediate Impact in Sacramento, NBA, http://njjewishnews.com/kaplanskorner/2010/02/11/profile-omri-casspi/

[6] Mannur, "Model Minorities Can Cook," 87.

[7] Warren Belasco and Philip Scranton, eds., *Food Nations: Selling Taste in Consumer Societies* (New York: Routledge, 2001), 2.

[8] Eytan Wallace, "An Interview with Omri Casspi: From Cholon to Sacramento," April 6, 2010, http://www.jewishjournal.com/sports/article/an_interview_with_omri_casspi_from_cholon_to_sacramento_20100406/

[9] Howard Beck, "From Israel to the N.B.A., Missing the Hummus," *New York Times* (18 July 2009) http://www.nytimes.com/2009/07/19/sports/basketball/19casspi.html

[10] Samantha Kwan, "Consuming the Other: Ethnic Food, Identity Work, and the Appropriation of the Authentic Self," Paper Presented at the Annual Meeting of the American Sociological Association, Atlanta Hilton Hotel, Atlanta, GA, Aug 16, 2003, http://www.allacademic.com/meta/p108203_index.html

[11] Noah Zaves, "Cheers for 'The Israeli' at Warriors' Jewish Heritage Night," February 20, 2010, http://www.eastbayreview.com/2010/Feb/bay-area-sports/000241

[12] Jacob Kamaras, "Israeli 'Hero' Graces N.J. Hardwood: Fans Relish the Chance to See Omri Casspi at Nets' 'Jewish Family Night,'" April 2, 2010, http://thejewishstate.net/april210casspi.html

[13] Jared Shelly, "Orthodox Pop Star Matisyahu Headlined Jewish Heritage Night at the 76ers Game on Jan. 13," January 14, 2010, http://www.jewishexponent.com/article/20417/

[14] Anna Chow, "Yo! Yao!: Critical Pedagogy and the Construction of an Asian American Identity," (Unpublished master's thesis, School of Education, Washington State University, Pullman, 2004).

[15] Jared Sexton, *Amalgamation Schemes: Antiblackness and the Critique of Multiracialism* (Minneapolis: University of Minnesota Press, 2008), 247.

[16] Lisa Lowe, *Immigrant Acts: On Asian American Cultural Politics* (North Carolina: Duke University Press, 1996), 88.

[17] Edward Shapiro, "The Shame of the City: CCNY Basketball, 1950-1951," in *Jews, Sports and the Rites of Citizenship* (ed. J. Kugelmass; Urbana: University of Illinois Press, 2007), 188.

[18] Ibid.

[19] Jon Entine, "Jews Sports, Jewish sports," July 2001, http://www.jewishmag.com/45mag/basketball/basketball.htm

[20] Scott Levin, "Kings Young Players Shine in Summer League Opener," July 12, 2010, http://www.examiner.com/sacramento-kings-in-sacramento/kings-young-players-shine-summer-league-opener

[21] Tom Ziller, "High Hopes for Omri Casspi in Sacramento," June 25, 2009, http://www.sactownroyalty.com/2009/6/25/925800/high-hopes-for-omri-casspi-in

[22] Ibid.

[23] Lee Jenkins, "Welcome, The King Of Israel," December 21, 2009, http://sportsillustrated.cnn.com/vault/article/magazine/MAG1164016/index.htm

[24] Brandon Hoffman, "David Stern's Legacy," January 29, 2009, http://ballerblogger.com/2009/01/29/david-sterns-legacy/

[25] "Amar'e Stoudemire Finds Out He's Jewish; Arrives In Israel," July 28, 2010, http://www.slamonline.com/online/nba/2010/07/amare-stoudemire-finds-out-hes-jewish-arrives-in-israel/

[26] Christopher Chavez, "Tracking The Truth: Amare Stoudemire On Hunt For Jewish Heritage," July 29, 2010, http://bleacherreport.com/articles/426841-tracking-the-truth-amare-stoudemire-on-hunt-for-jewish-heritage

[27] Trymaine Lee, "Black and Jewish, and Seeing No Contradiction," August 27, 2010, http://www.nytimes.com/2010/08/28/nyregion/28blackjews.html

[28] Donna Halper, "Black Jews: A Minority Within a Minority," http://www.jewishfederations.org/page.aspx?id=26506

[29]Brad A. Greenberg, "Jordan Farmar and the Jewish (Hoops) Future," April 23, 2009, http://www.jewishjournal.com/cover_story/article/jordan_farmar_and_the_jewish_hoops_future_20090422/

[30] For greater discussion, see David Theo Goldberg and Michael Krausz, *Jewish Identity* (Philadelphia: Temple University Press, 1993); Riv-Ellen Prell, *Fighting to Become Americans: Jews, Gender and the Anxiety of Assimilation* (Boston: Beacon, 1999); Jon Stratton, *Coming Out Jewish* (New York: Routledge, 2000).

[31] Stratton, *Coming Out Jewish*, 288.

[32] David Biale, "Jewish Identity in the 1990s," *Tikkun* 6 (1992):61.

[33] Quoted in Stephen Whitfield, *In Search of American Jewish Culture* (Boston: Brandeis University Press, 199), 203.

[34] Whitfield, *In Search of American Jewish Culture*, 230.

[35] Bernard Susser and Charles Liebman, *Choosing Survival: Strategies for a Jewish Future* (New York: Oxford University Press, 1999).

[36] Eric Goldstein, *The Price of Whiteness: Jews, Race, and American Identity* (Princeton: Princeton University Press, 2006), 210.

[37] Ibid., 211.

[38] Marc Dollinger, *Quest for Inclusion: Jews and Liberalism in Modern America* (Princeton: Princeton University Press, 2000), 224

[39] Ibid., 211.

[40] Nitasha Tamar Sharma, *Hip Hop Desis: South Asian Americans, Blackness and Global Race Consciousness* (Durham: Duke University Press, 2010), 27.